FRENCH POLITICAL PARTIES IN TRANSITION

FRENCH POLITICAL PARTIES IN TRANSITION

Edited by ALISTAIR COLE
Department of Politics
Keele University

Dartmouth

Aldershot · Brookfield USA · Hong Kong · Singapore · Sydney

Published by

Dartmouth Publishing Company Limited,
Gower House, Croft Road, Aldershot,
Hants. GU11 3HR, England

Dartmouth Publishing Company,
Old Post Road, Brookfield, Vermont 05036
USA

ISBN 1-85521-012-6

Printed in Great Britain by
Billing & Sons Ltd, Worcester

Contents

List of Tables

Notes on Contributors

Alistair Cole taught at the universities of Oxford, Caen and Aston before taking up his current position as a lecturer in Politics at Keele University. He has written widely on French politics. He is the joint author with Peter Campbell of *French Electoral Systems and Elections since 1789*, Gower, Aldershot, 1989. He is currently preparing a political biography of François Mitterrand.

John Gaffney is a senior lecturer in the Modern Languages department at Aston University. His main research interests are in French and British politics, in particular in relationship between language and political practice. He has also written extensively on aspects of political leadership and political culture. His books include: *The French Left and the Fifth Republic*, Macmillan, London, 1989, and *The Language of Political Leadership in Contemporary Britain*, Macmillan, London, 1990.

Paul Hainsworth is a lecturer in Politics at the University of Ulster. He has written extensively on French and European politics. He is the joint author, with Michael Keating, of *Decentralisation and Change in Contemporary France*, Gower, Aldershot, 1986. With John Loughlin, he is joint editor of the journal *Regional Politics and Policy*. He is currently editing a book entitled *The Extreme Right in Western Europe and the USA* (publication forthcoming with Pinter).

Susan Hayward is a lecturer in the French department at Birmingham University. She has published widely on French Cinema in American and British journals, and has also written extensively on French and British television, including analyses of the relationship between the state and television, television as a popular cultural medium and television genres. She is the co-editor with Ginette Vincendeau of *French Film:*

Texts and Contexts, Routledge, London, 1989. In her position as series editor of *National Cinemas*, she is currently preparing a book entitled *French National Cinema* (publication forthcoming with Routledge.

Andrew Knapp taught at the universities of Oxford and Paris, before taking up his current position as a lecturer in the French Studies department at Reading University. He is the author of numerous articles on French politics, notably in the journals *West European Politics*, the *Journal of Communist Studies*, and *Electoral Studies*. He is currently working on a monograph of the RPR (forthcoming publication with Gower).

Gino Raymond has taught at a number of institutions in Britain and France, and is currently a lecturer in the Department of French Studies at Bristol University. His research interests encompass both politics and literature. He has written on the Communist Party in France, the dilemmas faced by committed writers in France, and is presently working on a study of the cultural assumptions behind the French presence in Vietnam.

James G. Shields taught at the universities of Glasgow, Caen and Aston before taking up his present position as a lecturer in French Studies at Warwick University. He has published articles and book chapters on contemporary French politics and on aspects of 18th and 19th century French literature and thought. His current research projects include studies of French government policy under the Socialists and a book on Stendhal.

Main Abbreviations

AT	Amis de la terre
CD	Centre démocrate
CDP	Centre démocratie et progrès
CDS	Centre des démocrates sociaux
CERES	Centre d'études, de recherches et d'éducation socialistes
CGT	Confédération générale du travail
CNCL	Commission nationale de la communication et des libertés
CNIP	Centre national des paysans et des indépendents
CSA	Conseil supérieur de l'audiovisuel
EEC	European Economic Community
EMS	European Monetary System
ENA	Ecole nationale d'administration
FN	Front national
HA	Haute autorité
INSEE	Institut national d'études statistiques et économiques
LCR	Ligue communiste révolutionnaire
LO	Lutte ouvrière
MEP	Mouvement d'écologie politique
MRG	Mouvement des radicaux de gauche
MRP	Mouvement républicain populaire
MSI	Movimento Sociale Italiano
ORTF	Office de la radio-télédiffusion de France
PCF	Parti communiste français
PR	Parti républicain
PS	Parti socialiste
PSD	Parti social-démocrate
PSU	Parti socialiste unifié
REEL	Réalisme, efficacité, espérance, liberté
RI	Républicains indépendents
RPF	Rassemblement du peuple français
RPR	Rassemblement pour la République

RTF	Radio-télédiffusion de France
SDP	Social-Democratic Party
SFIO	Section française de l'internationale ouvrière
SMIC	Salaire minimum interprofessionnel de croissance
SOFRES	Société française d'enquêtes par sondages
SPD	Sozialedemokratische Partei Deutschlands
UDC	Union du centre
UDF	Union pour la démocratie française
UDR	Union des démocrates pour la République
UDT	Union démocratique du travail
UDV^{e}	Union des démocrates pour la Ve République
UNR	Union pour la nouvelle République
UNM	Union pour la nouvelle majorité
UPF	Union pour la France
URC	Union du rassemblement et du centre

Preface

The idea behind *French Political Parties in Transition* germinated from the belief that there is no serious study which adequately deals with changes which have occurred in the party system in the 1980s, despite the existence of excellent individual party studies. This book does not claim or, indeed, attempt to supplant the existing body of literature on the French party system, but rather to complement and update it. Although it is concerned primarily with French political parties in the 1980s and 1990s, the earlier period figures prominently in certain of the chapters. The authors hope to have broken genuinely new ground, while acknowledging the quality of much of the existing literature.

The 1980s were arguably a critical decade in the history of the French Fifth Republic. They were years of ideological and political transformation, of institutional innovation and of policy experimentation. In Chapter One, Alistair Cole assesses the evolution of the party system from 1974 to 1990, laying particular emphasis on its changing contours and structure. In a second contextual chapter, Susan Hayward assesses the challenge represented by the mass media, in particular by television, for leading French politicians in a highly personalised, presidentially-orientated political regime. In Chapter Three, Gino Raymond pursues the apparently relentless decline of the PCF throughout the 1980s; in Chapter Four, John Gaffney considers in detail the transformation of the French Socialist Party away 'from its earlier rally-style presidentialism' of the 1970s to 'a more sober governmentalism' in the 1980s and 1990s. Paul Hainsworth then charts the surprising rise of the French Greens, from being a cluster of minor warring sects to becoming a powerful *contestataire* movement by the end of the decade. In Chapter Six, Alistair Cole considers the centre-right UDF from a variety of perspectives, in particular as an example of a confederation of political parties, and as the latest historical manifestation of the 'Orleanist' right. In Chapter Seven, Andrew Knapp undertakes an exhaustive, highly original, analysis of the neo-Gaullist RPR. Finally, in Chapter Eight, James Shields considers the remarkable ascension of the extreme-right National Front and its effects on the party system as a whole.

Each author has interpreted his or her chapter in accordance with the prerogatives of individual style, and scale of priorities. Notwithstanding this, a number of common themes reappear throughout the chapters:

* *Electoral fortunes*: including reasons for electoral performance, sociology and geography of party electorates.

* *Institutional constraints and opportunities*, in particular the extent to which different French parties are organised in terms of presidential imperatives.

* *The party organisation*: state of the organisation (party members), democratic or authoritarian structures, importance accorded to the *élus* (holders of public office) vis-a-vis the permanent party organisation, influence of municipal power.

* *Ideology and policy:* certain party ideologies were transformed during the 1980s (PS, arguably RPR), whereas others were resistent to change (PCF), and still others in the process of refinement (FN, Greens).

* *Intra-party rivalries*: factionalism has long been prevalent in certain French parties, especially the PS. By the early 1990s, the PCF, UDF, and RPR were all afflicted by severe internal tensions.

* *The wider context of Western Europe*: while *French Political Parties in Transition* is concerned with French parties, numerous European comparisons are made in order to situate the study within a comparative context.

For reasons of space and practicability, it has not proved possible to extend the study to include the minor parties. As editor of this exciting book, I would like to take this opportunity to thank warmly each of the various contributors for having produced consistently high quality work and for meeting ambitious deadlines. On a personal level, I would like to extend my gratitude to Martin Harrison, who carefully read my chapter on the UDF and suggested welcome improvements. Finally, my thanks go to my secretary Pauline Weston, for her patience in responding to my incessant demands for assistance.

Alistair Cole, University of Keele, August 1990.

1 The Evolution of the Party System, 1974-1990

Alistair Cole

The study of French political parties in the Fifth Republic has enjoyed a rich and illustrious tradition. Indeed, there is an abundant literature in English on the subject.[1] The central focus of *French Political Parties in Transition* is upon the development of parties in the 1980s and 1990s; it is not proposed to retrace in any detail in this chapter the evolution of the party system in the first two decades of the Fifth Republic, which has been extensively dealt with elsewhere. Rather we shall summarise the main developments of the 1960s and 1970s before outlining the *contours* and *structure* of the party system in the 1980s and early 1990s.

A pattern of bipolarisation between rival right- and left-wing coalitions gradually replaced the fragmentation which had characterised the party system in the Fourth Republic. A number of causes were frequently cited to explain the development of bipolarisation. These included:

* The politico-institutional structure of the Fifth Republic. In particular the enhanced prestige of the presidency as modelled by de Gaulle in between 1958-69, the bipolarising pressures of direct election of the presidency after 1962, and the strengthening of executive government in the constitution of the Fifth Republic in 1958, which stimulated the emergence of stable government coalitions, and in turn more purposeful oppositions.[2]

* The historical role performed by Gaullism and the development of the strategies of other parties in response to this. The emergence during the 1960s of Gaullism as a federating force of the right eventually forced the disunited left to react in order to secure its own survival. Greater electoral cooperation between Socialists and Communists gradually materialised from 1962 onwards against the common threat represented by Gaullism. Although the 'opposition centrists' (composed of conservative and centrist politicians left over from the Fourth Republic) maintained the pretence of independence throughout the 1960s, they eventually rallied in stages to the Gaullist-led majority from 1969 onwards.[3]

* The growing secularisation of French society in the post-war period has been accompanied by a weakening of the significance of religion as a pointer to voting

behaviour.[4] Certain commentators pointed to the combined effects of secularisation, economic expansion, and social and political change as encouraging the emergence of social class as the central political cleavage during the 1970s, giving a structural basis to left-right bipolarisation. Class-based voting patterns certainly reached new heights during the 1970s, particularly since the cross-class appeal of classic Gaullism was greatly weakened after the departure of the General. This type of class-based analysis - especially the variety which argued that there was a 'sociological majority' for the left - was at best premature, however.[5] In fact, the 1980s were to be characterised by a growing electoral volatility, especially prevalent amongst the new social groups produced by rapid postwar socio-economic change (best symbolised by the *cadres*), as well as those most threatened by social change (industrial workers, artisans and shopkeepers).[6]

* Certain observers argued that the return to the single-member constituency, second-ballot electoral system in legislative elections had forced the parties of the left and right to form pacts to fight the common enemy, as well as marginalising the centre and constraining it to choose between the Gaullist-led majority, or the left in order to survive.[7]

Whatever importance to be accorded to these various explanations, a combination of them had certainly encouraged a steady rationalisation and bipolarisation of the party system. On the second ballot of each presidential election since 1965, with the exception of that of 1969, a candidate of the non-Communist left confronted a representative of the moderate right, Gaullist or non-Gaullist.[8] In parliamentary elections, bipolarisation could be measured by the decreasing number of triangular and four-cornered contests on the second ballot after 1962; in fact this was synonymous with the gradual rallying of the centrists to the Gaullist-led majority. The number of straight left-right duels on the second ballot increased steadily throughout the 1960s and 1970s, so that by 1978 (by which time the previously independent centre had been absorbed into President Giscard's centre-right UDF) triangular and four-cornered contests had virtually disappeared. Political competition took place increasingly between rival left-wing (Socialist-Communist) and right-wing (Gaullist and Giscardian) electoral coalitions. Each coalition was subject to severe internal strains, since each involved an internal struggle for ascendency between *frères-ennemis*. Despite their conflictual character, however, each coalition was guaranteed a minimum of electoral cohesion by aversion to the opposing camp, and by the electoral self-interest of both partners.

The strength of presidential institutions as shaped by de Gaulle transformed the direct presidential election into the decisive election of the Fifth Republic from 1965 onwards. This had an important effect upon the performance of parties in parliamentary elections: it gave a strategic advantage to those parties which could hope to elect presidential candidates. It also transformed the character of most of the parties, making them primarily into rallies around their 'presidential' leaders. This theme, along with a number of others, will be a recurrent one in the ensuing chapters. Before considering the fortunes of the individual parties, however, it is essential to situate them within the context of an evolving party system, within which, in the course of the 1980s, many of the presuppositions underpinning the study of French parties in the first two decades of the Fifth Republic were radically called into question. In the present chapter, we shall consider the evolution of the structure of the French party system in the post-Gaullist period: namely, the contours of the party system from 1974-81, the party system in the 1980s and prospects for its development in the 1990s.

The Contours of the Party System, 1974-81

The relentless development of bipolarisation between left and right reached a new stage in the 1974 presidential election, when the remaining so-called 'opposition centrists' declared their support for the conservative Valéry Giscard d'Estaing. Giscard's narrow election as President against François Mitterrand, candidate of the united left, represented a watershed in the history of the French right: Gaullism could no longer claim to federate the right as it had under de Gaulle and appeared temporarily to do so under Pompidou. By swallowing the independent centre, the balance of political gravity of Giscard's majority shifted towards the more centrist elements of the presidential coalition: Giscard's Independent Republicans, the 'Christian Democrats' (Centre of Social Democrats, CDS, after 1976), and the Radicals. This was at the expense of the Gaullist Party, which continued, however, to provide the bulk of pro-government deputies. Giscard owed his election in no small manner to the rebellion within the Gaullist Party's ranks organised by Jacques Chirac, who led a group of 43 Gaullist deputies in support of Giscard against the official Gaullist candidate Jacques Chaban-Delmas. In return, Giscard named Chirac as his first Prime Minister in 1974: his rationale was not only to ensure that the bulk of Gaullist deputies supported the new President, but also to split the Gaullist Party into pro- and anti-Giscard factions, of which Giscard hoped eventually to absorb the former into a new Giscardian presidential party. This calculation ran against the personal ambition of Chirac: having ensured Chaban-Delmas's defeat in 1974, Chirac now offered himself as the saviour of the Gaullist Party (see Chapter Seven for detailed development).

The Giscard-Chirac honeymoon was ended abruptly in August 1976, when Chirac resigned as Prime Minister. This occurred ostensibly in protest against his lack of power, but probably in order to consecrate Chirac's ambition of transforming the old Gaullist Party into a new dynamic, energetic organisation which could recapture undisputed leadership of the right, and act as a springboard for his presidential ambition. From 1976-81, Chirac's RPR (see below) and Giscard's various supporters (UDF from 1978) fought a bitter internecine battle to consolidate or regain leadership of the right-wing coalition. During the years of the Giscard presidency, personality rivalries seriously damaged the right's cohesion. No one leader emerged with sufficient authority to be the uncontested leader of the right-wing coalition. The centrifugal pressures created by rival presidential ambitions thus greatly damaged the right's cohesion from 1974 onwards, in a way which would have been inconceivable in the 1960s when de Gaulle presided over France's destiny, and the old Gaullist Party acted as the great federating force of the right.

Under the impact of Giscard's victory and of the success of Mitterrand's new PS, the centre of gravity within the rival presidential coalitions appeared to shift in favour of the more centrist elements, Giscard's supporters in the UDF (from 1978) and Mitterrand's PS. This movement was, however, unequal: it was more marked on the left than on the right. Within Giscard's presidential majority, the bitter battle for supremacy fought between Giscardians and Chirac's neo-Gaullists was inconclusive. The creation of the UDF in 1978 represented a new step in relation to the rationalisation of the party system: the various non-Gaullist parties of the centre and right merged together into one presidential confederation, in an attempt to counter-balance the strength of the disciplined RPR. From its origins as a loose coalition to fight the 1978 legislative elections, the UDF was always more of an electoral cartel than a genuine political party: that it survived throughout the

1980s testified both to its electoral efficiency and to the need to organise the various formations of the centre right into a relatively cohesive formation.

Throughout Giscard's presidency, the once-omnipotent Gaullist Party fought a rearguard action to attempt to recover the influence it had lost to Giscard in 1974, and to restore its position as undisputed leader of the right-wing coalition. On balance, neither Giscard's UDF, nor Chirac's RPR managed to impose its domination on the French right during the Giscard presidency: although the RPR maintained its edge in the legislative contests of 1978 and 1981, Giscard twice (in 1974 and 1981) distanced the official Gaullist candidate in presidential elections. Once Chirac had resigned as Prime Minister in 1976, the RPR moved into a position of semi-opposition to Giscard, relying on its discipline and organisational strength to attempt to overhaul and disorientate Giscard's composite support. This did not extend, however, as far as the RPR voting a motion of censure against Raymond Barre's (1976-81) government. That the RPR remained the more powerful party in legislative elections both in 1978 and 1981 partly reflected the extent to which the Gaullists had become political notables with solid local roots (somewhat like the conservative notables they had originally replaced).

Whereas the situation on the right was somewhat confused during Giscard's presidency, the development of bipolarisation in the 1970s clearly favoured Mitterrand's PS as the more central element on the left, at the expense of the PCF, the main party of the French left since 1945. The success of Mitterrand's PS during the 1970s (after the long stagnation of the old Socialist Party, the SFIO, since 1958) is analysed in detail in Chapter Four. By the 1974 presidential election, it appeared obvious to most observers that the PS-PCF alliance based on the common programme of government signed between Socialists and Communists in 1972, had not only given renewed credibility to the united left as the only alternative to the Gaullist-led coalition, but had strengthened the PS as the more central element within the alliance. The reinforcement of the PS had been at the expense of the stagnation of the PCF, which had expected to benefit from the alliance. The strengthening of Mitterrand's PS was an indispensable precondition for the victory of the left: it was the only means of reassuring moderate voters that the left would not be dominated by the PCF in the event of victory at the polls. The supremacy of the PCF within the left had given an insuperable ideological advantage to the right ever since 1958: the menace of communism should the left ever win power was regularly evoked by right-wing politicians to scare undecided voters away from the left. The emergence of the PS as the more important, and later dominant force of the left from the mid-1970s onwards was of fundamental importance in enhancing the left's chances of winning power.

Once that it had became obvious by the mid-1970s that Mitterrand's PS was the main beneficiary of the left-wing alliance, the PCF decided to terminate the experiment. In September 1977, some six months before the legislative election of 1978 which the left was expected to win, the PCF and PS failed to agree on terms for the 'updating' of the 1972 common programme demanded by the Communists.[9] The PCF preferred to break off the left-wing alliance based on the common programme (a detailed policy manifesto), rather than participate as a junior partner with the Socialists in a united left-wing government, in all probability constrained to manage capitalism. Until the eve of the second ballot in 1978, it was even unclear whether the PCF would agree to the left's traditional mutual-withdrawal agreement. Henceforth, the central objective of PCF strategy was to attempt by all means to restore its position as the leading party of the left. This destructive strategy was relatively successful in 1978 and the party managed to salvage defeat out of the jaws of victory: despite opinion polls predictions, the UDF-RPR alliance returned a comfortable majority of deputies.

The structure of the party system in 1978 continued to discriminate against the left. The right-wing coalition had a natural advantage for as long as the PCF remained either the dominant force, or at least as powerful a force as the more moderate PS. The PCF remained far too strong in 1978 (over 20 per cent) to permit undecided voters the luxury of supporting the left. Electoral bipolarisation reached its apogee in the 1978 legislative election, at which four parties of roughly equal political strength (PCF, PS, UDF, RPR) divided voter preferences evenly between left and right. This structure was labelled the *quadrille bipolaire*. In essence, the system could be called bipolar because in the supreme contest, the second ballot of a presidential election, only two candidates could run, representing respectively the right and the left. This was reproduced on a smaller scale in the second ballot of parliamentary elections, which by 1978 involved virtually everywhere straight left-right contests between the best-placed candidate in each camp: second-ballot agreements between allies to withdraw were vital to securing adequate parliamentary representation. The system was a quadrille in that the first ballot accommodated two major parties within each camp, the PCF and PS on the left, the UDF and RPR on the right. Within the quadrille, certain commentators postulated that the more central elements (PS, UDF) were at an advantage, since they could more effectively compete for the vital floating vote. We have argued above that while this mechanism undoubtedly favoured the PS on the left, the situation on the right was far more complex, with no one political formation emerging as the clear victor.

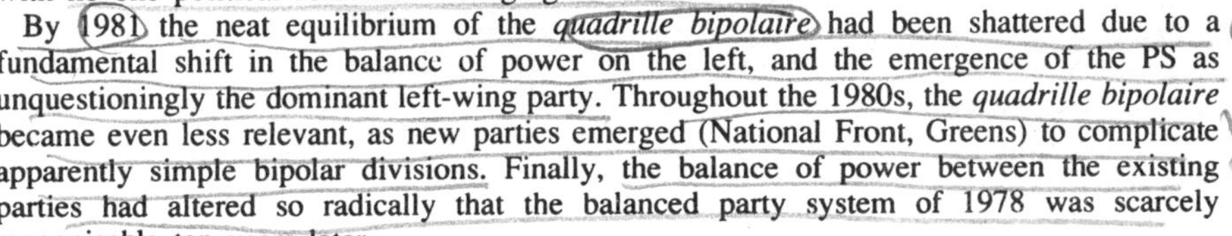

By 1981 the neat equilibrium of the *quadrille bipolaire* had been shattered due to a fundamental shift in the balance of power on the left, and the emergence of the PS as unquestioningly the dominant left-wing party. Throughout the 1980s, the *quadrille bipolaire* became even less relevant, as new parties emerged (National Front, Greens) to complicate apparently simple bipolar divisions. Finally, the balance of power between the existing parties had altered so radically that the balanced party system of 1978 was scarcely recognisable ten years later.

The Party System in the 1980s

In 1978, the Fifth Republic celebrated its twentieth anniversary in a frenzy of political excitement occasioned by that year's legislative elections: indeed political commentators used the imagery of civil war to describe the passions aroused and the sense of belonging to one or the other political camp.[10] In 1988, by contrast, the three main candidates in that year's presidential elections adopted a similar political discourse and stressed the virtues of consensus.[11] In the intervening ten years, the contours of the party system had shifted radically. The neat equilibrium of 1978 was short-lived: it was replaced in 1981 by a still bipolar but far more uneven party system in which one party - the PS - clearly dominated the left (at the PCF's expense), but where the right was split into two divisive, dispirited camps, the centre-right UDF, and the neo-Gaullist RPR, neither of which managed to dominate.

The presidential and legislative elections of 1981 led certain commentators to refer to a new period of dominant party rule, the PS taking over in the role performed by the Gaullist Party during the 1960s. Mitterrand's victory in the 1981 presidential election was heralded as the harbinger of fundamental change in the French party system. Few politicians, especially on the right, had believed that Mitterrand could overturn Giscard. The implications for the party system were considerable. The fierce struggle for influence on the left between Socialists and Communists was decided in 1981 in favour of the former. On the first ballot of the 1981 presidential election, Mitterrand obtained some 10 per cent more than the Communist candidate Georges Marchais, whereas only two per cent had separated the parties in 1978 (see Appendix 1). Mitterrand's 1981 victory was made possible precisely because of the left's disunity on the first ballot: it enabled him to appear a credible candidate in the eyes of hesitant voters who had previously believed the right's claim that the PS would be beholden to the PCF should the left win a major national election. The existence of separate PS and PCF candidates in 1981 convinced a vital proportion of the electorate that Mitterrand was genuinely independent of the PCF, whereas in 1974, as a united-left candidate, Mitterrand's autonomy in relation to the Communists had been far less certain. Giscard's unpopularity and a confused desire for change did the rest. For left-wing voters, Mitterrand continued to represent a powerful symbol of alliance between Socialists and Communists. Indeed, the sectarian attitude adopted by the PCF after the 1978 legislative election alienated a fraction of Communist voters which saw in Mitterrand the only candidate able to secure victory for the left. The PCF failed in its objective of ensuring Mitterrand's defeat in the 1981 election: around one-quarter of 1978 PCF voters backed Mitterrand from the first ballot. Moreover, on the second ballot, vote transfers to Mitterrand from first-round PCF supporters were excellent, despite unofficial attempts made by the Communist leaders to sabotage Mitterrand's victory. The institutional advantage enjoyed by the Socialist left at the expense of the PCF was clearly demonstrated in 1981, more explicitly than in 1974 when Mitterrand had stood as candidate of the united left. Only a representative of the Socialist left, able to compete for the vital centre vote, stood a realistic chance of defeating the right on the second ballot of a presidential election. A Communist candidate had no chance of victory in a presidential contest due to the overwhelmingly negative image of the PCF within French society. For this reason, the PCF had always previously attempted to back united-left candidates (Mitterrand in 1965 and 1974) rather than present their own challengers.

Whereas Mitterrand owed his victory to the left's disunity, Giscard could blame his defeat upon the guerilla warfare that RPR leader Chirac had waged against him since 1976. After a bitter election campaign, President Giscard emerged as the representative of the right-wing coalition on the second ballot, confirming the advantage given to the presidential incumbent by 'legitimist' voters. The animosity created by the first-round campaign, however, meant that vote transfers from first-round Chirac supporters to Giscard were lamentable: only 73 per cent of Chirac's first-round electors backed Giscard on the second ballot (with 16 per cent abstaining, and 11 per cent opting for Mitterrand).[12] Had all of Chirac's first-round electors transferred to Giscard on the run-off, the outgoing President would have been reelected. The disunity of the right secured Mitterrand's victory in 1981, even more so than the favourable outcome of divisions on the left.

Mitterrand's presidential victory was confirmed in the legislative elections of June 1981. By dissolving the conservative-dominated National Assembly elected in 1978, and by calling for the electorate to 'give the President the means to govern', Mitterrand signified his final acceptance of the presidential institutions bequeathed by de Gaulle. The PS obtained an absolute majority in the legislative elections of June 1981, only the second occasion on which one party (rather than a presidential coalition) had obtained an overall majority in the Fifth Republic, the other being the Gaullist landslide of 1968. The 1981 legislative election result confirmed the theory of the 'decisive election', whereby the victor of an initial decisive contest (referendum or presidential election) was virtually assured of obtaining an enhanced victory in a succeeding legislative election: a proportion of opponents preferred to abstain rather than contradict the nation's original choice.[13]

Although the form of left-right bipolarisation persisted in 1981, the balance of power within each coalition had altered, dramatically on the left, less so on the right. The *quadrille bipolaire* no longer adequately described the structure of the party system. The PS polled over twice as many votes as the PCF, whereas the parties had been almost evenly matched only three years earlier (see Appendix 1). The UDF and RPR combined to fight the election under the banner of the Union for the New Majority (UNM), dividing almost evenly the number of constituencies contested by each party. The near-equality between RPR and UDF could not disguise the fact that Chirac had inherited the leadership of the new opposition from the discredited Giscard. By providing for the first transfer of power between the right and the left, most analysts agreed that the 1981 elections had fully legitimised the Fifth Republic. The regime had finally come of age.

The basic pattern of Socialist domination of the left remained intact throughout the 1981-88 *septennat*, the PCF gradually being reduced to a marginal force on the extreme left (see Chapter Three). Despite Socialist domination of the left, however, the PS electorate was revealed to be highly unstable and volatile. This was confirmed by a series of elections (1982 cantonal, 1983 municipal, 1984 European, and 1985 cantonal), in which the PS fared poorly, exploding the myth that it had become a 'dominant' party. The PCF fared even worse, becoming reduced to a rump of less than 10 per cent by the 1986 legislative election.

The left's experience in government until 1986 shattered many of the myths both Socialists and Communists had retained in opposition, as well as the prospect of anything more than purely opportunistic alliance between the two parties in the future (see Chapters Three and Four). In terms of the party system, the brief spell of Socialist-Communist government between 1981-84 had cataclysmic repercussions on the left. The PCF's capacity to resist the PS was finally revealed to be an illusion. Even at the depths of PS unpopularity in 1984 (at the height of the church schools crisis), the PCF offered no serious alternative left-wing strategy to that of the PS. During its period of participation in government, the PCF was neither really a party of government (despite the presence of Communist ministers), nor a party of opposition (the party being forced, initially at least, to assume a degree of collective responsibility for the decisions of the Mauroy government). Despite its attempts to sabotage Mitterrand's victory in 1981, the PCF leadership had been constrained to accept the President's invitation to join the second Mauroy government, formed after the PS landslide in June 1981: to have refused would have been met with utter incomprehension by the mass of pro-unity PCF voters. The PCF's brief experience as a party of government was not, however, a entirely fruitful one: Communists held only a small minority of ministerial offices (four out of 44) and the party was scarcely in a position to influence the content of government policy.[14] Whereas Socialist ministers gained most of the credit for the more audacious reforms of the first two years (1981-83), the four Communists were inevitably associated with helping to administer the government's economic austerity policies from 1982 onwards. Participation in government led to a growing divorce between the PCF ministers and hardliners in the party leadership, who were resolved that the Communists could only aspire to recover a leading influence on the left should the PS be humiliatingly defeated in 1986. The party finally quit the government in July 1984, after Mauroy's resignation and the nomination of Laurent Fabius as Mitterrand's second Prime Minister.

The repercussions on the PS of the left's experience in power were still more profound (because more important). The party's experience is dealt with in detail in Chapter Four, but brief comment must be made here. The Socialist *quinquennat* destroyed many illusions somewhat complacently maintained by Mitterrand's PS during its decade of opposition prior to 1981. The transformation of the Socialist Party in between 1981-86 was multifaceted:

two major aspects will be mentioned briefly here, but there were others. Firstly, under the impact of government experience (especially after the left's economic U-turn of 1982-83), the party underwent an ideological *aggiornamento*, abandoning many of the 'lyrical illusions' it had believed in while in opposition, and committing itself to a programme of moderate social reform, counterbalanced by the necessary modernisation of the economy and society. This process (which followed the Socialists' practical apprenticeship in government) culminated at the PS Toulouse Congress in October 1985, at which the party declared itself to be a party in the European social-democratic tradition, a label it had stoutly resisted when in opposition. Secondly, the PS was forced to conform to the prevalent model of the presidential party in the Fifth Republic, the *parti de godillots* (party of bootlickers) bequeathed by de Gaulle's UNR. Despite declaring itself to be a new-style democratic and participatory party while in opposition, the PS generally acted as a classic presidential party in the tradition of the Fifth Republic, subordinating itself directly and indirectly to the orders of 'its' President, François Mitterrand.[15] The party could exercise only a limited influence on the content of government policy. It was indicative of the relationship which existed between the different partners of the Socialist tryptic (president-government-party) that the party's ideological transformation followed the government's practical apprenticeship of the constraints involving in governing the country. The party rapidly gave up any pretence that it could give a lead to government activity, rather than follow its orders. The combined effect of transformations within both party and government was that by 1986 the PS, matured by its first five-year term in office, had acquired the image of a responsible party of government, the natural alternative governing party to the formations of the mainstream right. It had come to occupy that position shared by most of its fraternal parties within the Socialist International.

The evolution of the situation on the right after 1981 removed the French party system still further from the *quadrille bipolaire* of 1978. Notwithstanding Chirac's presidential setback in 1981 (see above), the RPR could claim a degree of victory in defeat: Giscard's discredit after losing to Mitterrand enabled Chirac to impose his leadership on the right, and to lead a new uncompromising opposition to the left from 1981 onwards.[16] The shock of the right's defeat was nonetheless considerable: the RPR, inheritor of the Gaullist tradition, was totally excluded from any share in executive power for the first time in the Fifth Republic. The RPR was able to capture the leadership of the right-wing opposition by its intransigent tactics and by calling into question the left's legitimacy to govern; the disorganised UDF proved no match alongside the disciplined neo-Gaullist party. During the first two years of frenzied social and economic reform (1981-83), the RPR appeared as a party of opposition *par excellence*, a disciplined, coherent alternative to the left. This stance proved to be an electorally fruitful one: once that public opinion had begun to swing against the left (as early as January 1982) the RPR found that it had positioned itself perfectly to lead the right's challenge, which eventually led to the RPR-UDF victory of March 1986. The high point of RPR success against the 'Socialo-Communist' government came with the 1983 municipal elections, symbolised by the opposition's conquest of all 20 Paris *arrondissements*, and by Chirac's triumphal reelection as mayor of Paris (see Chapter Seven). The RPR's aggressive style of opposition soon demonstrated its limits, however. It was best suited to the early phase of the left's administration (1981-83), when radical social and economic reform caused growing anxiety amongst the *déçus du socialisme*, those floating voters who had supported Mitterrand in 1981, but who rapidly became disillusioned by the left. Once that the Socialist-led government had moderated its economic policy and the pace of social reform (the economic U-turn of 1983), and especially once that the PCF had left the government in July 1984, the RPR's intransigent style of opposition became less effective, the party being sandwiched between the more extreme National Front and the centre-right UDF. The new-style socialism of Jacques Delors or Laurent Fabius could not be made to appear the same as the economic profligacy and social impatience of the 1981-83 period. In addition, from 1983 onwards Chirac's RPR had to face serious competition from a reinvigorated UDF with two *présidentiables* at its head, Giscard and Barre (see below).

It might be argued that the very intransigence of the RPR facilitated the breakthrough of Le Pen's National Front (FN) from 1983-84. It was the RPR which first promoted with most urgency themes such as immigration, or insecurity as major political issues in an attempt to mobilise opinion against the left; the popularisation of these issues from within the political mainstream arguably legitimised Le Pen's movement, which first attracted major national support in 1983-84 as an ultra-conservative reaction to the left-wing government.[17] Once that the FN's national breakthrough had occurred in the 1984 European election, the RPR, a party preparing for power in 1986, could not seriously compete with the Front on Le Pen's favourite themes. As it was, RPR ambiguity towards Le Pen had already alienated a proportion of centre-right opinion. The success of Le Pen's movement in 1984, and 1986, as well as the UDF's gradual recovery, limited the extent to which Chirac's RPR could channel the left's unpopularity into support for itself. Undoubtedly, the RPR emerged as a victor in the 1986 elections, but its victory was less dramatic than it might have hoped for three years earlier.

The disciplined, cohesive RPR was at least a real party; the UDF could not pretend as much. The UDF was formed by President Giscard in 1978 in an attempt to give greater organisational cohesion to his various supporters, and to stand up to the RPR. The UDF united those various conflictual tendencies today grouped (somewhat inaccurately) under the title of the centre right: old-style Conservatives (PR), Christian Democrats (CDS), Radicals, Social Democrats (ex-SFIO) and various minor groups. The survival of the UDF throughout Mitterrand's first *septennat* surprised many commentators, given the combined pressures placed upon the confederation by presidential, personal and ideological rivalries. Its efficiency as an electoral cartel in legislative elections was the UDF's principal justification during the Mitterrand years. The UDF's confederal structure enabled the centre-right parties to maintain a degree of cohesion alongside the RPR, especially in the electoral negotiations preceding the 1986 and 1988 legislative elections. But it was completely unable to contain the emergence of rival *présidentiables* within its ranks. In fact, its loose structure and lack of effective organisational discipline encouraged rival potential candidates (Giscard, Barre, latterly Léotard) to pursue their presidential ambitions, since there was no effective federal organisation which could be used by those in control to crush unwelcome presidential bids. This marked the UDF apart from the RPR, PCF, FN, and, arguably, the PS. From the end of 1982 onwards, the UDF became dominated by rivalries between Giscard and Barre. The former's failure to recover in the opinion poll ratings gradually enabled the latter to establish his claim to be the best non-Gaullist centre-right candidate. Presidential rivalries between Giscard and Barre were reinforced by their irreconcilable analyses in relation to *cohabitation*, tactically accepted by Giscard but vigorously rejected by Barre. The only way of preserving the UDF's continuing existence was by refusing to make any definite decisions (on *cohabitation*, on the presidential candidate, or on policy), or at least by postponing these decisions until the latest possible moment.

The emergence of the FN in the 1984 European election further complicated the traditional bipolar classification of the party system.[18] The significance of the FN in relation to the overall political system is analysed in Chapter Eight. Le Pen's breakthrough had serious strategic implications for the other formations of the right. The issue of how to deal with Le Pen created new tensions both within and between the UDF and RPR, superimposed upon pre-existing presidential and political divisions. These were concentrated over whether the mainstream right should in any circumstances ally with Le Pen, as well as the attitude the established parties should adopt to the new issues forced to the forefront of the political agenda by the Front's success (such as immigration, or security). At a local level, both the RPR and UDF made tacit deals with the FN in municipal by-elections, which the national leaderships far from unambiguously condemned (see Chapter Eight). Such alliances with the FN (albeit unofficial local alliances) seriously divided both the UDF and RPR. By holding forth the prospect of parliamentary representation for the Front, the introduction of proportional representation for the 1986 election created favourable circumstances for the extreme-right movement. It also reprieved the mainstream parties from having to consider the issue of alliance with the FN.

Thus from 1984 onwards, there existed a tripartite division of the right. The persistence of this tripartite division complicated the opposition's task in the 1986 legislative election, and eventually facilitated Mitterrand's reelection in 1988.

The 1986 Legislative Election

In 1985, President Mitterrand responded to the prospect of almost certain defeat for the PS at the 1986 legislative election by replacing the old second-ballot majoritarian electoral system with a single-round system of 'proportional representation', based on party lists and small constituencies centred on France's 100 metropolitan and overseas departments.[19] Since its reintroduction in 1958, the second-ballot system had generally overrepresented the party or coalition with the most votes and greatly exaggerated the electoral consequences of swings in opinion. Mitterrand calculated that proportional representation would minimise the effects of any such anti-governmental swing, limiting the likely defeat suffered by the PS, the presidential party, and - by assuring the National Front of parliamentary representation - possibly even preventing the UDF-RPR from obtaining an overall majority of seats.

Despite Mitterrand's Machiavellian tactics, the UDF-RPR tandem won the 1986 legislative election with over 42 per cent of the vote and a slender overall majority of seats (see Appendix 1). The PS performed honourably, surpassing its proclaimed objective of 30 per cent, although it polled less than any previous presidential party since 1958. By 1986, the party system had evolved from the *quadrille bipolaire* of 1978 (four parties of roughly equal strength) to something resembling an uneven bipartisan structure, with two major political forces (UDF/RPR versus PS) flanked by two minor ones (FN and PCF). Despite the existence of two powerful 'extreme' minorities, the PCF and the FN, the broad contours of the French party system now approached the model of moderate polarised pluralism prevalent in a number of West European countries, whereby two competing poles (parties or coalitions) of the social-reformist left and the moderate right provided the mainstay of political competition and choice.[20]

Notwithstanding its partial recovery from the nadir of 1984, the left's overall total represented its worst performance since 1962. The PCF's lamentable result was its worst since 1932, forcing it to rely on its Parisian heartland (and pockets of resistance elsewhere) and its core working-class electorate. The PS emphatically confirmed its domination of the left: although the two parties had polled roughly the same number of votes in 1978, the differential rose to 2:1 in favour of the PS in 1981, and to 3:1 in 1986. But it was unclear how President Mitterrand, whose Socialist Party had been soundly defeated and who had consistently been the most unpopular President of the Fifth Republic, could hope to recover before the next presidential election. The RPR-UDF tandem, running joint lists in 60 mainland departments, obtained the narrow overall majority the polls had been predicting, while the FN polled almost exactly the same number of votes as the PCF and confirmed its existence as a national political force.[21]

Cohabitation, Presidentialism, and the Party System, 1986-88

The 1986 election, fought under a restrictive system of proportional representation, created the impression that the mainstream right had won only a narrow overall victory (such as in 1967), whereas under the old second-ballot system there would have been a crushing UDF-RPR majority, and the political significance of the result would undoubtedly have been greater. Mitterrand's ability to portray the result as a narrow right-wing victory, rather than as an overwhelming rejection of his presidency lessened the pressures upon him to stand down as President, which might otherwise have proved irresistible. In the longer term it enabled him to stage a political recovery as the arbiter-President of *cohabitation*. It is not proposed here to analyse the period of *cohabitation* for its constitutional detail; this lies outside of the boundaries of the current chapter. Rather, we shall attempt to outline the extent to which, in spite of the weakening of presidential power during *cohabitation*, presidentialism and the forthcoming presidential election dominated the strategies of the French parties from 1986-88.

The importance of presidentialism as an organising principle continued strongly to characterise the French party system during *cohabitation*. As in previous presidential elections, the autonomy of the candidates reduced the control that their sponsoring parties could hope to exercise over them: to a greater or lesser degree, each candidate based his electoral campaign upon the notion of *rassemblement*, the ecumenical appeal beyond the political space represented by any one political tendency. This made it unlikely that any political party could control its candidate during the election campaign.

In the 1988 presidential election, only in the case of André Lajoinie and the PCF was the candidate clearly subordinate to the leadership of the sponsoring party.[22] Mitterrand's decision whether or not to stand again in 1988 was an intensely personal one, which did not in practice depend upon a formal nomination procedure within the PS. Indeed, the PS was largely excluded from any influence during Mitterrand's campaign. The RPR remained essentially a powerful electoral machine, whose main function was to promote Chirac's presidential bid and to organise for victory. Barre, in the Gaullien overtones characteristic of his campaign, openly denounced all parties as divisive, and suggested that no serious presidential candidate should pay any attention to party. His campaign suffered as a result (see Chapter Six). Finally, despite evidence of internal divisions within the National Front, few doubted that Le Pen completely mastered the far-right organisation in the 1988 campaign. In fact, the presidential elections of 1988 demonstrated more starkly than ever before that presidential candidates had to appeal beyond the boundaries of 'their' natural electorates, which led them to distance themselves from their sponsoring parties. It also illustrated, however, that the infrastructure provided by a political party remained an important factor in running an effective campaign.

The impact of presidentialism was felt in other ways too. The approach of the presidential election affected the internal cohesion of all the main parties. In relation firstly to the PCF, the internecine rivalries separating the party's official candidate Lajoinie from the unorthodox Pierre Juquin probably owed more to the dialectics of conflict within the small Communist world than it did to the principle of presidentialism. The orthodox PCF leadership deliberately selected an uncharismatic, orthodox candidate, Lajoinie, who would toe the party line, and subordinate his campaign the orders of the party's General Secretary Marchais. Lajoinie was opposed by Juquin, a long-time advocate of cooperation between Communists and other 'progressive' forces (Socialists, Greens, and small groups of the extreme left). He was expelled from the party in October 1987 for his pains, and subsequently stood as a independent Communist candidate in the 1988 presidential election (see Chapter Three).

Secondly, the PS. Mitterrand's successful positioning as the President of all of the French during the period of *cohabitation* severely limited the autonomy that could be displayed by the PS, the presidential party even in opposition. The party was constrained to follow 'its' President, the arbiter-President of *cohabitation,* despite the fact that it could exercise little influence over whether Mitterrand decided to stand again, or over the content of his platform once he had declared his candidacy. Meanwhile, Mitterrand's hesitations before declaring his renewed candidacy in March 1988 encouraged rival potential candidates (notably Michel Rocard and Jean-Pierre Chevènement) to pursue their campaigns while awaiting Mitterrand's decision, thereby fuelling internal tensions. In fact, the PS was forced to start its campaign for the April-May presidential election without knowing which candidate it would be backing.[23] The 1988 election thus clearly illustrated the continuing subordination of the PS to its historic leader, as well as the party's marginalisation during the campaign.

The corrosive effects of rival presidential ambitions were most visible on the right. The proximity of the 1988 presidential election revealed the extent to which rivalries between the main candidates on the right (Chirac, Barre, Le Pen) had a damaging effect upon the cohesion of Chirac's government, within which the UDF participated as a junior partner alongside the RPR. Despite having only a slender overall majority, Chirac's government pushed through a programme of radical reform, best characterised as a French version of Reaganite or Thatcherite economic liberalism and political conservatism.[24] Chirac's strategic calculation in accepting to form a government of *cohabitation* under a Socialist President had been that his only chance of restoring his position as undisputed leader of the right-wing coalition before the next presidential election was to adopt the 'courageous' choice of governing in unpredictable circumstances: he counted not only upon the success of government policies, but also on the reflex of legitimacy within the right-wing electorate to outdistance Barre, the divider. His strategy was eventually partly vindicated, at least in that he won the first-round primary against Barre. Unlike the latter in relation to the UDF, Chirac completely mastered the RPR, the axis party of the conservative administration. His recovery to overtake Barre as the leading right-wing candidate illustrated that Chirac was able to mobilise the conservative electorate on the first round more efficiently than Barre, although most polls suggested that the latter would have been a better second-round candidate against Mitterrand.

The UDF was by far the most divided of the main political formations. Barre's candidacy revealed more lucidly than ever how the UDF structure was a primarily a loose confederation of centre-right parties with different objectives rather than a coherent political entity: whereas the CDS and one fraction of the Republican Party (PR) campaigned actively for Barre, another fraction of the PR and most of the Radical Party barely concealed their preference for Chirac. The final obstacle to a right-wing victory in 1988 was the continuing existence of the National Front, and its charismatic leader Le Pen. Analysis of the composite nature and protest character of Le Pen's exceptional vote on the first round of the 1988 presidential election lies outside of the boundaries of this chapter.[25]

The 1988 Elections and the Party System

On 8th May 1988, Mitterrand was reelected as President, the first time that any French politician had been popularly reelected to the presidency in the Fifth Republic. Mitterrand's reelection illustrated a number of lasting trends in relation to the party system of the 1980s, as well as indicating several new features. The first ballot of the 1988 presidential election demonstrated more clearly than ever Socialist domination of the left. In presidential terms, the PCF, whose candidate Lajoinie received less than 7 per cent, had become a virtual irrelevance (see Chapter Three). Mitterrand's success was predicated upon his practice as the arbiter-President of *cohabitation,* during which he had successfully created a new image: that of Father of the nation, presiding over the interests of all French people above the partisan rivalries represented by political parties.[26] The key to Mitterrand's electoral success in 1988 lay in the extent to which he attracted an important fraction of centre-right voters from the first ballot, who might normally have been expected to vote for Chirac or Barre. This centre-right support helped offset a degree of discontent amongst traditional PS supporters, on account of the centrist orientation of Mitterrand's campaign. Notwithstanding this, the myth of the union of the left retained all its potent force on the second round: second-ballot transfers from PCF, extreme-left and Green voters in Mitterrand's favour were excellent, marking a stark contrast with the disunity of the right.

Since the mid-1980s, the French right had been faced with a similar dilemma to that confronting the left opposed to de Gaulle in the 1960s: a divided right had to face a left clearly dominated by one party - the PS - which in favourable circumstances could unite electoral support from extreme left to centre right. The 1988 presidential campaign clearly revealed the extent to which the right's divisions contributed to Chirac's defeat (as they had done so for Giscard in 1981). The tripartite division of the right on the first round severely complicated the task of the leading right-wing candidate on the second ballot. In order to secure victory, Chirac had to attract the virtual totality of both Barre's and Le Pen's voters, an act of political acrobacy which proved impossible to accomplish. Nominally majoritarian on the first ballot, as in 1981, the French right was gravely weakened by its own divisions.[27]

By 1988, the symmetry of the party system was almost the mirror opposite to that of the 1960s. The dominant party of the 1960s, de Gaulle's UNR, had been replaced by a fractious and divided opposition, insufficiently united to combat the common enemy, and rent by rivalries between *présidentiables*. The existence of the FN acted as a repellent to hesitant centrist-inclined voters, of whom a proportion preferred the Socialist left to the classical right-wing formations (UDF and RPR) on account of the perceived compromises made by the latter with Le Pen's movement or ideas. By contrast, the left, sorely divided in the 1960s between a dominant PCF (repellent to most voters) and an impotent non-Communist left, had become increasingly the domain of a Socialist Party mellowed by the experience of power, flanked by a marginal, largely irrelevant Communist Party to its left.

Mitterrand's campaign in the 1988 presidential election had been fought around the theme of *l'ouverture*, the promise to open up the presidential majority beyond the confines of the left. That he had able to employ such a concept so successfully testified to the decline of left-right bipolar sentiment within the electorate. Once elected President, Mitterrand named his erstwhile rival Michel Rocard as Prime Minister. In itself, the choice of Rocard testified to the President's apparent anxiety to be consistent with the political discourse he had adopted during the campaign: Rocard had consistently been the most popular Socialist politician amongst UDF and RPR voters.[28]

Once named as Prime Minister, Rocard engaged in a series of initial negotiations in an attempt to incite the centrists in the CDS and elsewhere to join his government: these negotiations failed. The centrists, aware of the conservative character of the 'centre' electorate, were unwilling or unable to switch alliances overnight, in the style of the Fourth Republic (see Chapter Six). The President responded by dissolving the National Assembly elected in 1986 some five days only after his triumphal reelection, effectively burying any realistic prospect of a new majority based upon an alliance between the PS and the centrists. Mitterrand's presidential campaign had promised an opening to the centre; instead the classic bipolar electoral alliances of the Fifth Republic were hastily resurrected. The old PS-PCF alliance was given a new lease of life, mainly because deputies from both parties had become used to considering such an alliance as indispensable for their re-election. There was no political cohesion in the PS-PCF alliance, whatever its electoral virtues. By 1988, PS domination within the 'alliance' was virtually complete: despite a partial Communist recovery from the presidential contest, PS or 'presidential majority' candidates obtained more votes than PCF candidates in 95 per cent of first-round primaries.[29]

The mainstream right-wing formations (UDF [including the CDS], RPR) responded to Mitterrand's dissolution by announcing the creation of the *Union du rassemblement et du centre* (URC), led by Giscard. URC declared its intention to present one right-wing candidate from the first ballot in virtually every constituency, in an attempt to minimise the disunity which might otherwise have reigned between RPR, UDF and CDS candidates. The right thereby remained faithful to its established Fifth Republic practice.[30] The renewed UDF-RPR alliance illustrated its efficiency, suggesting that the French right performed better in legislative elections (where it could rely on the strength of incumbent deputies) than in presidential contests, during which fierce personal rivalries damaged the right-wing candidate's chances on the second ballot. For the first time, the UDF returned more deputies than the RPR: this was a testament to the effectiveness of Giscard's leadership, as well as of Chirac's discredit after his severe electoral defeat, and to the more centrist location of the UDF (typified by the frequently excellent performances of CDS candidates).

The theory of the 'decisive' election (presidential contest or referendum) being followed almost automatically by a victorious general election was called into question by the 1988 legislative result. Rather than elect a convincing (but not excessive) majority for the President, as Mitterrand had demanded, the French electorate returned a mitigated verdict: there was certainly a relative PS majority, and an absolute electoral majority for the left (PS and PCF). Despite being the largest party, however, the PS failed to obtain an overall majority of seats; a minority Socialist-led administration flanked by opponents on its left (PCF) and its right (UDC, UDF, RPR) resulted from the election. The weak relative majority given to the PS was interpreted by many commentators as testifying to the electorate's refusal of a return to the pre-1986 style absolute presidency, such as Mitterrand himself had decried during the 1988 presidential campaign.

In terms of the contours of the party system, the 1988 elections repeated the pattern established in 1986, albeit with marked differences in support for individual parties: two major social-reformist (PS) and moderate conservative (URC) formations were flanked by significant minor parties on the extreme right (FN) and the extreme left (PCF). There could no longer be any illusion as to the political cohesion of the traditional left-wing alliance: the second Rocard government formed in June 1988 was from the outset fiercely contested by the PCF. In political terms a price had to be paid for the comfort of the PS-PCF electoral alliance, since it made any rapprochement with the centre extremely difficult in the short term. The favourite explanation of the 1988 legislative election result was that a majority of the French people had been determined to prevent Chirac's election in the presidential election, but was now equally determined to prevent Mitterrand holding all the reins of power, and thus 'corrected' its presidential vote in favour of the right.

The Party System in the 1990s

Michel Rocard's second government, formed on 30 June 1988, could claim to be an original one in the context of the Fifth Republic: half of its ministers were not Socialists, but were either dissident UDF (such as Jean-Pierre Soisson, former Secretary-General of the Republican Party, and Jean-Marie Rausch of the CDS), or else were 'apolitical' representatives of civil society. Despite this, the key ministries were held by prominent Socialist politicians, often the same ministries as these personalities had occupied under Laurent Fabius (Mitterrand's second Prime Minister from 1984-86). The CDS refused to join Rocard's government, but as a sign of their new autonomy the centrists formed themselves into the Union of the Centre (UDC) parliamentary group and proclaimed their intention of offering a 'constructive opposition'.

The period opened by the formation of the second Rocard government in June 1988 remained of uncertain contours two years later. Despite the failure of the centrists to rally to Mitterrand's majority, Rocard appeared determined to adopt a consensual approach towards the art of governing, and to search for bipartisan agreement on policy wherever possible. The new political discourse adopted by Rocard received a favourable echo within public opinion, so much so that after one year in office, Rocard was by far the most popular of Mitterrand's four Prime Ministers. His ability to attract support for a number of policies across party lines, especially within the electorate, meant that no political commentator could dismiss the long-term possibility of a lasting political realignment being brought about by the practice of 'government by consensus'. Notwithstanding this, once the initial impetus had given way to a more stable practice of government, older patterns of opposition gradually reasserted themselves: the European election of June 1989 was of considerable importance in this respect, since it demonstrated the limits to centrist autonomy (see Chapter Six).

By the early 1990s, the party system in France displayed a number of prominent features:

* It appeared more apparent than ever that traditional bipolar electoral alliances no longer accurately reflected the real divisions between France's political parties. But it was unclear what, if anything, could replace these traditional alliances. During the first two years of Rocard's administration, a political discourse advocating *l'ouverture* had not led to any lasting political realignment, based on Socialist-centrist governmental and electoral alliances. Indeed, the PS-PCF alliance was partially resurrected in time for the municipal elections of March 1989. The rather poor performance of joint Socialist-Communist lists, by comparison with autonomous PS, or 'presidential majority' lists, indicated a reaction against their lack of political credibility.[31]

* The sudden emergence of the Greens in 1988 and 1989 illustrated that the party system had to be analysed in terms of being an active evolving structure, rather than

a static range of pre-established political positions. The breakthrough of the Greens in the 1989 municipal elections and the spectacular confirmation of their strength in the European election of June 1989 was interpreted in numerous manners, which are considered in Chapter Five. Undoubtedly, their success represented part of a European-wide movement, based on the new saliency of the environment as a political issue. Within the context of the French party system, however, their success might be interpreted as one more sign of the inability of the mainstream parties to articulate new political demands. Certain commentators argued that the success of the Greens testified to the growing degree of alienation from the political system experienced by a minority of the French electorate.

* The PCF remained a marginal force on the extreme left, riven by internal divisions, above all determined to ensure the Socialists' defeat in the future. Notwithstanding the favourable opportunity for expanding on the left created by Rocard's centrist political discourse, the PCF proved itself incapable of exploiting discontent with the new government. The speed with which developments in Eastern Europe shook the old Communist world to its foundations was unlikely to leave the PCF unaffected, despite the leadership's attempts to suppress all calls for *glasnost* within the party.

* The PCF had previously acted as the protest-party *par excellence*; this role had gradually devolved to the National Front. By the end of the decade, the FN had illustrated its capacity to survive in each different sort of political contest that the regime had to offer. It had defied numerous predictions of its imminent demise, and had become a permanent part of the political landscape.

* Socialist domination of the left appeared to be henceforth irreversible. The French left had become more akin to its counterparts in most other West European nations in this respect: only in Italy did the Communist Party retain something of its former glory, despite changing its name. The first two years of Rocard's government illustrated, however, that the Socialist Party was as divided as ever. These divisions were given their full expression at the Rennes Congress of March 1990, where Mitterrand's protégés Fabius and Jospin fought a bitter, inconclusive battle for supremacy (see Chapter Four) in the optic of *l'après-mitterrandisme*.

* The situation on the centre right of French politics remained confused. Despite the CDS's loyalty to its traditional allies in the UDF and RPR in the municipal elections of March 1989, the decision to run an autonomous list for the European election of June 1989 provided adequate illustration of the centrists' continuing quest for an identity separate from that of its UDF partners. However, the poor performance of the independent centrist list led by Simone Veil in an apparently favourable election was followed by the CDS's decision to participate in the new UDF/RPR confederation, the Union for France (UPF), formed in June 1990.

* The French right continued to suffer from serious structural difficulties: to the now traditional locational divisions (centre right, central right, extreme right) were added those created by the emergence of a new generation of dynamic, ambitious politicians determined to challenge the established UDF and RPR leaderships (Chapters Six and Seven), as well as the ever-present danger of presidential rivalries as a corrosive force. Both the UDF and RPR were seriously internally divided: by

early 1990, the traditionally monolithic RPR was tearing itself apart, as policy and personality-based factionalism created a confusing array of shifting intra-party alliances of the type usually associated with the PS. In June 1990, in recognition of the potentially fatal effects of untrammelled and unregulated presidential rivalries, the RPR and UDF agreed to institute a system of US-style primaries to designate a single candidate before the next presidential election.

Conclusion: Are Parties In Crisis ?

Rather than concentrating upon the performance of individual parties, by the end of the decade certain commentators were openly calling into question the ability of the party system as a whole effectively to formulate responses to new problems, or to cope with managing the nation.[32] Some went so far as to evoke a crisis of parties as representative institutions, a hypothesis by no means limited to France. Opinion surveys began to register a profound deception with the political system on the part of a substantial minority from around 1983-84 onwards. This was first reflected in the rise of the National Front as an anti-system party, and latterly in growing abstention rates, culminating in the June 1988 legislative election, which registered the highest rate of abstention (34.25 per cent) since the beginning of the Third Republic. The latest manifestation of this movement was the breakthrough of the Greens.

According to the tenets of this pessimistic thesis, the French political system is afflicted by a profound malaise, predicated upon a reaction against broken and unrealistic party promises by left and right (see below), dissatisfaction with the artificial bipolar basis of political competition (which no longer corresponds to the electors' aspirations), as well as with the perceived incapacity of left and right to resolve France's economic problems, and a widespread perception that all politicians are corrupt.[33] By the end of the decade, there was clear evidence from opinion polls that many French voters had grown tired of older ideological divisions and programmes, especially after the heightened expectations and subsequent disappointments created by the 'dual alternation' of 1981-82 and 1986-87. At issue was not merely the incongruity between oppositional discourse and governmental practice, but also the capacity of the political sphere to act in an autonomous manner in relation to the central problem of managing the economy.

The failure of the Socialists' radical reform programme of 1981-82 to combat unemployment, to relaunch the economy, or to redistribute wealth had disillusioned a fraction of the left-wing electorate. The incongruity between the promises made throughout the 1970s (as expressed by the optimistic slogan *changer la vie*) and the practical effects of the Socialists' reform programme (the government being forced to recognise the primacy of economic constraints over social objectives) was painful for many voters who subsequently formed part of the *deçus du socialisme*. The Socialists in power were unable to satisfy the party's rhetorical demands made while in opposition during the 1970s. The reaction against the left was all the more keenly felt because these illusions had been maintained for so long (see Chapter Four). The right suffered from a similar inability to match theoretical claims with practical results: what it defined as 'liberalism' did not automatically have all the effects its advocates had claimed, such as a rapid reduction in unemployment, or an immediate economic recovery. When in opposition from 1981 to 1986, the right - especially Chirac's RPR - had engaged in a similar process of ideological mobilisation to that of the left in the 1970s in an attempt to lead opinion against the left-wing government after 1981.[34] In the UDF-RPR common platform of January 1986, upon which the parties fought the 1986 legislative election, the right proposed an all-encompassing alternative to the left's statism, in the form of a gallic version of Reaganite economic liberalism and social and political conservatism (see Chapters Six and Seven). Chirac made the mistake of believing that the French electorate had voted in March 1986 for an all-embracing alternative to the left, which the polls had never suggested to be the case. Despite the popularity of certain measures (such as privatisations), in its haste to reform French society Chirac's government seriously misread the state of French opinion, and created the impression of a government governing in the interests of one social class. In both cases, opposition parties had created false expectations, which were promptly disappointed once that these parties gained power.

The left-wing French tradition of proposing comprehensive ideological solutions was thus imitated by the French right in order to mobilise support against the 1981-86 Socialist government. But all ideological solutions emerged discredited from the dual alternation of 1981 and 1986. Neither left nor right had been able to resolve what is perhaps France's most pressing economic problem - unemployment - by their respective panaceas, although both could point to relatively successful anti-inflationary policies. Each of the mainstream candidates paid heed in 1988 to the limits of political action, and the need to avoid making too many detailed commitments or unrealistic promises. Rocard's attempt to create a new style of government by consensus might be regarded as a clear recognition of the constraints which weigh upon any government's freedom of manoeuvre, and an acceptance of the need for greater harmony between discourse and governmental practice.

The political situation created by Mitterrand's re-election had all the hallmarks of being a period of transition. Few would predict the eventual outcome.

Notes

1. See in particular Bell, D.S., *Contemporary French Political Parties*, Croom Helm, London, 1983; Frears, J., *Political Parties and Elections in the French Fifth Republic*, Hurst, London, 1977; Williams, P.M., and Harrison, M., *French Politicians and Elections, 1951-1969*, Cambridge University Press, Cambridge, 1970; Wilson, F., *French Political Parties under the Fifth Republic*, Praeger, New York, 1970.

2. On the author's evaluation of the importance of these various explanations, see Cole, A., and Campbell, P., *French Electoral Systems and Elections since 1789*, Gower, Aldershot, 1989.

3. See Ysmal, C., 'L'impossible centrisme', *Politique Aujourd'hui*, no. 10, January 1989, pp. 85-96.

4. On the influence of religion as a determinant of voting behaviour, see Michelat, G., and Simon, M., *Classe, réligion et comportement politique*, FNSP, Paris, 1977. France remains an overwhelmingly Catholic country, at least nominally, but the proportion of devout practising Catholics, who overwhelmingly favour right-wing parties, has declined substantially. In 1983, the polling organisation SOFRES (*Opinion publique*, 1984) classified 14 per cent of the population as 'regularly practising' Catholics (21 per cent in 1974, circa 25 per cent in 1965). For occasional (17 per cent in 1983) and non-practising (52 per cent) Catholics, religion is of less or little significance in influencing patterns of voting behaviour; in theory, these electors are less likely to be influenced by religion, more by social class, ideological preference, issues, region etc. Secularisation was commonly held as one explanation behind the rise of the PS in the 1970s. See Johnson, R.W., *The Long March of the French Left*, Macmillan, London, 1981, Chapter Six. Those who profess no religion (14 per cent in 1983) overwhelmingly favour left-wing parties.

5. On the greater scope, if not intensity, of class voting in the 1970s, see Johnson, op. cit., Chapters Five and Six. The notion of a 'sociological majority for the left', the inevitable consequence of the development of the *salariés* (salaried workers in a situation of non-independence) resulting from the decline of agriculture and the growth of the tertiary sector, was frequently expressed in a pseudo-Marxist manner by Socialist politicians in the 1970s.

6. For a comprehensive survey of the electorate in the 1970s see Capdeveille, J. et al., *France de gauche vote à droite*, FNSP, Paris, 1981. For an update on electoral volatility in the first half of the 1980s, see Dupoirier, E., and Grunberg, G., *Mars 1986: la drôle de défaite de la gauche*, FNSP, Paris, 1986; Lancelot, A., and M-T., 'The Evolution of the French Electorate', pp. 77-99, in Ross, G. et al., *The Mitterrand Experiment*, Polity Press, Oxford, 1987. The usual English translation for *cadre* is that of a manager. This is rather narrow: besides management, the *cadres* include: the teaching profession, engineers, the scientific and literary professions, technicians, social and medical workers, and various smaller categories. No socio-professional category was exempt from considerable volatility in its voting behaviour patterns during the 1980s. Threatened social groups - workers, small independents (especially shopkeepers) - were disproportionately represented within the National Front electorate.

7. See Cole and Campbell, op. cit., Chapter Two for an examination of the merits of this argument. On the right, from 1962-73, only one candidate generally carried the label of the presidential majority from the first ballot onwards. Up until (and including) 1973, this was usually a Gaullist, sometimes an Independent Republican. This 'rule' was only breached in 1978, when RPR and UDF fought each other on the first ballot to carry the torch of the presidential majority into the second. In 1981 and 1988, united first-round candidacies returned, subject to pre-electoral deals between the parties based on the presupposition of equality between them. In the 1986 proportional representation election, UDF and RPR ran joint lists in 60 departments, usually the smaller ones, where they alternated leadership according to local strength. In 36 other metropolitan departments, usually the larger ones, UDF and RPR ran separate lists. The situation was somewhat more complicated on the left: from 1962 onwards, Socialist and Communists agreed to 'mutual withdrawal' pacts, according to which only the best placed left-wing candidate proceeded to the second round. This mechanism gradually favoured the Socialists: whereas the PCF had arrived ahead in three-fifths of constituencies in 1962, by 1988 PS candidates won through to the second ballot in 95 per cent of instances. This competitive electoral mechanism greatly exacerbated tensions between the two parties. In 1986, fought under proportional representation, PS and PCF competed everywhere.

8. The only exception to the rule of left-right confrontation was in 1969, when the left's disunity meant that no left-wing representative won through to the second ballot. The Gaullist Pompidou faced the centrist Alain Poher.

9. See Johnson, op. cit., pp. 181-189, for a detailed examination.

10. See Frears, J., and Parodi, J-L., *War Will Not Take Place: the French Parliamentary Elections of March 1978*, Hurst, London, 1989.

11. See Gaffney, J. (ed.), *The French Presidential Elections of 1988: Ideology and Leadership in Contemporary France*, Gower, Aldershot, 1989.

12. Figures from SOFRES post-election poll, *Le Nouvel Observateur*, 16-22 May 1981.

13. On the 'decisive election', see Cole and Campbell, op. cit., pp. 96, 128, 164.

14. See Biffaud, O., 'Le piège et le déclin', *Bilan du septennat*, Le Monde: dossiers et documents, May 1989.

15. See Charlot, J., 'Le président et le parti majoritaire', *Revue Politique et Parlementaire*, no. 905, pp. 27-42, August 1983.

16. At the 1981 legislative election, UDF deputies anxious to keep their seats were only too willing to strike a bargain with the stronger RPR, according to which all outgoing deputies received the backing of both formations. The composite nature of the UDF thus facilitated the RPR's task in reimposing its leadership on the right after the 1981 presidential election.

17. See Schain, M.A.,' The National Front in France and the construction of political legitimacy', *West European Politics*, vol. 11, no. 1, pp. 229-252, April 1987.

18. See Shields, J.G., 'The French far right in the ascendent', *Contemporary French Civilisation*, Fall/Winter, 1987, pp. 39-52; Charlot, M., 'L'emergence du Front national', *Revue Française de Science Politique*, vol. 36, no. 1, February 1986, pp. 30-45.

19. For detailed examination, see Cole and Campbell, op. cit., Chapter Eight; see also Knapp, A., 'Proportional but bipolar: France's electoral system in 1986', *West European Politics*, vol. 10, no. 11, April 1987.

20. See Pulzer, P., 'Is There Life After Dahl?', in Kolinsky, E. (ed.), *Opposition in Western Europe*, Croom Helm, London, 1987.

21. The effect of the changed electoral system ought not to be exaggerated: the use of proportional representation in the 1986 election did not prevent the RPR-UDF from obtaining an overall majority. At best, the switch away from the old second-ballot system, towards a list-based system of proportional representation encouraged greater party autonomy, and liberated parties from politically embarrassing alliances they might otherwise have been forced to consider under the old second-ballot system. There was no longer any necessity for Mitterrand's PS to conclude an electoral pact with the PCF, which would have lacked all political credibility. President Mitterrand likewise calculated that the FN might return a sufficient number of deputies to prevent the UDF/RPR from obtaining an overall majority. This did not occur, but the new system did enable the FN to elect 35 deputies and maintain a high political profile, which was likely to embarrass the mainstream right in the run-up to the next presidential election.

22. See the contributions on Lajoinie, Mitterrand, Chirac, Barre and Le Pen in Gaffney, op, cit.

23. See Cole, A., 'The French Socialist Party in transition', *Modern and Contemporary France*, no. 37, January 1989, pp. 4-11.

24. On the RPR's ideological evolution in the course of the 1980s, see Baudouin, J., 'Le moment néo-libéral du RPR: essai d'interprétation', unpublished paper presented to the Third National Congress of the French Political Science Association at Bordeaux, 5-8 October 1988.

25. See Shields, J.G., 'Campaigning from the Fringe: Jean-Marie Le Pen', in Gaffney, op. cit., pp. 140-157.

26. See Cole, A., 'François Mitterrand: from Republican Contender to President of All the French', and 'La France Unie: François Mitterrand' in Gaffney, ibid., pp. 37-56, 81-100.

27. Chirac had illustrated sufficient ambiguity towards Le Pen during the 1988 presidential campaign (refusing any alliance, but repeating themes associated with the extreme-right leader) that he alienated the support of a fraction of centre-right voters from the first ballot, and that of a minority of Barre's voters on the second round. In addition, although he was forced to bid for support from potential (or actual) FN voters, Chirac was unable to capture the support of more than two-thirds of Le Pen's first-round electorate, confirming the composite nature of this electorate, and the protest-vote character of Le Pen's 14.4 per cent in April 1988.

28. Certain commentators analysed Mitterrand's whole campaign discourse as a Machiavellian tactic to attract the support of centre-right electors, without having any intention of 'opening up' his presidential majority.

29. Although the PS emerged as the largest party in seats, the RPR-UDF coalition actually received more first-ballot votes (see Appendix 1), and the overall left (PCF, PS) and right (URC, FN) totals were virtually identical.

30. Only in 1978 did the various formations of the right-wing coalition agree to a generalised pattern of first-ballot 'primaries'.

31. See Cole, A., 'The French municipal election of 12th and 19th March 1989', *Modern and Contemporary France*, no. 39, October 1989, pp. 23-32.

32. See, for example, Duhamel, O., and Jaffré, J., *Le nouveau président*, Seuil, Paris, 1987, Chapter Two.

33. See Baudouin, op. cit.

Bibliography

Bartolini, S., 'Institutional constraints and party competition in the French party system', *West European Politics*, vol. 7, no. 4, October 1984.

Bell, D.S., and Shaw, E., *The Left in France: Towards a Socialist Republic*, Spokesman, Nottingham, 1982.

Bell, D.S., *Contemporary French Political Parties*, Croom Helm, London, 1983.

Bell, D.S, and Criddle, B., *The French Socialist Party: the Emergence of a Party of Government*, Clarendon Press, Oxford, 1988.

Borella, F., *Les partis politiques dans la France d'aujourd'hui*, Seuil, Paris, 1975.

Braud, P., 'Etre le parti du président: délices et maléfices', *Projet*, no. 209, February 1989.

Capdeveille, J., *France de gauche vote à droite*, FNSP, Paris, 1981.

Charlot, J., 'Du parti dominant', *Projet*, no. 48, September-October 1970.

Charlot, J., *Les partis politiques en France*, FNSP, Paris, 1986.

Charlot, J., 'La transformation de l'image des partis politiques français', *Revue Française de Science Politique*, vol. 36, no. 1, February 1986.

Charlot, J., 'Les mutations du système de partis français', *Pouvoirs*, no. 49, 1989.

Cole, A., and Campbell, P., *French Electoral Systems and Elections since 1789*, Gower, Aldershot, 1989.

Frears, J., *Political Parties and Elections in the French Fifth Republic*, Hurst, London, 1977.

Gaffney, J., *The French Presidential Elections of 1988: Ideology and Leadership in Contemporary France*, Gower, Aldershot, 1989.

Johnson, R.W., *The Long March of the French Left*, Macmillan, London, 1981.

Machin, H., 'Stages and dynamics in the evolution of the French party system', *West European Politics*, vol. 12, no. 4, October 1989.

Le Monde, *Les clivages politiques*, Le Monde: dossiers et documents, March 1988.

Offerlé, M., *Les partis politiques*, PUF, Paris, 1987.

Portelli, H., 'Les partis et les institutions', *Pouvoirs*, no. 49, 1989.

Quermonne, J-L., 'La présidence de la République et le système des partis', *Pouvoirs*, no. 41, 1987.

Ross, G. et al., *The Mitterrand Experiment*, Polity Press, Oxford, 1987.

Von Beyme, K., *Political Parties in Western Europe*, Gower, Aldershot, 1985.

Williams, P.M., and Harrison, M., *French Politicians and Elections, 1951-1969*, Cambridge University Press, Cambridge, 1970.

Wilson, F., 'The revitalisation of French parties', *Comparative Political Studies*, vol. 12, no. 1, April 1979.

Wilson, F., *French Political Parties under the Fifth Republic*, Praeger, New York, 1982.

Wright, V., *The Government and Politics of France*, Unwin Hyman, London, 1989.

2 French Politicians and Political Communication

Susan Hayward

In France over the last twenty years there has been a radical shift in politicians' perceptions of the relevance of television to elections, be they presidential, general or even local. The French were not the first to understand the importance of television in this area, the USA in the 1950s was the forerunner. However, France was the first West European country to capitalise on the ability of television to mediatise the political message effectively on a massive scale. In fact, as this chapter will go on to demonstrate, it could be claimed that television, more so than any other media, has played a major role in the legitimation of what has come to be termed 'presidentialism' and its changing style. Appropriately this process began with de Gaulle. Almost at the very beginning of the Fifth Republic, it was he who saw the political potential of television to mediatise his message on a massive scale (by 1962 the number of television sets in France had more than quadrupled since 1958 from 800 000 to four million sets). The message was first and foremost, although the mediatisation of his person came as a natural consequence. To accusations that he was making history on the small screen, de Gaulle countered that television was a state organ that must necessarily be invoked to redress the balance of anti-governmental bias in the written press. At this time, the French broadcasting authority, the *Radio-télédiffusion de France* (RTF), subsequently renamed the *Office de la radio-télédiffusion de France* (ORTF), was entirely state-owned and was under the direct control of the Minister of the Interior, thus interventionism was a straightforward exercise of state authority imposed upon the institution. In this first stage of mediatisation, television performed the role of transmitting the ideology of the state. And in this respect, at least where television was concerned, presidentialism was about making history.

Under President Giscard, television was relieved of its somewhat demagogic function and given a resolutely more personalising role to play. Indeed, in his thinking of politics in terms of images to be acted out, Giscard displayed a supreme mastery of the medium of television and revealed a modernity of vision that appealed to the electorate of 1974. During his mandate, Giscard used television first to mediatise his person (fire-side chat, pullover, open shirt etc...) and second, as a platform from which to attack his opponents and detractors (the Bokassa affair for example).[1] In both instances, in terms of mediation, state ideology was subsumed to the individual, and television - in this second stage of its political evolution - played a vital role in the personalisation of presidentialism. In the circumstances this personalisation is not that surprising given that Giscard did not have a true party to lead but rather a consortium of centrists, nor indeed a platform based on doctrinal lines. Even more significant, however, was his forsaking history, a flaw in his thinking that has made him forgettable.

During this whole period, watching from the side lines was François Mitterrand, the presidential hopeful and veteran campaigner in two of the three elections prior to the 1981 presidential contest (1965, 1974). He had waged and lost a bitterly contested election in 1974 against Giscard and, whilst it may be true that television does not make an election, in Mitterrand's case in 1974 it certainly did not prevent him from losing it. In the televised debate prior to the second round of the presidential election, Mitterrand was to learn some hard lessons about self-mediation, scoring off one's opponent clearly and avoiding neatly laid discursive traps. In 1981, Mitterrand was a man well prepared (by the advertising magnate Jacques Séguéla amongst others) to do mediatic battle with his old rival and, by adapting many of Giscard's televisual tactics and adding one or two of his own, he stole the incumbent's fire. Again, to claim that it was television which gained Mitterrand the 1981 presidency would be too strong, but it is certain that the floating voters who in percentage numbers could sway the outcome were left unimpressed by Giscard and more convinced by Mitterrand's performance. At this third stage in its evolution, television gave a reflection on political discourse as duopolistic and a reflection on presidentialism as *alternance* (i.e. it reminded viewers that the constitution of the Fifth Republic allowed for the left just as much as the right to be elected with equal legitimacy to executive and legislative power without in any way endangering the institutions of the Fifth Republic).

By the 1988 presidential contest, the mediatisation of elections had reached such proportions that commentators were heard saying that the media hype all but occulted the political debate. There was some truth in this in that some of the *présidentiables* (Le Pen, Mitterrand, Waechter and Chirac) but not all (Barre, Laguiller, Lajoinie, and Juquin) were more concerned with positioning themselves to correspond to what they perceived as the electorally desired image rather than entering into confrontational debate over platforms. And, in the end, Mitterrand was the most successful in projecting the image of the man of state. Curiously, he achieved this by combining two of his predecessors' mediating tactics. He successfully conflated the personal (Giscard) with the historical (de Gaulle): personal in that, during the election, he was an individual not seemingly aligned to a political party (the PS was very much in the background); historical in that he was mediated as the symbol of *La France unie* and the embodiment of France's patrimony (republicanism) since the Revolution.

By 1988 the electorate had become so media-literate that an unmediated candidate would be poorly received. André Lajoinie (PCF), Arlette Laguiller (LO) and Barre refused to mediatise their campaigns and certainly in Barre's case this cost him dear. By way of contrast, a marginal candidate who did not ignore television's potential to get a message over to a mass audience was Antoine Waechter, the Green candidate. Indeed, in the run up to the 1988 presidential election the Green Party, sensing it had a potentially significant electoral following, was not adverse to shedding its former somewhat *folklorique* (sandals and home-knitted sweaters) image and moving up-market in its positioning. Strong on the good showing of its presidential candidate, at least in terms of successfully conveying the Greens' message, the party repeated its successful mediatic policy in its campaigns for the legislative elections of June 1988 and the European election of June 1989.[2]

From the above we can see that where presidential elections are concerned television can be used successfully to project an individual and indeed a message provided the image and the message correspond. So how to use the media is of crucial importance. But what are the merits of this media in the light of parliamentary elections? How useful is television in projecting a party's political message? As we shall go on to show, the PS in the 1986 legislative election certainly obtained the result consonant with its electoral slogans proving that negative campaigning (where campaigning is targeted against the opposition, as in 1986) is not necessarily the best tactic to follow if you are on the losing side.

Television is not the media for putting over complex messages, therefore a political message must be simplified, and mediatically packaged. Again the 1980s and especially the legislative campaign of 1986 saw a recognition by the major parties of the importance of packaging. Furthermore, minority parties (most especially the FN) were quick to seize upon the merits of simplicity.

Getting it right has now become the job of the advertising world, of the image-makers and media experts. Mediatising elections has meant that all presidential candidates need a *conseiller de communication* and that all the main parties have media units within their organisations.[3] As a result of these intense media pressures, political discourse, at least where its dissemination is concerned, has undergone an important evolution and has moved inexorably into the consumer market. Parliamentarianism is out, live broadcast democracy is in. Such is the impact of television that it is the way in which politics are communicated that is uppermost in politicians' minds. This is not to say that television forms the political, far from it. And as Jean-Jack Queyranne (spokesman for the PS) states 'the content of the campaigns... has become modified under the influence of the political situation and not from increased mediatisation.'[4] The message is the politic certainly, however, the presentation is the mediatic. How far, indeed, electioneering style has evolved from the early primitive television campaign style of 1965 (the first election campaign to be televised) when politicians read their texts from a piece of paper and the camera did not move.

In this chapter, three aspects of the influence of television on elections will be examined (bearing in mind the adage that, doubtless, election campaigns also have an impact on television). First, the influence of television on electioneering style and political discourse; second, candidates' positioning in the light of the media's exigencies; and, finally, the demands television places on politicians to get their oratorical skills around the right kind of televisual language.

However, before coming to this analysis one very important point needs to be made about the relationship between the state and television and how it is only since 1981 that there has been any change (for the better) in that relationship. As we have explained above, since the mid 1960s, the importance of television in electoral campaigns in getting the political message and personal image over has become steadily recognised, hence an ensuing ambivalence towards television on the part of political parties and most especially politicians. Since 1962, the struggle for control of the media (manifesting itself through state intervention, autocensure etc) by Presidents, Prime Ministers and party leaders has been notorious. It has been as if they believe that the politician who has a hold on the media is more assured of being elected. Giscard, the most blatant interventionist of all the Presidents of the Fifth Republic, was to find by 1981 that this belief had less founding in fact than he had led himself to believe. In the end, it took a Socialist President, François Mitterrand, to make any significant gesture to decouple state and television. Consonant with his electoral platform, he introduced legislation (through his government) to institute a governing body for broadcasting. This body was called the *Haute autorité* (HA) and part of its remit was to act as watchdog during election time and ensure that all parties were evenly represented in terms of air-time. At this stage air-time was in direct proportion to either the percentage of votes received, for the presidential elections, or the number of seats held, for parliamentary elections. During the *cohabitation* period of 1986-88 the

Commission nationale de la communication et des libertés (CNCL), the new body replacing the HA, had similar responsibilities, although air-time was now equally distributed amongst all presidential candidates (15 minutes each over the electoral period). Presently, it is the turn of the latest of these governing bodies, the *Conseil supérieur de l'audiovisuel* (CSA), to carry forward this torch of liberalisation. The effect of this equality of air-time has meant that minority parties do get a voice and in some cases (Le Pen, the Greens) a surprising ballot result.

Television and Electioneering Style

Television is a medium that is in constant flux. At the simplest level for example it is a constant flow of images, a constant renewing of images. It is also a very conservative medium and more inclined to stick to the same recipes of success where its programmes and scheduling are concerned. It is therefore reasonable to say that television is about the process of change (flow of images) and about showing something if not different, then differently (different styles, ways of showing the same narrative - take the different types of cop series for example). Political personages or parties must be able to answer to the mediatic demands placed upon their message-delivery by this paradoxical nature of television. They must be able to prove that their platforms are about change and modernity, or in the case of presidential hopefuls that they are the incarnation of these two criteria. They must also demonstrate that they are mindful of the republican tradition and the institutions which constitute that tradition. To be seen to embody only one at the expense of the other will be costly indeed. Of all the Presidents since the first televised presidential election of 1965, only Mitterrand appears to have understood the need constantly to upgrade one's image whilst simultaneously grounding it in republican tradition. De Gaulle failed to be modern. Over the years of his two consecutive presidencies he had built himself into an epic, but by 1969 he was no longer believable. France had become modern as a result of its spectacular postwar economic expansion (involving a massive programme of industrialisation), which came to fruition in the 1960s during de Gaulle's two presidential terms. However, by the late 1960s, the General no longer corresponded to the necessary image of modernity, and television exposed that he was no longer at the measure of modern society (the unsuccessful referendum of April 1969 did the rest). Giscard's fall from favour was similarly due to a failure to renew. His 'ordinary bloke' approach in 1974 won him an electorate satisfied with the image projected. However, over the seven years of his presidency, this image became thoroughly worn out because he constantly staged the same image projection ('ordinary children' having breakfast with him, 'ordinary dustmen' - mostly Magrhebins - having tea with him, etc). The punishment for repetition is dismissal, people get wise to the *trucage* and get tired of it. On a completely different scale of importance this lack of renewal is the problem which confronts Georges Marchais, General Secretary of the PCF (and the PCF in general). Marchais is all used up mediatically.

Television, then, is about how the politicians and parties project their image and message. Not exclusively, of course, for there are the political rallies, but here too there is a change. The epoch of the mass meeting, although not over, has met an ending in its purpose and style since television has become the mass-communicator. The *tribune* (mass meeting) still serves to rally the faithful, but it no longer takes place in some undistinguished hall or a large square (as in the days of Léon Blum and the Popular Front) where more than just the party supporters came to hear the message. Rather it is now staged (under strict security in most cases) under huge marquees or in great big conference centres with a podium and elaborate backdrop. The reason for this evolution is not just a matter of security, it is also televisual. The meetings are newsworthy and clips will be shown as part of a news item on the 8 o'clock evening news. A second effect of television with regard to the modernisation of electioneering style is, then, this spectacularisation of the *tribune* and its decline as the major platform from which to launch a political programme.

The impact of television in this respect is worth noting for it touches upon the whole issue of the illusion of intimacy and how it is constructed. Within a *tribune* setting in general the great majority are present out of a sense of solidarity. A *tribune* creates a sense of intimacy through the physicality and realness of the presence of both the audience and the individual politician (or group of politicians). In this instance the individual is perceived as being within the reach of the mass, the illusion of intimacy being based on the belief of accessibility. Now, with television something quite other occurs. Firstly, television gives the spectator a sense of intimacy with the politician through the use of close-ups - emotions, facial gestures can be closely scrutinised - but this intimacy is of course totally false and far more illusory than with the *tribune*. Second, and more importantly, whilst this individualised accessibility is going on, the opposite is also occurring: television has made it possible for all audiences to be within the grasp of the politician (which is the converse of what happens in a *tribune*). What is also of interest with regard to France is that, up until the legislative elections of 1986, all audiences who turned on their television set were indeed within the reach of politicians (because all channels were state-owned) and all channels had to give coverage of the election campaigns. However, by 1986, thanks to a liberalisation of the channels, only three out of the then six channels were state-controlled, so the individual had a choice. If, for the audiovisual world, Mitterrand's first presidency is to remain famous for only one thing then it may well be for this demassification of the political message (i.e. it is no longer omnipresent, there are alternative discourses available at the same time).

We have already stated that, with regard to elections, television is about how the individual creates and continues to renew his or her persona, but one or two further points need to be made in this context. If Marchais and his party have failed to recognise this necessity to renew, then such is not the case for a formerly inept televisual communicator, the now twice-elected President of the Republic, François Mitterrand. By 1981, Mitterrand had changed enormously: he was rounder (he got rid of his heavy side-burns which accentuated the rectangularity of his face), he got rid of his brown suit (and brown-rimmed glasses) and went for the more mediatic republican blue suit (a blue which goes over particularly well on television), he found his own style of expression, that of a *conteur* (talking his politics through as if they were short narratives, using anecdotes by way of illustration, etc), he used formulas to throw his opponent (a trick of Giscard's which he learned in fact to turn to his advantage in the 1981 debate). In the 1981 elections Mitterrand played at being himself ('I say what I think' he often retorted to Giscard's taunting tactics during the debate) thus showing his sincerity and honesty (what the French call 'le test du parler vrai') all of which Giscard proved not to be up to. First, he was the rather tarnished incumbent (a number of scandals and his arrogance in dealing with them had greatly detracted from his image of 'ordinariness') and, second, he showed a certain disdain and *hauteur* towards his opponent Mitterrand during the debate, an unforgivable positioning where the spectator/electorate is concerned who like a good fight but no upper or under-handedness. In this famous debate, Mitterrand came over as a man of character for, crucially, he had at long last understood that a televised debate is about two rivals on show, a conflict of personalities, and not about ideology. In 1974, Mitterrand was still a man of the *tribune*, his discourse was grandiloquent, by 1981 he had come to grips with the fact that television was concerned with individual address (the individual coming into the living room via the screen, thanks to the illusion of intimacy discussed above) and not collective address which belongs in the *tribune*. Of the parties on the left it is the PCF with Marchais at its head which persists with the tribunal address on television and, when its discourse enters into a conflictual mode, it is over ideology not personalities that Communist politicians argue with their interlocutor. On a metaphorical level Marchais's dress code serves to illustrate this immobilism. Although it is obviously not true, Marchais appears to be wearing the same tweed jacket he has had since the beginning of 1981, in any event he is still sporting the same cut and colour of cloth.

On the question of Mitterrand's grandiloquence it is worth noting that in his 1988 presidential campaign he managed to reintroduce it as part of his image construction and in the most convincing manner. The way in which it was introduced was consonant with his image of man of state (one of the many facets of his image construction, a point to which I shall return) and this in turn served to reinforce his legitimacy to the presidency. Instead of arrogantly stating that he had after all been President for seven years and could rightly claim to be a man of state, his campaign video for the second round had clips of him giving speeches at various summit meetings during his first seven-year mandate. Superimposed (emblazoned even) over these images of him exercising his executive position (head of defence, head of international affairs) were key words such as 'peace', 'credibility', 'independence', 'firmness', 'disarmament', 'security', 'Rights of man' and 'solidarity' - grand rhetoric signifying a great statesman.

A third effect of television on electioneering style is, as was pointed out in the introduction, that television has democratised political discourse. Television is in a permanent mediation role between the political system and the electorate - through the news, through political affairs programmes and through the various *Magazines politiques* where journalists put questions to an invited political personality. In its role as the site of arbitrage, it has become a political institution in and of itself, in much the same way that a referee is part and representative of the sporting institution. The role of the journalist in setting the agenda for discussion in these *Magazines politiques* is a significant one. The journalist in question will orientate the interview around two factors. First, a straw poll of the electorate as to their most pressing preoccupations and, second, an agenda agreed upon between journalist and politician (usually a compromise). The politician, in the meantime, will endeavour to put over the message or messages which he or she considers uppermost. This triumvirat positioning of political debate may (and often does) prevent a squaring of the circle: the discussion may well start off with a regard to the electorate's concerns, but soon it shifts its focus and brings on line issues which politicians and journalists alike consider to be vital. In other words, the tendency is to fix the political agenda according to what politicians and journalists (because they cover what politicians say) think is important or think preoccupy the electorate, with the result that the electorate may well be left disaffected. This may not particularly disturb politicians during the fallow non-campaign time. However, during electioneering time it is crucial for politicians to ensure that the agenda matches the concerns of the electorate or they will lose credibility (in much the same way as the image of politicians must match up to the opinion the electorate holds of them).

Of all the grands *présidentiables* in the 1988 election, it was surely Barre who suffered most from this loss of credibility. The most important issues for the electorate at that time were unemployment and training and yet Barre, in trying to establish his difference from Chirac (the other major candidate of the right), focused on three specificities, only one of which (unemployment) bore any relation to the major preoccupations of the day. His first specificity dates back to March 1986 and to the whole period of *cohabitation* which he consistently attacked in order to distinguish himself from Chirac. However, this issue was a lost cause because the electorate had seen it work. Banking his difference on a non-starter was far from strategically sound and, in this instance, it brought with it the inference that Barre was not a man of compromise and was lacking in institutional flexibility (something which the electorate had appreciated during the *cohabitation* period). He also misfired on his second marker, his economic specificity. His reputation as one of France's best economists could have been a pulling card, but abstract economic and fiscal matters were low priorities for an electorate concerned with the more immediate problem of getting people into jobs.

Chirac also talked in similar ways to Barre about unemployment by placing it in the context of economic solutions. However, his miscalculation of electoral preoccupations only became transparently evident in the second round and nowhere more clearly so than in the televised debate with Mitterrand. In this debate only half as much time was devoted to education/training and unemployment as was to immigration and security. Since these latter issues were closely identified with Chirac's platform, the over-debating of them would be more likely to count against Chirac, for his lack of sensitivity to the needs of the electorate, rather than against Mitterrand.

Of the three heavy-weight presidential candidates, it was Mitterrand who came over as the least out of touch with popular opinion. His diversified image appealed to the electorate and not just the PS voters and in orientating his specificities around the top priorities without pretence to simple solutions he made clear, on two counts (image and message), his distinctiveness from his opponents. It would seem that Mitterrand had found the way to counter allegations that television electioneering had reached a crisis point where political discourse was concerned in that it had emptied it of all meaning. The effect of television on political discourse, most critics alleged, was to have centred it. Most discourse on television had become safe and homogeneous with each party or politician speaking the other's discourse. Unwilling to take risks, nobody would say unpopular things, the allegations continued. Left (PCF) and right (FN, RPR & UDF) complained that ideological debate had disappeared (they were saying this as early as 1986) and that all real distinction between the two camps had been erased. In ten years, they claimed, political discourse had moved from too much ideology to none at all. Mitterrand's trump card was doubtless to agree that the effect of the *alternance* and subsequently of *cohabitation* had led to a realistic centring of political discourse and that *rassembler* meant uniting all of France not just the left or the right. In effect, in his mediatic message he was saying, that's what the electorate want and that's what I can give them: *La France unie*. The various candidates of the right were unable to articulate this centrist message as effectively as Mitterrand, the arbiter-President of *cohabitation*: Barre discovered the centrist space already occupied by the incumbent President, whereas Chirac became trapped by his increasingly Lepenist rhetoric. Neither, of course, was the PCF. Thus, paradoxically, by centring the Socialist political discourse and by being re-elected on the strength of that discourse, Mitterrand placed the cachet of legitimacy on the politics of *alternance* within the constitution of the Fifth Republic.[5]

One further aspect of the influence of television on political discourse during election-time is the spectacularisation of the political message and by extension all symbolic acts of the political arena, such as the second-round debate, the *mise-en-scène* for news items or, indeed, the moment of election results and eventually the moment of the hand-over of power. Debates in general, ever since the famous Chirac-Fabius debate of

1985, have been commodified by the media into a sporting event - most especially a boxing match, exceptionally a slugging match (as with the Le Pen-Lajoinie scrap on La «5» in 1987) - with only one possible winner as the outcome. Television news coverage as we have seen elicits fanciful stage-setting, the most fanciful perhaps being Chirac's mobile television studio with which he travelled round France at the beginning of his '88 presidential bid - he subsequently dropped the idea in favour of a more moderate *mise-en-scène*.[6] Election-night sees the television studios either metamorphosing themselves into a cardboard facsimile of the National Assembly or local town hall depending on the election (this is A2's predilection), or into a glitzy Hollywood mirror-panelled studio (as adopted by TF1); in both arenas political personalities representing opposing camps are invited in to do combat - once again the modality of the debate is structured very much as a boxing match. Last, but not least, the televising of the symbolic change of power is redolent with spectacular promise. The most memorable of this particular event is probably the May 1981 *alternance*. On the one side, Giscard made a lonely departure from the Elysée (with much pathos he slowly said his goodbye and then, equally slowly, rose to his feet, walked away from the viewer to the back of the room to finally exit left); on the other, Mitterrand, surrounded by thousands of rejoicing supporters, makes his way on foot to the Panthéon and then, in solitude, visits the graves of brave Socialist heroes depositing a single rose on their sepulchre.

One way or another television has made spectacle an integral part of the electioneering process, small wonder then that all politicians and political parties desirous of success will need a communication strategy that will help their positioning.

Television and Political Positioning

There are three major 'musts' central to any communication strategy. First comes knowledge of the climate and terrain: politicians must be aware of the state of public opinion in all its diversity and the image the public have of them. Second, candidates must have a language all can understand and must therefore simplify their expression but not to the point of rendering it meaningless and empty. Finally, candidates must adopt a multi-media strategy and not just focus on television: recent studies have shown that two out of three voters read or scan election leaflets.[7] In this light it is easy to see why, of all of the 1988 presidential hopefuls, Mitterrand and Le Pen were the most successful. Le Pen's message was simple and clearly stated and appealed to 14.4 per cent of voters, his image, words and actions all matched up (so no confusion there as to what one was voting for), and his lack of television exposure (in relation to the three heavy-weights and even the PCF) forced him to make exponential use of the printed media (most importantly leafleting).[8] Mitterrand's message was diversified as was his image and responded simultaneously to dominant concerns in public opinion and to sectorised opinion; he had a clear message, *La France unie*, he deliberately decided to low-profile his television campaign by not over-exposing himself on the small screen (contrary to Chirac's tactic), he kept his pamphlet message short and straight to the point reserving his epistolary and literary skills for his *Lettre à tous les Français* (a long document published in *Le Monde* and *Libération* in which he laid out thoughts for the future of France).

At the beginning of the presidential campaign, Barre's communication strategy was all at sixes and sevens. In fact he appeared to have none at all. His initial positioning, a refusal to mediatise his image and a refusal to be associated to a party (thus snubbing the UDF), lost him a lot of ground and grass-root support. In interviews on television, he had no apparent interview strategy. The most exemplar of this error in mediatic thinking was his *Questions à domicile* in June 1987, although subsequent programmes of this genre revealed the same tendencies in poor campaign strategy. In this particular programme he came over as meandering and long-winded. There is some irony attached to this: at the beginning of the programme he stated that he did not prepare for television programmes because he believed in spontaneity, but his ponderous, slow delivery revealed him as anything but spontaneous. In later programmes, this image of the rather stuffy elderly professor (which his rotund physique does little to dislodge or contradict) was further compounded by his over-scientific (*langue de bois*) answers to some questions.[9] His reserved and sober campaign plus his inability to appear close to the concerns of the electorate meant that he was perceived as distant, arrogant even (on *L'heure de vérité* in April 1988, he stated 'people criticise me for not being critical of myself'). By deliberately ignoring the campaign strategy 'musts' he successfully marginalised himself into becoming the 'implicit candidate' (*candidat implicite*), as opposed to the explicit Chirac, and by constantly decrying the nefariousness of mediatising one's campaign he effectively became the spectator to his own.

In the legislative elections of 1986 and 1988, it could be argued that the PS conducted similarly disastrous campaigns. This seems especially true of the 1986 parliamentary elections. Admittedly the PS was fighting the campaign on the defensive. The Socialists knew they would lose their majority and their main target was damage-limitation. This meant that they were targeting a 30 per cent electoral return. Prior to the official campaign, the PS were standing at 26 per cent. The four per cent they made up in the actual election (there was only one round in the 'proportional' election of March 1986) would seem to be far more readily attributable to the bipolarising effect of the campaign than it was to their televised campaign. There were three essential problems with the campaign. In the first instance, the party political broadcasts were targeted negatively, based as they were on the slogan *Au secours! la droite revient* (help! the right is returning), which everyone knew. It was clearly a redundant message, one which compared unfavourably with the success of the British Conservative Party's negative targeting of Labour and the SDP over successive general elections. However, although the sketches were done humorously enough, the slight touch of 'hysteria' in the images meant that the humour back-fired. In the second instance, the juxtaposition between certain images and discourses gave a discordant, even schizoid tone to the message. Choosing to use, at the beginning of the clip, images of the rural village and its church reminiscent of Mitterrand's 1981 presidential campaign of *la force tranquille* was a tactical error. It implied that the PS was looking back to the Mitterrand and the PS of 1981, a fatal form of *arrièrisme*, especially given the subsequent economic austerity policies which that period engendered. When the talking heads came on, there was talk on the one hand of modernisation and a social plan and then, on the other, of following the example of *l'histoire du bon jardinier* (the diligent labourer). These two semantic fields just clashed head on, thus not enabling the message to come over clearly at all. It will not come as a surprise therefore that the last of the three weaknesses in the 1986 Socialist campaign was its inability to square the party's priorities with those of the electorate. In this instance it was the RPR/UDF alliance that got it right. To the PS's expressed concerns with purchasing power, *ouverture* and *rassemblement*, the allied right's platform countered with policies that 'the electorate wanted' (to quote Michel Noir) - what counted most was security and employment. To the PS's *arrièrisme* came the RPR's confident slogan for the future: *Vivement demain!*

Again, in the 1988 legislative election, it would appear that the PS somewhat mismanaged its campaign. The PS determined not to crow or campaign with arrogant confidence in the wake of Mitterrand's successful re-election as President (as they had done in 1981), but rather to play its cards modestly. In effect, on all party fronts the whole campaign was very low-key, but the PS campaign was undoubtedly the most understated. The central plank to their platform was *l'ouverture* and in most of their campaign talk they were asking the electorate for a majority but not too great a one. In the end, they did not even obtain a clear, out and out, majority so it could be said that they got a little less than they bargained for. It should also be pointed out that the message of the opposition RPR/UDF coalition was very much a centrist one as well, so that there was little to distinguish the rival parties (thus confirming in a way Le Pen's allegation - and incidentally that of the PCF and the Greens - that there was little to choose between the major parties; *bonnet blanc, blanc bonnet* was Le Pen's favourite expression in this context, a phrase originally coined by Marchais). Television, as mediator of this political discourse, enabled the message of centrist politics to get through to the electorate who voted accordingly.

The right tried to interpret the results of the 1988 legislative election as a vote of no-confidence in Mitterrand. The PS interpreted the results as confirmation that the electorate wanted a centre left/centrist-inclining government and not the return of the brash and arrogant style of 1981. Had it realised in advance how low the turn-out to vote was going to be (34.5 per cent abstentionism, a record level since 1870), the party would have campaigned with a bit more vigour. At the time it was felt that the electorate was vote-weary (which may well have been the case). It should also be noted, however, that the second round of the elections coincided with the live television broadcast of the final of the men's French Tennis Open - apparently the box at home offered a far more enticing sporting fare than the ballot box.

If, as we argued earlier, the effect of television on political discourse is to have centred it over the last decade it must also be clearly stated that it has done so in the light of the evolution of the political situation over that same period. As Jean-Jack Queyranne says:

> Little by little the political actors are obliged to adopt a moderate, perhaps more realistic course. Especially since television gave them, over this period, a great deal of air-time in which to exhaust their traditional discourse and cleanse their messages and physical attitudes of all asperity.

As Queyranne goes on to point out, it is not just television that has played a role in this centring of political discourse but responses by left and right alike to the emergence of the National Front:

> It is quite clearly the threat of a significant extreme-right vote which appeared for the first time in 1984 that has obliged moderate parties to adopt a similar anti-racist discourse which in turn has presently engendered a fragmenting of the traditional right. This is one of the fundamental elements in the evolution of the campaigning style most noticeably on television: a major political event, the emergence of the National Front, has imposed a break with traditional political discourse (which was) rather mechanical in its setting up of two opposing models of society each time an election was in sight.

Television then provides a reflection of this process of centring. However, it is also true that the main objective of campaigning is to bring out differences between political tendencies. It is clear from what we have said above that it is going to be less easy to accomplish this differentiation in legislative elections, where it is the party's message that has to be put across, than it is in presidential elections which pitch individual candidates against one another. It is clear too that if political discourse has become less oppositional (with the exception of the extreme right and left of the political spectrum), then differences will have to be marked through personal qualities.

In the 1988 presidential election, it became rapidly evident, from a comparison of the first-round election broadcast spots of the front-running candidates, that Mitterrand was well aware of the need for distinctiveness and was equally well able to project it. By contrast, both Barre and Chirac positioned themselves in relatively similar ways and in conformity with the traditional practices of an election broadcast. Thus the candidates were introduced via a short clip (Chirac on his estate in Corrèze for example) or a statement by a well-known personality eulogising the presidential hopeful. This introduction was followed by an interview of the candidate, interspersed with 'testimonies' from appropriate members of the public.

Mitterrand successfully positioned himself as the only candidate who could unite France, exploiting the prestige of his presidential incumbency to this end. In order to achieve this, he projected a diversified, multi-dimensional image. This was intended to demonstrate both that he had depth and that he was the site of the many aspects of France, i.e. that all France was united in his person. This multi-dimensionality was clearly inscribed in the subliminal message of the video clip that preceded his interview. In this clip (edited by Jacques Séguéla) 800 images flash by in a total of 90 seconds. This excitingly fast-edited photo-montage links together images starting from the 1789 Revolution and proceeding all the way through great moments in France's social, cultural and political history. The whole message is summed up by the last shot which is of Mitterrand's election poster: a dignified three-quarter profile of the President-candidate and inscribed beneath the slogan *La France unie*. The message and connotations are clear: Mitterrand is the legitimate site for this great republican heritage and the man who can unite France in all its diversity. The three-quarter face profile shot at the end marks him out as a man of destiny of almost mystic proportions. As Barthes remarks on political positioning in his essay 'Photography and Electoral Appeal':

> A three-quarter face photograph suggests the tyranny of an ideal (in Mitterrand's case the ideal of a united France): the gaze is lost nobly in the future, it does not confront, it soars, and fertilises some other domain, which is chastely left undefined. Almost all three-quarter photos are ascentional, the face is lifted towards a supernatural light which draws it up and elevates it to the realm of a higher humanity; the candidate reaches the Olympus of elevated feelings, where all political contradictions are solved...[10]

His image took on mythological proportions whereby the viewer apprehended the meaning of Mitterrand as the site of France past, present and future. Over the weeks of the official campaign, Mitterrand was seen on the television screen masterfully revealing with the greatest naturalness the many images which construct his persona. He was all generations united in one, the embodiment of the *génération Mitterrand*. He was the patriarch of all generations, who would guarantee France its unity and continuity. He was the gentleman farmer (on his farm at Latche), the man of letters (*Lettre à tous les Français*), humanist, philosopher, teacher, lawyer. His credentials as man of state were irrefutable.

Neither Chirac nor Barre were able to counter Mitterrand's multi-dimensional image with any conviction. Barre, with his slogan *Barre: du sérieux, du solide, du vrai* (Barre: solid, serious, true) came over as woodenly as did the connotations of these dull uncatchworthy words. Chirac's slogan *Nous irons plus loin ensemble* (we will go further together) seemed to suffer from the same indecisiveness as did the candidate's campaign strategy: he switched course half way along the way from a somewhat brash image-projection to a more tempered and restrained one. After all, the slogan does beg the question where are we going? Furthermore, he made the drastic decision to focus his attention on television only, thereby falling into the mediatic trap of over-exposure which in turn opened his image up to public scrutiny with all the risks that such a positioning can bring with it. The viewer ended up with two conflicting images of Chirac rather than any sense of depth and diversity. Television news reportage revealed an aggressive politician who would go to extraordinary lengths to obtain media coverage for his law and order stance; conversely his broadcast spots, in their effort to project him as the problem-solving Prime Minister-candidate, attempted to reveal a more all-rounder image.[11] This lack of consistency only served to expose the limitations of his candidacy and begged the question which is the real Chirac?: the tough law and order guy or the man who has an answer to everything - a Jacques of all policies? Thus for Chirac, television served to expose his inconsistencies and for Barre his wooden immobilism. Jumping Jack Flash, the *distributeur automatique de promesses* (the 'automatic distributor of promises', as Mitterrand labelled him) and Barzy the bear (as *Le bébête show* called Barre) were hardly the measure of the quasi-mystical image of Mitterrand.

Television and Language: Getting the Message Over

Television, because it is firstly a visual medium, has changed the way a message must be delivered. Television is a constant flow of images and the viewer relies on the images first to deliver the message. This means that little attention span will be available for verbal accompaniment. News items are constructed around this principle which is why they are delivered in short pithy sentences. Studies have shown that the attention span for viewers is for an average sentence length of twenty words. Once that limit is surpassed the spectator is more than likely to tune out. Thus a politician has to be careful to avoid oratory and rhetoric - linguistic skills more suited to parliament. Speed of delivery is also a crucial factor. Television broadcasters average about 140 words per minute. The astute politician must not deliver that fast or s/he will be perceived as a *vedette de l'écran* (a screen star) and not a serious politician. Conversely the delivery must not be too slow or else the politician will be perceived as unmodern: predictably Barre, with his average of 88 words per minute, fell into this category. And, finally, the politician will need to employ a modernist discourse if he or she is to be listened to.

Before 1981, Mitterrand fell at each of these hurdles which is why Giscard could, in the 1974 debate, so perfunctorily dismiss his opponent as *un homme du passif* (a man in the past tense). However, by 1981 he had polished his image and improved his delivery. Now it was his turn to bring out the withering formula 'M. d'Estaing vous êtes un homme du passé' (Mr d'Estaing, you are a man of the past). His sentences were short and to the point: 'j'entends mener ce débat comme je le veux' (I intend leading this debate as I wish) and the pace of his delivery had considerably speeded up to around 100 words per minute. By the 1988 election, Mitterrand had greatly expanded on his communication skills: he varied his rhythm of delivery - for example when taking on his role as *conteur* his speed slowed down to 95wpm, he punctuated his sentences with gestures or gentle smiles to make them easy to follow and thus gave the impression of clarity of purpose and thinking.

In his debate with Chirac, he constantly shifted his discursive tactics, thus making it impossible for his fast-talking opponent (120wpm) to land any effective blows. The evolution in Mitterrand's discourse over the seven years of his first presidency showed too that in 1988 he held a modernist discourse which was in touch with the political climate and that he was not afraid of *le parler vrai* (frank-speak).[12]

Curiously, if we turn our attention to two of the minor presidential candidates, Le Pen and Lajoinie, it can be demonstrated how, in some respects, Le Pen's positioning and specificity had certain parallels with Mitterrand's, and Lajoinie's with those of Chirac and Barre. Le Pen was also the man of *le parler vrai*, even more forcefully than Mitterrand: his 'je dis ce que je veux' (I say what I want), had echoes of Mitterrand's 'je dis ce que je pense' (I say what I think); he talked of himself as 'l'enfant du peuple' (child of the people), whereas Mitterrand positioned himself as 'le père du peuple' (father of the people). Le Pen's discourse was modernist in so far as it contrasted strongly with Lajoinie's discursive immobilism and *arrièrisme*: the PCF candidate talked of agriculture and the steel industry as if there had been no change since the 1930s.[13] Le Pen forged his image as leader of *la droite nationale populaire* (the popular nationalist right) and the image of his party as *la nation de la France* (compare Mitterrand words: 'mon parti c'est la France').[14] Le Pen, too, managed to establish his distinctiveness from all other candidates: he was the little guy, the outsider, the polemicising tele-evangelist (claiming to be the defender of moral values held by the Pope and Reagan) crusading against the heavyweights. His discourse was both modern and imbued with the past so that he too became a site for France ancient and modern (the France of Jeanne d'Arc, Pétain, Laval and Poujade). There however any comparison with Mitterrand ended. For Le Pen was also the macho-man (journalists talked of his *propos viril*) that Chirac attempted to be. Finally, Le Pen was the unrepentant pugilist who, much like Marchais and Lajoinie, accused journalists of bad faith in their questioning.[15]

In terms of linguistic tactics, Le Pen, almost without exception, personalises questions addressed to him. In so doing, he positions himself as victim of the journalist's aggression and occasional disdain. From this deliberately cultivated defensive position, Le Pen is able to steal the offensive and launch forth with his ideology. In so doing, of course, he side-steps the questions themselves. His hard image remains unscathed, his positioning unassailable. Small wonder Le Pen is often able to display his sense of humour - he holds the cards and can say what he wants. Such is not the case for any other politician, and that is what makes Le Pen's campaigning style so distinctive.

Conversely, in his 1988 presidential campaign Lajoinie had, mediatically speaking, nothing distinctive to offer. His discourse and his rhetoric were carbon copies of his leader's. His answers were as long and as digressive as those of Marchais (lasting often upwards of five minutes) and were delivered in that familiar soap-box style. The image of the PCF remained, therefore, unchanged despite having a different presidential candidate from 1981. When Lajoinie claimed to be in possession of modern policies he was completely unbelievable. Over the campaign period, Lajoinie's style revealed in fact that he was more a mouthpiece for the PCF than a candidate in his own right. So inept was he in debating tactics that, when confronted with Le Pen, his whole approach (accusatory tones, virulent attacks on Le Pen's person and integrity) left the impression that he was even more pugilistic than his opponent. Clearly he made the mistake of personalising the debate rather than seeing it as a conflict of two personalities expressing opposing visions of society. On a more elevated tone of debating styles, this was Chirac's mistake in his confrontation with Mitterrand. Lajoinie and Chirac joined ranks again in the ease with which they fell into traps of their own making: hoping to set up their opponent for a fall, the whole effort backfired and it was they who were caught totally by surprise. The agitated morphology of their persons (pointing, gesturing vociferously etc.), their lengthy and forceful attacking discourse revealed their unmediatic selves almost immediately. And, finally, long preambles at the beginning of a *Magazine politique*, to which Lajoinie was far too prone, were a recipe for disaster - far better the quick witty quip or formula.

Elections and Television: Some Conclusions

In terms of brevity of response and a calm exterior, it is certainly the leading representatives of the PS - especially since the 1986 parliamentary election - who have found the right measure, revealing a mastery of the medium that is almost consensual in its manifestation. And yet, this has not, where parliamentary elections are concerned, necessarily guaranteed an over-ridingly strong electoral return. We have suggested that, whilst of course the political situation must be the major factor to be taken into consideration, negative or non-positive campaigning can have adverse effects on election results. The electioneering style adopted by the Socialist Party seems to lack the confidence which paradoxically, in two successive presidential elections, their de facto leader François Mitterrand has appeared to have in abundance.

The argument is not that the PS is getting the message over badly, but that the message that is coming over has, in its realism, reaped what was sown. Again Jean-Jack Queyranne is instructive on this point:

> A specific governmental culture has led us... to adopt a deliberately didactic discourse, to explain our policies to the French. The constraints of management, realism, the constant desire for reform have played a fundamental role in the evolution of the style of our campaigns... And that appeared clearly on the television screens.

It would appear also that the electorate is not presently disposed to great ideological swings and that any campaign run on that basis will not, in the 1990s, see a growth in its electoral following. Thus television, in centring the debate, has largely echoed popular electoral practices. Over the period of *cohabitation*, Mitterrand had proved that he could sustain his presidential authority within the electorate as the embodiment of national unity without intervening in legislative functions. His 1988 campaign was run along those lines: his image was that of leader of the nation and it convinced a majority to return him to the Elysée.

In this last respect, television has played a vital role in tracing the evolution of the signification of presidentialism over the period of the Fifth Republic. In the 1960s and 1970s, television served to valorise the authority of the directly-elected President (how else could it not, given that television was part of the state machinery?). Over the 1980s, the image of presidentialism it has projected has been an evolving one, reflecting the progressive separation of the two powers (executive from the legislative). It is interesting, and not without coincidence, that the 1980s also witnessed an uncoupling of television and state. That both institutions, the presidency and television, should be subject to such a process of continual change constitutes a remarkable evolution for the democratic legitimacy of the Fifth Republic. It would seem that Mitterrand may have the last word, after all, over de Gaulle's constitution which invested the President with executive powers strong enough to intervene on legislative matters. At that time, Mitterrand was strongly opposed to any such arrogation of power; now, almost thirty years later, his revenge - if such it is - must be sweet.

Notes

1. This was not just American influence. Giscard's predecessor Pompidou was the first to invite cameras to his country estate to film him going about his daily doings.

2. In fact, Waechter did marginally less well than Brice Lalonde in the 1981 presidential elections (3.78 per cent vs 3.87 per cent). However, the impact of Waechter's campaign was felt in subsequent elections, indicating that his presidential bid had galvanised a significant minority behind the Greens' cause: in June 1989 for the first time ever the French Greens secured representation in the European parliament.

3. It is ironic that when at last - for the 1988 presidential elections - the PCF conceded on the necessity of having a media adviser, it chose, first, to maintain the existing name of its department of communication i.e. *le département de propagande* and, second, to call on the services of the modest and retiring Alsacian Francis Wurtz as campaign manager. Wurtz, a former Protestant converted to catholicism, and a member of the PCF is described by *Le Monde* as being almost Lutheran in his manner. Hardly the persona one would expect to be handling the campaign of the equally uncharismatic presidential candidate André Lajoinie.

4. This quotation and all subsequent references to Queyranne have their source in a letter he wrote in response to a questionnaire sent to the PS. This questionnaire was sent (in August 1988) to all the major parties; however, the PS was the only one to have answered by the time of writing this chapter.

5. Possibly, if any one thing was responsible for making this centre ground available for Mitterrand to step into and claim it, it was the effect of Le Pen on the political environment.

6. For more detail on the campaigning styles of the candidates see Hayward, S., 'Television and the French Presidential Elections 1988' in Gaffney, J. (ed.), *The French Presidential Elections of 1988: Ideology and Leadership in Contemporary France*, Gower, Aldershot, 1989, pp. 58-80.

7. Cayrol, R., *La nouvelle communication politique*, Larousse, Paris, 1986, p. 83.

8. According to Le Pen, he and the FN were the victims of 'une injustice médiatique' because he and his party had had the least televisual exposure - here is his list of the number of television appearances on *Magazines politiques* (which he produced in January 1988):

RPR/UDF	112
PS	71
PCF	21
FN	9

9. As Barre himself recognised, in *Le monde en face* in March 1988, 'television sometimes pushes one to speak too scientifically because one is unsure of the audience and how to pitch the discourse.

10. Barthes, R., *Mythologies*, Paladin, London, 1989, p. 100.

11. In a televised interview with Christine Ockrent, Mitterrand - making an indirect comment on Chirac's behaviour - termed his rival's law and order stance as concealing *une agitation ambiante*, an ambiant restlessness.

12. *Le Monde*, in an article entitled 'Les 14 juillet de M. Mitterrand' notes how, over his first mandate, Mitterrand's choice of key words pointed to the evolving political climate (*Le Monde* collated this lexicon by watching Mitterrand's yearly interview on television with Yves Mourousi):

1981	rassembler
1982	sens de solidarité
1983	redressement national et justice sociale
1984	pas de promesses, pas d'engagement, pas de perspectives magnifiques
1985	cohabitation, respect des institutions
1986	garant de l'indépendance nationale (he is speaking of his role as he saw it then)
1987	je ne cherche pas de récompenses, je cherche à faire mon devoir

Source: *Le Monde*, 14 juillet 1987.

13. Lajoinie's thirties discourse was epitomised by his use of expressions such as 'les travailleurs doivent baisser la tête', the workers must bow their heads.

14. Mitterrand made this statement in a televised interview with Christine Ockrent (*Le monde en face*, 7 April 1988).

15. In his first major televised interview, Le Pen retorted to tough journalistic questioning: 'je ne suis pas venu ici pour que vous me placiez sur le bûcher...' (I haven't come here so that you can roast me alive). This was an invidious choice of terms given his appropriation of Joan of Arc. *L'heure de vérité*, 13 February 1984.

Bibliography

Barthes, R., *Mythologies*, Paladin, London, 1989.

Blumler, J.G., and McQuail, D., *Television in Politics: Its Uses and Influences*, Faber & Faber, London, 1968.

Brusini, H., and James, F., *Voir la vérité: le journalisme de télévision*, PUF, Paris, 1982.

Cayrol, R., *La nouvelle communication politique*, Larousse, Paris, 1986.

Fiske, J., and Hartley, J., *Reading Television*, Methuen, London, 1978.

Hartley, J., *Understanding News*, Methuen, London, 1982.

Hayward, S., 'Television and the Presidential Elections April-May 1988', in Gaffney, J. (ed.), *The French Presidential Elections of 1988: Ideology and Leadership in Contemporary France*, Gower, Aldershot, 1989.

Masterman, L., *Television Mythologies*, Comedia, London, 1984.

Mermet, G., *Démocrature: comment les médias transforment la démocratie*, Aubier, Paris, 1987.

Missika, J-L., and Wolton, D., *La folle au logis: la télévision dans les sociétés démocratiques*, Gallimard, Paris, 1983.

Le Monde, *Le nouveau contrat de François Mitterrand*, Le Monde: dossiers and documents, May 1988.

Ranney, A., *The Channels of Power: The Impact of Television on American Politics*, Basic Books, New York, 1983.

Rolot, C., and Ramirez, F., *Choisir un président*, Ramsay, Paris, 1987.

Smith, A., *The Politics of Information*, Macmillan, London, 1980.

3 The Party of the Masses and its Marginalisation: The Communist Party

Gino Raymond

The 1980s was a decade during which the French Communist Party (PCF) was faced with the continuing challenge of adapting to change, within its own ranks and in the wider social sphere. In one respect, the election of the Socialist candidate François Mitterrand to the presidency of the Fifth Republic in 1981 enabled the PCF to start the decade with a notable historical achievement: it returned to government after a thirty-four year absence. The second government headed by Pierre Mauroy accommodated four Communist ministers within its ranks: Charles Fiterman as Minister of Transport, Anicet Le Pors as the equivalent of a Minister in charge of Civil Servants, Jack Ralite as Minister for Health and Marcel Rigout as Minister with responsibility for Further Education and Vocational Training.

The decision of the PCF to enter into an agreement with the PS in June 1981 and subsequently to participate in government was partly motivated by a desire not to be perceived as a party sliding into sterile opposition, at a time when, paradoxically, it described the measures proposed by the Socialists as insufficient. There was, however, a belief on the part of the PCF leadership that a Communist presence in government would prevent the party from becoming marginalised, and that the right claimed by its representatives in parliament to make constructive criticism of the government would enable the party to maintain its individual profile. It was not long before the pseudo-optimistic expectations of the PCF leadership were frustrated.

The austerity measures introduced by the Socialists in 1982 strained the willingness of the PCF to support its governmental allies. The European elections of 1984 were a severe blow to the fortunes of the left and reduced the PCF's share of the vote from 20.5 per cent in the 1979 European elections to 11.3 per cent. Notwithstanding the record number of abstentions (43 per cent), this was regarded by the PCF leadership as evidence that support for the Socialist-led government was a liability. President Mitterrand replaced Pierre Mauroy with the right-wing Socialist Laurent Fabius a few days after the result of the election was known. For its part, the PCF Central Committee decided on 19 July to try and secure a commitment from Fabius to stimulate the economy, notably investment and employment. In view of what it perceived as his refusal to make this commitment, the PCF ended the participation of its four ministers in government. The experience of government during Mitterrand's first term as President was therefore not a prelude to a greater and more secure presence in national politics for the PCF, but marked instead the beginning of a decade of fluctuating fortunes and unease at the grass-roots of the party.

Electoral Fortunes and the Communist Constituency

The performance of the PCF in elections during the 1980s showed it to be a party in gradual decline:

Table 3.1
Electoral performance of the PCF since 1981[1]
(percentage of PCF vote at first ballot)

Type of election	Year	Vote
Presidential	1981	15.6
Legislative	1981	16.2
European	1984	11.3
Legislative	1986	9.8
Presidential	1988	6.76

In the first round of the legislative elections of 5 June 1988, there was a slight revival in the fortunes of the PCF when it polled 11.32 per cent.[2] In the first round of the cantonal elections that followed on 25 September, the PCF share of the votes cast was 13.39 per cent[3], but the downward trend was soon to re-establish itself. The municipal elections of 12 and 19 March 1989 were a critical test for the Communists, given the traditional strength of their roots in local government. In the final calculation of municipalities which changed hands, grass-roots support for the PCF was shown to have diminished. The PCF lost control of 14 towns with more than 20,000 inhabitants and twenty-two towns with between 9,000 to 20,000 inhabitants. It was left in control of 258 towns with more than 3,500 inhabitants, compared with 325 such towns before the elections.[4] In the European election of 18 June 1989, there was confirmation of the fragility of the support for the PCF at national as well as local level when the Communist list led by Philippe Herzog obtained only 7.72 per cent of the votes cast.[5]

In the post-war period the PCF has recruited its members in all the departments of France. The greatest concentration of its membership and its strongest electoral support has come traditionally from the 'red belt' departments in the south-east Paris region, the industrial north, the northern and western areas of the Massif Central, and the Provence and Rhône valley area. Approximately 50 per cent of PCF voters are working class and in the partial census taken in 1979 11.8 per cent of its members were shown to be under twenty-five, 39 per cent between the ages of twenty-six and forty, and over 35 per cent of them women.[6] This geographical and sociological profile had, however, become subject to a number of notable changes as the party entered the 1980s, and that process of change continued throughout the decade.

As the PCF approached the watershed of the 1980s, certain factors converged to underline the increasing structural frailty of the party. The municipal power bases which were noted for their erstwhile impregnability were forced to weather the effects of social and demographic change. Conurbations in which the party was entrenched were also the centres of population which were among the most affected by the social changes which began to manifest themselves clearly in the 1960s: changes in the patterns of employment;

population flows and the consequences for traditional working-class areas; the growth of a post-industrial society and its impact on traditional working-class allegiances. All of the foregoing factors rendered the task faced by the PCF of renewing its electoral base in urban areas more arduous. The party's loss of support demographically became demonstrable by the middle of the 1980s. Its electoral appeal to voters between the ages of eighteen and thirty-four declined from 21.4 per cent in 1978 to 11.5 per cent in 1984, whereas among those aged sixty-five or over it increased marginally, from 11.5 per cent to 11.8 per cent.[7]

When the focus is narrowed on the support for the party from its membership, the foundation which sustains the existence of communism in France is shown to have exchanged its rock-like immutability for a more fragile nature. In 1978, the almost - certainly exaggerated figure given by the PCF for the number of membership cards taken up was 702,864.[8] A decade later, the party's General Secretary, Georges Marchais, claimed that the PCF could mobilise a membership of 600,000 behind the Communist candidate in the presidential elections of 1988, André Lajoinie. However, scrutiny of the figures released by the party itself regarding its membership suggested that Marchais's assertion was informed by an unjustified measure of optimism. In an analysis of the PCF's claims, one of the party's critics calculated that notwithstanding the 45,000 new members which it purported to have recruited in 1987, the total figure for paid-up party members in 1987 was approximately the same as the total established for the previous year, thus leading to the surmise that the new members recruited in 1987 simply replaced those who had left. In addition, close scrutiny of the financial statement produced by the Central Committee at the party's 26th congress in December 1987 indicated a substantial disparity between the total number of party members and party funds, implying therefore that a significant number of subscriptions were not being renewed and that official claims by the PCF about the size of its membership were exaggerated.[9] The reasons for the development of structural weaknesses in the PCF's representation geographically and demographically were partly due to societal factors beyond the party's control but, as the non-renewal of membership in the party suggests, the PCF itself had not shown sufficient alacrity and imagination in responding to internal pressure for change. More particularly, the party's ideological orientation, expressed through its organisational structure, failed to satisfy the desire among members for the freedom to express a greater diversity of opinion and engage in debates that might have an impact on party policy. The consequence for the PCF during the 1980s was an ever more visible challenge to its organisation from within, which damaged its credibility vis-à-vis the French electorate as a whole.

The Internal Pressure for Change

The organisational principle which characterises the PCF is 'democratic centralism'. As it is defined by the party, this principle does allow for discussion: within each party unit; within all advisory committees; and in the party press. But majority decisions are binding on all and the decisions of higher bodies are binding on lower bodies. This principle does not accommodate the presence of 'factions' within the party, i.e. the operation of groups within it who, under the pretext of democracy, flout majority decisions.

The democratic centralism of the PCF operates in a structure whose basic unit is the 'cell', of which there are three types: workplace, residential and rural. Considerable ideological importance is placed on the workplace cell, testament to the PCF's claim to be the 'party of the working class'. The cells of a given geographical area belong to a section and elect a Section Committee (*Comité de section*). The sections of a given department belong in turn to a departmental federation and elect a Federal Committee (*Comité fédéral*). At a national level, the National Congress is regarded as the party's supreme authority and is convened every three years. One of its tasks is to elect the party's executive, known as the Central Committee, which in turn elects the Politburo (*Bureau politique*) and the Secretariat. The relationship between the party organisation and its *élus* (local councillors and deputies) is encapsulated in the principle that they have the same rights and duties as other party members and are consequently subject to party control. In keeping with this and as a purported safeguard against careerism, the salaries of these representatives are paid into the party.

The limitations placed on the grass-roots membership and parliamentary representatives by the PCF's organisational structure led to the growth of internal opposition to the immobilism of the leadership, which crystallised in a manner clearly damaging to the party during the year leading up to the presidential election of 1988. The unequivocal manifestation of this internal pressure for change had, however, been presaged at the beginning of the decade. The 1970s had ended on an electorally sour note for the PCF. In the first round of the legislative elections of March 1978, for the first time in their post-war history, the Communists, with 20.6 per cent of the vote, had to concede their position as the premier party of the left to the Socialists, who had obtained 22.6 per cent of the vote. In the aftermath of the breakdown of the common programme with the Socialists in September 1977 (see Chapter One), opposition developed within the PCF directed against the manner in which the leadership had defined the party's electoral strategy, and in particular its relationship with other left-wing parties. These voices challenging the leadership, such as the members of the PCF university branch at Aix, became known as the *contestataires* and sparked off a debate whose terms of reference went beyond questions of party strategy and initiated discussion of the fundamental issue of democracy within the party. It had become clear to the *contestataires* that although the organisation of the party allowed the decisions of the leadership to filter down through the strata of the party and be obeyed, it was far less flexible in allowing the views of the membership to percolate upwards and influence the decisions being taken on their behalf.

The profile of the discussion was raised by the written contributions of Communist intellectuals like Louis Althusser and Jean Elleinstein, and in response to the demand for debate within the party, the PCF leadership organised a series of discussion meetings on 9 and 10 December 1978, which provided a forum for some of its sternest critics among the four hundred intellectuals who attended. This kind of initiative had not occurred for several decades and although disagreements with the leadership's management of the party's affairs and policies were expressed, the consensus which emerged ultimately was one which supported the essence of the leadership's policy.

Not all of the critics, however, were placated and pressure from within the party for structural changes leading to greater democracy increased throughout the 1980s, reaching a climax in the prelude to the 1988 presidential election. The beginning of the decade was marked by the activities of one *contestataire* who refused to be satisfied by the leadership's concessions on debate within the party. Henri Fiszbin had been the Paris district secretary of the PCF and a Central Committee member, resigning from the latter body in 1979. In May 1981, together with François Hincker, he founded *Rencontres communistes*, a group comprising PCF dissidents and others. The reaction of the party was to expel Fiszbin and Hincker in October of the same year. The justification advanced by the leadership for this sanction was that these *contestataires* had expressed their criticisms in the bourgeois press instead of the party press. The discontent among the party's intellectuals was underlined by the departure that year of Elleinstein and Etienne Balibar. In addition to this frustration at its attitude towards the membership, a forum for the expression of discontent with the leadership's stance towards the Socialists was established through the founding of the Union in Struggle (*L'Union dans les luttes*). This was a body created by Socialist and Communist intellectuals who wished to make the restoration of left-wing unity a priority, and who rejected the PCF line which accused the PS of shifting to the right.

As the 1980s progressed, a qualitative change occurred in the demands emanating from within the PCF. Disagreements over the means of achieving party policy deepened into disagreements over the essence of that policy. Figures emerged, from the upper echelons of the party as well as from the ranks, who were not only reformist but also *rénovateur*, i.e. prepared to demand a renewal of the party's appraisal of its aims through, if necessary, a radical rethinking of some of its basic premises, such as democratic centralism. The Central Committee member Pierre Juquin, speaking in Limoges in June 1984, argued the case for a debate within the party about the way in which it was managed, and one which would treat no aspect of party affairs as sacrosanct or beyond question. More specifically, Juquin suggested that the party's democratic centralism was something that could be revised positively. In what subsequently proved to be a watershed speech at the party's 25th Congress in February 1985, Juquin made an overt call for a 'PC rénové', a reconstructed Communist Party in which the concept of democratic centralism would be radically expanded to accommodate the will to self-management. What placed further pressure on the PCF leadership was that Juquin was not without sympathizers on the Central Committee, notably Marcel Rigout and Félix Damette.

The leadership was placed more firmly on the defensive by the PCF's poor performance in the legislative elections of 1986, when the party obtained under 9.8 per cent of the votes cast. The criticism this elicited from discontented members found a new outlet in the Marxist Circles (*Cercles marxistes*), the Communist discussion groups which were organised, according to one *rénovateur*, in at least ten towns to discuss issues raised by *rénovateur* criticism of the party.[10] The leadership reacted aggressively to the rising clamour of criticism and in an interview on the television channel *Antenne 2*, on 14 January 1987, Marchais castigated the *rénovateurs*, labelling them the *liquidateurs* of the party. A reply came from Marcel Rigout in the form of a written statement, in which he described Marchais's condemnation of the *rénovateurs* as a manifest blow to the unity of the party, and on 27 January Rigout announced his resignation from the Central Committee of the PCF. Four days later, *rénovateurs* from fifteen departments met in Paris and established themselves organisationally by forming a Coordinating Committee (*Collectif de coordination*). It thus became clear that as the party began to look forward to the presidential challenge of 1988, it also had to contend with a *rénovateur* movement that had not only taken root within the party, but also assumed an organisational cogency.

As events developed on the ground, an additional complication manifested itself which rendered the leadership's management of the party's affairs more problematical. The membership was not simply divided between a majority who supported the party line and a minority who favoured the increasingly autonomous approach of the *rénovateurs*; it also included an element which wanted to remain within the party while at the same time being highly critical of PCF management and strategy. One such element, led by Daniel Garipuy, was to be found among the Communists of Toulouse, who came under the regional authority of the Haute-Garonne department. Unlike Claude Llabrès, the well-known *rénovateur* from Toulouse who had resigned from the Central Committee in September 1987 and who was later excluded from the PCF, Garipuy and other *contestataires* wanted to pursue change from within but cast serious doubts on the leadership's assertions about its membership. For example, they contested figures illustrating the purported strength of the membership in the federation of Haute-Garonne, arguing that it had decreased from 11,000 in 1979 to 3,500 in 1987 and that the real challenge facing the party was the need to address the causes of this decline and arrest it.[11]

As the most prominent advocate of their cause, Pierre Juquin had signalled to the PCF leadership in November 1986 the determination of the *rénovateurs* to transform the party from within and below. The inflexibility of the party was, however, to frustrate this ambition and as the presidential election of 1988 drew closer, Juquin distanced himself from the leadership. He did not attend the Central Committee meeting in May 1987 which approved unanimously the choice of André Lajoinie as the party's presidential candidate, and in the following month he resigned from the Central Committee. On 12 October he announced his decision to stand as a candidate in the presidential election and two days later he was excluded from the party. On 24 October the National Coordinating Committee of the *rénovateurs* (COCORECO) met in Paris and elected Claude Llabrès at its head. Consequently, the PCF found itself entering the prelude to the second presidential campaign of the decade facing a challenge wholly without precedent: in addition to traditional right-wing rivals, the PCF candidate would be faced with a former high-ranking member of the party hierarchy supported by an organisation of former PCF members, some of whom had once had similarly impressive Communist credentials.

The organisational rigidities which had so complicated the relationship between leadership and base were also a factor which inhibited the ability of the PCF candidate in the 1988 presidential election to define himself in individual terms, and thus inspire the confidence of the French electorate in him as a candidate genuinely capable of taking over the reins of presidential power. Lajoinie had been chosen in preference to better known Communist figures like Georges Séguy, the former General Secretary of the CGT trade union, and Anicet Le Pors. Lajoinie was portrayed by the party, and portrayed himself, as a man of quiet diligence and simplicity who was unique among the presidential candidates in his ability and enthusiasm for talking directly to the people about their most pressing concerns.[12] Lajoinie's background and his progress through the party hierarchy to the leadership of the PCF's parliamentary group in the National Assembly suggested, however, that the decisive factor determining his choice as the party's presidential candidate was his fidelity to the line elaborated and handed down by the leadership.

Born of peasant stock in the Corrèze in 1929, Lajoinie rose through the party ranks initially through service to the party's agricultural concerns. He followed the courses organised for party members and in 1976 became responsible for the Communist weekly journal for farmers, *La Terre*. 1978 saw him elected as a deputy representing a constituency in the department of Allier and in February 1982 he joined the Central Committee of the party on the occasion of its 24th Congress. He was thus an individual whose social and intellectual identity had been profoundly shaped by the party and whose loyalty to it would be unswerving. Consequently, from the moment he was adopted by the Central Committee as the PCF's presidential candidate, some observers interpreted his selection as a signal that the basis of Lajoinie's appeal would be indistinguishable from the policy platform constructed by the leadership and enunciated by Marchais.[13]

The organisational constraints faced by a Communist presidential candidate constitute, however, only one of several factors that undermine his success. Allied with the general hostility of the electorate to the PCF, the institutions of the Fifth Republic make the prospect of a Communist presidential candidate being elected effectively nonexistent. This fact, combined with the generally decisive outcome of presidential elections, served to heighten the public's perception of the PCF during the 1980s as a party lacking in political credibility, thereby also colouring the attitude of the French electorate towards the party in legislative contests and further weakening its performance. The opposition of the PCF leadership to direct presidential elections is informed by an awareness of the dangers they pose for the party. As the results of the presidential elections of 1981 and 1988 suggested, when faced with a choice between a Communist or a Socialist candidate, an important number of PCF voters are tempted to exercise the *vote utile* and thus vote 'usefully' on the first ballot for the left-wing candidate with the best chance of being elected on the second. Since in order to be elected on the second ballot this candidate must be capable of attracting support from beyond the traditional ranks of the left-wing electorate, it must be the Socialist.

Even if organisational constraints were to be loosened upon the Communist candidate, the latter would still find himself in the paradoxical situation of representing a party that questioned the legitimacy of the post to which he aspired, as it is defined in the constitution of the Fifth Republic. Rivalry with the PS, an ambiguous attitude towards the presidency and the evolution of party politics were key factors constituting the external pressure on the PCF to change and which, as a result of its failure to do so sufficiently, contributed to its marginalisation.

The External Pressures for Change

i) The PCF-PS Rivalry

The PCF's relationship with the PS during the 1970s and the 1980s was characterised by alliances, disagreements and uncomfortable electoral accommodations. At the root of this unhappy relationship for the PCF was the fact that the PS was highly successful in not only stealing the PCF's clothes ideologically, but also the votes of its members. The PCF entered the 1970s with a strategy based on pursuing 'political' and 'economic' democracy in France. The events of 1968 had provided a powerful impetus for this and the manifesto produced by the party's Central Committee in December of that year was an important expression of this approach. A crucial means for implementing the strategy was to be found in an alliance with the PS, marked in 1972 by the agreement of both parties to a common programme of government. From this point onwards, however, the Communists were to find themselves ideologically outsmarted and tactically wrong-footed by their Socialist allies. Whereas the Communists were unable to use the opportunity of alliance with the PS to focus more sharply on what they understood by a pluralist Socialist society, either in the party's manifesto or in Marchais's best seller *Le défi démocratique*, the Socialists harnessed their energies to produce an increasingly appealing vision of democratic socialism in France.[14] The PCF proved itself incapable of competing with the PS in that sphere; it had always envisaged the left alliance as a means of consolidating its ideological and political hegemony, rather than as the occasion to compromise fundamentally with 'social democracy'. By signing the common programme and thereby approving its radical prescriptions, the PS had done much to enhance its credibility vis-à-vis the left-wing constituency as an alternative to the PCF in the pursuit of a society governed by socialist values. In the draft version of the common programme produced by the PS, the party declared its commitment to Marxist ideology and affirmed its determination to lead the country to a point in its history where the transition to socialism would become 'irreversible'.[15] Furthermore, by being swifter than the PCF in incorporating the May-68 inspired notion of *autogestion* (self-management) among its policies, the PS was able to exploit the popular mood of a powerful left-wing constituency in post-1968 France. The PS had thus successfully embarked on a process of dislodging the PCF from its hegemonic position on the French left.[16]

The PCF found itself in the position of being constantly forced to react to the successful initiatives of the PS instead of pre-empting PS policy initiatives with its own. The success of the Socialists in six legislative by-elections in October 1974 was a motivating factor behind the PCF's attempt to update its strategy during its 21st (extraordinary) Congress in November 1974. In an endeavour to rival the appeal of the PS message to the masses, the final document of the congress contained a brief section on 'socialisme aux couleurs de la France'. By the time of its 22nd Congress in February 1976 the PCF was making a calculated effort to prevent further loss of support to the PS by adopting a 'Eurocommunist' stance. A major ideological obstacle was overcome when the party declared that the transition to socialism which would result in an enlarged democracy would be achieved solely through universal suffrage, implying therefore that it would be neither historically ineluctable nor irreversible. The PCF attempted to define a model of socialism that was no longer comparable with the Soviet Union's and to this end it affirmed that its vision of socialism was synonymous with liberty itself. To prove its democratic credentials, the PCF dropped the erstwhile ideological touchstone of the 'dictatorship of the proletariat' in favour of 'democratic socialism'.

Unfortunately for the PCF the PS was already firmly camped on the terrain of democratic socialism and the plans to rival the appeal of the Socialists failed to convince the electorate as a whole, and even some PCF members themselves. The decline in the party's ideological cohesion reached a point which was sufficiently alarming in 1977 for the leadership to decide to reorganise the 'Propaganda' section in order to reduce the uncertainty among ordinary members regarding the party line. The end of the Union of the Left in 1978 brought the competition between the PCF and the PS more blatantly into the open. The task confronting the Communists was clearly how to package and convey their policies in a way that would enable them to make up the ground lost to the Socialists. The PCF tried to regain the initiative by defining its strategic perspective in the conceptual framework provided by *socialisme autogestionnaire*.[17] As it approached the threshold of the 1980s, the PCF cast itself as the genuine party of *autogestion*, in contrast to what it criticised as the shallow pretensions of the Socialists. But this very pattern of emulation and virulent criticism undermined the efforts of the PCF to restore its credibility vis-à-vis the electorate of the left and necessitated another campaign of 'clarification' by the Communist leadership to make the party line more comprehensible to the membership.

After accepting to join the PS-led government formed in the wake of Mitterrand's victory in 1981 (see below), the PCF renewed its efforts to formulate a clearer expression of its particular vision of Socialist society. Throughout the 1980s the PCF's political vocabulary became increasingly dependent on appeals to the people for dialogue and mutual involvement, in an endeavour to lose its tarnished image as the party of dogma and intolerance.[18] The problem lay in the manifest incongruity between *autogestionnaire* theory and a largely sectarian practice. Notwithstanding its persistent attempts to distance itself from its negative image the PCF failed to revitalise its appeal: this was substantially due to its inability to embrace a new vision of socialist society which was distinctly its own and which could rival the vision being conveyed by the PS. The Communists thus found themselves doubly disadvantaged: fearing the loss of further ground to the Socialists they felt forced to attack what they saw as unwarranted compromises by the Socialist-led government, but in so doing underlined their own lack of a credible alternative, and the dilemma posed by their participation in government.

For all the party's ideological posturing, it could not escape the central contradiction posed by its participation in government from 1981-84. The PCF's brief experience as a party of government was not an entirely happy one: Communist ministers were in a small minority within the second and third Mauroy governments. The Communist ministers were scarcely in a position to influence the content of government policy. Whereas Socialist ministers gained most of the credit for the more audacious reforms of the first two years (1981-83), the four Communists were inevitably associated with helping to administer the government's economic austerity policies from 1983 onwards. Participation in government led to a growing divorce between the PCF ministers and hardliners in the party leadership. The ex-ministers, especially Le Pors and Rigout, were in the forefront of the *contestataires* once the party had quit office in July 1984.

After leaving office, the party reverted to its older *ouvrieriste*, anti-PS stance, relying upon what remained of its organisational strength (in particular its control of the CGT trade union federation) to attempt to destabilise the Fabius government. In vain: by 1984, the PCF lacked the organisational and political strength seriously to worry the Socialist government. President Mitterrand's introduction of proportional representation in 1985 for the 1986 legislative election dispensed the PCF from having to consider the formality of an electoral alliance with the PS for the first time since 1962. The party's largely negative strategy was severely sanctioned by the French electorate in March 1986: with less than 10 per cent, the PCF not only declined to its 1932 level, but was on the same level as Le Pen's National Front (see below). The issue of what function the PCF performed was raised with more acuity than ever after the party's lamentable performance in March 1986. It lay at the root of the *contestataire* movement and Juquin's candidacy in the 1988 presidential election.

Faced with new depths of unpopularity and the schism created by the Juquin candidacy, the PCF attempted to rely upon its once-powerful organisation to mobilise grass-roots support for its candidate, André Lajoinie. Communist Party members were exhorted to exploit with greater vigour the opportunities provided by the *points de rencontre*, the meeting points set up by the party outside factories, offices, supermarkets etc., which allowed the ordinary public to meet party members and thus provide them with the chance to express the party's views. At the same time, Lajoinie made every endeavour to condemn the policies of the Socialists. During the course of a broadcast on the radio station RTL on 21 February 1988, Lajoinie rejected categorically the prospect of Communists once again accepting ministerial posts in a Socialist-led government in order, as he put it, to implement the policies of the right.

As the campaign entered the final weeks before the first round of voting, Lajoinie's inability to secure more than 5 or 6 per cent of voting intentions suggested that the electorate was not persuaded by PCF tactics or convinced by the Communist alternative. Moreover, what emerged from the Central Committee meeting of 8 March was that too many PCF members themselves were unmotivated and confused. During the course of the meeting, Jean-Claude Gayssot, the man responsible for party organisation, identified a 35 per cent deficit in the number of party members who should have been engaged in promoting Lajoinie's campaign. Another Central Committee member evoked the belief among many ordinary members that *désistement* in favour of Mitterrand in the second round had already been decided, whereas in fact no such commitment had been articulated. These facts further underlined the possibility of substantial numbers of PCF voters opting for the *vote utile* in the first round and thus casting their vote for Mitterrand. In view of this Marchais was forced to stress the need to inform PCF voters of their obligation to work and vote for their candidate in order to avoid what he believed had been Mitterrand's ambition since he assumed the leadership of the PS in 1971: a first-round majority in a presidential election which would thus fatally undermine the PCF as a credible left-wing alternative to the PS.

During the final weeks of the campaign, Lajoinie demonstrated the difficult balance the Communists were attempting to strike by resting their campaign both on a positive promotion of their policies and the negative tactic of constantly criticising the PS, in the hope that this would situate them in advantageous contradistinction to their left-wing rivals. Lajoinie's appearance on the television programme *L'heure de vérité* on 23 March came shortly after Mitterrand had announced his decision to seek a second term as President, and his performance showed a more than usually marked concern to mount an action against the Socialists as well as advancing his claim to the presidency. After outlining the principal policy objectives defining his campaign, Lajoinie attacked Mitterrand and the Socialists more pointedly than ever. Mitterrand's commitment to disarmament was treated as hollow by Lajoinie, who reminded viewers that the PCF was the only party which had refused to vote for increases in the defence budget. As for Mitterrand's vision of the single European market and his declared pursuit of social harmony, according to Lajoinie they were simply pronouncements that masked the intention of the Socialists to facilitate the exploitation of the workers by right-wing economic interests.

The fact that the results of the first round of the presidential elections on 24 April 1988 left Pierre Juquin with only 2.10 per cent of the votes cast (substantially less than Antoine Waechter, the Green candidate, with 3.78 per cent) was little comfort to the PCF, for whom Lajoinie's 6.76 per cent represented a historic low. Marchais's explanation for the failure of Lajoinie's campaign was that many Communist voters had opted for the *vote utile* and voted for Mitterrand in the first round. The PCF's 11.31 per cent share of the votes cast in the unscheduled legislative elections of June 1988 partially substantiated Marchais's thesis, since the bastions which had seemed reluctant to support Lajoinie in the presidential election were the ones responsible for the revival in the party's fortunes in the ensuing legislative contest. Both in the interim period and subsequently, however, the PCF's failure to revise its attitude positively towards the PS cost it credibility within its own ranks and vis-à-vis the wider left-wing electorate. In mid-May the internal opposition to the PCF leadership which was polarising around Marcel Rigout, Claude Poperen and other former leading members of the hierarchy, began to articulate its opposition to the leadership's policies. One of their major demands was a less sectarian approach to the struggle for change according to socialist values, but the inflexibility of the leadership's reaction to this and other internal demands for changes in attitude was made manifest in *L'Humanité* on 17 May, which characterised the critical element which had gathered around Rigout and Poperen as a kind of clannish recidivism which the revolutionary workers movement in France had long outgrown.[19] In the same issue of *L'Humanité*, the Politburo of the party asserted that it was the Socialists who had turned their backs on the project to pursue change through concerted action by the left, arguing that Mitterrand had provoked the legislative elections in order to engineer an alliance with a right-wing party in order to implement right-wing policies. The leadership had therefore deemed it necessary for the PCF to articulate a 'different voice' for left-wing voters to heed in the legislative elections.

One of the anxieties of the PCF leadership with regard to the legislative elections was that the party's parliamentary representation might drop from 35 to below 30, the constitutionally fixed threshold for the existence of a parliamentary group. During the week before the second round of the legislative elections on 12 June the PS signalled that the threshold in question could be revised downwards and the PCF declared its decision to abide by the practice of *désistement* vis-à-vis the PS. Although Communist fortunes enjoyed a revival relative to Lajoinie's performance in the presidential elections, the party's representation in parliament nonetheless declined to 27 seats. The Socialist policy of opening up towards the centre had benefitted the PCF and, more importantly, so had the concentration of votes in its traditional bastions, but in statistical and demographic terms the general erosion of working-class support for the PCF had continued.[20] More than ever the party was forced back upon its Parisian heartland and pockets of support elsewhere. This, however, was attenuated by the mixed fortunes of the PS and left the PCF with an unexpected degree of leverage. Unable to amass the support of more than 276 representatives out of a total of 577, the PS was therefore dependent either on the PCF, or the CDS in order to operate with an overall majority. The PCF's reaction was to relaunch the idea of left-wing unity, but this was surrounded by such ambiguities as to suggest that the suspicion felt by the Communists towards the PS remained essentially unaltered. Marchais's appeals for left-wing unity were combined with a categorical rejection of the possibility of Communist participation in a Socialist-led government and criticism of what the PCF regarded as Socialist austerity measures.[21]

Between 1981-84 the PCF had supported and participated in PS-led governments; since then the party had receded into a more hardline opposition to its Socialist rivals. After the 1988 elections, the PCF once again expressed an inclination for 'selective support', although it reserved its right to opt for 'constructive opposition' should it deem such an attitude necessary.[22] PCF support for the wave of public sector strikes that occurred during the autumn of 1988 was interpreted by some observers as an attempt by the Communists to use their leverage in order to procure favourable local agreements with the PS prior to the next critical electoral hurdle for the PCF: the municipal elections of 1989.[23] The performance of the PCF in the municipal elections of March 1989 showed, however, that their tactics had failed to damage the PS or gain the confidence of the left-wing electorate. There was a record level of abstentionism, 27.2 per cent against 21.6 per cent in 1983, but unlike 1977 and 1983 the municipal elections of March 1989 did not constitute a protest vote against government policy. There was a marked increase in the PCF-PS 'primaries' in large towns (over 20,000 inhabitants), up from 27 in 1983 to 144 in 1989, but whereas the PS emerged from the elections having erased the reverses of 1983 and increased its local representation still further, the PCF lost another 48 communes with over 9,000 inhabitants in addition to the 33 similar communes it had lost in 1983, thereby registering a 37 per cent drop in its municipal representation over a period of 12 years.[24] That it retained control of so much of its municipal patrimony, however, was a considerable relief both to the party leadership, and to sitting Communist mayors, able to draw on well-tested reserves of loyalty unavailable to the party's presidential candidate Lajoinie in 1988. In retrospect, those in the PS who had argued for a tougher negotiating stance vis-à-vis the PCF over local agreements had been proved right, given Socialist advances in Communist municipalities like Petit Quevilly and Les Mureaux.[25]

The competition provided by a tactically astute and revitalised PS was a major component in a complex of factors resulting in the marginalisation of the PCF. As was suggested by the attitude of the Communists to the Socialists during the presidential campaign of 1988, the former had failed to reconcile themselves fully to the fundamental institution of the Fifth Republic and the style of politics it imposes: the presidency.

ii) The Challenge of Presidentialism

From the moment of its inception, the PCF had disagreed with the extent of the powers which the Fifth Republic confers on the President. This disapproval was made manifest by the banner headline of *L'Humanité* on 29 September 1958, 'La constitution monarchique adoptée', proclaiming the PCF's criticism of what it saw as the arbitrary and quasi-monarchical powers of the French President under the new constitution. During the ensuing years the PCF found ways of working within the constraints of the system and making the ideological accommodations which, for example, allowed it to participate in a Socialist-led government. Once out of government, however, the PCF could return to far less muted criticism of the constitution from which government derives its powers.

At its 25th Congress (1985) the PCF adopted a resolution which marked an end to the strategy which had characterised its attitude towards governmental office during the preceding quarter century. According to the resolution, the cooperation with the PS which had brought the left to power had been a mistake and had resulted in too many compromises at the expense of the PCF. Consequently, after the Congress the party's political activity was going to be marked by autonomous action among the masses with a view to creating a *nouveau rassemblement populaire majoritaire*.[26] In his report to the 25th Congress, Marchais explicitly condemned the way he believed the constitution of the Fifth Republic permitted power to be concentrated in the hands of one individual. Calling for a democratisation of the institutions created by the constitution, Marchais outlined five objectives: a parliament with greater power over legislation, notably its inception; a more powerful Prime Minister, and therefore greater independence of the government from the President; a less direct role for the President in the exercise of power, and a greater definition of his role as a ceremonial guardian of the republic's institutions; real decentralisation, and effective debureaucratisation. These objectives were supported by nine specific proposals which included a non-renewable seven-year term for the President, a change in the voting system to allow any candidate with more than 10 per cent of the vote in the first round to stand in the second round, a more narrowly defined presidential right to dissolve parliament, and more power for parliament to decide the order of business.[27]

In the presidential elections of 1981, the high-profile campaign fought by Marchais had failed to bring the success hoped for. In 1988 the PCF made a point, publicly and repeatedly, of its refusal to compromise with the tactic it condemned in the other parties of concentrating on an American-style packaging of their candidates in order to achieve maximum impact in the media at the expense of a genuine analysis of the programmes they were advocating. In contrast to his rivals in the campaign, Lajoinie's appeal was to be an integral aspect of the appeal of his party as a whole and of its message. He was portrayed by the PCF as the kind of candidate who would forego the self-seeking rivalry of his presidential adversaries in order to project the policies determined by a political collectivity for the collective benefit of French society. The terms for the campaign were thus not only set by the PCF Central Committee and articulated by its General Secretary, they were set in such a way as to accommodate two figures at the head of the presidential campaign: the presidential candidate himself, Lajoinie, and the person who defined the nature of the PCF's participation in the elections, Marchais.

In his report to the PCF's 26th Congress in December 1987, Marchais referred to the institutional obstacles Lajoinie would face.[28] In Marchais's opinion, the presidency had begun to resemble an elected monarchy, not only because of the power concentrated in the hands of the President but also due to the fact that since the President's mandate is obtained directly from the people, this had fostered a widespread belief that the office of President conferred a legitimacy that could not be challenged by any other democratic institutions. In deciding how to vote, the French electorate was therefore guided principally by the choice of individual rather than policy. Furthermore, Marchais affirmed, the form of electoral choice offered to the French people would pressure them into resorting to the *vote utile*. In short, electors would be discouraged from voting for the candidate with whom they identified in favour of the possible winner least unacceptable to them. Marchais concluded that such a system could not fail to handicap any candidate and party pursuing radical change. But by portraying Lajoinie as the presidential candidate who embodied the collectivist and consultative virtues that would check the drift to right-wing presidentialism, the PCF leadership could deny the legitimacy of presidential power and its manifestations while, without apparent contradiction, putting forward a candidate in the presidential elections.

The unfolding of the campaign illustrated, however, the electoral dangers consequent upon a failure to adapt to presidentialism. Throughout the campaign, observers could only become more firmly convinced that Lajoinie's prospects of emerging as a genuine *présidentiable* capable of inspiring the confidence of the French electorate were terminally undermined by his democratically centralised persona.[29] On the hustings and in the media, the shadow of Marchais made it all the more difficult for an already lacklustre candidate to shine. During the month of February 1988, it was noted in *Le Monde* that Marchais had made five major appearances on television whereas Lajoinie had made only two. This tendency for Marchais to eclipse Lajoinie was of fundamental importance in creating the impression that the choice of Lajoinie as the PCF's presidential candidate had not diminished Marchais's role as the real guiding force within the party. Lajoinie's result added substance to the argument that the Communists had failed to establish a credible alternative to presidential-style politics and that their refusal of presidentialism had cost them dearly.

iii) The Evolution of Party Politics.

The PCF's failure to adapt to presidentialism undermined not only the fortunes of its presidential candidates but also its fortunes in the game of party politics, by denying it the kind of injection of vigour enjoyed by the PS. The attitude of the PCF expressed a general shortcoming vis-à-vis the institutions of the Fifth Republic which limited the advantage the Communists could take of the osmosis which occurred between parties and institutions as the republic entered the 1990s.

The constitution of the Fifth Republic recognised the legitimate existence of political parties, but claimed to exclude them from power by predicating a double separation, between governmental and parliamentary power, and the state and political parties. In a system where the indivisible authority of the state came to be vested in the President (whatever ambiguities were contained within the constitution) parties were defined as elements of civil society representing particular interests. This Gaullist-inspired notion of the role of parties was particularly strong during the presidencies of General de Gaulle (1958-69) and his successor, Georges Pompidou (1969-74). A decisive turning-point was reached in 1974 under the presidency of Valéry Giscard d'Estaing, when for the first time the parties constituting the parliamentary majority were represented as such in the government. Giscard d'Estaing departed further from the Gaullist tradition by instituting regular meetings with the leaders of the parties comprising the parliamentary opposition as well as the majority, in order to keep them abreast of presidential policy. It was in keeping with this new departure that he made an abortive attempt to launch the idea of state funding for political parties.

The election of Mitterrand in 1981 was another evolutionary step eroding the Gaullist separation between the state and political parties. He was the first President elected as the official candidate of a party. As both President, and elder statesman of the PS, Mitterrand personified the convergence between the institutions and the parties of the republic, often acting as a kind of arbiter between the parliamentary group and ministers, and ministers themselves. The victory of the right in the legislative elections of March 1986 marked a kind of apogee in the osmosis between the institutions and the parties of the Fifth Republic, but in quite a different manner to the kind which obtained in 1981. This time, the crucial arbitration was performed by the leaders of the new right-wing majority in parliament, elected by proportional representation. Until the compatibility of the presidential and the parliamentary majority was restored in the legislative elections of June 1988, Mitterrand was therefore limited to operating within the parameters of his presidential preserve as the embodiment of the state, faced with the ascendancy of party and parliamentary power during that period in the life of the republic.[30]

As the evolution in the relationship between the parties and institutions of the Fifth Republic suggests, it was incumbent upon parties wishing to enhance their presence on the political stage and extend their influence to accept the institutions of the republic and work through them to their advantage. The PCF's attitude towards presidentialism, its withdrawal from Socialist-led government and robust affirmation of its subsequent disinclination to participate, were factors which inhibited its ability to capitalise on the evolution in question. And during the 1980s, departures from the *quadrille bipolaire* which characterised the second-ballot electoral system did not bring the PCF the benefits it might have hoped for (see above, p. 7 for an explanation of the *quadrille bipolaire*). The use of proportional representation instead of the majority system in the 1986 legislative elections could have been expected to benefit smaller parties like the PCF, as well as freeing it from the constraints of 'republican discipline' implicit in second-ballot deals with the PS. As the results illustrated, however, the tendency to bipolarity outweighed the potentially fragmenting tendencies of proportional representation. Inasmuch as the PCF was freed from the constraints of republican discipline, so the PS was free to mobilise left-wing voters behind its banner alone. In addition, the reasonably united strategy of the RPR and the UDF further enhanced the sense in which the central contest was one between an incumbent governing party and an aspiring government coalition. And notwithstanding the pull it was able to exert on some issues raised in the campaign, the PCF remained on the periphery of the main bipolar struggle.[31]

Partly through its own volition and partly through circumstances which it could not alter, the PCF during the 1970s and 1980s found itself unable to profit as other parties had done (notably its great rival on the left) from the evolution in party politics. But one challenge that put the onus more squarely on the PCF's own capacity for intellectual regeneration was the challenge posed by new ideas and changing times.

New Ideas and Changing Times

Notwithstanding the failure of his campaign in the 1988 presidential election, Pierre Juquin articulated ideas which elicited a wide and sympathetic reaction among the members of the PCF, even if they did not agree with the way he envisaged implementing them. In his book *Autocritiques*, Juquin had criticised the failure of the Communist movement to accommodate the need for individuality.[32] It had relied too much on terms that were ideologically fixed, such as the 'masses' and the 'class struggle', and which led to a conception of the individual in which he or she was indistinguishable from the mass. As he re-iterated in *Fraternellement libre*, the prevailing interpretation of communist ideology in France needed to be intellectually renewed and reorientated towards the transformation of society's values so as to allow the human person ultimately to assume a free and fulfilled sense of individuality.[33]

After the presidential elections of 1988 were over, it emerged that Claude Poperen had written to the leadership of the PCF before the second round and in his letter had unequivocally underlined the need for the intellectual and organisational changes which Juquin had stressed, if the party's decline was to be arrested. Poperen argued that economic changes and the evolution in the condition of the working class made it vital for the party to respond to the 'increasing demand for individuality'. As for the party's organisation, it had to alter in order to accommodate genuine debate which provided the members with the real possibility of influencing policy in order to be a 'democratic centralism worthy of the name'. These changes could only be concomitant with a willingness to dispense with 'incantatory discourse' and the 'repetition of certainties with no foundation in real life'.[34] Poperen's questioning of democratic centralism in particular, illustrated the continuation of a tendency that characterised the extent to which the political culture underpinning the PCF was weakening. Democratic centralism had been a fundamental part of the membership's belief that the PCF was not a party like any other, but had a quasi-revolutionary role as the united organ of the French working class. It was also an ideological means of cementing the mass party and the leadership.[35] The persistent expression of a desire to reform democratic centralism was indicative of the new scepticism felt amongst the membership regarding this central organising principle, as well as their disaffection with the leadership.

As the PCF approached the end of the 1980s, however, the leadership could review a decade during which it had overcome a number of important challenges to its authority: Pierre Juquin had quite clearly failed to define an electorally credible alternative to the PCF; the *rénovateurs* under Claude Llabrès, bereft of their base in the PCF, found themselves edging ever closer to the PS; while the *reconstructeurs*, isolated behind Marcel Rigout and Claude Poperen, were left to cling tenuously to the hope of reforming the party from within. Yet the objective facts which governed French political life remained unaltered. The re-election of Mitterrand to a second term as President indicated that the simplisms which so often characterised the PCF line were no longer adequate. In spite of French society's slide to the right, the French electorate had voted for a man of the left. Paradoxically, although Mitterrand had been elected as a personification of change in 1981, in 1988 he was re-elected through a conservative response to the prospect of an excessively rapid progression down the road to free market liberalism, and the failure of the anti-presidentialist campaign of the Communists was indicative of their inability to judge the mood and the wishes of the electorate.

Having apparently neutralised the Communist critics who had emerged before and during the presidential election of 1988, the PCF leadership could not have expected an expression of dissent from within its own circle which implicitly criticised its strategy during that campaign and its general ideological orientation thereafter. Absent from the Central Committee meeting of 13 October 1989 due to his convalescence after a road accident, Charles Fiterman - formerly a minister in the Mauroy government and a close associate of Marchais - sent a written exposition to the Central Committee of what he perceived to be powerful arguments for change. Fiterman criticised the PCF's tendency to play the role of 'Monsieur Plus', its tactical inclination to raise the stakes politically for the sake of distinguishing itself from other parties, and argued that it would be preferable for the party to pursue the dynamics of progress and left unity instead of lapsing into polemics. In view of the changes that had occurred in France, Fiterman advised his colleagues to rethink their position on nationalisation and the mixed economy, and of the crucial need to espouse 'universal values'.[36]

Fiterman's proposals found few supporters among the 130 or so Central Committee members at the meeting, with the notable exception of another former minister in the Mauroy government, Anicet Le Pors. On 19 October 1989, when the PCF leadership gathered the First Secretaries of the federations which constitute the party nationally, Jean-Claude Gayssot elucidated the leadership's reaction to the positions taken by Fiterman and Le Pors. He characterised the proposals put forward by the latter as a 'step backwards' and encapsulated the leadership's attitude to change by arguing that if the counsels of Fiterman and Le Pors were to be followed, there would have to be a change of 'policy, strategy and party'.[37] Fiterman refused, however, to relinquish his position of considered criticism vis-à-vis the PCF's leadership and its strategy. He developed his ideas further, for the benefit of the party's Central Committee, in February 1990. Fiterman countered any accusations that he was a lackey of social democracy by asserting his disquiet at the accommodations the Socialists had reached with monied interests, arguing instead that the PS would never be able to rally the left in its entirety and that there still remained a vacuum to be filled by a party of revolution. It was incumbent on the PCF to seize that opportunity, but it could only do so, Fiterman argued, if it could divest itself of its seige mentality and the consequent inclination to regard any divergence of opinion as heretical. More importantly, the party had profoundly to revise what it understood by the principle of democratic centralism.[38]

As the decade drew to a conclusion, however, the PCF found it harder to resist the momentum of change on the international scene than the pressure for change from within its own ranks. The collapse of the Communist establishments of eastern Europe during the autumn and winter of 1989 forced the PCF to redefine its international perspective. During the Central Committee meeting of 15 December 1989, Maxime Gremetz presented a report which acknowledged some deficiencies in the PCF's attitude to its sister parties in eastern Europe. According to the report, this was due partly to a failure of foresight and partly to ignorance of the real situation in those societies. The report condemned those Communists in the USSR and elsewhere who had tried to hinder the process of destalinisation and thus helped to create a gulf between the Communist Party and the people which was inimical to the freedoms of the latter.[39] But, unlike the Communist Party of Italy, which during the preceding month had decided to change its name and create an image that was less tainted by the negative connotations which had become popularly associated with the very name 'communism', the PCF persisted with its familiar line of analysis. It criticised the plans for privatisation and austerity envisaged in countries like Poland and Hungary, arguing that historically, social democracy had proved its inability to advance the cause of socialism and that the nations in question should not be seduced by the market economy at a time when capitalism was at its most morally bankrupt. Almost in spite of himself, however, in April 1990 Marchais was forced to admit that the PCF had in the past been 'duped' by the Soviet Union into maintaining a naively optimistic vision in relation to 'real socialism' as historically practised in the USSR and eastern Europe.[40]

Notwithstanding its singular analysis of world events, the PCF entered the final decade of the twentieth century knowing that it still occupied a strategically important place on the left of national politics. Although the PS had gained in strength at the expense of the PCF, it still could not take the bastions of the latter, and as long as the electoral system remains fundamentally unchanged the two parties can envisage a continuing dependence on each other in order to secure the best representation possible. The challenge the PCF must address if it is to reverse its decline, is whether it is willing and able to renew itself organisationally and ideologically, or whether it is willing, in effect, to resign itself to an ineluctable process of marginalisation by falling back on entrenched positions and within traditional bastions.

Notes

1. Figures include overseas territories and departments, hence there are marginal inconsistencies between these figures and those presented in Appendix 1. Dainov, E., 'Problems of French communism 1972-1986', *West European Politics*, vol. 10, no. 3, July 1986, p. 375; *L'élection présidentielle*, Le Monde: dossiers et documents, May 1988.

2. *Les élections législatives*, Le Monde: dossiers et documents, June 1988.

3. 'Le mois politique', *Revue Politique et Parlementaire*, no. 938, November-December 1988, p. 72.

4. Le Gall, G., 'Novations et paradoxes des municipales 89', *Revue Politique et Parlementaire*, no. 940, March-April 1989, p. 11.

5. See Biffaud, O., 'Le PCF atteint par la culture de l'échec', *Le Monde*, 21 June 1989.

6. Adereth, M., *The French Communist Party: A Critical History 1920-1981*, Manchester University Press, Manchester, 1984, p. 290.

7. Ranger, J., 'Le déclin du Parti communiste', *Revue Française de Science Politique*, vol. 36, no. 1, February 1986, p. 50.

8. Figure given in *L'Humanité*, 9 January 1979.

9. Milon, R., 'Le PCF est toujours un parti passoire', *Est et Ouest*, no. 50, January 1988, p. 29.

10. Cardoze, M., 'PCF: le destin du courant critique', *Revue Politique et Parlementaire*, no. 27, January-February 1987, p. 8.

11. Samson, M., 'PC: divorces à la toulousaine', *Libération*, 31 October 1987.

12. Lajoinie, A., and Passevent, R., *A coeur ouvert*, Messidor, Paris, 1987, p. 170.

13. Jeambar, D., 'Présidentielle: l'ombre de Marchais', *Le Point*, 25 May 1987.

14. Marchais, G., *Le défi démocratique*, Grasset, Paris, 1973.

15. Parti socialiste, *Changer la vie: programme de gouvernement du Parti socialiste*, Flammarion, Paris, 1972, pp. 8-14.

16. On the success of Mitterrand's PS in appealing to the new social groups produced by post-war social and economic change (*les couches moyennes salariées*), and in ideologically outmanoeuvreing the PCF, see Bell, D.S., and Criddle, B., *The French Socialist Party: The Emergence of a Party of Government*, Clarendon Press, Oxford, 1988.

17. A concept the party had previously vigorously condemned as a *gauchiste* utopia. It was always unclear what the PCF understood by *le socialisme autogestionnaire*. The party claimed in 1977 to have broken with its traditionally statist thinking and to be proposing the kind of socialism in which institutions and groups would be left to govern their own affairs, and the role of the state would be reduced to one of guide and coordinator. However, the party's tough stance adopted in negotiations

with the Socialists in the run-up to the 1978 legislative elections called into question its sincerity, as, indeed, did the PS and the CFDT. The party demanded that the subsidiaries of the nine major industrial groups whose nationalisation was foreseen by the common programme should themselves be taken into public ownership. The common programme had been vague on this subject. The Communists' demand would have greatly extended the scope of the left's nationalisation programme, and probably ensured the defeat of the PS-PCF alliance at the legislative election of March 1978. Mitterrand realised this and refused what he considered to be a suicidical proposal.

18. The 24th Congress in 1984 claimed to have broken with the old thinking which envisaged socialism in terms of 'models', opting instead for a socialist project that would be fulfilled through a piecemeal approach to France's problems and the central plank of which would be a *stratégie autogestionnaire*.

19. Biffaud, O., 'M. Marcel Rigout se joint à M. Claude Poperen pour critiquer la direction du PCF', *Le Monde*, 18 May 1988.

20. Le Gall, G., 'Printemps 1988: retour à une gauche majoritaire', *Revue Politique et Parlementaire*, no. 936, July-August 1988, p. 17.

21. Lavau, G., 'Le Parti communiste tire sa carte du jeu électoral', *Libération*, 13 June 1988.

22. Biffaud, O., 'Le juge de paix de la gauche', *Le Monde*, 14 Juin 1988.

23. Schneider, R., 'PC-PS: le retour du bras de fer', *Le Nouvel Observateur*, 24 November 1988.

24. Le Gall, 'Novations et paradoxes des municipales 89', p. 10.

25. Colombani, J-M., 'La victoire des hérétiques', *Le Monde*, 14 March 1989.

26. This might be somewhat loosely translated as the 'new popular majority'. Its linguistic ambiguity reflected its political obscurity.

27. Bauby, P., 'Le révisionnisme institutionnel du PCF', *Revue Politique et Parlementaire*, no. 919, September-October 1985.

28. Published in *L'Humanité*, 3 December 1987.

29. Dubois, J-P., 'Quand André endort Georges', *Le Nouvel Observateur*, 7 April 1988.

30. Portelli, H., 'Les partis et les institutions', *Pouvoirs*, no. 49, 1989.

31. See Knapp, A., 'Proportional but bipolar: France's electoral system in 1986', *West European Politics*, vol. 10, no. 1, January 1987, p. 107. See also Cole, A., and Campbell, P., *French Electoral Systems and Elections since 1789*, Gower, Aldershot, 1989, Chapter Eight.

32. Juquin, P., *Autocritiques*, Grasset, Paris, 1985, Chapter Nine.

33. Juquin, P., *Fraternellement libre*, Grasset, Paris, 1988, p. 28.

34. Biffaud, O., 'M. Claude Poperen appelle les communistes à une prise de conscience', *Le Monde*, 11 May 1988.

35. Newman, W., 'Conflict and cohesion in the British Labour Party and French Communist Party', *West European Politics*, vol. 10, no. 2, April 1987.

36. 'L'ancien ministre invite les communistes à "un énorme travail idéologique et politique" ', *Le Monde*, 15-16 October 1989.

37. Biffaud, O., 'La direction mobilise ses secrétaires fédéraux contre MM. Fiterman et Le Pors', *Le Monde*, 21 October 1989.

38. Algalarrondo, H., 'Fiterman: le défi paisible', *Le Nouvel Observateur*, 15 February 1990.

39. Biffaud, O., 'Le PCF ébauche une autocritique', *Le Monde*, 17-18 December 1989.

40. *The Times*, 14 April 1990.

Bibliography

Adereth, M., *The French Communist Party: A Critical History 1920-1984*, Manchester University Press, Manchester, 1984.

Becker, J-J., *Le Parti communiste veut-il le pouvoir?: la stratégie du PCF de 1930 à nos jours*, Seuil, Paris, 1981.

Burles, J., *Le Parti communiste dans la société française*, Editions Sociales, Paris, 1981.

Burles, J., Martelli, R., and Wolikow, S., *Les communistes et leur stratégie*, Editions Sociales, Paris, 1981.

Cardoze, M., *Nouveau voyage à l'intérieur du Parti communiste français*, Fayard, Paris, 1986.

Elleinstein, J., *Le PC*, Grasset, Paris, 1976.

Fauvet, J., *Histoire du Parti communiste français*, Fayard, Paris, 1977.

Gaffney, J., *The French Left and the Fifth Republic*, Macmillan, London, 1989.

Gaudard, J-P., *Les orphelins du PC*, Belfond, Paris, 1986.

Gayssot, J-C., *Le Parti communiste français*, Messidor, Paris, 1989.

Juquin, P., *Autocritiques*, Grasset, Paris, 1985.

Juquin, P., *Fraternellement libre*, Grasset, Paris, 1988.

Kriegel, A., *Les communistes français*, Seuil, Paris, 1970.

Lajoinie, A., and Passevent, R., *A coeur ouvert*, Messidor, Paris, 1987.

Laurens, A., and Pfister, T., *Les nouveaux communistes aux portes du pouvoir*, Stock, Paris, 1977.

Lavau, G., *A quoi sert le PCF?* Fayard, Paris, 1981.

Pronier, R., *Les municipalités communistes*, Balland, Paris, 1983.

Pudal, B., *Prendre parti. Pour une sociologie historique du PCF*, FNSP, Paris, 1989.

4 The Emergence of a Presidential Party: The Socialist Party

John Gaffney

In May 1981, François Mitterrand was elected the first Socialist President of the Fifth Republic with 51.8 per cent of the vote, beating his rival, Valéry Giscard d'Estaing, the incumbent President, by over a million votes. In order to secure a sympathetic parliamentary majority, Mitterrand dissolved the National Assembly. Six weeks after his own election, the Socialist Party (PS) swept to power with an absolute majority of seats in the National Assembly.

The results of May and June 1981 were remarkable for two reasons. First, the right had held power in various forms since the creation of the republic in 1958, and, until the 1981 presidential election campaign itself, it was generally assumed that the sitting President would win again, thus demonstrating the apparently unyielding grip of the right on the reins of power. Second, not only did François Mitterrand win the presidential election, the Socialist Party's victory in the ensuing legislative elections surpassed all expectations: with only one exception (the Gaullist landslide of June 1968 following the student uprising of May) no single party had ever gained an outright majority in the Fifth Republic. And it was the received view that if the left ever were to take power then it could only be in the form of a Socialist/Communist alliance. The dual reality, therefore, of a Socialist President of the Fifth Republic and a victorious Socialist Party in the National Assembly changed perceptions of the republic and of the scope for the left within it.

The Socialists held power from 1981 to 1986 and again from 1988. Their former First Secretary, François Mitterrand, has been President continuously since 1981. In the course of the 1980s, however, there was a series of changes within the party system which had major effects upon how the system functioned (see Chapter One). We shall divide the following study into four chronological sections: 1971-81, which covers the period between Mitterrand's becoming the leader of the PS and his first presidential election victory; 1981-86 which saw the Socialist government move from the 'lyrical illusion' phase of 1981 to the pragmatic reformism and economic realism of the mid-1980s; 1986-88 which saw the party return to opposition while maintaining its new, competent, reformist image - and at the same time trying to contain and resolve the internal leadership rivalries which were threatening party stability; and, finally, the post-1988 period which saw Mitterrand returned to the Elysée Palace as President for a second term, and the Socialists returned to government after the legislative elections called in the wake of Mitterrand's presidential election victory of May 1988.

In each of these phases, the evolving relationship between the party and Mitterrand himself was of crucial significance. We shall be concerned with this relationship between party and person throughout our analysis.

The Road to Victory

Between the beginning of the 1970s and the end of the 1980s a bizarre inversion took place in terms of Mitterrand's relationship to the PS. What became a passionate love affair, in which, in the eyes of the Socialists, he came to stand on an equal footing with Jaurès and Blum, began as a marriage of convenience.[1] Schematically, Mitterrand, the only credible presidential candidate on the left by the late 1960s, would give the party power, in return for its, the only nationally credible party or grouping on the centre left by the early 1970s, helping him gain the presidency.[2] The nature of his actual leadership of the PS in the 1970s and his symbolic leadership in the 1980s was such as to eventually make Mitterrandism and socialism near-synonyms.[3] However, given French socialism's history, its national and local implantation, and its ideology, the change did not simply involve the party's abandonment of its traditional identity and its embracing of a 'catch-all' identity reminiscent of Gaullism at an ideological level and the US Democrats or Republicans at an organisational one. The party organisation which Mitterrand led from 1971 had much of the same internal structure, and local implantation, and many of the same second-rank leaders, as it had before he became its leader (section one).[4] All national political parties, as well as possessing an organisational structure to sustain them over time, must also possess a doctrine or philosophy to orientate the party, define its relationship to power and offer (in differing degrees) to its activists, members, and potential electorate a view of life, and of the relationship between morality and politics, and a referential context for the elaboration of policies (section two). In the context of the PS between 1971 and 1981 these dual organisational and ideological imperatives had to accommodate themselves to the main imperative of Fifth Republican politics, namely, the gaining of the presidency (section three). Let us, then, examine these issues in turn.

The Party Structure

The PS does not, as do most European socialist and social-democratic parties, have a trade union connection. Consequently, its internal structure is based upon the organisation of a direct membership which, throughout the 1980s, hovered around the 200,000 mark. The basic organisational unit of the party is the section which has between 5 and 250 members.[5] The section sends representatives to the departmental (roughly equivalent to a county in the UK) Federal Congress (*Congrès fédéral*) using proportional representation to reflect the currents of opinion within the section. The Federal Congress elaborates and debates policy resolutions (and selects delegates) for the National Congress (*Congrès national*). The biennial Congress elects the Directing Committee (*Comité directeur*) of the party, which in turn elects the Executive Bureau (*Bureau executif*) and the National Secretariat (*Secrétariat national*). The composition of the Directing Committee is based upon the percentage of delegates' votes cast for each of the national motions circulated in the federations before the Congress (proportional representation operates, therefore, at virtually all levels of the party, though not at the most prestigious National Secretariat level where the 14 or so members are drawn from the majority of the Directing Committee). We can make three points here concerning the effect of these structures on the nature of the PS. The first is that the number of delegates sent by a federation to Congress (and therefore its voting power) is dependent upon the members in the federation. The large federations have, therefore, a significant influence on the party (traditionally the Nord and Bouches-du-Rhône federations). The second is that because of the way policy debates (votes for the Congress motions) are linked to power in the party (election to the Directing Committee, Executive Bureau and Secretariat), the party is unofficially organised into several currents which become associated with a motion and vie for votes at the National Congress. A related factor, perhaps the most important one of all, is that the 'currents' (there are normally between three and five strong currents in the party at any one time) have come to be associated with individual leaders within the party, and the motions with their leading signatory (the most successful being, in the 1970s, the Mitterrandist current). The hierarchical nature of the currents, moreover, is compounded by the fact that the motions themselves are invariably drawn up by the leaders of the currents and their collaborators.

The Party Ideology

The PS shares along with, for example, the German SPD, the British Labour Party, and the Spanish Socialists the principal aims of the Socialist International: the emancipation of working people, freedom of expression, women's rights, equality, solidarity with liberation movements, and so on; the state to secure or help to secure these aims, along with decentralisation of power to local communities, a redistribution of wealth, in short, the panoply of aims and objectives informing twentieth century democratic socialism. In the French case, because of the wider political culture and history of France, certain other emphases not found to the same degree in other European parties pertain (some of which contradict other elements of French socialism): a very strong commitment to national defence (which has seen the PS adapt to France's general acceptance of its nuclear force); a stronger commitment to state intervention and centralised control inherited from Jacobinism (which has vied with an almost equally strong decentralising current of opinion within socialism to the point where observers could speak of two cultures); a traditional hostility (less declared in the present period) to the Catholic Church; a strong and romantic relationship to the history of republicanism; and, in spite of its traditional hostility to militarism, a revolutionary heritage from the nineteenth century and, therefore, an ambiguous relationship, if not to revolutionary violence, then to its rhetoric and mythology of liberation; and, finally, a strong relationship throughout the twentieth century to Marxism (though this latter always informed the party's rhetoric more than its policies).

Traditionally, these various ideas and approaches were expressed through the tendencies or currents of opinion inside the party. Organisationally, these vectors of opinion within the party can be described as factions, and generally speaking it has been the play of factions which has characterised the internal life of the PS and contributed to its political orientation.[6] As we mentioned above, some of the factions became associated with geographical areas of strong local implantation, and with their leaders, the best recent examples being Pierre Mauroy's Nord federation and, in the 1960s and 1970s, Gaston Defferre's Bouches-du-Rhône federation. To a certain extent, factions were sustained by the proportional representation applied to the election of the Directing Committee. By the mid-1970s, there were five major factions or currents (or sub-currents) in the party: the Mitterrandists (self-explanatory, though incorporating a whole range of attitudes from the extreme left to the extreme right within the party); the Mauroyists (traditional municipal socialism); the Defferrists (similar to the Mauroyists but incorporating the arcane politics of Marseille bossism); the CERES group which constituted the extreme left of the party and therefore most sympathetic to the PCF; and the Rocardians, the party's modernist, social democrats (and least sympathetic to the PCF).[7] The Mauroyists (and their forerunners in the Nord) and the Defferrists had kept the old Socialist Party (SFIO) alive through its difficult years, and brought much of the old socialist tradition, and traditional legitimacy, into the new party; the CERES group kept the French Marxist tradition alive; the Rocardians spoke for the new modernism; the Mitterrandists for all of these things plus a particular allegiance to Mitterrand himself. In this way, the ideological vivacity of the party was maintained while it adapted to the exigencies of presidentialism. We can say, therefore, that factionalism in the PS has sustained it since the party's creation in 1905 both ideologically and organisationally, ensuring (most of the time) that the heterogeneity of the party remained an asset rather than a danger to party unity. Commitment to presidentialism, however, was to change the nature of factionalism.[8]

In the Fifth Republic, therefore, the Socialist Party, especially from 1971 onwards, maintained a lively ideological orientation which was underpinned organisationally by the activity of the factions. The leftist orientation of the party was further maintained by the signing of the common programme of government with the PCF in 1972 (an unworkable governmental programme which nevertheless kept the PS committed to a left-wing alliance and away from centrist alliances which would have split the party); alliance with the strong PCF (see Chapter Three) being seen as necessary given the electoral system of the Fifth Republic.[9]

The most far-reaching adaptation was to the presidentialism of the regime. It was clear to the PS and to the left generally that unless it had a nationally known, credible, and respected figure at its head, it could not entertain the idea of winning the presidency of the republic. By adapting to presidentialism, however, the PS was to undergo changes at all levels of its activity: factional, electoral and ideological, this last especially given that all socialist parties are, in principle, opposed to the notion of personal power. The reward, however, was ultimately electoral success and the dominant position in the party system throughout most of the 1980s. Before examining this period, let us look in more detail at the effects of presidentialism on the party itself.

Presidentialism

It is clear from this brief overview that organisation and ideology and strategy are inextricably, though problematically, linked to one another in the PS. In the Third, Fourth and early Fifth Republic this relationship of organisation and ideology to strategy was relatively non-contentious: the strategy being simply that of maintaining municipal implantation and gaining seats in parliament. In the post-1971 PS, this strategy remained but was overlain with the one mentioned earlier: the promotion of Mitterrand as a potential President. As this strategic orientation developed it had far-reaching effects upon the activity of the currents of opinion and factions. We can note three here. In the first place, the wave of allegiance to Mitterrand meant that he enjoyed the support of the majority of the factions for the greater part of the 1971-81 period, overt criticism of him or the proposal of a different strategy becoming tantamount not to mere doctrinal disagreement but to leadership betrayal.[10] This was reinforced by a very particular use of the notion of the 'Epinay line' (that is, the commitment made at the Epinay Congress in 1971 - when Mitterrand took the leadership - to the 'Union of the Left' with the Communist Party). At a declared level, allegiance to the Epinay line meant commitment to the Union of the Left; at an undeclared level it meant personal allegiance to Mitterrand, even after the Union of the Left collapsed in 1977 through disagreements between the PS and PCF over the updating of the symbolic common programme.[11]

Second, Mitterrand himself, in order to gain a presidential-style freedom of manoeuvre from the weighty democracy of the party's structures, and to present his ideas and political persona to the electorate without fear of being called to order by the organisation itself, developed a large parallel network, inside the party, of officers responsible to him alone. In this way, he presidentialised his own faction while circumventing the potential control of other factions.

Third, factional development in such a context meant the relative presidentialisation of the other factions (or else their relative marginalisation, e.g. CERES - or incorporation, e.g. the Poperenists - into other factions). If any faction was to entertain taking the leadership (from, or after, Mitterrand) and/or offering a potential presidential candidate, it logically needed a *présidentiable* of its own. This personalisation of factions (encouraged by the media and the developing prominence of second-rank leaders as the party came closer and closer to power) meant that even though many of the ideas underpinning and informing factions and their concomitant input into policy elaboration were not destroyed, the factions became more and more the focus of leadership struggles within the party. The most celebrated example of this was Michel Rocard's attempt to gain the presidential nomination for 1981 after the left's defeat in the 1978 legislative elections which followed the breakdown of the Union of the Left in September 1977. This affair not only generated the acute personal hostility of much of the party towards Rocard's attempt to contest Mitterrand's position at a moment of vulnerability (1978-81), but also saw the clear emergence of other second-rank leaders who could contest, in their turn, Rocard's claims while promoting their own standing inside both their own factions and the party as a whole (e.g. Jean-Pierre Chevènement, whose current had gained over 25 per cent after the 1975 Congress, Laurent Fabius, and Lionel Jospin). We shall examine this problem in more detail in section three of this chapter. Here we can conclude with the observation that the party's acceptance of Mitterrand as its leader in 1971 for the specific purpose of promoting him as its presidential candidate in the context of the Union of the Left meant that the internal life of the party was affected to an unforeseen degree: Mitterrand accepted the presidential nature of politics within the republic, the party accepted Mitterrand, and the factions themselves ultimately internalised the presidential imperative.[12] All other considerations - such as the Union of the Left itself - became secondary.

The rally quality of the PS which had in the 1970s gone from strength to strength in terms of by-election victories, the near success of Mitterrand as presidential candidate in 1974, the sweeping gains in the 1977 municipal elections, and a dramatic growth in the party's membership and national standing (it was by 1978 the largest single party in parliament) - all of this achievement was considerably dampened by the failure of the now quarrelling left to win the 1978 legislative elections.[13] The situation was exacerbated by the aftermath of the 1978 elections which saw Mitterrand's extra-party popularity falling while Rocard's rose and Mitterrand's reversion to a more Machiavellian approach inside the party in order to retain power.[14] Many commentators in May 1981 argued that it was Giscard d'Estaing who lost the election rather than Mitterrand who won it. This to a certain extent was true. Nevertheless, the party, thanks to the Mitterrand strategy and the successes of the 1970s, was in a position to field a worthy candidate against the incumbent President. More significant for the purposes of our analysis, however, was that once Mitterrand had won, all the enthusiasm of the 1970s returned and carried the PS to power in the Assembly, reviving all the expectations of the previous decade, and bringing into government a radical reformist party on a wave of popular enthusiasm.[15]

After the legislative elections, the left held 70 per cent of the seats in the National Assembly (269 PS, 14 MRG, and 44 PCF). Neither electorally nor in terms of commitments entered into was the victorious PS obliged to share power with the once *incontournable*, now declining, PCF. Nevertheless, the Communists were offered four ministerial portfolios in the new government (all of them minor ones). Such a move not only ensured PCF acquiescence (until 1984) in what was to become a far more unpopular government than could have been anticipated by predictions about the normal effects of office upon a government's popularity, it also reassured a whole generation of activists (and to a lesser extent voters) who had come to see the Union of the Left as a myth to be aspired to - the true alternative to the uncaring capitalism that had ruled for a quarter of a century. Moreover, the transcendental, near-revolutionary rhetoric of the 1970s remained and reflected the party's own belief not only that it needed to 'keep left' to avoid the siren calls of the centre, seen as so detrimental to the party in the past, but that it could effect irreversible political, social and economic change in French society.[16]

In the context of such enthusiasm and self-confidence, three related and forbidding realities would accompany any and every government initiative in the months following the new President and party's victory: the electorate expected not only radical but successful change, an expectation which had been encouraged by the party in order to get it into power; any failure (let alone a series of them) would plunge the government into unpopularity of a particular kind - that of an electorate that felt it had been cheated.[17] Because of the right's dominance since 1958, the PS had had no experience of power, apart from the Fourth Republican government experience of one or two of its leaders (Mitterrand among them) who had held ministerial office a quarter of a century earlier.[18] Linked to both of these realities was a third, and the most insurmountable in terms of the Socialists' intentions: the left came to power at the moment the economy was plunging into recession.

The Price of Victory

It lies beyond the limits imposed by a chapter of this length to treat in great detail the period 1981-86 from a policy perspective.[19] Bearing in mind our preoccupation in this chapter with the interactive relationship between Mitterrand, the First Secretary, and the party itself, we shall examine in this section the effects of what became overnight a new triangular relationship between party, government and President. Dependency upon Mitterrand was not overcome; in fact in many ways, given his new status and the need to restrict the possibility of rivals emerging for the 1988 presidential nomination, the dependency increased. Nevertheless, the 1981-86 period saw the party shift from its earlier rally-style presidentialism to a more sober governmentalism, that is to say, from its perception of itself as a left-wing rally behind an inspired leader whose victory would produce massive and progressive social change, to that of a party representative of a huge grouping of French citizens and providing rational, competent and incrementalist government.[20] The realities of government were to be the motor of this change. Given, however, the harshness of those realities in the early 1980s coupled with the welter of expectations which the crusading PS had, in part, fostered, the journey from idealism to pragmatism was a difficult one and involved a dramatic reappraisal of the PS by French opinion. The fact that the party ultimately survived and prospered from the reappraisal demonstrates the relative solidity of the structure elaborated in the 1970s. Let us look at the period from a governmental perspective, a party perspective and at how the Socialists prepared for defeat in 1986 and their return to opposition.

The U-turn

The left came to power in France as the French economy entered a period of recession. By early 1983, the franc had been devalued three times (October 1981, June 1982, and March 1983). In the space of barely a year it became painfully clear that spending one's way out of a crisis was not a viable strategy in an economy now part of a global economy which itself was not adopting a policy of reflation. Reflation in an economy which was not geared up to respond to demand meant massive import penetration (without, in fact, a concomitant export rise - first because industry was not able to produce sufficient goods, and second because the potential overseas markets were closed, their governments applying a policy of economic rigour). Neither in terms of the electorate which had given the Socialists victory (large sections of which expected significant economic and social change after twenty-five years of right-wing government), nor in terms of the party which had created an image of itself as a victorious rally which would transform capitalism, was the new Socialist government prepared (economically, organisationally or ideologically) for the economic recession it was propelled into (and in some ways exacerbated).

In the five years they were in power between 1981 and 1986, the Socialists achieved much. In many ways a new, less authoritarian, more innovative political culture was created, and in social policy much was done or at least begun to redress the manifest inequalities within French society.[21] It was the results of its economic policy, however, which gave the first and lasting body blow to the government's popularity, and which provided the single most important cause of the government's misfortunes and, eventually, of the party's reappraisal of itself and its place in the French polity.[22]

When the Socialists came to power in 1981 the only economic policies the party had were the common programme of government signed with the PCF in 1972 and whose updating had caused so much discord between the PCF and PS in 1977, and the irrelevant and unreadable *Projet socialiste* published in 1980. The central key to both was nationalisation, a means of major state intervention in the economy. By September 1981, the extent of nationalisation was agreed (essentially reflecting Mitterrand's electoral promises in his election campaign): all large privately-owned banks, the largest industrial groups, Thomson, Compagnie Générale d'Electricité, Rhône-Poulenc, Péchiney, Honeywell-Bull, and Saint-Gobain, the steel companies Usinor and Sacilor, plus some key firms such as Matra and Dassault (aeronautics and armaments), and CGCT (telecommunications) were to be nationalised. The result was an increase for the public sector in French industry from 8 per cent to around a quarter. In banking, state ownership moved from around two-thirds to almost all.

The details and fortunes of the nationalisation programme have been dealt with elsewhere.[23] Here we can make two related points in terms of our analysis. The first is that the nationalisation programme cost the new government 40 billion francs in compensation, thus increasing the state's debt and bringing into its budget a whole series of firms, many of which were doing very badly because of the recession.

The second is that, paradoxically, the Socialist government ultimately proved its economic credibility by using the nationalisation programme to further - to the extent that such terms have a meaning - not socialism but capitalism. The very process of taking over ailing industries and increasing significant state intervention in industrial strategy through the nationalisation of the banks meant that, when economic policy changed (from 1983 these industries were less part of an overall plan for the restructuring of the economy along socialist lines, but were to be returned to profit within a given period, in most cases by 1985), the nationalised industries were in a good position to respond. As early as 1983, the policy of getting the huge electronics industry to return to profits was applied.[24] Nationalisation may have been a blunt instrument and meant for another purpose, but the relative modernisation and restructuring of industry was achieved.[25] The new realism was reflected in the elaboration of the 9th Economic Plan (1984-1988) which now spoke of industrial modernisation, decentralisation, training, research and development, and innovation, and no longer of the Plan as a tool for the radical transformation of society.[26]

When Jacques Chirac returned to power as Prime Minister in March 1986 he privatised most of the firms nationalised by the Socialists. These firms, however, returned to the private sector in profit, often restructured, and with a new modern-looking management, a redefinition of their aims and their relation to government and the outside economy.

The concerted action of the Socialist government after 1983 meant that by 1986 the balance of payments was in equilibrium and inflation was down to five per cent. In terms of reforming the industrial infrastructure, the Socialists went even further than Valéry Giscard d'Estaing and Raymond Barre in de-industrialisation and the promotion of new high-tech industries. The price for these changes, however, was slow growth and high unemployment - the kind of issues governments lose elections over.

Irrespective of the merits and demerits of the nationalisation programme, the movement of industries from or to state control does not of itself alter economic performance. Nor necessarily does a redistribution of wealth. And in terms of a sound and thought out economic policy per se, the PS did not really possess one. The reflation of the economy was, as we have said, largely a political response to electoral success and expectations. Only after 1983 and three devaluations was a more rigorous monetary and industrial policy applied. Growth between 1981 and 1986 was half what the Socialists had predicted (a predicted growth that was to have paid for the government's reform programme). Having said this, by the time the PS left office, inflation was down, unemployment had indeed risen but at a lower rate than in, say, the UK, and the economy was beginning to expand modestly. The point, however, was no longer one of whether the government was doing well after having done badly, but that the criteria by which the Socialists were now judged, or judged themselves, had altered significantly, essentially from a socialist to a social-democratic perspective. Let us look at how the party itself responded to these developments.

The Party in Power

It was the problems confronted in the economic domain which, to a large extent, transformed the party unambiguously into a social-democratic party. Nevertheless, in the social and administrative domain, the 1981-86 government put forward a whole series of proposals which breathed fresh reformist air into the social and administrative structures governing a still hierarchical and centralised France. The intention was to redistribute wealth, raise wages, tax the rich, raise or introduce other benefits while keeping inflation down, and, as it were, service these reforms with faster growth. The assumption that unemployment would go down through increased government spending, lower interest rates, and a raising of the income of the lower paid did not, for all the reasons we have discussed, prove to be a correct one. There was, however, a whole series of measures which had significant effects upon individual and collective life. The main measures and reforms included:

* A series of measures in favour of equality and justice for women;
* Reducing the working week to 39 hours;
* Lowering the retirement age to 60;
* Raising the minimum wage;
* Increasing paid holiday to five weeks;
* Increased research spending;
* A wealth tax;
* Decentralisation of powers to elected bodies;
* Extension of workers' rights.

Some of these measures were not of momentous importance and, besides, the economic situation militated against their complete success. They were, moreover, countered by cuts in public expenditure and social security, by increases in the cost of telephone, gas and electricity after March 1983, and by foreign currency restrictions. Nevertheless, these measures had a symbolic value in that they indicated the desire of the PS and its government to address the issues of social justice and equality. In a word, the difficulties of the 1981-86 period and the realities of power, rather than divide the party, converted it to Rocardian social democracy. At the same time, of course, this did not involve any admission of such a change.

Rocard himself did not gain personally from the reorientation - though he was to do so four years later in 1988. Rather, it claimed a victim in the form of the incumbent Prime Minister, Pierre Mauroy. The resignation of Mauroy in July 1984 (specifically over the government's handling of the church schools issue, but in fact as a result of the need for a scapegoat for the government's misfortunes since coming to office) and the subsequent resignation of the Communist ministers represented a kind of rejection of old-style socialism with its municipal and union of the left orientation which Mauroy ostensibly represented, and the ushering in of a new dynamic modernising socialism. As subsequent developments in the late 1980s were to show, the reality was more nuanced than this and the 'old' and the 'new' continued to coexist (no doubt necessarily - see conclusion of this chapter) into the 1990s.

More telling of the nature of the PS in government was its virtual continuation of the preceding regime's policies on foreign policy, nuclear energy production, national defence, and arms sales, several issues which contributed to the gradual rise of a contestatory ecology movement in the course of the 1980s.[27] The Socialist government was, therefore, not only reformist rather than revolutionary in domestic policy, but its foreign policy differed little from Giscard, Pompidou and de Gaulle's.

The 1981-86 period saw the party adapting unwillingly but inevitably to the new conditions, and to the need, quite simply, to show solidarity with an embattled government. The Valence Congress of 1981 was the party's first after the May and June election victories. It is true that here the revolutionary rhetoric remained. Nevertheless, in retrospect we can see that this was the last gasp of such pre-governmental language. In fact, such language, when contrasted with what the government was actually doing (even the 1981 measures were little more than an attempt at mild reflation and a measured redistribution of wealth), masked the PS's inability to be other than an uncritical support to the government and the President. And in spite of the rhetoric, the Valence Congress passed a single resolution which hid all the internal division and demonstrated even further the party's supportive rather than combative role. And from Valence onwards, unanimity became the norm; and as we shall see, the barely disguised factional conflict within the party owed much more to conflict over presidential nominations than over ideological rectitude. By the mid-1980s, ideological debate, such as it existed, was between different kinds of reformism, and, as we shall see below, even these debates were strongly informed by personal loyalties and preferences.[28] Michel Rocard's gaining 29 per cent of the mandates in October 1985 at the Toulouse Congress was a vote in favour of both a particular approach to politics and a particular post-Mitterrand leader or President. In terms of this presidential factor, a further point to make concerning the party/government/president relationship is that the second two elements also underwent a series of interesting changes in the 1981-86 period. Here we can look at just one of the developments, perhaps the most important, the relationship between the President and the Prime Minister.

One of the abiding question marks over the left's attainment of power concerned the nature of the relationships within the executive: in a word, would President Mitterrand who had himself attacked the Bonapartist nature of the Fifth Republic allow power to move back towards the Prime Minister (responsible to the National Assembly) and his government?[29] It is true to say that in the 1981-86 period Mitterrand was less 'monarchical' than his predecessors, intervened less directly in the day to day running of government.[30] Indeed, he allowed a climate to develop where government ministers themselves began to develop a national profile.[31] Having said this, it is also true to say that by and large Mitterrand did nothing to change the fundamental centrality and authority of the presidency. And at a personal level, the allegiance of ministers was to him rather than to either Prime Minister (Pierre Mauroy and Laurent Fabius), and when there were disagreements, as between Prime Minister Fabius and President Mitterrand over the visit of the Polish leader, General Jaruzelski, in December 1985, the subordination of the former to the latter was clearly illustrated.[32]

As the scheduled 1986 legislative elections approached, however, it was clear from opinion polls that the Socialists were themselves on schedule for defeat, and possibly - given the electoral system - a dramatic one, whose severity might be such that the President would have little choice but to resign - a situation which would see Chirac installed in the Elysée with a possible absolute majority of RPR MPs in the Assembly. The Socialists (their new realism here expressed as sheer opportunism) decided to deploy an exercise in electoral damage limitation in order not to lose all the glittering prizes they had won five years earlier.

Defeat

A series of factors enabled the PS to go into the legislative elections of 1986 with a justifiable degree of equanimity. We can list six of them here. First, and ingeniously, the government introduced a form of proportional representation for the 1986 elections.[33] The effect of this single-round system was to save the PS from searching for alliances. Second, the three Mauroy administrations between 1981 and 1984 became undeniably unpopular. Mauroy's replacement by Mitterrand's young protégé, Laurent Fabius, offered to the public the image of a renovated, modernised, go-ahead party, and Fabius and his new ministerial team were able to project themselves as responding to the new challenges of the mid-1980s.

Thirdly, and linked to the second point, was the dual factor that the Fabius government's policies were an implicit though public rejection of the economically unsound earlier period (although, in reality, the government's recognition of the impossibility of 'reflation in one country' dates from 1982), and placed enormous emphasis on the notion of modernising the economy in order to better arm France for European competition, and so on. In fact, this modernising theme not only had undoubted appeal among the electorate but also offered to the party a kind of rallying theme to fill the vacuum left by the collapse of so many myths and good leftist intentions, and to forestall the encroaching ideological aridity of the party.[34]

Fourthly, it is the case that, as the elections approached, opinion was beginning to rise again in favour of the government; not enough to save the Socialists from electoral defeat, but enough to ensure that the outgoing government (many of whose members had become, as we said earlier, well-known public figures) left office as a coherent, professional team capable of providing leadership at some point in the future.[35]

Fifthly, the economy too was beginning to pick up as France began to move out of the depths of the recession of the early 1980s. The fruits of the Fabius government's actions would not be seen until after the elections, but by 1985 inflation was down to five per cent, and the party and government were not seen as leaving office humiliated by a confident opposition and the disastrous results of their own economic policies, but rather as having gone from being inexperienced and in part irresponsible to becoming a mature party of government. Its 'cure of opposition' would continue this process.

Finally, the party remained, and would remain after the elections of 1986 and on into the 1990s, the largest single party in France (in terms of seats in the National Assembly). Such an entrenched national presence meant quite simply that the PS had become a formidable political presence whether in opposition or in government. In Weberian terms, disenchantment had been dramatic and deep; in practical terms, the PS was the only alternative to the political right.

The right-wing coalition came to power in 1986 on a tide of popularity for what was called at the time 'neo-liberalism'. In the French case, this seems in retrospect to have been something of a fad - the role of the state and the inability of the French private sector to effortlessly absorb a privatised public sector being too much in evidence. Nevertheless, the right was clearly in the ascendant. The right's victory, however, was not a great one and the new government's majority in the National Assembly was slender and not substantial enough to force Mitterrand's resignation.[36] Moreover, the proportional representation system had allowed the extreme-right National Front into the Assembly, a factor which put great stress upon divisions within the mainstream right. Mitterrand was thus able to begin to play upon these divisions while he set about reviving his popularity with the electorate. This process and prospect would force the PS into unconditional public support for the embattled (and, later, highly popular) President, a support very similar to the kind it had been obliged to demonstrate for its own embattled rightwards-moving government after 1982. Between 1986 and 1988 Mitterrand remained in isolated powerlessness (while his popularity began to soar); the right took over the reins of power; the left returned, with dignity, to opposition and preparation for the next presidential elections in 1988. The PS had been beaten and been sanctioned, but now it was not only the sole alternative to the right, but had become once again, in the eyes of the electorate, a credible alternative. The condition of remaining so, however, was linked, once more, to its acquiescent subordination to Mitterrand's own political fortunes.

The Socialists in Opposition, 1986-88[37]

It is ironic that the two factors characterising the Socialist Party by the mid-1980s seemed to be in direct contradiction to one another. On the one hand, the party was politically successful, and the government drawn from its ranks had been clearly able, despite more than twenty years in opposition, to learn to govern the country. The party had developed a national implantation, and electorally was being voted for by both a young and a growing female electorate, both highly significant electoral constituencies. In terms of its personnel, moreover, it had leaders within it as capable as those of any of its fellow socialist and social-democratic parties of Western Europe. On the other hand, and in direct contrast to this, the party also exhibited a helpless dependence upon Mitterrand which paralysed it, gagged it, threatened to empty it of ideas and ruin its electoral successes overnight if Mitterrand's fortunes fell. From 1986, moreover, the party began to see its formerly healthy factionalism reduced to debilitating personal squabbles. We have seen how these two contradictory characteristics were in fact interlinked. In this section we shall look in closer detail at the effect of this phenomenon upon the development of the party in the 1986-88 period, at how the party prepared for the presidential elections of 1988 and at how it fared in the legislative elections triggered by Mitterrand's success in May 1988. We shall argue that these three essential moments of the *cohabitation* period are linked to one another and are revealing both of one another and of the nature of French socialism as it entered the 1990s.

Personality Politics and Factionalism

In the 1986-88 period the party underwent severe internal fractioning and saw revealed hitherto covert divergences, divergences which placed considerable strain upon the party.[38] Let us list the main forms these took, and their effect upon ideology and organisation.

The first major lines of division followed the currents themselves. We have already seen how these had become more than ever rallies around alternative leader figures. In the post-March 1986 period, this tendency was developed even further (the fusion of currents A and B (Jospin/Mauroy) was in part an attempt to counter the strongly centrifugal nature of current activity). The main actors in these developments were the 'Mitterrandist' current, led by the First Secretary, Jospin; the 'Mauroy' current; CERES, now called *Socialisme et république* (Chevènement); and the Rocardian current. The currents, organised around their leader, held their own meetings. In the case of the Mitterrandist current, this led to accusations of a secretive leadership by other currents (given that its leader was also the First Secretary of the party - and whatever his intentions, it was clearly difficult at this time to distinguish Jospin's role as current leader from his role as party leader). Developments such as this led in their turn to an increased focus upon the currents as strategic sites for the promotion of individual leaders (and within the currents themselves, sub-currents, obeying the same principle of a doctrinally justified leadership focus, also developed around particular figures).

The national leaders doubled their current activity with particular 'high-profile' activities of their own. These activities involved a continuous stream of television and radio appearances, press releases, international and domestic travel. Fabius's many visits through 1986 and 1987 to speak at party federation meetings are a good example of this. Conversely, of course, silence or inactivity were equally symbolic forms of leadership intervention, the best example being Rocard's muted activism during the March 1986 legislative elections. Many leader-orientated groups had their own clubs and regular newsletters which paralleled the party's activity and mainstream literature.

Inside and outside the main currents, there also developed a series of *entourages*, or *relais* or *équipes* around leaders, which often extended well beyond the party itself, and some of which were very elaborate, especially the network around Rocard. These networks involved all the current leaders and other national leaders, especially ex-ministers (in status terms the two ex-Prime Ministers, Mauroy and Fabius, enjoyed a particular respect here).[39]

These leaders also had *groupes d'experts* working for them. The best examples of this trend were the several groups working under Claude Allègre (totalling 300 people) for the First Secretary, Jospin. Ex-Prime Minister Mauroy (who also enjoyed the support of the Léo Lagrange sport and leisure clubs and the *Revue Politique et Parlementaire*), ex-ministers Delors, Delebarre, Bérégovoy, Dumas, Rocard and others had their own offices, personal secretariats, advisers and so on. And Mitterrand established his own secret network of relations with several of these groups after his loss of communication with the Socialists through governmental and ministerial channels after March 1986.

The informal meetings between leaders also informed power relations within the party. Given the focus upon the importance of individual leaders, these meetings had even more influence because they were informal and 'private'. The most important of these, of course, were those between Mitterrand and Rocard (November 1986 and April 1988). Also significant, however, were the meetings between other leaders and the, often imagined, alliances between them which gave rise to a whole series of rumours involving axes of power between national leaders.

The First Secretary's response to the immediate development of all this intra- and extra-party activity in the wake of the March 1986 legislative elections was to stress that his 'club' was the party itself.[40] However, one of the most significant factors concerning this or any other club was that it in fact offered little contribution to the arguments surrounding doctrinal renewal, little to the arguments concerning alliances and no contribution at all to the problem of how the party should prepare for the 1988 presidential elections.

By bringing the party's Lille Congress forward by six months to April 1987, the First Secretary's nominal separation of doctrinal and organisational concerns from those of leadership (the selection of the presidential candidate for 1988) was an attempt to cope with some of the problems posed by the developing internal rivalries. Because of the continuing importance of unity, little resistance to such an initiative could be shown by other national leaders, and Jospin enhanced his own position by showing that he was able to call competing leaders to order in the name of socialism as a doctrinal and organisational reality. There was also an attempt to deal with the problem by calling for the reorganisation of the Directing Committee in order to allow the multiplicity of national figures (ex-ministers) to play a part inside the party apparatus, and 'thematic commissions' to be created within the party. Victory in 1981 and five years of rule seemed to have created an army top heavy with generals, and generals, moreover, who, lacking an overall strategy, spent their time fighting amongst themselves.

The Presidential Campaign[41]

The compromises made within the party - essentially those with and by the Rocardians - meant that the internal divisions triggered by the return to opposition and in the context of the approaching presidential election were contained within reasonable and relatively private limits. The party was therefore able to approach the presidential elections with Rocard as a declared candidate who would probably withdraw whenever the 'real' candidate, Mitterrand, declared himself (which he did not do until 22 March 1988). In a very bizarre way, therefore, Rocard, the single most isolated figure within the party, filled the vacuum left by Mitterrand's absence from the campaign and pre-campaign of 1987 and 1988.

In terms of the party itself, however, this situation was debilitating now, not only because of the intense personalised factionalism, but also because the party's role in policy elaboration was under real threat. By the mid-1980s, it was a fair and damaging question to ask, what exactly did French socialism now stand for? The ideological debate, such as it was, between 1986 and 1988 had produced a campaign document, *Propositions pour la France*, which neither of the candidates would use: Rocard as candidate would not use a document whose most important ideas - those on the economy - were drawn up largely by sections of the party with which he had been in dispute even before he joined the party in 1974; Mitterrand would not, as the new Father of the Nation figure, use any partisan document. And his subsequent manifesto, the *Lettre à tous les Français*, was a highly personalised document which bore no relation at all to the *Propositions*.[42] We can say, therefore, that ideologically the PS was marginal to the presidential election. Indeed, when Mitterrand did declare his candidacy, his campaign made very little reference to socialism, and even less to the PS - even the party's famous symbol, the rose in the clenched fist, was excluded from Mitterrand's campaign posters. In terms of a legislative programme too, the party could offer very little, not only because Mitterrand's autonomy from the party meant that he ignored the *Propositions*, but because there was no certainty concerning what action he would take in terms of the nomination of a prime minister and the dissolution of parliament. Apart from a few dissident voices (Jean Poperen, for example), the party as a whole had little choice but to support the idea that the PS should exert no pressure on Mitterrand regarding dissolution or the choice of the Prime Minister. In any case, if he were to choose a member of the Socialist Party as his Prime Minister, it was almost certain that it would be Michel Rocard.

The only remaining area in which the PS could offer its services was that of organisation. Even here, however, its role was negligible. During the campaign, Mitterrand himself kept his distance from the PS, and there was virtually no contact between the party and the campaign headquarters. In symbolic terms, the *Génération Mitterrand* (his campaign slogan) went beyond the parameters of the non-Communist left; and electorally, Mitterrand did not need to campaign for the PS vote - this was assured. What he needed was to convince traditional Communist supporters and centrist supporters to vote for him on the first round - and too close an identification with 'his' party would be a hindrance to this. This is the logic of all presidential election campaigns. In the case of the PS by 1988, it demonstrated just how far along the presidentialist road the party had travelled. In the campaign between the two rounds, the activists turned out in their thousands to welcome Mitterrand, and his verbal collusive reassurance to them that he remained a socialist (and that they knew it) was all they could hope for - and all they seemed to ask for - in terms of evidence of Mitterrand's enduring socialism.

On 8 May, Mitterrand won the presidential elections with 54 per cent of the vote, named Rocard his Prime Minister and dissolved the National Assembly.

The 1988 Legislative Elections

On 16 May 1988, as it entered the legislative election campaign, one week after Mitterrand's own astounding success, the PS found itself in a curious position. In government between 1981 and 1986 it had undergone an internal evolution which demonstrated that it was a pragmatic, reformist party of the centre left. Mitterrand's presidential campaign of 1988, moreover, had called repeatedly for an *ouverture* (opening towards the centre). Within the logic of this, the Elysée attempted to impose a certain proportion of 'presidential majority' candidates (non-PS personalities who had rallied to the President) upon the PS campaign organisation. However, most of the established centrists shied away from any deal with the PS or the President (for fear of being annihilated at the polls). In spite of all Mitterrand had said about *ouverture*, therefore, there was an immediate return to traditional alliances (see Chapter One). Moreover, any PS gesture towards the centre (essentially, the CDS) at this point would have been anomalous, the electoral system itself making this virtually impossible (the 'presidential majority' candidates - not helped by local PS organisations - did extremely badly). And as with the voter, so with the parties: old allegiances - and especially old fears - endured; in the PS itself, the fear of the 'third force' (the PS moving to the centre) had become inbred; yet on the threshold of his second presidential term Mitterrand was actively pushing the party towards it. Throughout the 1970s and, especially, the 1980s, the party had supported Mitterrand totally; during the 1988 presidential election campaign it virtually effaced itself. In the ensuing legislative election campaign, he was implicitly asking the party to make itself even less significant. Disarray among party activists and a certain refusal to cooperate was the result.

There was a good illustration of this latter point when the party leadership became vacant on 11 May, with the appointment of First Secretary Jospin as Education Minister in Rocard's government. Mauroy's election against Mitterrand's protégé Fabius demonstrated clearly the party's hardening attitude and retreat into defence of the *vieille maison* against the siren calls of an American-style Democratic Party. Mauroy, the last of the major pre-1971 Socialists, now embodied the traditional 'keep left' spirit in the PS. The government offered 40 seats to MRG candidates and others. Under internal pressure this was later reduced to 16 (plus those centrist ministers already members of Rocard's government).

We shall comment below on the reasons for the PS's failure to gain an outright parliamentary majority in the elections of 5 and 12 June. Here we can say that after the first round the party had no alternative but to renew its alliance with the Communists. Did it jump willingly or was it pushed by the circumstances of the moment into an alliance which at the national level had been dead for over a decade? In fact, both interpretations are true: many in the party saw the Union of the Left as the only guarantee of the PS's continuing socialism; others believed that the Union of the Left was electorally acceptable given that the PCF was no longer the fearful partner it had been ten years earlier; still others felt that the alliance was inevitable given the prevailing circumstances and that after the elections the PS would rethink its own identity and alliance strategy for the future. In fact, the election results demonstrated clearly that the PS's hegemonic pretensions were overstated, that the realignments of the next decade would be complex, and that although in a very strong position - still France's largest single party - the PS could not dictate the rules of the game.

There were three essential reasons why the PS did not gain the overall majority which it and everyone else had anticipated; each illustrates the complexity of the interplay of presidential and party considerations within the political system.

The first reason was tactical. Valéry Giscard d'Estaing's immediate creation of the URC (*Union du rassemblement et du centre*) for the duration of the campaign meant that the RPR-UDF alliance would have only one candidate in each constituency. The candidate could therefore hope to draw on an electorate that went from the centre across to the boundary with the extreme right. Giscard's move also withdrew from the PS the possibility of any local deals with centrists, leaving it with only the 'presidential majority' candidates who were new, often forced upon local PS constituencies, and much resented by the party at the local level.

The second concerned electoral geography. Although Mitterrand had won with a resounding 54 per cent, he had done so, unlike in 1981, from a centrist position. His voters too were drawn from all parts of the electoral spectrum and were therefore unlikely to vote unequivocally for the PS (from which he had in any case significantly distanced himself). It should be remembered that the PS vote in March 1986 was only 32 per cent. The 54 per cent vote for Mitterrand on 8 May 1988 was a personal and not a party endorsement, and in fact Mitterrand's supra-partisan position was an implicit criticism of the sectarianism of his own party.

The third reason was ideological. Not only had the PS been forced, over an eight-year period, to lose its ideological edge (the hallmark of activists, so necessary in campaigns), but it had been pushed, as we have seen, into an even more marginal role during the presidential election campaign itself. As it entered the legislative campaign, its image, and self-image, were confused: was it simply the President's party (which the President had seemed to disdain)?; or was it a socialist party in its own right, fighting for its own aims? The confusion of activists and electorate turned into the significant demobilisation of both: the abstention rate of the 1988 legislative elections was the highest recorded in the Fifth Republic, an abstention which was particularly marked, moreover, among traditionally left-wing voters.[43] When Mitterrand declared, just before the first-round vote, that rule by one party was not a good thing, the party was paralysed with disbelief. If he was trying to minimise the *size* of a PS majority so that it did not also entrap him, he succeeded only too well. The left's electorate and the PS's activists, drawn into a half-hearted alliance with the PCF, and fighting as if for only a relative majority in order that socialism itself accord credibility to the political centre, thereby not dominating the political agenda, gained just that, a relative majority. Twelve seats short of an overall majority, the new Socialist government had a very difficult task ahead of it.

Whatever else the electoral results of 5 and 12 June 1988 demonstrated about the PS, it was clear that by the end of the 1980s even the most successful political party of the 1970s and 1980s could not pretend to encapsulate within itself the wishes of a majority of the French; only the President could do this. In fact, Mitterrand's second-round vote was 3,000,000 votes more than all six leftist candidates in round one. For this reason alone, the party remained in a relationship of subordination to him.

It is clear from our review of the 1981-86 period that after coming to power in 1981, the PS learned a series of cruel lessons: the rapid dissipation of euphoria; the doctrinally unpleasant decisions of the post-1982 period; having to stand alone after the departure of the PCF ministers from government in 1984; an inexorable decline in the popularity of the party, the government, and, in the 1982-86 period, the President; defeat at the polls in 1986; and, after this, serious internal factionalism coupled with a dearth of stimulating ideological debate, and its replacement by a war of the chiefs (or *sous-chefs*). After all this, relative victory was accorded to the party but only because their leader was re-elected to the presidency, and this without the party's help. For our analysis, what is of paramount interest is that all of these developments can be traced to the pre-1981 period: the wild promises of the 1970s helped carry the party to power (and held it together) but the price was paid very soon after taking office; the acute personal rivalries of the post-1986 period were the ultimate result of the party's normative acceptance from 1971 of the presidential principle within the republic (and which too had brought it victory).

In the aftermath of Mitterrand's overwhelming victory and the party's relative one, it was clear that a new phase had begun. From 1988, there was once again a Socialist Prime Minister and (quasi-) homogeneous Socialist government which rested upon a relative majority in the Assembly. In such a situation, the party's room for manoeuvre was even less than it had been in 1981, and we have already seen how little the party could influence the government in the 1981-86 period.[44] What is more, the government which the party was being constrained to support after 1988 was clearly centre-orientated. The Prime Minister, Michel Rocard, had, moreover, been the *bête noire* inside the party for nearly fifteen years, both for his *lèse majesté* towards Mitterrand in the late 1970s and his declared 'realism' and disapproval of the party's earlier claims to quasi-revolutionism. The post-1988 government, however, remained stable and supported by the PS because, whether enthusiastically or reluctantly, the PS had itself become a party of government, that is to say, in the political context of the Fifth Republic, unashamedly social democratic - it could now hardly lay claim to any other tradition. In this way, it entered upon the second great socialist experiment of the Fifth Republic, the Rocard government of 1988.

The Socialists in Government since 1988

Irrespective of the disappointment at failing to gain an overall majority on 12 June 1988, irrespective of the nomination of the party's eternal 'outsider', Michel Rocard, as Prime Minister (rather than a mainstream PS politician), irrespective of the party's almost bystander role over the previous two years, and irrespective of the ideological aimlessness of the party in the 1980s, the PS was once again the party of government, that is, the party supplying to government its ministers, advisers and so on; and it was still the largest party in France and would be crucial to any future alliances of the left or centre left; in a word, the PS was the most important party on the French political scene as the Fifth Republic entered its fourth decade. Let us look then at Michel Rocard's government, and assess its character and contribution to French politics. Given our preoccupation throughout this chapter with the party and its relation to the presidency and government, we are concerned here less with the legislative record of the government than with how it differed in character, style and intention from its 1981 predecessor; with the changes in the relationship between President, Prime Minister and party; and finally with the prospects for the Socialist Party and government into the 1990s.

The Rocard Government

The first point to make about the nomination by Mitterrand of his old rival Michel Rocard as Prime Minister is that the choice was not an obligatory one. The choice of Rocard demonstrated the extent to which politics and French socialism had evolved in the Fifth Republic: Rocard's nomination, although he was a socialist, was a response to public opinion; and he was the embodiment of 'ouverture'. In fact, Rocard was arguably the first popular Prime Minister of the Fifth Republic.

Two related features of Rocard's 1988 government are worth noting here. The first is that the impression was given of a team which was getting down to work immediately, and the impression was sustained. Most of the new ministers now knew the corridors of power from their 1981-86 experience. This was in marked contrast to the situation in 1981. 1981 was characterised essentially (and disastrously) by a particular leftist myth of change: that change could be instantaneous, total, and irreversible. 1988 was also characterised by an originally leftist myth: in this case that change was necessary and desirable but would be incrementalist, cautious and unpretentious.[45] The second and related point concerns the Prime Minister. All of Rocard's speeches as Prime Minister, though not devoid of emotional content, were calming; they called for hard work, patience, realism concerning expectations, and so on. Here again the contrast with 1981 was stark: not only were Rocard's speeches ideologically neutral, their tone was such as to offer a new kind of politics: minimal public interventions by ministers (giving the impression of a government working away at problems); a restrained and straightforward style (allowing any grandiose style to be the domain of the President); and a refusal to behave or be seen to intervene dramatically in moments of social tension or apparent crisis. The style was reminiscent of the Fourth Republican politician, Pierre Mendès France, though occasionally - and this is the disadvantage of such a style - Rocard's apparent calm was sometimes interpreted as evidence of a lack of commitment, will and orientation. From inside his own party such accusations took the form of his lacking a project or a 'grand design' for France. Occasional highly publicised television interviews with the Prime Minister were deployed as methods of maintaining his public profile, and afforded him a means of explaining his softly-softly approach and style. In this context two features stand out, the first being his strict loyalty to the President, both through professions of such and the absence of any hint of criticism; the second, his insistence on his own government's equally strict loyalty to him.[46]

In the main, Michel Rocard's second government, formed on 23 June 1988, was identical to his first: of its 49 members, 26 were PS, 3 MRG, 6 'Barrist' UDF, and 14 'technical' (that is to say, non-partisan representatives of 'civil society').[47] The Executive Bureau of the PS formally expressed its concern over the inclusion of centrists in Rocard's government, and although the party was clearly concerned by such a move towards the centre, and would continue its critiques in various muted expressions throughout the Rocard government, two factors militated against any concerted party criticism of the government. The first was the inescapable reality of the situation itself: Rocard's government reflected what the country had expressed in votes; a dominant PS without exclusive dominance. Criticism of such a situation would have discredited only the PS in public opinion. The second was that the PS's 'keep left' orientation served ultimately simply to keep the government in place (the centrists, who from 1988 constituted a group autonomous from the right which sometimes abstained from voting against the government, remained, nevertheless, de facto in the opposition). With the PCF, the left did have an absolute majority, and the party could continue, where necessary, the old Union of the Left as an ever-present option if not as an overall strategy. This problematic circumstantial alliance became a means of maintaining the Socialists in government while pushing through their centrist policies. Like all Fifth Republic governments before it (1986-88 excepted), Rocard's was demonstrably the President's government, its guiding principle (or its ideological alibi, depending on how one views politics), Mitterrand's *Lettre à tous les Français*. Rocard, therefore, could in no way be seen as a rival to or negation of Mitterrand; his distinctiveness suggested rather a complementarity between the two main members of the executive.

In spite of the government's difficulties, in particular the widespread public sector strikes in the government's first year of office over grievances which had been building up over the previous two years, a relative majority in the Assembly, continuing unemployment, and the dangers to the economy presented by West German competition in the run-up to 1992, Rocard's government remained popular and, more miraculously, stable. In fact, it remained stable because it was intrinsically unstable. It navigated between majorities (a deal here with the Communists, a deal there with the centrists - one of the best early examples being PCF abstention on the 1989 budget voted in November 1988).[48] At times it even acted as if defying what was a non-Socialist majority in the Assembly to vote against it; any such early dissolution following the bringing down of the government probably benefiting the Socialists. And most observers and polls concluded that Rocard's government was doing what most competent, pragmatic, reformist governments would do in the circumstances even with an overall majority. In its first year, in spite of its newness and the peculiar circumstances of a relative majority, the government effected or initiated legislation on: major reforms of the penal system, a minimum wage, a wealth tax, investment in education, a major scientific research and development programme, regional development plans, reform of the civil service, and preparation for the single European market. Moreover, unemployment was down, as was inflation.

Such reforms and activity were those of a centre-left government moving the country towards modernisation and preparation for 1992, in the declared context of the need for social protection and social solidarity. Gone was the rhetoric of radical reform, gone indeed were the calls for such reform inside the party itself. Let us look at how the party itself responded to the new situation.

The Party

By 1988 the PS was, as we have seen, in a strange position. It was a strong national party and the party of government, but one, however, which was not certain of its own orientation or even its identity. The election to the leadership of the party of Pierre Mauroy over Laurent Fabius in May 1988 was in part a response to this: Mauroy's election was both a demonstration of party uncertainty and an assertion of the continuing importance of the PS as an organisation with a historical tradition, and one that should be maintained rather than capriciously abandoned in the name of modernisation. As we have seen, however, much had already been abandoned; there was indeed a serious problem surrounding the party's role in the 1990s.

The defeat of Fabius also had a personal angle: anticipation of the post-Mitterrand period saw the Mitterrandist current splitting into factions or constellations of factions and individuals around Mauroy, Fabius and Jospin, and outside the Mitterrandist current, around or against Rocard. Fabius's defeat was Jospin's and Rocard's victory. This illustrates that the party was already responding to the next presidential election, seven years into the future. The Rennes Congress in 1990 continued and accentuated the developing personal rivalries to the point where doctrinal debate, even policy debate, was ignored, and the hall resounded only to personal and unsubstantiated claims and counter-claims to socialist authenticity.

A further feature of the party's position vis-à-vis the government was that the Prime Minister, outside his own minority current, had been - in part because he was the darling of the opinion polls - the least liked and most distrusted leading figure in the party. This was one of the advantages to Rocard of the PS's failure to gain a crushing victory in the legislative elections: the party was not in a strong enough position to dominate him. Given, however, a) his need of the party's support, and b) Mitterrand's dominant influence, it is interesting to note that many of the leading figures of the PS and many of 'Mitterrand's men' were in extremely strong positions within the government, and owed their loyalty to the President rather than to the Prime Minister. The most notable cases of this were Lionel Jospin who became Education Minister (and number two in the government) and Pierre Bérégovoy, Minister of Finances and an old ally of the President. Thus, Rocard was surrounded by a network of ministers who were party 'elephants' and/or the President's men. Rocard's success, moreover, would be their success, and with the 'promotion' of Jospin to a high ministerial position, Fabius's reserve position outside Rocard's government but in a nationally prominent position (failing to gain the leadership of the PS, he obtained the presidency of the National Assembly), and the continuing national presence of PS figures like Bérégovoy or Jacques Delors, then President of the

European Commission, there remained, from the beginning of Rocard's government in May 1988, a range of rivals whose central aim was the party's presidential nomination (especially Fabius, Jospin, Rocard, and Delors) for the presidential elections scheduled for 1995. Inevitably, however, because of his position as Prime Minister, and given that the Rocardian view of government was now shared by nearly everyone in the party, given also his continuing popularity in the country, Rocard's status within the party increased from 1988 onwards. He was received at the 1990 National Congress, for example, with a generalised enthusiasm unsurpassed by any of his rivals.

In government, Rocard coped with being surrounded by potential rivals by making himself its main spokesperson, and in his letter sent to all his ministers on 24 May 1988 and published by all the national newspapers three days later, he affirmed the need for 'governmental solidarity' i.e. allegiance to him and a prohibition on public criticism and any subtle public undermining of him by any of his ministers.[49]

Once again, moreover, the government's own potential instability became an asset to the Prime Minister. Concerted criticism from figures within the PS in order to redress the balance of authority in favour of the party would have provoked a possible crisis of confidence in the government. There was some muted criticism, particularly from the new party leader, Pierre Mauroy, but in the main the party had little alternative but to support the government. The political logic was such that if the opposition parties brought down the government before it had had time to prove itself, this would almost certainly have rebounded to the PS's favour; if the PS, through lack of solidarity, had contributed to the same, the effect on the PS at ensuing elections would most likely have been very serious.

All in all, the party entered Mitterrand's second seven-year term in a more realistic yet more uncertain state than it entered upon his first. The party had been shaken by its failure to achieve an overall majority, and its move towards a more realistic social-democratic position was clear evidence of its recognition of the realities both inside the party and in public opinion. However, no political party thrives on realism alone, and in the case of the PS the abandonment of an unrealistic revolutionism was not followed by the development of an alternative discourse. The Marxist rhetoric had gone but was not replaced by anything substantial (other than a somewhat modish commitment to modernisation). The ideological stock of the party was dangerously low, and was inadequately filled by a surreptitious war of position between the various rivals for the presidency, a conflict which absorbed all debate. Let us look at what this augurs for the party in the 1990s.

Prospects

As we have seen, the French Socialist Party entered the 1990s with a series of advantages and disadvantages. Let us draw these together here and look at each in turn.

The fact that the Socialists governed France for most of the 1980s and into the 1990s is proof enough of their success. Their leader and President, moreover, was accorded by the French electorate fourteen unbroken years in office. These facts point not only to the PS's strength but also to its nodal position on the political spectrum, and with the PCF in constant decline (a situation which creates difficulties for the PS in terms of creating successful local alliances), PS occupation of the political spectrum from the centre across to the extreme left is beyond doubt.

Second, the PS is the one party with up to half a dozen *présidentiables*. It is true that this involves time-consuming and debilitating squabbles within the party. In spite of this disadvantage, and as long as intra-party rivalry does not become too public, this situation also means that the PS can offer permanently to the public a series of potential Presidents,

Prime Ministers and ministers. Perhaps even more importantly, this situation saves the PS from leadership rivalries with other parties, which is the case with all the parties on the right and arguably one of the major factors in Jacques Chirac's defeat in the presidential elections of 1988.

A third advantage for the PS is that it remains a strongly nationally implanted party with, by French standards, a relatively high membership, and is the heir of a long and rich political tradition that is part of the French political landscape. This last remark brings us to the disadvantages.

One of the immediate effects on the PS in the aftermath of Mitterrand's re-election to the presidency was the demoralisation of the party and the disarray of some of its electorate in the legislative elections of 1988, these misfortunes caused by, first, the PS and its supporters' failure to understand exactly where the President was trying to make them go, and, then, hesitation about whether, having once understood, they wanted to go there. In electoral alliance with the PCF, the PS was being asked to endorse a near centrist line and welcome the ideas (and personnel) of centrists who, for years, had been their arch-enemies in the constituencies and town halls of France.

A second and related disadvantage for the party in the 1990s is the growing split between the new PS elite and the party's rank and file. The Parisian-based, well-educated, professional politician often stands in marked contrast to the ordinary party member whose powers even to select candidates have been gradually undermined by central party headquarters and, in the 1988 legislative elections, by the Elysée. Not only candidate selection but all levels of party activity have, over the last twenty years, gradually moved upwards in terms of decision-making: from members to current leaders, from currents to the central leadership, from the party leadership to government departments and their advisers, and from government to the presidency and its advisers. Such developments are the inevitable consequence of national success. Nevertheless, in a party whose only organisational and ideological base is its membership, such an orientation of decisions will accelerate disaffection and demobilisation. And a strong party base and support have proved indispensable in Fifth Republican politics, in spite of presidentialism; and in Mitterrand's case was the sine qua non of success.

The third and, again, related disadvantage - and perhaps the hardest to identify - was the ideological draining of the party in the second half of the 1980s. This was in part the result of the realities of power (and having only a relative parliamentary majority the party's governmental expression could only strive for consensus through its efforts to navigate other parties' ideas). This however is not the whole explanation. If this were the case, there would have been before 1988, as there normally is when parties find themselves returned to opposition, a fundamental reappraisal of the party's doctrine in the 1986-88 period. The ideological aimlessness of the PS goes far deeper than an imposed pragmatic social democracy, and is linked to the choice it made in 1971. *La ligne d'Epinay* had originated as a strategic orientation to the Union of the Left but by the late 1970s had become almost exclusively focused upon personal allegiance to François Mitterrand as First Secretary. Since his attaining of the presidency of the republic there have been two related developments. The first was an increase in dependency upon him, and the developing inability to elaborate ideas (especially in the 1986-88 period, the very time when the party should have been renewing its ideas). The second development was the gradual emergence of a whole range of personal strategies which involved all the major currents and sub-currents and this to the extent that virtually all activity within the party in the late 1980s and early 1990s is traceable to the personal ambitions of rival *présidentiables* or their *entourages*. This has very debilitating effects for the ideological renewal of the party, and the 1990s will be characterised by the way in which the party resolves this problem: how, in the context of a presidential system in which the PS is in a very strong position, the party is to impede the development of outright presidentialism within its own ranks, a development which will without doubt stifle the party's ability to come to terms with and develop its own social democracy. In the 1980s the PS learned the exigencies of realism; in the 1990s the party needs once again to deploy a considerable effort of imagination if it is to avoid a stagnation of its ideas while its rival leaders box each other and the party to an ideological standstill.

Conclusion

The PS's success has been due in large part to its willingness to adapt to a new system - in this case, presidentialism. The contrast with the PCF is stark (see Chapter Three).

Electorally, the PCF now stands at around 5 per cent, and is well and truly a 'minor' party. There are many reasons for this, but one of the essential ones is its failure to adapt to presidentialism. This situation also allowed the PS to become more overtly social democratic. This in turn, apart from the defection of Communist voters to it, has also meant a greater willingness on the part of centre and centre-right voters to entertain voting for the PS. Nevertheless, the decline of the PCF has left the PS with a problem, that is, with such a weak (occasional) partner, the left cannot cross the 50 per cent threshold. In the 1986 legislative elections, for example, the combined left gained only 44 per cent of the vote, the lowest since 1968. After 1986, it was clear that the PS would need another 5,000,000 votes to win power. It did gain them, in a manner of speaking, when Mitterrand was re-elected President. But it was clear that the vast majority of these votes came from the centre.

We have argued at different points in this chapter that the party's move towards presidentialism was one of the main factors underlying its gradual lessening of interest in doctrine and the content of its socialism. Another has been the changing attitudes in the French electorate throughout the period of the Fifth Republic. This has been described - from as early as the 1960s - as the depoliticisation of the French.[50] This assertion begs many questions but what is clear is that there have been many changes in the social composition of French society and a rise in life styles - individualism in particular - which do not fit well with traditional socialism, communism, Gaullism and so on.[51] The PS's shift in attitudes is in part a response to this - as evidenced by its growing pragmatism, unpretentious language and more realistic approach.

The party remains strongly implanted nationally, but continuing success in the post-Mitterrand era could push the party towards the doctrinal sterility of the Radical Party in the Third Republic. It is true that given the circumstances: the 1982 austerity, the impending defeat of 1986, the need to rally behind Mitterrand, and, after 1988, a government with only a relative majority, the party has been unable to assert authority over the President, the government, or indeed the economy, and has been continuously constrained to play a supporting role. Nevertheless, the challenge facing the party in the 1990s and a prerequisite to the survival of its identity as it moves into alliances with others, is - having recognised the stubbornness of economic facts, and the unwillingness of the French to embrace adventurist left-wing rhetoric - to deepen its reflection upon and commitment to its social democracy. The PS has been plagued by an identity crisis since its creation in 1905. Traditionally, however, this never deterred it from searching for one. In the 1990s and into the next century, the ideological reappraisal of a party which is now the linchpin of political power in France is the necessary prerequisite to the party's remaining strong in ideas, and, thereby, in a productive relationship with its membership and its electorate.

Notes

1. Jean Jaurès (1859-1914), founder of the Socialist Party in 1905, and claimed by both the socialist and communist traditions in France as the father of modern French socialism. He was assassinated in July 1914. Léon Blum (1872-1950), Socialist Party leader and Prime Minister of the Popular Front in 1936. Deported to Germany in 1943, Blum returned a hero at the end of the war. He became Prime Minister again for a brief period in 1946.

2. In the late 1960s/early 1970s there was also a short-lived but concerted attempt by the left-wing of the Radical Party led by Jean-Jacques Servan-Schreiber to re-group the forces of the centre left. See Nordman, J-T., *Histoire des radicaux*, La Table Ronde, Paris, 1984, pp. 455-489. Gaston Defferre, Mayor of Marseille, was the only other viable Socialist presidential candidate in the 1960s. After his very poor showing in the 1969 presidential elections, he abandoned his presidential pretensions and rallied to Mitterrand.

3. See Gaffney, J., *The French Left and the Fifth Republic*, Macmillan, London, 1989, pp. 178-183.

4. After 1971, there was, nevertheless, a certain renovation (by and large Mitterrand supporters), an expansion of the party in terms of both membership and national implantation, and the gradual emergence of a younger generation of second-rank leaders.

5. Some sections are based in the workplace, some in the universities, but the overwhelming majority are based in the locality. The development of workplace sections *(sections d'entreprises)* after 1971 was intended to signify the new party's determination to be more than a presidential party. Such preoccupations were especially strong amongst leaders and supporters of the left-wing CERES faction.

6. See Cole, A., 'Factionalism, the French Socialist Party and the Fifth Republic: an explanation of intra-party divisions', *European Journal of Political Research*, vol. 17, no. 1, January 1989, pp. 77-94.

7. Defferre's current became a sub-current of Mitterrand's in the course of the 1970s.

8. On the social composition of PS factions see Bell, D.S., and Criddle, B., *The French Socialist Party: The Emergence of a Party of Government*, Clarendon Press, Oxford, 1988, p. 258.

9. The bipolarity of the polity was due to three factors: 1) the electoral system; 2) the existence of de Gaulle who forced the parties into acquiescence or hostility towards him; and 3) the presidentialism he began and others subsequently developed.

10. See inter alia Bell and Criddle, op. cit., pp. 222-248. CERES between 1975 and 1979, and the Rocardians between 1979 and 1981, were in opposition to Mitterrand but both acquiesced at various times in his leadership, and subsequently fell into line after 1981.

11. Gaffney, op. cit., pp. 180-181.

12. It was assumed that the first presidential elections after Epinay would take place in 1976. President Pompidou's death in office in 1974 changed the situation completely, forcing Mitterrand - who failed to win against Giscard d'Estaing in the unscheduled 1974 elections - into a seven-year 'shadow' presidency.

13. The conflictual nature of left unity was inevitable: the near-success of 1974 was dependent upon left unity; such success itself, however, sowed seeds of disunity, given that the PS benefited much more than the PCF from it.

14. The starkest example of Mitterrand's Machiavellianism was his willingness to associate with his strongest critics, CERES, in 1979, in order to counter a challenge from Rocard and Mauroy at the Metz Congress. Mitterrand also had to contend with Rocard's significantly greater popularity in the opinion polls between 1978 and 1981 (see Bell and Criddle, op. cit., p. 103).

15. The PS round one vote was 37.5 per cent, 10 percentage points up on Mitterrand and the Left-Radical Michel Crépeau's vote combined.

16. For an interesting discussion of this point see Bell and Criddle, op. cit., pp. 146-147.

17. See Gaffney, op. cit., pp. 176-177.

18. This unfamiliarity with governmental power was slightly mitigated by the fact that the party had ir many areas held local power continuously throughout the Fifth Republic. Also many of its leader were high-ranking civil servants with many contacts in government, the civil service, business an industry.

19. See inter alia Gaffney, J. (ed.), *France and Modernisation*, Gower, Aldershot, 1988, esp. Chapter 4, 6, 7, 8, and 9.

20. See ibid., pp. 176-211.

21. See inter alia Duhamel, A., *La république de Mitterrand*, Grasset, Paris, 1982; Gaffney, *France an Modernisation*; Ross, G. et al. (eds.), *The Mitterrand Experiment*, Polity Press, Oxford, 1987; July S., *Les années Mitterrand*, Grasset, Paris, 1986; Machin, H., and Wright, V. (eds.), *Economic Polic and Policy-Making under the Mitterrand Presidency: 1981-1984*, Frances Pinter, London, 1985; an Mazey, S., and Newman, M. (eds.), *Mitterrand's France*, Croom Helm, London, 1987.

22. A small illustration of the chain reaction of economic misfortune that the government was involve in: the increased SMIC (minimum wage) raised employment costs. The employers countered thi by cutting jobs and output. In the context of a mildly reflated economy such a situation stimulate a consumer boom which was satisfied by a dramatic increase in imports.

23. See inter alia Rhodes, M., 'Industry and Modernisation: an Overview' in Gaffney, *France an Modernisation*, pp. 66-95; Holmes, P., 'Broken Dreams: Economic Policy in Mitterrand's France in Mazey and Newman, op. cit., pp. 33-55; and Stoffaës, C., 'The Nationalizations, 1981-1984' i Machin and Wright, op. cit., pp. 144-169.

24. See Rhodes, ibid.

25. For the illustrative example of information technology, see Green, D. (1988), 'The Political Econom of Information Technology in France', in Gaffney, *France and Modernisation*, p. 131.

26. Holmes, P., and Estrin, S., 'Planning for Modernisation' in Gaffney, *France and Modernisation*, pp. 110-123.

27. The Greenpeace Affair, moreover, began in July 1985 with the blowing up by French secret agents of the ship the Rainbow Warrior which was protesting against French nuclear tests. One man was killed in the explosion.

28. CERES continued for a while as a partial exception to this centripetal rule, although much of its activity was subsequently directed at combatting Rocard's ambitions rather than offering alternatives to reformism.

29. Mitterrand, F., *Le coup d'état permanent*, Plon, Paris, 1965.

30. Weekly private meetings, however, took place throughout the 1981-86 period between Mitterrand and other key figures, the Prime Minister and the party First Secretary in particular.

31. Before 1981, the idea of ministers having a high national profile was almost unheard of: there were one or two examples in Giscard's *septennat*, and perhaps only André Malraux before that.

32. Nor did the power of the National Assembly increase to any great extent, and when the government needed to (due to lack of time, for example), it did not hesitate to use article 49, clause 3 of the Constitution to push government bills through, even though it had denounced this measure for over twenty years.

33. The introduction of proportional representation had been urged in Mitterrand's *110 propositions* of 1981, but had not been heard of since Mitterrand's election. The decision to introduce it occasioned Rocard's resignation from government as Minister of Agriculture in April 1985.

34. The notions of *la rupture avec le capitalisme, changer la vie*, and, especially, *autogestion*, had been fundamental to the ideological cohesion of the party in the 1970s. With government, they disappeared completely from the socialist lexicon.

35. This phenomenon of a team of successful ex-ministers coming back into party life after March 1986, created a deluge of interpersonal rivalries at the top of the party hierarchy, and no small amount of problems for First Secretary, Jospin. See Gaffney, J., 'French socialism and the Fifth Republic', *West European Politics*, vol. 11, no. 3, July 1988, pp. 42-56.

36. The distribution of seats in the 1986 legislative elections was as follows: PCF, 35; PS, 209; MRG, 7; FN, 35 (a total of 286); RPR/UDF, 291.

37. For a thorough overview of the PS in the 1986 period see Hanley, D., 'President's men or party of government? The French Socialist Party in 1988', *Modern and Contemporary France*, no. 35, October 1988, pp. 3-15.

38. For a more detailed and theoretical treatment of this issue see Gaffney, J., 'French socialism and the Fifth Republic'.

39. Mitterrand and Rocard created the precedents for these *équipes*; and the PS experience of government and ministerial *cabinets* between 1981 and 1986 generalised them.

40. *Le Nouvel Observateur*, 4 April 1986.

41. See Gaffney, J. (ed.), *The French Presidential Elections of 1988: Ideology and Leadership Contemporary France*, Gower, Aldershot, 1989.

42. See Cole, A., 'La France Unie? François Mitterrand' in ibid., pp. 81-100.

43. The abstention rate in the legislative elections (5 and 12 June 1988) was 34 per cent for round o 30 per cent for round two.

44. This lack of influence was mitigated to a certain extent by the government's need for PS suppo A good early example of this was government concessions to the PS parliamentary group over t elaboration of the 1990 budget. Even here, however, the PS's influence was less than it appeare given that it was supported by the President himself who used the party to exert pressure on government to pay more attention to 'social' issues and less to 'economic' ones.

45. It is noteworthy that the four main axes that the government declared would guide its actic Education, the quality of urban life, those excluded from social and economic progress, and relationship between the bureaucracy and the consumer, were all long-term projects which, althou 'social' in intention, offered the image of a sustained, incrementalist, pragmatic programme.

46. Rocard enhanced his own position vis-à-vis both his government and the PS by always referring justification of his actions to Mitterrand's *Lettre à tous les Français*, rather than to the PS's ov campaign document *Propositions pour la France*. See also Rocard's authoritative letter to ministers on 24 May 1988 (subsequently published in the national press).

47. The most significant centrist ministers were the long-standing supporter of Raymond Barre, J Soisson (Employment), and the arguably right-of-centre J-M. Rausch (Overseas Trade).

48. Rocard's government's task was also helped by the very significant divisions in the opposition, main one being the CDS's ambivalence towards outright opposition.

49. Ironically, the first victim of Rocard's demand for governmental solidarity, a demand designed minimise the possibility of factional rivals like Jospin undermining him, was a minister representati of Rocard's dearly-held 'civil society', the Minister of Health, Léon Schwartzenberg, who was sack in July 1988 for voicing his own attitude to Aids screening without having gained the Pri Minister's approval.

50. This is mirrored, moreover, by a social class dimension. The internal embourgeoisement of the pa is relentless as one moves up the hierarchy. The working-class represents 35 per cent of PS vote 15 per cent of its membership, 5 per cent of its activists, 3 per cent of its leadership, 1 per cent its MPs, and 0 per cent of its ministers; see Bell and Criddle, op. cit., p. 205.

51. See Rémond, R. et al., *La démocratie à refaire*, Editions Ouvrières, Paris, 1963.

Bibliography

Alexandre, P., *Le roman de la gauche*, Plon, Paris, 1977.

Alternances, 'La gauche dans le rétroviseur', no. 2, 1986.

Balassa, B., 'Après cinq ans, bilan de la politique économique et sociale', *Commentaire*, vol. 9, no. 33, Spr 1986.

Bell, D.S., and Criddle, B., *The French Socialist Party*, Clarendon Press, Oxford, 1988.

Birnbaum, P., and Leca, J., *Individualism*, Oxford University Press, Oxford, 1990.

Bizot, J-F., *Au parti des socialistes*, Grasset, Paris, 1975.

Bourgine, R., 'Austerité socialiste, l'expérience cruciale', *Perpsectives*, no. 7, May 1983.

Bussery, H., 'Réhabiliter les services publics', *Projet*, no. 215, February 1989.

Cayrol, R., and Ysmal, C., 'Les militants du PS: originalités et diversités', *Projet*, no. 165, May 1983.

Cayrol, R., 'Le godillot et le commissaire politique', *Projet*, no. 161, January 1982.

Chevènement, J-P., and Motchane, D., *Clefs pour le socialisme*, Seghers, Paris, 1973.

Club Jean Moulin, *Un parti pour la gauche*, Seuil, Paris, 1965.

Cobham, D., 'French macro-economic policy under President Mitterrand', *National Westminster Bank Quarterly Review*, February 1984.

Cole, A., 'Factionalism, the French Socialist Party and the Fifth Republic: an explanation of intra-party divisions', *European Journal of Political Research*, vol. 17, no. 1, January 1989.

Colombani, J-M., 'La gauche à l'épreuve', *Le Monde*, 5, 6, 7 April 1983.

Desjardins, T., *François Mitterrand: un socialiste gaullien*, Hachette, Paris, 1978.

Dreyfus, F., *Histoire des gauches en France: 1940-1975*, Grasset, Paris, 1975.

Duhamel, A., *La république de Mitterrand*, Grasset, Paris, 1982.

Duhamel, O., *La gauche et la Vᵉ République*, PUF, Paris, 1980.

Evin, K., *Michel Rocard ou l'art du possible*, J-C. Simeon, Paris, 1979.

Faire, *Qu'est-ce que la social-démocratie?*, Seuil, Paris, 1979.

Faure, J., 'La nouvelle politique économique et la crise', *Société Française*, no. 4, October 1982.

Frank, R., 'La gauche sait-elle gérer la France?', *Vingtième Siècle. Revue d'Histoire*, no. 6, June 1985.

Frears, J., 'The 1988 French Presidential Elections', *Government and Opposition*, vol. 23, no. 3, Summer 1988.

Gaffney, J. (ed.), *France and Modernisation*, Gower, Aldershot, 1988, esp Chapters 4, 6, 7, 8 and 9.

Gaffney, J., *The French Left and the Fifth Republic*, Macmillan, London, 1989.

Gaffney, J. (ed.), *The French Presidential Elections of 1988*, Gower, Aldershot, 1989.

Gaffney, J., 'French socialism and the Fifth Republic', *West European Politics*, vol. 11, no. 3, July 1988.

Gerstlé, J., *Le langage des socialistes*, Stanké, Paris, 1979.

Guerrieri, S., 'Il congresso di Lilla del partito socialista francese', *Materiali e atti*, no. 9, October 1987.

Guidoni, P., *Histoire du nouveau Parti socialiste*, Tema, Paris, 1973.

Hamon, H., and Rotman, P., *L'effet Rocard*, Stock, Paris, 1980.

Hanley, D., 'President's men or party of government? The French Socialist Party in 1988', *Modern and Contemporary France*, no. 35, October 1988.

Hargrove, C., 'Thatcher-Mitterrand', *Revue des Deux Mondes*, vol. 1982, no. 2, February 1984.

Harrington, M., 'Mitterrand's term: a balance sheet', *Dissent*, Winter 1987.

Harrison, M., 'France under the Socialists', *Current History*, vol. 83, no. 492, April 1984.

Harrison, M., 'The French economy in disarray', *Contemporary French Civilisation*, vol. 8, no. 1-2, Winter, 198

Haudeville, B., 'Politique industrielle et politique économique générale', *Revue d'Economie Industrielle*, vol. 23, no. 1, 1983.

Hoffmann, S., 'Mitterrand: the triple mystery' *French Politics and Society*, vol. 6, no. 2, April 1988.

Hurtig, S., *De la SFIO au nouveau Parti socialiste*, Armand Colin., Paris, 1970.

Jaffré J., 'Le parti socialiste et l'opinion depuis 1981, la chute et les chances d'une remontée', *Pouvoirs*, n 36, 1986.

Jenson, J., and Ross, G., 'The tragedy of the French Left', *New Left Review*, no. 171, October 1988.

Johnson, R.W., *The Long March of the French Left*, Macmillan, London, 1981.

July, S., *Les années Mitterrand*, Paris, Grasset, 1986.

Lavau, G., 'Les effets de vingt ans de gaullisme sur les partis de gauche', *Espoir*, no. 37, December 1981.

Lefournier, P., 'Ceintures de tous les pays, serrez-vous' *L'Expansion*, no. 206, 6 January 1983.

Machin, H., and Wright, V. (eds.), *Economic Policy and Policy-Making under the Mitterrand Presidenc 1981-1984*, Frances Pinter, London, 1985.

Macshane, D., *François Mitterrand. A Political Odyssey*, Quartet, London, 1982.

Manent, P., and Machin, H., 'Two views of the Mitterrand presidency, 1981-1988', *Government and Oppositic* vol. 23, no. 2, Spring 1988.

Marensin, J., 'A propos de l'ouverture au centre', *Commentaire*, vol. 11, no. 44, Winter 1988.

Mauroy, P., *C'est ici le chemin*, Flammarion, Paris, 1982.

Michel, P., 'Un Français sur deux désapprouve', *L'Economiste*, no. 1555, 22 January 1983.

Mitterrand, F., *Le coup d'état permanent*, Plon, Paris, 1965.

Mitterrand, F., *Ma part de vérité*, Fayard, Paris, 1969.

Mitterrand, F., *Un socialisme du possible*, Seuil, Paris, 1970.

Mitterrand, F., *La rose au poing*, Flammarion, Paris, 1973.

Mitterrand, F., *La paille et le grain*, Flammarion, Paris, 1973.

Mitterrand, F., *Politique*, 2 vols., Fayard, Paris, 1977 and 1983.

Monsen, R.J., 'French Socialists march to the right', *Challenge*, vol. 27, no. 4, October 1984.

Mazey, S., and Newman, M. (eds.), *Mitterrand's France*, Croom Helm, London, 1987.

Northcutt, W., 'The changing domestic policies and views of the Mitterrand government 1981-1984', *Contemporary French Civilisation*, no. 2, Summer 1985.

Nugent, N., and Lowe, D., *The Left in France*, Macmillan, London, 1982.

Parti communiste français and Parti socialiste, *Programme commun de gouvernement*, Editions Sociales, Paris, 1972.

Parti socialiste, *Le projet socialiste*, Club Socialiste du Livre, Paris, 1980.

Pfister, T., *Les socialistes*, Albin Michel, Paris, 1977.

Pfister, T., 'Le nouveau paysage politique', *Revue Politique et Parlementaire*, vol. 90, no. 935, June 1988.

Plassard, J., 'Les équilibres économiques généraux en France et la politique conduite depuis mai 1981', *Revue d'Economie Politique*, vol. 93, no. 5, October 1983.

Plassard, J., 'Conjuncture de l'économie française: hésitations de la politique économique et financière', *Chroniques d'Actualités de la SEDEIS*, vol. 34, no. 4, April 1986.

Poperen, J., *L'unité de la gauche: 1965-1973*, Fayard, Paris, 1975.

Portelli, H., 'L'intégration du parti socialiste à la cinquième République', *Revue Française de Science Politique*, vol. 34, no. 4-5, October 1984.

Portelli, H., 'Les contraintes de la Ve', no. 3, *Politique Aujourd'hui*, January 1989.

Portelli, H., *Le socialisme français tel qu'il est*, PUF, Paris, 1980.

Rémond, R. et al., *La démocratie à refaire*, Editions Ouvrières, Paris, 1963.

Rocard, M., *Parler vrai*, Seuil, Paris, 1979.

Rony, J., 'PS: gérer l'hégémonie', *Politique Aujourd'hui*, no. 3, January 1989.

Ross, G., and Daley, T., 'The wilting of the rose', *Socialist Review*, vol. 16, no. 3-4, August 1986.

Ross, G. et al. (eds.), *The Mitterrand Experiment*, Polity Press, Oxford, 1987.

Sachs, J., and Wyplosz, C., 'The economic consequences of President Mitterrand', *Economic Policy*, April 1986.

Salomon, A., *P.S.: La mise à nu*, Laffont, Paris, 1980.

Schifres, M., and Sarazin, M., *L'Elysée de Mitterrand. Secrets de la maison du prince*, Moreau, Paris, 1985.

SOFRES, *Opinion publique - 1984*, Gallimard, Paris, 1984.

SOFRES, *Opinion publique - 1985*, Gallimard, Paris, 1985.

SOFRES, *L'état de l'opinion - 1988*, Gallimard, Paris, 1988.

SOFRES, *L'état de l'opinion - 1989*, Gallimard, Paris, 1989.

Williams, S. (ed.), *Socialism in France*, Frances Pinter, London, 1983.

Wilson, F.L., 'Socialism in France: a failure of politics not a failure of policy', *Parlimentary Affairs*, vol. 38, no. 2, Spring 1985.

5 Breaking the Mould: the Greens in the French Party System

Paul Hainsworth

Since the early 1970s, ecological and environmental forces have threatened to penetrate the mainstream of French party politics only to be thwarted by divisions, organisational weaknesses or circumstances. More recently, however, in the late 1980s, the Greens (*les verts*) have emerged as a relatively durable, united and timely political movement. In this chapter, it is proposed to examine the nature of contemporary French political ecology on various levels: evolution, electoralism, sociology, structures, leadership and strategy. At the same time the impact of the Greens on the French party system shall be assessed. In the latter context, the Greens have established their identity as a resolutely autonomous political force, independent of other political organisations and suspicious of any alliances likely to compromise this status.

'Neither right nor left' - nor, indeed, centre - has become the catchphrase of the French Greens and the dogged pursuit of this strongly articulated strategy-cum-principle since 1986 has been largely correlated with the various electoral breakthroughs of the movement, notably in the 1989 municipal (March) and European (June) elections. The 1989 results, whilst attracting much publicity and some surprise, must be seen against the background hinted about above, that is almost two decades of electoral and other activities throughout alternating periods of government embracing right or left or, exceptionally from 1986 to 1988, right and left. Consequently, a familiar slogan of the Greens and their ecological forerunners calls for a genuine *alternative* as opposed to a mere bipolarised *alternation* of the traditional political parties. In this limited respect, we can make obvious - but guarded - parallels with the National Front in so far as both the Greens and the extreme right pose as the *real* alternatives to the existing political formations - PS, RPR, UDF, PCF - referred to by both as 'the gang of four', albeit a term invalidated somewhat by the decline of the French Communist Party (PCF). A second parallel worth noting is that the National Front and French political ecology arrived on the electoral scene simultaneously, with the 1973 legislative and 1974 presidential elections constituting the first national contests for each nascent movement. For political ecologists, this signalled the dawn of an electoralism comprising sixteen years of national electoral shares of the poll ranging from about one to (almost) five per cent. The National Front was even less successful in its first decade of electoralism but broke through spectacularly, suddenly and repeatedly between 1983 and 1989. Political ecology, in the form of the Greens, had to wait until the 1989 elections before making any really significant challenge to established party politics and, as with the

National Front, the European elections provided the occasion. Initially, it will be useful to examine the fortunes of political ecologists prior to the Greens' success in order to situate the contemporary movement.

Political Ecology: Evolution and Electoralism

To a large extent, French political ecology in the 1970s (at least) was a child of the May 1968 events in France. Many of the themes of this period fed into the 'young' political ecology of the next decade. These included anti-statism, anti-authoritarianism, direct democracy, libertarianism and hostility towards traditional institutions and structures. Also, in the 1970s, the anti-nuclear protest movement preoccupied ecologists and perhaps at times appeared synonymous with the ecologist cause. However, as Tony Chafer[1] explains:

> From a movement the sole argument of which appeared to be a principled refusal of nuclear energy based on fear due to the risks inherent in the nuclear cycle, the anti-nuclear movement has evolved into a movement which now provides a comprehensive social and political critique of the nuclear society and proposes an alternative model for the future development of a non-nuclear society.

We discuss the ideology of political ecology below. Suffice to note here that the first conspicuous landmark in the rise of political ecology was the agronomist Réné Dumont's bid for the French presidency in 1974. Of course, the intention was not to win - Dumont polled 1.37 per cent of the poll - but to propagate and popularise ecologist ideas. Yet, 'while giving impetus to the movement, Dumont's campaign also highlighted splits within it. Many groups did not agree with the entry of ecology into the political arena and refused to support Dumont, preferring to confine their activity to local campaigns'.[2] The question of to be or not to be 'political', and under what format, characterised the movement in the years ahead. Despite the unprecedented success of the Greens the matter has not been resolved convincingly. Nevertheless, following Dumont's candidacy, political ecology developed.

After 1974, the green lobby mobilised primarily against President Giscard's nuclear policy.[3] The 1977 municipal elections, too, witnessed an impressive ecologist performance with the movement contesting a limited number of constituencies and achieving from about five to thirteen per cent therein, including an average of ten per cent in Paris, where urbanisation was the key issue. Shortly after these elections however, in July 1977, the violent confrontations of the anti-nuclear protesters and forces of law and order at Creys-Malville prompted some rethinking within the broad movement. According to one viewpoint:[4]

> The violence of the demonstration led to a profound feeling of disappointment and betrayal in the movement. The extreme left, for whom the anti-nuclear movement was primarily a vehicle for the overthrow of the bourgeois state, had led the movement up a blind alley, and a reassessment of tactics and objectives was needed.

In the late 1970s, therefore, several basic questions circulated within ecologist circles: how political and electoral should the movement become? On what bases was it possible to unify the movement? What relationships, if any, should the movement have with other social movements such as regionalists, trade unions, women's movements and the lobby for *autogestion* (self-management)? Electoralism proceeded amidst the quest for identity and soul-searching. In 1978, the ecologist movement polled its highest number of voters (0.6 million, 2.18 per cent of the poll) in the legislative elections, with *Ecologie 78* serving as the main umbrella organisation for many candidates. Further, this provided the impetus for the 1979 European election, when *Europe écologie* polled 4.39 per cent (890,000 votes), marginally below the elusive five per cent quota required for French seats in the European Parliament.

Throughout the 1970s, anti-nuclear campaigns and electoral contests served as major foci of ecologist activity but neither were able to promote a cohesive single political structure or significantly distract the state from nuclear policies. Nevertheless, the experiences of this decade led eventually, in 1980, to the creation of the Movement of Political Ecology (MEP), which aimed to provide a durable political structure to surpass the ad hoc arrangements hitherto. The MEP militants aspired to create a specific 'political space' for the movement which would enable political ecologists to fight elections in a greater state of preparedness. As current Greens' 'leader' Antoine Waechter was to remark later, the 'French ecologists have spent their time building houses and then knocking them down again'.[5] For the 1981 presidential election, for instance, new organisational forms were necessary.

In 1981, choice of candidate proved to be a labyrinthine and tortuous process summing up the best (diversity, democracy, debate) and the worst (factionalism, fratricide) in the movement. Various names were proffered (including Dumont and undersea explorer, Jacques Cousteau) and others declared their interest (notably the President of *SOS - environnement*, Jean-Claude Delarue, and the ex-PCF intellectual, Roger Garaudy) but, ultimately, Brice Lalonde, leader of *Amis de la terre* (AT), the French Friends of the Earth organisation, was elected via a democratic, decentralised process involving an Ecologist Liaison Committee and the three main prongs of the movement, that is the MEP, AT and the so-called 'third college' of unorganised environmental associations. Lalonde viewed ecology as a contemporary social movement which needed to ally with other movements and even political parties in order to be effective. His critics inside the movement - including the MEP and, currently, the Greens - have since accused him of trying to push political ecology towards the left, thereby undermining the potential autonomy of an ecologist political force. In turn, Lalonde has questioned the alleged utopianism of some of his ecologist contemporaries whilst equally warning against the specific creation of an ecologist political party (see below). For the 1981 presidential election, however, enough unity of purpose prevailed to enable Lalonde to achieve a creditable one million plus votes (3.8 per cent of the poll). Significantly, for the second ballot of the election, Lalonde respected the autonomy of the movement and offered no clear advice to voters - despite his undisguised left-oriented sympathies - but the defection of ecologist first-ballot voters facilitated François Mitterrand's victory over Giscard. Approximately forty-six per cent of the million plus ecologist voters switched to Mitterrand, twenty-four per cent backed Giscard and twenty-six per cent abstained. The results confirmed the perception of ecologist voters as 'leaning to the left without toppling over'.

With the alternation of governments in 1981, ecologists hoped for a receptive hearing. In some respects, there were changes and a dialogue emerged. Controversial military (Larzac) and nuclear power (Plogoff) installations were arrested and sympathetic, respected spokespersons were given ministerial briefs for the environment - Michel Crépeau, leader of the Left-Radicals (MRG) and Huguette Bourchardeau, candidate in 1981 for the small Unified Socialist Party (PSU). Ultimately, though, the Socialist administration's commitment to nuclear options and the limited budget for the environment placed French ecologists primarily in the opposition role.[6] In fact, by 1982, there was dissatisfaction with Socialist rule and little expectation that the PS's slogan, *changer la vie*, would apply to ecological issues. Opposition to the experience of Socialist rule and the dynamic of unity around Lalonde's candidacy, at least, provided the context for the various prongs of the political ecology movement to sign a five point agreement, in October 1982, based upon the following important principles: political autonomy; no dual membership (that is, belonging to other political parties simultaneously); majority rule (with respect for minorities); individual, as opposed to group or organisational, membership; and representation for the regions within the movement's structures. Significantly, these features were carried over into the Greens two years later. Initially, a major convention was to follow the 1982 agreement with a view to ratifying it fully and preparing for the 1983 municipal elections. This proved unmanageable for the movement and the elections were fought under various guises and tactics. With only limited resources and activists, ecologists contested only their strongest areas achieving 0.58 per cent overall, a modest result yet, via the PS's new electoral reform to introduce a measure of proportionality into municipal elections, over three hundred ecologists of sorts were elected to municipal office. In fact, the elections were both an interlude and an impetus in the process of trying to unify the French ecology movement. In May 1983, at Besançon, and January 1984, at Clichy, key steps were taken to create a single party-cum-movement.[7] Even so, division and disunity characterised the political ecology movement. This was illustrated vividly in 1984 when the French ecologists might comfortably have entered the European Parliament but, crucially, ecologist votes were spread across two Euro-lists: *La liste des verts - Europe écologie*, led by well established militant ecologists, Didier Anger, Yves Cochet and Solange Fernex, and *La liste entente radicale écologiste (ERE) européenne*, led by Lalonde in conjunction with MRG, centrist and ecologist support. The lists received 3.4 per cent (678,826 votes) and 3.31 per cent (664,403 votes), respectively, again both below the five per cent quota mark.

Les verts

Despite overall disappointment, some political ecologists could draw comfort from the Euro-elections' promotion of the Greens as a potentially autonomous political force. Prior to the election, in January 1984, the Greens were born as a unifying political force.[8] Basically, the Greens combined two movements: the *Verts-parti écologiste*, formerly the MEP, and the *Verts-confédération écologiste*, born in the early 1980s as a consortium of various minor forces (mainly ex-MEP and ex-Friends of the Earth). The Greens' official full title reflected the compromises inherent in the process of unification - *Les verts confédération écologiste - parti-écologiste*. This step towards unification and political party formation did not please all ecologists. For instance, as we have already suggested above, certain environmental associations as well as Friends of the Earth were hostile to these organisational developments. Disagreements were less over policy and ideology than organisation, leadership and strategy.[9] For example, prominent ecologists like Anger and Lalonde both drew their inspiration from May 68 and favoured a left-oriented strategy. In turn, Yves Cochet looked respectfully across the border at *Die Grünen*'s alternative left, eco-socialist strategy. On this point, Lalonde differed since, to him, creation of ecologist political parties was a contradiction in terms. For Lalonde, party was synonymous with the very evils which the movement sought to contest - discipline, hierarchy, centralisation, power seeking, institutionalisation and so on. Lalonde supported a looser, federal, alliance-making organisation, depicting political ecology as the visible point of a much bigger, deeper social movement. Unsurprisingly, therefore, Lalonde and the Greens parted company in the mid-1980s. Lalonde's alternative Euro-list was interpreted as a betrayal of the movement but the decisive step occurred in November 1986. From this date onwards, Antoine Waechter and others staged a highly successful coup within the Greens, effectively committing the movement to the resolutely autonomous 'neither left nor right' line.

After 1986, then, Waechter and his supporters' independent line increasingly dominated the Greens, ushering in a phase of tangible success as the movement won voters, members and diverse electoral offices. Indeed, the regional elections of 1986 had helped to launch Waechter's rising star since he was one of only three Greens elected to the new regional councils. Since the early 1970s, Waechter had been active in his native Alsace within environmental and nature associations. In March 1986, two of the Greens' three regional councillors were elected in Alsace, testifying to the strength of political ecology in the region. The other, Didier Anger, was returned in Basse-Normandie. According to one observer of the Greens, the effect of the regional elections was to provide the Greens with their highest elected offices, assist in the legitimation of the movement and predestine Waechter to an important role in the Greens in the years ahead.[10] Indeed, Waechter's success could be contrasted with certain failures within the movement. For instance, thirty to forty Green regional councillors were hoped for and between four to eight deputies in the French National Assembly, courtesy of the proportional representation voting system adopted by the Socialists for the concurrent general election. Moreover, insufficient political capital was derived from the Chernobyl effect and the notorious sinking of the Greenpeace Rainbow Warrior vessel in Auckland Harbour. In these circumstances, therefore, Waechter represented new hope for the Greens.

Subsequently, Waechter warded off 'red-green' challenges from Anger and Cochet to capture the Greens' nomination for the 1988 presidential election. In addition, the autonomist line was consolidated within the Greens via democratic support from the party's General Assembly. Next, with increasing professionalism, the Greens established Waechter's political identity with the electorate at large. According to Waechter, the aim in the presidential election was to lay the foundation for the forthcoming municipal and European elections in 1989 where, realistically, seats could be won. Suffice to note here that Waechter, with 3.8 per cent and one million plus votes, emulated Lalonde's performance seven years earlier. This time, however, the ecologist candidate could draw upon a support structure already in place and unlikely to disintegrate following the presidential election. As in 1981, the ecologist candidate was not the master of his votes on the second ballot. Many abstained but many, too, went to François Mitterrand and relatively few to Jacques Chirac, the Gaullist right-wing candidate - again illustrating the tendency of ecologist voters to lean to the left, whatever the strategy of the movement.[11] Still, these trends were not unexpected. The municipal elections would provide a more severe and revealing test of the Greens' autonomist strategy since the electoral laws permitted second-ballot challenges depending upon first-ballot returns.[12]

1989: The Year of the French Greens

With Waechter's good showing in the presidential election the Greens experienced an unprecedented wave of enthusiasm, attention, sympathy and membership. Resources were still too meagre to support more than a token presence at the hastily convened (June 1988) legislative elections so, officially, the Greens abstained, opting for the Autumn cantonal elections as a means of keeping up the momentum, albeit in selected areas. In the 1989 municipal and European elections the movement boasted its most significant political gains to date.

In the municipal elections, the Greens polled only 1.47 per cent and, ultimately, claimed only 0.27 per cent of France's municipal councillors. Yet, their success could be pin-pointed easily. First, the Greens were able to field twice as many candidates as in 1983, indicative of the growing strength of the movement. Officially, the Greens boasted more candidates than members. Second, the Greens achieved over thirteen hundred local councillors, below Waechter's target of three thousand but well above 1983 figures.[13] Moreover, the Greens had twice as many seats as the National Front. Third, the elections represented a triumph for the Greens', and Waechter's autonomist line. With first ballot scores of over ten per cent in many constituencies, the Greens were able to maintain their lists on the second ballot, rather than merge with or defer to other parties. Instead of thereby declining, as many observers predicted, the Greens improved their share of the vote in most cases. A vote for the Greens was seen as a 'useful' vote. Moreover, where alliances and mergers were made with the left, the Greens fared less well - disappointing in the immediate but vindicating the neither left nor right strategy against 'red-green' exponents. According to Guillaume Sainteny, the progression of the Greens' votes from first to second ballot constituted their real success in the municipal elections.[14] Interestingly, too, where the Greens polled some votes on the first ballot but not enough (that is, ten per cent) to maintain a second-ballot presence, it is instructive to note the flight of second-ballot Green voters: 42 per cent to the left, 15 per cent to the right and 45 per cent abstentions.[15] Again, these figures confirm the left bias of ecologist voters but equally - and more disturbing for other political parties - reveal a political space beyond the left versus right axis. Also, with the National Front maintaining perforce a second-ballot presence in areas of strength, the combined effect of both these political movements was to cause triangular and quadrangular contests, militating against bipolarisation in the political system.

Accused of 'sectarianism' by some critics, Waechter professed not to be against local alliances with other parties - except the National Front - provided clear, written, public agreements could be struck, *contrats de municipalité* accommodating the Greens' demands. In the event, various mergers and alliances were made, mainly, although not exclusively, with the left in several large towns - Lille, Dunkirk, Aix, Avignon, etc. - legitimating the Greens in the process, in a fashion not dissimilar from National Front legitimation in recent years.[16] According to one interpretation, these arrangements promised a phase of red-green *cohabitation*, rather than *union*, possibly along the lines of 'the German model' of comparable alliances. Simultaneously, Waechter professed his movement's receptivity to political *ouvertures*, if key preconditions were met such as denuclearisation, an environment minister with 'teeth' and the authorisation of the referendum by local/popular initiative. Proportional representation and curtailment of arms sales to the third world were items high on the Greens' priority list, too.

The question of *ouvertures* spilled over into the European elections. Twenty of the 81 places on the Greens' Euro-list went to outsiders, with three in 'electable' positions. Amongst the causes taken up therein were regionalism (with the Corsican autonomist, Max Simeoni, in third place), second-generation immigrants, non-violence, the third world and the unemployed. Besides Waechter, the list included prominent, veteran leaders of political ecology, Anger, Cochet, Fernex and Dumont, most of these in 'electable' positions. The municipal election results were promising enough for the Greens to expect to surpass the five per cent barrier in the European elections and enter the European Parliament for the first time. The opinion polls concurred with Waechter's estimation of five to ten European deputies for the Greens.

In various ways, the European stage in 1989 was a fitting platform to demonstrate and enhance the Greens' political maturity. Compared to 1979 and 1984, the movement could now claim a greater degree of unity, direction and tangible success. As with the National Front in 1984, conditions were favourable to the Greens' challenge: a proportional representation voting system; a 'second order' election affording the opportunity of voting Green without bringing the government down; the immediate precedent of promising local election results; voter identification with the movement's main campaign issues; a certain disillusionment with traditional political parties; a recognisable and acceptable enough leader; and so on. Furthermore, the holding of the fifth conference of European Greens in Paris shortly before the European election and Waechter's appearance on the prestigious *L'heure de verité* television programme were signs of the growing influence of the movement. Consequently, the Euro-elections were a resounding success for the Greens, who emerged as a new component of the French party system.

In June 1989, the political ecology movement polled its highest ever share of the poll, 10.59 per cent, and number of voters, 1.9 million, sufficient to elect nine European deputies, including two fellow travellers. Moreover, the results demonstrated an increasing 'nationalisation' of the Greens' vote as over five per cent was polled in each French department and over ten per cent in half. Traditional areas of strength (see below) and regionalist enclaves (Corsica) were the most profitable areas but, clearly, the Greens were now reaching the parts other political ecology movements had failed to touch. Moreover, the scale of the victory enabled the French Greens to wrest the European leadership of the movement from the German Greens at Strasbourg - with implications thereby for the future strategy and direction of the movement - and sever formal links with the European Rainbow Group in order to create a more cohesive eco-political force. Waechter's mediatisation continued whilst, also, he became chairperson of the European Parliament's Regional Policy and Planning Committee. Waechter now aspired to make the Greens France's third largest political force, ahead of the National Front (11.73 per cent in June 1989), behind the PS and the united right. For the PS, this aspiration threatened to impede the Socialists' goal of reaching forty per cent of the poll in future elections. However, to all parties the Greens' performance was a warning and, according to Waechter, the Euro-elections were a triumph for the Greens' independent strategy and a vote for new environmental policies within the main political parties.

The Greens: Voters, Party and Leader

As we noted above, the MEP leadership had hoped to create 'a new political space' in French politics with which voters might identify as their primary political choice. The Greens hoped to emulate this goal and the 1989 elections were clearly a step in the right direction. In this section, we shall examine the character of the Greens placing emphasis upon the voters, structure and leadership of the movement.

Geographically, the strongest areas of support for political ecology are to be found in the west and east of France, notably Alsace, Brittany and Basse-Normandie.[17] Also, above average levels of support are evident in parts of the Rhône Valley, Ile-de-France and Nord-Pas-de-Calais. Weakest areas are the centre and centre-west. In 1989, the Greens performed well in areas of long-standing ecological activity. In many cases, local factors prevailed: opposition to the Loire dam, the Strasbourg metro, acid rain in Alsace, coastal pollution and port developments in Brittany, nuclear power installations in various places, uranium mining in Limoges, Euro-Disneyland in Marne-la-Vallée and so on. However, the Greens did especially well where local factors could be combined with established organisation on the ground.

In contrast to the National Front's vote, the Greens' vote was very much a positive espousal of the environmental cause rather than a neo-Poujadist protest against the government of the day.[18] Indeed, generally, Green voters were even more favourably, than unfavourably, disposed to the Mitterrand presidency, albeit critical where it concerned the environment, unemployment, purchasing power and social matters. Of course, to some extent, the Greens' vote amounted to a protest against the traditional 'political class' and a concomitant tendency to look elsewhere for qualitative change. In 1988, though, the ecologist electorate continued to demonstrate a left-wing bias ultimately helpful to Mitterrand (against Chirac). By 1989, albeit in different electoral circumstances, the Greens' vote was beginning to exhibit more autonomist leanings with less overlap with the left.[19] All in all, the Greens were able to take from the left, right and centre, at the same time as mobilising abstentionists and attracting new voters to a significant degree. Indeed, in the latter two cohorts, the Greens performed better than rivals. According to a SOFRES enquiry, in April-May 1989, the Greens took 47 per cent of their support from the 18-34 age group, with the average age of the ecologist voter comparatively low at thirty-eight, promising omens for the future.[20] As regards social and/or professional class, the Greens drew primarily from the middle classes - teachers, students, social workers, professionals and intermediary layers but with an ability to draw in sizeable proportions of white- and blue-collar workers. Many of the social layers which sponsored the rise of the Socialist Party supported the Greens. Also, the Greens' electorate is proportionally more feminine than masculine, although as regards members the pattern is reversed, with male easily outnumbering female adherents by about two to one.

As the electorate of the Greens increased so did the membership. Between 1984 and 1988, membership oscillated around the 1,000 to 1,300 mark, rising to about 1,700 in 1988, 3,000 by April 1989, and over 5,000 after the European elections.[21] One source even reported 5,000 new members since the municipal elections.[22] Certainly, since the movement is decentralised and membership applications continued to flow in, these figures underestimate actual membership. Nor does membership include the wider reservoir of sympathisers and fellow travellers put by one source at 80,000 persons.[23] After the 1988 presidential election, applications for membership were forthcoming particularly from teachers, the retired and former members of the extreme left, such as the PSU, with the average age of Green members mirroring that of Green voters. With the influx of new members there were some expectations that this might affect the democratic character of the Greens' organisation.

From birth, the Greens' structures rested upon statutes set out in a small eight page booklet. At the base of the movement, there are local groups - akin to PCF cells or PS sections - feeding into departmental and regional structures. Essentially, the structures were designed to incorporate direct democracy, regional representation and collegial, as opposed to single, leadership. The provision of an authoritative General Assembly reflected the direct democratic basis of the movement. Any member could put forward structural changes provided one-tenth of the membership, spread across one-third of the regions, supported the motion. In truth, the Assemblies were sometimes chaotic but, arguably, the medium was as important as the result. According to Waechter, the Greens were not *un parti comme les autres* and exhibited a more democratic edifice than other formations.[24] Waechter himself strongly supported the internal democracy of the movement. After all, through it, he had been able to commit the Greens to the *pur et dur* autonomist line in 1986. In November 1989, the Greens' Annual General Meeting again confirmed Waechter's hegemony within the movement.

The Annual General Meeting of the Greens helps elect the National Council, the 'parliament' of the movement. One quarter of the sixty or so members were elected at the annual General Assembly with the other three quarters elected by the regions to maintain the decentralised bias. At the apex of the structure is the Executive College (circa twenty members) elected annually via the National Council and led by four spokespersons assisted by various officers therein (Treasurer, Secretary, Campaign Manager and so on). Significantly, the Greens shied away from electing a single leader although circumstances, notably the presidentialism of the French Fifth Republic, have cast Waechter in this role.

The question of leadership is crucial to any political party or movement but particularly delicate within the sphere of French political ecology. Traditionally, the Greens have been opposed instinctively and philosophically to the concept of a single leader, interpreting this as the essence of other political parties and incongruous with the democratic, participatory ethos of the movement. Over the years, though, various individuals may be seen to have led the cause of political ecology. Dumont, of course, helped to launch political ecology with his 1974 presidential candidacy but, since, has played mainly a supportive role. In turn, Lalonde's appetite for publicity and his undoubted media skills were an asset to the movement but disturbed many rank and file members. Moreover, at crucial times, Lalonde appeared divisive whilst his recent recycling via accession to ministerial office in 1988 served to confirm critics' suspicions about his principles and motives.

In contrast, Waechter has acquired a reputation for dourness, excessive observance of democratic structures and reluctance for leadership. Lalonde views him as 'an archaic boy scout' in view of Waechter's long-standing active commitment to nature and environmental causes in Alsace.[25] The French correspondent of an English newspaper depicted the Greens' spokesman as 'this serious, cold-eyed environmentalist, as grey as he is green'.[26] For Daniel Boy, Waechter is 'not too charismatic, but sufficiently mediatic'.[27] Other commentators tend to highlight his dislike for politics. Yet, Waechter has been active in virtually all major elections over the past two decades. Indeed, in terms of winning office, he has been successful: municipal councillor for Mulhouse, regional councillor for Alsace and French European deputy. Also, we have already noted the strength of his autonomist line within the Greens. Waechter, too, is often seen as a 'fundamentalist' within the movement and represents principally the environmentalist component of political ecology. Moreover, through his influence, the Greens have acquired a reputation for seriousness, managerial efficiency and realism, moving political ecology away from the post-68 leftism of the 1970s:

> The great ecologist battles of the 1970s - the Plogoff nuclear power station in Brittany or the Larzac army base - were fought by Woodstock-style mass gatherings. The new generation of Greens fights in committee, with briefcases full of documents to support its arguments.[28]

Marie-Thérèse Pagel, a regional secretary of the Greens, has also maintained, 'we prefer responsibilities to power', a simultaneous expression of political maturity and critique of other political forces.[29] Historically, political ecologists had stressed their hostility towards the state; in the 1980s, the Greens began to occupy positions within the state's orbit to promote their cause. At this point, it will be instructive to discuss briefly the ideology and policy basis of the French Greens.

Ideology

Basically, French political ecology is a confluence of multiple, varied influences and experiences drawing from extremely politicised activists on the extreme left to anti-political environmentalists. Attempts to pigeon-hole the movement succintly are prone to failure. Hence, observers have tended to emphasise the eclectic nature of the movement. Chafer and Prendiville, for instance, portray the political ecology movement as 'an extremely diffuse affair' based on a synergetic belief system incorporating diverse sources: humanism, individualism, personalism, utopianism, reaction, regionalism, anti-materialism and so on.[30] Again, the same authors point to the essential unity of the movement as regards the ideological underpinnings:

> The most marked disagreements were largely over organisation, leadership and strategy, rather than policy... the critique of productivism and consumerism, the demand for new forms of work, for a less wasteful and polluting style of life and for the achievement of a more balanced relationship between man and nature, based on conservation and the careful exploitation of the resources of the planet through development of renewable technologies and energy sources, formed a somewhat diffuse, but nevertheless largely agreed, ideological basis for policy formation within the movement.[31]

Elsewhere, Eric Dupin discerns four basic components of the movement: environmentalists, anti-nuclearists, third world campaigners and exponents of alternative politics and society.[32] However, these categories are not watertight or comprehensive, they both overlap and omit whilst providing a strong flavour of the Greens' make-up.

The Greens are an umbrella organisation with members coming from different access routes: nature associations, extreme-left groups and parties, anti-nuclear struggles, established political parties, third world solidarity organisations, militant Christian movements and so on. Certainly, in the context of France's developing party system, the Greens are capable of decimating the effectiveness of the extreme left (PSU, LCR, etc). In turn, the extreme left accuses the Greens of attacking the evils of the capitalist system without fundamentally questioning the system itself. The extreme left shares the view with traditional political parties that ecology is too important simply to be left to the ecologists. Of course, this stance represents an attempt to regain control of the agenda from the Greens and even sow the seeds of division therein. What essentially unites the Greens is a belief that the political parties have failed to take ecological questions seriously enough. Therefore, the Greens propose a genuine, qualitative, alternative.

Essentially, the Greens' vision is of a more humanised, peaceful, participatory, democratic, cleaner and greener society. Consequently, the Greens question such concepts and processes as industrialisation, growth, planning, consumerism, technocracy, third world development, nuclearisation, urbanisation and progress. A particular target of criticism for the Greens is the role and, for some, even the concept of the state, perceived as centralised, hierarchic, bureaucratic and technocratic. The Greens' critique of established political parties rests, in part, upon the perception of these as de facto accomplices of state power. The Greens' alternative model of development and organisation rests upon such measures as wider, democratic decision making (via the referendum by popular initiative, further decentralisation, *autogestion*, a Europe for the regions, etc) and solidarity with the less well off, within and without France. Initially, as suggested above, the anti-nuclear struggle, May 68 style libertarianism and anti-political environmentalism characterised the ecology milieu of the 1970s. Increasingly, though, the Greens have taken on board other issues such as unemployment, the economy, multiculturalism and job sharing. For the 1989 elections, the Greens produced an information pack of leaflets covering various specific areas of concern as well as municipal and European election manifestos. As regards the latter, the key themes in the Greens' European election campaign were encapsulated in the title of the manifesto, *Les verts et l'Europe. Pour une Europe des régions et des peuples solidaires*. Besides the themes of environmental protection, alternative energy strategy, the quality of life and anti-nuclearism, the manifesto urged solidarity with the third world, the regions, the unemployed, the young and the old. Simultaneously, the Greens expressed strong reservations about the Single European Act, fearing that the tearing down of barriers will be at the expense of ecological and social needs. On the question of European integration, the Greens have clashed with the pro-integrationist Brice Lalonde who has used the issue to support his critique of them as retrogressive and reactionary. Whilst both Lalonde and the Greens see themselves as political ecologists, disagreements persist about the way forward. For Lalonde, a movement allied to other pressure groups and working with political parties remains the best means of mobilising support. For the Greens, politics and independence are the current and correct yardsticks to guide the movement into the 1990s.

Conclusions: To The Future - A Movement For The 1990s?

The 'long march' to political success is an analogy applied to the experience of various political movements. In France, for instance, the PS, the FN and the Greens fit into this perspective. After about a decade and a half of moderate to poor electoral returns for political ecologists, the 1986 (regional) and 1988 (presidential) elections paved the way for the more tangible rewards of 1989. To what extent have the Greens fulfilled their purpose? How might we sum up the appeals of the movement? Also, what are the prospects for the future?

In November 1988, Waechter set out five measurable targets for the Greens:

* 3,000 local council seats in March 1989;
* representatives in the European Parliament;
* a significant number of departmental councillors in 1991;
* 30 regional councillors in 1992;
* more optimistically, depending on the reintroduction of proportional representation, deputies in the French National Assembly.

Whilst the municipal elections yielded less arithmetic gains than hoped for, the 1989 elections, municipal and European, established the ascendancy of the Greens. The political discourses of other political parties, too, increasingly reflect the ecological and environmental dimension as Green issues are now assuming more importance in the electorate at large. Of course, as with the National Front, electoral triumphs and political clothes' stealing serves further to enhance the legitimacy of the movement. Opinion polls, too, reveal growing sympathy with Green politics although many voters still see the Greens as a limited environmental body rather than as an organisation with a viable, comprehensive blueprint for society.[33]

The revaluation of ecological themes plus the increasing respectability, legitimacy and efficiency of the Greens point to the durability of the movement as a significant force in French party politics in the 1990s. Moreover, there is enough proportionality in the electoral system at a municipal, regional and European level to expect continued elected office. Furthermore, the Europeanisation and internationalisation of environmental issues (for instance via the Single European Act) and the Greens' caucus at the European Parliament are useful platforms for the movement. The relative youth of the Greens' electorate, access to higher and wider education, the disillusionment with traditional parties, the persistence of ecological crises, the multiplier effect of 'green waves' outside France, improved financial status, increasing membership and so on are all factors capable of playing into the hands of the Greens. Indeed, the explanations put forward for the Greens' municipal success are still valid: 'the ecologist vote represented a new form of protest vote against the incumbent Socialist government; it reflected the new saliency of the environment as a political issue (a phenomenon not limited to France); it expressed a reaction against the commitment of the main parties to a model of economic growth; it was the latest manifestation of rejection of the political system and the established political parties'.[34] Indeed, with the Greens in contention, it seems difficult for the PS to achieve its target of 40 per cent of the electorate in the near future. However, on the less positive side, the Greens face various problems, mainly brought upon by rise of the movement. In conclusion, therefore, potential hurdles to future success must be noted.

First, how does the Greens' organisation react in the short and long term to *entriste* tactics notably from former alternative left forces anxious to become hitched to the Greens' rising star? Second, to what extent will the new waves of members necessitate internal reform, possibly impinging upon the movement's democratic structures? Third, how does the movement balance the inevitable mediatisation of Waechter and increasing 'partyisation' of the Greens with its customary hostility towards politics, parties and the leadership principle? In this vein, to what extent will the Greens evolution towards political party status be a smooth and manageable process? Fourth, divisions still exist within the Greens although success and Waechter's influence have papered over these. Still, partisans of a more left-oriented stance remain inside the Greens and represent potential threats to the loose unity of the movement, anchored around Waechter's autonomist strategy. Fifth, to what degree will rivals, such as the PS, be able to recuperate Green themes and expose the programme of the movement as utopian? In 1988, the nomination by Prime Minister Michel Rocard of Brice Lalonde as Minister of State for the Environment represented an obvious concession to the ecologist lobby. Alternatively, it can be seen as a means of demobilising support for the Greens and appropriating ecology as a left-wing-cum-PS value. Waechter sees Lalonde as a hostage to the Socialist government and a compromiser of issues fundamental to the movement. In turn, Lalonde preaches 'realism' and defines the government as France's most pro-ecologist one to date. Furthermore, threatening for the Greens is Lalonde's recent projected launch of a brand new ecological organisation, *Génération écologie*, structured differently from the Greens, alliance-oriented and sympathetic to the idea of dual membership.[35] To paraphrase René Dumont, Lalonde - as poacher turned gamekeeper - is more concerned to ecologise the politicians whereas Waechter seems intent on politicising the ecologists, albeit within autonomist parameters. Last, in June 1990, the executive of the PS opted for a less proportional system of elections for the French regions. Reforms along this line would work against multi-partyism and, therefore, dilute Waechter's goal of thirty regional councillors and deprive the Greens of useful positions.

Nevertheless, despite the above reservations, the prospects for the Greens' continued success are objectively good and the movement's main campaigning issues are unlikely to dissipate or be resolved overnight. Paradoxically, then, one of the threats to the major French political parties in the 1990s will emanate from a milieu opposed instinctively to party politics but obliged to 'go political' and contributing towards the transformation of the bipolarised system in the process.

Notes

1. Chafer, T., 'The Anti-Nuclear Movement and the Rise of Political Ecology' in Cerny, P. (ed.), *Social Movements and Protest in Contemporary France*, Frances Pinter, London, 1982, p. 203.

2. Ibid., p. 205.

3. See Ardagh, J., *France Today*, Harmondsworth-Penguin, London, 1990; Frears, J., *France in the Giscard Presidency*, Allen and Unwin, London, 1981.

4. Chafer, op. cit., p. 207.

5. *Financial Times*, 17 June 1989.

6. Ardagh, op. cit.

7. *Le Matin*, 24 May 1983; *Le Monde*, 25 May 1983; *Le Quotidien de Paris*, 8 June 1983; *Combat Nature*, June 1984, pp. 4-5; Chafer, T., and Prendiville, B., 'The Emergence of the Green Movement in France. Structures and Attitudes within the French Green Movement', unpublished paper presented to the joint sessions of the European Consortium for Political Research (ECPR) conference in Paris, April 1989.

8. *Combat Nature*, No. 62, June 1984, pp. 4-5.

9. Prendiville and Chafer, op. cit., p. 2.

10. Sainteny, G., 'Le vote écologiste aux élections régionales', *Revue Politique et Parlementaire*, No. 927, January-February 1987.

11. *Le Nouvel Observateur*, 23-29 March 1989.

12. Bridgford, J., 'The French municipal elections of March 1989', *Parliamentary Affairs*, Vol. 42, No. 3, Autumn 1989.

13. Sainteny, G., 'Les verts: limites et interprétation d'un succès électoral', *Revue Politique et Parlementaire*, No. 940, March-April 1989.

14. Ibid.

15. *Politis*, 24-30 March 1989.

16. See Schain, M.A., 'The National Front in France and the construction of political legitimacy', *West European Politics*, vol. 10, no. 2, April 1986.

17. *Vert-Contact*, 18 March 1989; Sainteny, 'Les verts: limites et interprétation d'un succès électoral'; *Combat Nature*, No. 86, August 1989.

18. Sainteny, ibid.; *Le Point*, 3 April 1989.

19. *Politis*, 2-8 June 1989.

20. *Le Monde*, 28-29 May 1989.

21. *Politis*, 2-8 June 1989; *Le Quotidien de Paris*, 24 March 1987; *Combat Nature*, February 1989; *Le Nouvel Observateur*, 23-29 March 1989; *Le Figaro*, 29 June 1989.

22. *La Croix*, 8 August 1989.

23. *Politis*, 2-8 June 1989.

24. *Le Quotidien de Paris*, 2 June 1989.

25. *Le Quotidien de Paris*, 27 March 1988.

26. *The Financial Times*, 17 June 1989.

27. *Le Nouvel Observateur*, 23-29 May 1989.

28. *The Financial Times*, 17 June 1989.

29. *Politis*, 30 December-5 January 1989.

30. Chafer and Prendiville, op. cit.

31. Ibid., pp. 2-3.

32. *Libération*, 31 May 1989.

33. *Le Monde*, 12 July 1989.

34. Cole, A., 'The French municipal elections of 12th and 19th March 1989', *Modern and Contemporary France*, No. 39, October 1989, p. 27.

35. *Le Point*, 6 April 1990.

Bibliography

Ardagh, J., *France Today*, Harmondsworth:Penguin, London, 1990.

Bridgford, J., 'The ecologist movement in the French general election of March 1978', *Parliamentary Affairs*, vol. 31, no. 3, Summer 1978.

Bridgford, J., 'The French municipal elections of March 1989', *Parliamentary Affairs*, Vol. 42, No. 3, Summer 1989.

Chafer, T., 'The Anti-Nuclear Movement and the Rise of Political Ecology' in Cerny, P. (ed.), *Social Movements and Protest in Contemporary France*, Frances Pinter, London, 1982.

Chafer, T., and Prendiville, B., 'The Emergence of the Green Movement in France. Structures and Attitudes within the French Green Movement', unpublished paper presented to the joint sessions of the European Consortium for Political Research (ECPR) conference in Paris, April 1989.

Cole, A., 'The French municipal elections of 12th and 19th March 1989', *Modern and Contemporary France*, No. 39, October 1989.

Combat Nature

Frears, J., *France in the Giscard Presidency*, Allen & Unwin, London, 1981.

Hainsworth, P., 'The re-election of François Mitterrand: the 1988 French presidential election', *Parliamentary Affairs*, Vol. 41, No. 4, Winter 1988.

La Croix

L'Express

Le Matin

Le Monde

Le Nouvel Observateur

Le Point

Le Quotidien de Paris

Les verts (1989):

* *Avec les verts pour l'écologie* (policy pamphlets);
* *Projet municipal des verts*;
* *Les verts et l'Europe. Pour une Europe des régions et des peuples solidaires*;
* *Vert - contact (la lettre des verts).*

Politis

Sainteny, G., 'Le vote écologiste aux élections régionales', *Revue Politique et Parlementaire*, No. 927, January-February 1987.

Sainteny, G., 'Les verts: limites et interprétation d'un succès électoral', *Revue Politique et Parlementaire*, No. 940, March-April 1989.

6 The Return of the Orleanist Right: The Union for French Democracy

Alistair Cole

Of all the formations considered in French Political Parties in Transition, the Union for French Democracy (UDF) can perhaps lay the weakest claim to be a coherent political entity. Rather than a party in the conventional sense of the term, such as the Communists, Socialists, or Gaullists, the UDF is in reality a confederation of independent political parties. Two central themes dealt with in this chapter are the nature of the confederation as a form of political organisation (section four), and the impact of the personal, presidential rivalries spurred by the Fifth Republic upon the cohesion of this type of organisation (section five). Before looking at the UDF as a particular type of political organisation, however, we shall consider the history of the confederation (section one), its component parties and leading personalities (section two), and the ideas associated with it (section three). Finally, we shall evaluate the future prospects of the UDF, as well as those of the renewed centrist parliamentary group, the Union of the Centre (UDC), formed after the 1988 elections.

The creation of the Union for French Democracy (UDF) by President Giscard d'Estaing in 1978 had its origins in the presidentialism and bipolarising pressures of the Fifth Republic. It was originally a confederation of those non-Gaullist parties supporting Giscard's presidency. It comprised the conservative-inclined Republican Party (PR), the Christian-democratic Centre of Social Democrats (CDS), the Radical Party and various smaller formations. Giscard's immediate objective in forming the UDF was to organise his dispersed parliamentary supporters into a more coherent presidential coalition in an attempt to stave off defeat in the legislative election of March 1978.

The creation of the UDF was the logical culmination of the process whereby the 'opposition centrists' (as the Radical Party and the Democratic Centre, precursor to the CDS, were collectively known) rallied to support Giscard d'Estaing in the 1974 presidential election. Their support for Giscard came after some 15 years of opposition to the Gaullist-led governing coalition in both parliamentary and presidential elections. Independent centrists had attempted to construct a viable 'autonomous centre' alternative to both the Gaullist majority and the left at each legislative election since 1962. Their efforts had continually been frustrated, and they had rarely obtained enough support to elect more than a handful of deputies under the second-ballot electoral system. The process whereby the opposition centrists gradually rallied to the right-wing coalition has been adequately dealt with elsewhere.[1] It should be noted, however, that the centrists' decision to support Giscard in 1974 reflected a de facto convergence with the right-wing coalition which had existed since the early Fifth Republic. In fact, the 'opposition' centrists had generally allied with the parties of the presidential majority (Giscard's Independent Republicans, or the Gaullists) on the second ballot of legislative elections from 1962 onwards.

There had also been two unsuccessful attempts to elect centre candidates to the presidency, in 1965 and 1969. In 1965, Jean Lecanuet trailed behind François Mitterrand and Charles de Gaulle and was eliminated on the first ballot. In 1969, the centre candidate Alain Poher actually managed to win through to the second ballot, largely as a result of the left's chronic divisions, but was roundly defeated by Georges Pompidou (de Gaulle's successor) on the decisive second round. Neither candidate had stood a serious chance of being elected. The decision to support Giscard represented a final admission that the 'autonomous' centre could not effectively compete with either the right-wing coalition (composed of the Gaullists and Giscard's moderate Independent Republicans since 1962), or the PS-PCF alliance. In a rigorously bipolarising regime such as the Fifth Republic, the centre was called upon to choose its camp. Rather than attempt to elect one of its own to the presidency, far better in 1974 to support the moderate Giscard, the first time a non-Gaullist from within the traditional governing coalition had stood for the presidency. By supporting Giscard, the ex-'opposition' centrists hoped to be able to counter-balance the influence of traditional conservatives within the presidential majority should Giscard be elected.

The need to create the UDF in 1978 partly reflected the failure of Giscard's own political party - the Independent Republicans - to organise his supporters efficiently.[2] After his election as President in 1974, the Independent Republicans (as Giscard's supporters had labelled themselves since 1962) had expected to benefit in a quasi-automatic manner from being the presidential party. They regarded themselves as the natural pole around which the President's other supporters should regroup. Such an analysis was not shared, however, by the two other main non-Gaullist components of Giscard's majority, the 'Christian Democrats', or centrists (whose two fractions united to form the CDS in 1976) and the Radicals. Giscard's Independent Republicans were no match for Jacques Chirac's reinvigorated Gaullist Party, relaunched as the Rally for the Republic (RPR) in December 1976. In May 1977, the old Independent Republicans transformed themselves into a new-style Republican Party (PR), with the objective of providing a serious structured rival to Chirac's RPR for ascendency on the right. The PR did finally succeed in uniting most pure Giscardians into one organisation, but it was unable to transform itself overnight into a convincing party able to recruit grass-roots activists, or provide a rallying-point for Giscard's centrist and Radical supporters.[3] The new party remained a classic cadre party, heavily reliant upon its sitting deputies, senators and mayors to provide the rudiments of a party organisation. It was no match for the disciplined party machine of the RPR, and was regarded with suspicion by Giscard's other parliamentary supporters, the CDS and the Radicals.

Despite their mutual suspicion, Giscard's various parliamentary supporters in the PR, the CDS and the Radical Party were constrained to come to some form of electoral agreement before the 1978 legislative election, once it became clear that neither Giscard, nor Chirac would envisage the traditional pattern of single 'presidential majority' candidates from the first ballot. Under the second-ballot electoral system, the existence of separate PR, CDS, and Radical candidates, all competing with the RPR for leadership of the 'majority' coalition on the first ballot, would undoubtedly have had disastrous consequences for Giscard's supporters. As the strongest single party, the RPR would have led the right virtually everywhere on the first ballot to face the left alone on the second. The politico-institutional system of the Fifth Republic (in particular the manner in which the electoral system had come to operate by 1978) and the prevailing atmosphere of internecine struggle between Giscard and Chirac combined to promote the creation of the UDF as a matter of electoral and political necessity. The UDF proved its worth as an electoral cartel in 1978: it polled almost as many votes as the RPR despite the fact that it had been formed only six weeks before the first ballot. Moreover, the desperate first-round competition between UDF and RPR did not prevent the two formations from coming to an electoral agreement for the second ballot, and defeating an even more disunited left.

The influence of presidentialism on the creation of the UDF had been obvious: even the name of the federation was an extension of Giscard's political testament *La démocratie française* (1976). The President had originally envisaged the UDF not merely as an electoral cartel to save his parliamentary majority in 1978, but as the basis for the emergence of a great moderate centre-right party, which would fulfil the role of the dominant presidential party that the Gaullists had performed during the 1960s. Unlike the latter, however, the UDF was an imperfect presidential party. It lacked any real organisational capacity for mobilising support at the grass-roots level, and was far too divided to portray a unified political message to the electorate. In addition, as measured in terms of the number of its deputies, it did not even constitute the 'majority of the majority', let alone a dominant party along the lines of de Gaulle's UNR, or later Mitterrand's PS. Giscard's presidency undoubtedly suffered from his inability to structure his supporters into a cohesive presidential party able to provide him with powerful logistical and organisational support to counteract his rivals. The weakness of the UDF became obvious in the course of the 1981 presidential campaign: Giscard largely excluded the UDF parties from any involvement in his campaign for reelection, thereby remaining faithful to the 'above-partyism' of the presidential function.

For as long as Giscard remained in office, the UDF could scarcely aspire to an independent existence: its role was not to propose policy, but to defend presidential initiatives. The cohesion provided by the presidency prevented internal rivalries within the UDF from assuming their later proportions. Nonetheless, the resistance from all quarters within the UDF to a genuinely fused presidential party testified even during his presidency to the limitations of Giscard's presidential domination of the UDF.

The Giscardians in the Republican Party regarded themselves as part of a natural governing élite. The challenge of opposition came as an unwelcome and unpredictable surprise. Indeed, once the UDF had lost the cohesion created by occupying the presidency, there was a real possibility that it might disintegrate under the force of its own centrifugal pressures. But the electoral logic which had lain behind the creation of the UDF in 1978 remained intact in 1981: in a bipolarising political system, the component parties of UDF would probably be obliterated if they did not cooperate with each other, as well as with the RPR. The expected PS advance (as the new presidential party), and the surprise created by Giscard's defeat made most UDF deputies only too willing to accept Chirac's leadership of a renewed UDF-RPR coalition.[4] The UDF emerged greatly weakened from the 1981 legislative election, with just 63 deputies, half of its 1978 total (124). Its performance would undoubtedly have been worse had each party fought the election under its own colours.

During the entire period of Mitterrand's first *septennat* (1981-88), the history of the UDF as a separate political formation independent of the parties which composed it was strictly limited to a number of spheres: essentially these related to the preparation of elections, and the activities of UDF deputies. That the UDF survived at all after the traumatic events of 1981 surprised many commentators. Despite pressures from certain elements to quit the confederation, these gradually subsided as public opposition to the PS-PCF government developed in intensity. In November 1981, the Radical Party opted to remain within the UDF, as did the CDS at its congress of May 1982. Faced with persistent rivalries between the PR, still dominated by Giscard's supporters, and the CDS, it was decided in 1981 that the UDF should retain its confederal structure, which left each individual party with the greatest amount of autonomy. Grandiose ideas relating to the creation of a new dominant party of the centre and right were quietly shelved.[5]

A common reaction within the UDF against the PS-PCF government provided a solid source of cohesion for member parties, and gradually tied them closer to each other and to the RPR. Serious sources of cleavage rooted in the recent past remained, however, in particular in relation to the personality of Giscard d'Estaing. In April 1982, Giscard returned to the UDF's Political Bureau (*Bureau politique*), much to the chagrin of the CDS and the Radicals. A new generation of supposedly pro-Giscard politicians took control of the PR in September 1982, with François Léotard taking over as leader, supported by Giscard; and the UDF Pontoise Congress in October 1982 was subsequently transformed into a pro-Giscard rally, despite assurances to the contrary having been given to the CDS.[6] On an electoral level, the UDF repeatedly illustrated its value as an efficient cartel, arbitrating between the rival claims of constituent member parties, and securing a series of agreements with the RPR. Despite its electoral advances in the 1982 cantonal and 1983 municipal elections, however, critics increasingly argued that the UDF had ceased to exist as an independent political formation with its own specific policies and identity. They pointed to the UDF's self-effacing U-turn over the 1984 European election for evidence to support this conclusion: after having repeatedly asserted the UDF's intention to run its own list in 1984 - favourable territory in a non-decisive election fought under proportional representation - Giscard finally gave in to the demand formulated by Chirac and Simone Veil (head of the UDF list in 1979) for a joint RPR-UDF list. The new PR leader, Léotard, signalled his disgust by resigning as UDF vice-President and threatening to run his own list. Despite eventually backing down, the episode marked the beginning of a new rivalry between Giscard and his former protégé Léotard.

The 1984 election represented a watershed, at least in so far as the UDF gave in to RPR pressures for a joint list, when a more self-confident organisation might have been expected to present a separate list as in 1979. In practice, from 1981-86, the confederation favoured promoting the overall objectives of the opposition as opposed to developing the specific identity of the UDF. The theme of unity between the RPR and UDF, in the run-up to the 1986 legislative election, was constantly marshalled by Giscard, as well as by Chirac. This was in part a response to the spectacular rise of Raymond Barre (Giscard's Prime Minister from 1976-81) in the presidential ratings since 1982: in order to counter-balance Barre's growing influence, as well as to position himself favourably as a *présidentiable* able to unite the whole opposition, Giscard sought to create a privileged RPR-PR axis. Underlying the theme of 'union' lay an engagement by both UDF and RPR that they would form a government of *cohabitation* after the 1986 elections. Giscard and Chirac thereby demarcated themselves from Barre, who vigorously opposed *cohabitation* in the name of defending the presidential institutions of the Fifth Republic (see below). The imperative of unity with the RPR also dictated that the two formations agree upon a policy-manifesto. This materialised in February 1986, when the UDF and RPR signed a 'common platform of government', committing the opposition to a wide-ranging programme of economic liberalism.[7] This manifesto acted as the basis for the Chirac government's ambitious reform programme from 1986-88. In addition, union with the RPR involved a series of complex electoral negotiations prior to the 1986 legislative election, fought under a new electoral system based on a variety of proportional representation. In the interests of the 'union', the UDF negotiators attempted to reach agreement with the RPR for as many joint lists as possible.[8]

The UDF emerged greatly strengthened from the 1986 election (see Table 6.1), but was still clearly the junior partner of the RPR-UDF alliance, and subsequently of Chirac's government. The poor performance of those UDF candidates proclaiming their overt support for Barre was undoubtedly a setback for the latter's credibility: an over-concentration on institutional problems at the expense of political ones had been misunderstood by the electorate. Barre's problems were compounded by the ill-advised commitment made before 1986 that he would never vote confidence in a government of *cohabitation:* such a commitment proved impossible to respect, since it would have involved sabotaging the creation of the new UDF-RPR government. The UDF occupied a delicate position within Chirac's government. A number of pro-Barre CDS politicians were named to head technical ministries, where they could participate in government while preparing covertly to rally to support Barre at a later date.[9] But the core political ministries were dominated by the RPR, with Léotard's PR playing a willing second fiddle. This renewed PR-RPR axis was aimed not only against Barre, but also against Giscard, whose presidential ambitions conflicted with those of Chirac. Giscard was 'betrayed' both by Chirac, who systematically ignored Giscardians when composing his government, and by Léotard, whose lieutenants were preferred to those of Giscard. In fact, Léotard often appeared openly supportive of Chirac's presidential bid until the summer of 1987.[10] So opposed was the PR leader to either Barre or Giscard, that Léotard momentarily promoted the idea of his own presidential candidacy as the UDF's saving grace.

Throughout the period of *cohabitation* the UDF was paralysed by severe presidential rivalries, dealt with in detail below. Once Giscard had announced in January 1987 that he would not be standing again in 1988, there was little that could prevent Barre from obtaining the support of the UDF. Barre's severe defeat in April 1988 on the first ballot of the presidential election, followed by the breakaway of the centrist CDS to form its own parliamentary group in June 1988, called into question the future survival of the UDF in the form in which it had existed since 1978. These themes will be returned to in our final section, but first let us look in greater detail at the various families and leading personalities comprising the UDF

Families and Founding-Fathers of the UDF

The formation of the UDF in February 1978 was more of a marriage of convenience than a genuine and passionate love affair. The confederation brought together within a common organisation a range of parties with different historical origins, and to an extent with distinct political identities. In this section, we shall examine in turn each of the various families comprising the UDF, as well as the most prominent personalities associated with the confederation

The Republican Party (PR)

The Republican Party has always been the largest, most influential party within the UDF. The origins of the PR lay in the events surrounding the creation and consolidation of the Fifth Republic from 1958-62. In 1958, the National Council of Independents and Peasants

(CNIP), a loose grouping of conservative notables created during the Fourth Republic, rallied to support de Gaulle, along with virtually every other party. By 1962, it had declared its hostility to de Gaulle, on account of its opposition to the constitutional referendum of October 1962, which introduced the direct election of the presidency. However, a small group of deputies led by Giscard declared its support for the General, and the restyled Fifth Republic. From 1962 onwards, Giscard's Independent Republicans represented the bulk of the non-Gaullist fraction of the majority, providing critical support for the Fifth Republic, for de Gaulle and later for Pompidou. Despite originating in the conservative CNIP, most commentators considered that Giscard's Independent Republicans occupied a degree of political space to the centre of the Gaullist Party.[11] In return for support for the Gaullist-led majority, Giscard occupied the prestigious position of Finance Minister from 1962-66, and 1969-74.[12]

For as long as de Gaulle survived (1958-69) the Republicans were largely overshadowed, but they adopted an increasingly important profile during Pompidou's presidency. When Pompidou succeeded de Gaulle in 1969, he took the first steps towards extending the boundaries of the presidential majority beyond the traditional ranks of the Gaullists and the Independent Republicans to include one fraction of the 'opposition centre', Jacques Duhamel's Centre for Democracy and Progress (CDP). In the 1973 legislative election, the non-Gaullist fractions of the majority considerably narrowed the gap which traditionally separated them from the Gaullists. But the fundamental transformation in the balance of power between the Gaullists and non-Gaullists within the governing coalition occurred with Giscard's election as President in 1974. Giscard thus acted as the catalyst for the unity of the various diverse formations who wanted to belong to the governing presidential coalition against the PS-PCF alliance, but who had resisted for as long as Gaullism remained the dominant force on the right.

In May 1977, Giscard's Independent Republicans transformed themselves into the Republican Party. It was partly the failure of the PR to achieve its (over-ambitious) objectives (see above) which stimulated Giscard to create the UDF in February 1978, of which the Republicans formed the most important element. After 1981, no one in the party initially contested the primordial position of the ex-President. Anticipating the need to associate the new generation with the party leadership (in order to transform them into his allies), Giscard approved the succession of François Léotard to become General Secretary of the PR in September 1982. Léotard symbolised a new generation impatient for power, determined to resist the left as vigorously as possible. The new leadership declared its intention of transforming the PR into a genuine party with recognised patterns of membership recruitment and participation. Once the PR had broken the umbilical cord, the party began to adopt an increasingly autonomous stance under the influence of Léotard's leadership. His media appeal and youthful popularity made the new leader into a national politician in his own right, who in time committed the crime of *lèse-majesté* against Giscard. Léotard had limited success, however, in exploiting the dynamic image he had created to forge a new-style PR with a real grass-roots presence and genuine membership.

The PR has always been the strongest formation within the UDF: in 1988, it claimed 150,000 party members, 58 deputies, 54 senators, 13 mayors of large towns (over 30,000 inhabitants), and four European deputies: given the nature of the PR as a cadre party, however, its membership figures were almost certainly grossly over-exaggerated, as indeed they were for all other parties within the UDF.[13] Under Léotard's leadership, the party has invariably been closer to the RPR in terms of ideological and strategic analysis than to the CDS. The commitment to economic liberalism and to the dynamics of the free

Table 6.1
UDF deputies by political family

Party	1978	1981	1986	UDF88	UDC88
PR	70	30	61	57	1
CDS	30	21	43	11	37
Radicals	9	2	5	3	-
PSD	1	-	1	3	-
Clubs	-	-	-	-	-
Adhérents directs	-	6	16	16	1
Others *a*	14	4	3	-	2
Total	124	63	129	90	41

Source: Thiebault, op. cit., p. 17

a Mainly independent conservative notables given UDF support.

market has been especially pervasive amongst the *bande-à-Léo*, the small elite of party decision-makers supporting Léotard's leadership. On a strategic level, the PR has been intensely hostile to any notion of collaboration or compromise with the PS, setting it apart from one faction within the CDS. But it has been far more ambiguous in relation to the FN, occasionally lapsing into an anti-immigration discourse aimed at attracting support from potential FN voters. This has especially been the case in certain areas of PR strength in the south-east mediterranean, precisely those areas most receptive to Le Pen's message.[14] At the level of organisation, Léotard did manage a certain renovation of party structures but without fundamentally changing the nature of the PR as a cadre party, based on the power of its elected notables. Finally, in the run-up to 1988, the PR was more afflicted by presidential rivalries than any formation within the UDF. The party was in reality split four ways between those loyal to ex-President Giscard, those supporting Léotard, a minority opting for Barre and another minority more or less openly backing Chirac. These various elements combined to situate the PR as lying clearly on the right of the UDF, which corresponded to its self-image as a new type of conservative party, and a bitter adversary of the left.

The Clubs perspectives et réalités

The *Clubs perspectives et réalités*, formed by the ex-President in 1966, represent the most solidly pro-Giscard structure within the UDF. The clubs predated the formation of the UDF, and were a product of the club movement of the 1960s.[15] This national federation of clubs was a cross between a forum for philosophical reflection, and a network of political influence dominated by Giscard's supporters, absolutely loyal to the ex-President. It was in order to retain their specific character as organs of philosophical reflection that the clubs refused to join the Republican Party in 1977. Once within the UDF the clubs performed a primordial role in drawing up policy statements, a role recognised in UDF statutes in October 1983. Because of their ostensibly 'philosophical' character, the clubs could not be compared to the political parties coexisting within the UDF. But neither were they deprived of influence over UDF affairs: over 100 clubs existed throughout the country, often closely attached to the local Republican Party organisation. In recognition of their contribution to the UDF, the clubs were given two seats in the Political Bureau, the UDF's executive. After the 1988 legislative election, the clubs claimed seven deputies of their own, although in practice each was a card-carrying member of the PR.

The Centre of Social Democrats (CDS)

The CDS was founded in 1976. It reunified two parties which claimed the legacy of the Christian-democratic tradition in France, as inspired by the great Popular Republican Movement (MRP) of the Fourth Republic. These were the Democratic Centre (CD) led by Jean Lecanuet, the centrist presidential candidate in the 1965 presidential election, and the small Centre for Democracy and Progress (CDP), which had been formed in 1969 by Jacques Duhamel to allow a minority of centrists to rally to support Pompidou in the 1969 presidential election (against the official centre candidate Poher).[16] The CDS was always a somewhat unwilling partner of Giscard's presidential majority, unhappy with being allied with the conservative right as represented by the Republicans. It regretted its loss of autonomy, and retained a strong sense of its own identity (Catholic, social and European). For as long as Giscard remained at the Elysée, however, the CDS was bound to play a subordinate role within the UDF.

Despite early pressures from within the CDS to quit the UDF after the 1981 elections, the autonomists were defeated at the 1982 Congress, which elected Pierre Méhaignerie as leader, commonly regarded as being committed to the UDF. Along with its partners in the UDF and RPR, the CDS vigorously opposed the PS-PCF government, accusing it of political demagogy, economic irresponsibility and anti-clericalism (over the abortive reform of the private, mainly Catholic schools in 1984). One area in which agreement between the CDS and its partners was far from obvious, however, was in relation to who would be the UDF's best presidential candidate. From as early as 1983 onwards, the CDS declared its support for Barre. Barrism and the CDS became interchangeable concepts in the public mind, but the marriage was in most senses a strange one. The CDS, infected by the desire to become the presidential party, proved willing to follow Barre into uncharted waters in pursuit of the presidency. Although the centrists had been long-time fervent supporters of a return to a more parliamentary-style regime, for example, the CDS followed Barre religiously in his opposition to *cohabitation* in the name of defending the presidential institutions of the Fifth Republic. A similar shift took place in terms of policy (see section three). Such loyalty ultimately proved to no avail, not only because Barre lost the presidential election, but also because he took little account of the CDS (let alone the UDF) during his presidential campaign. The divisions born out of the 1988 presidential campaign (see Chapter One) coincided with the positive effect created by Mitterrand's new political discourse valorising *l'ouverture* to encourage the CDS to regain a substantial part of its autonomy. The creation of the UDC parliamentary group appeared to represent the triumph of the autonomist position within the CDS, and opened up a greater period of uncertainty than at any time during the previous decade (see final section).

The CDS is in most respects the second formation of the UDF. In 1988 it counted 48 deputies (37 within the UDC), 63 senators, 19 mayors of large towns (over 30,000 inhabitants), and a claimed, over-estimated, membership approaching 50,000.[17] Despite a long tradition of political activism stretching back to the MRP, the CDS is mainly a party of notables. Moreover its electorate (Catholic and rural) has noticeably been more conservative than either its leaders, or its activists. This constraint had always in the past dampened the reforming aspirations of its leaders and - in the last resort - induced the CDS to side with the conservative right, rather than the Socialist left.

The Radical Party

The largest of the minor formations within the UDF is the Radical Party which can claim to be the oldest French political party: it was formed in 1901 to defeat the perceived clerical threat to the Third Republic during the Dreyfus affair.[18] The old Radical Party acted as a pivotal force in the centre of French politics during the Third Republic, participating in virtually all governments from 1901 onwards. In spite of its principled anti-clerical origins, in the Third and then Fourth Republics the Radical Party gradually became synonymous with electoralism and political opportunism, despite the rare efforts of men such as Pierre Mendès-France and Edgar Faure. Notwithstanding its illustrious origins, the Radical Party has become an anachronism in the Fifth Republic, engaged in a process of inexorable decline. Even more so than the CDS, the party has fallen victim to the new institutional rules and bipolarising tendencies of the Fifth Republic. Before rallying to Giscard in 1974, the Radical Party had oscillated between allying itself with the left (in 1962, 1967 and 1968) and the centre (in 1973). Neither alliance proved electorally fruitful. In 1972, the Radical Party split into two separate parties, a minority forming itself into the Movement of Left Radicals (MRG) which joined the PS-PCF alliance, while the majority retained the party's official title and formed an alliance for the 1973 legislative election with Lecanuet's CD. This initiative represented the only serious attempt by a Radical leader, Jean Jacques Servan-Schreiber, to transform the Radicals into the axis of a non-Socialist opposition to the Gaullist-led majority. The new orientation was a blatant failure: the 'mainstream' Radicals returned only four deputies, compared with 13 for the MRG. In 1974, the Radicals recognised the futility of resisting the pressures of presidential bipolarisation and rallied to support Giscard against Mitterrand on the second ballot.[19]

In organisational terms, the Radical Party enjoys an extreme degree of flexibility. Like the old Independent Republicans, the Radical Party is a confederation of elected officials, rather than a pyramidical hierarchical party in which the central party organisation can impose its will on the base. The party remains organised in the tradition of being a collection of electoral committees based around prominent notables, representing somewhat different political constituencies in various areas of France. It is now barely more than a shadow of its noble ancestor: after the 1988 legislative elections, the party counted only 3 deputies, 17 senators, and 9 mayors in towns of over 30,000 inhabitants, while claiming (implausibly) 20,000 party activists.[20] The Radicals have been consistently over-represented within the UDF's governing organs in accordance with the confederal principle.

The Social Democratic Party (PSD)

The Social Democratic Party (PSD) is by far the smallest member party of the UDF. It is the successor of the Social Democratic Movement of France (MDSF), created by a handful of ex-Socialist politicians who refused the common programme signed between Mitterrand's PS and the PCF in 1972. It has effectively become a historical leftover, limited to a diminishing band of cold war warriors with a few pockets of electoral strength. Its over-representation within the governing bodies of the UDF is striking: despite its weakness, it has two members in the UDF's Political Bureau, and counted two ministers in Chirac's 1986-88 government. After the 1988 legislative election, the PSD could boast

3 deputies, 4 senators, 10 mayors in towns with over 30,000 inhabitants, and claimed some 4,000 party members. The 1989 municipal election seriously shook what remained of its electoral strength.[21]

Les adhérents directs

The *adhérents directs* (direct members) represent the only real concession to the principle of federalism within the UDF: that the UDF competes directly for members like any other party suggests that it was originally intended as more than just an electoral cartel. The idea that individuals could join the UDF directly, rather than any one of the component member parties, responded to Giscard's early notion that the UDF would be the basis of a new dominant party in French politics, gradually substituting itself to its founder members. Such conceptions were laid to rest after Giscard's 1981 defeat, when both the PR and the CDS made it clear that they were opposed to any extension of the rights of the direct members. The fact that it claimed less than 30,000 direct members in July 1988, 10 years after its creation, testified to the weakness of the UDF as a genuine federation or political party.[22] Although by definition independent, the direct members swung strongly in support of Barre before the 1988 presidential election. Their effectiveness as a force within the UDF has always been weakened by their composite character. Within the UDF's governing bodies, the direct members are treated as one of the minor parties, with two seats in the Political Bureau. This is an eloquent testimony to the failure of the UDF to transform itself into being a genuine federation or political party.

Leading Personalities

As much as being a confederation of independent political formations, the UDF is commonly associated in the public mind with a number of prominent political personalities. The force of presidential and personal rivalries within the confederation has been such that any analysis would be incomplete without a brief assessment of the main personalities attached to the UDF.

* *Valéry Giscard d'Estaing*

Giscard d'Estaing first entered parliament in 1956 as an Independent.[23] It was, perhaps, indicative of his privileged family background that he inherited his seat from his grandfather, in the tradition of a Third Republic notable. This, in conjunction with the fact that he could claim a distant royal lineage, and an elitist educational background confirmed Giscard in his belief that he formed part of a natural governing elite. He was, moreover, a perfect symbol of the symbiosis between administration and politics, a characteristic feature of the French Fifth Republic: a brilliant graduate of both *Polytechnique* and the *Ecole nationale d'administration*, Giscard started his career in the prestigious Finance Ministry as a civil servant, before becoming actively involved in partisan politics from 1956 onwards.

His position of support for de Gaulle in the October 1962 referendum earned Giscard and his rump of Independent Republican deputies the status of a ginger group within the presidential majority, but separate from the official Gaullists. In 1962, at the age of 35, he became Finance Minister, one of the top three posts in the governmental hierarchy. He held this post until 1966. From the origins of the Fifth Republic, Giscard's Republicans firmly supported the new regime, but equally made it clear that their presence as part of the presidential majority did not signify an unconditional acceptance of Gaullism. Indeed, the relationship with de Gaulle was a thorny one: in January 1966, after his re-election as President, de Gaulle refused Giscard the Finance ministry, reacting against the latter's growing national stature.

The three years of Giscard's crossing of the desert (1966-69) were years in which personal and political antagonisms were intensified between traditional Gaullists and Giscard's supporters. Giscard gradually came to represent an alternative centre of gravity for the presidential majority, more 'centrist', Atlanticist and European. From 1966 onwards, he adopted an overtly critical stance within the presidential majority. This was epitomised by his famous declaration in January 1967 that his attitude towards de Gaulle's majority was one of 'Oui, mais', critical, conditional support. This critical stance culminated in April 1969, when Giscard refused to support de Gaulle in the 1969 referendum: given the narrow result, his decision might have been crucial in explaining the General's defeat, despite the fact that four-fifths of Republican deputies refused to follow their leader's initiative. Eschewing his own candidacy in 1969, Giscard backed Pompidou for the presidency, and was rewarded by being renominated as Minister of Finance, a post he held until 1974. His election as President in 1974 represented one of the fundamental points of reference for assessing the development of the party system in the Fifth Republic (see Chapter One).

In the event of his failing to win another presidential election, Giscard will almost certainly be remembered as the first non-Gaullist President of the Fifth Republic, from 1974-81. The reformist momentum of the early Giscard years, considered in more detail below, gradually evaporated as a result of the natural conservatism of the President's electorate and as a consequence of the fact that his supporters never comprised more than a 'minority of the majority', the Gaullists remaining the senior partner throughout, at least as measured in terms of the number of deputies. Giscard's early political ascendency was further weakened by the fierce internecine competition that opposed the President's supporters and Chirac's RPR after 1976. By 1981, Giscard's presidency had degenerated into scandal and the partisan use of power, symbolised by the Bokassa affair of 1980, and his repeated, somewhat paranoic purges of the civil service.[24] It was commonly agreed that Giscard d'Estaing lost the 1981 election, much more than that François Mitterrand won it.

Throughout Mitterrand's first *septennat*, Giscard suffered repeated setbacks. His intended political comeback in 1982 (after his re-election as a deputy in the Puy-de-Dôme department) was marred by the breakthrough of Raymond Barre, his second Prime Minister, in the presidential popularity ratings. His attempt to promote a new generation of his protégés to take over the Republican Party turned sour, when François Léotard attempted (with some success) to transform the party into a vehicle for his own ambition. His faith in *l'union* and support for *cohabitation* was betrayed when Chirac ignored him after March 1986, preferring the young turks around François Léotard. He renounced the idea of a new presidential candidacy for 1988 as early as January 1987, conscious of the futility of ignoring public opinion. At the core of Giscard's misfortune lay his inability to recover public confidence in the opinion polls: for most voters he remained *l'homme du passé*, the man of the past ironically derided by Mitterrand in the 1981 presidential campaign. And yet, he remained rarely out of the public limelight, with sufficient credibility to perform a major national role, if not to stand for the presidency. This latter objective has appeared once again within reach since the joint discredit of Raymond Barre and Jacques Chirac in the 1988 presidential election. By mid-1990, Giscard had overtaken Chirac in the opinion poll ratings of hypothetical voting intentions on both first and second rounds of a future presidential election.

Throughout his career Giscard has attempted to construct a political image based upon modernity, competence, youth and *le changement sans risque*, the combination of moderate social change with a guarantee of political and economic stability. This personal image has been predicated upon the belief that the evolution of French society (in particular the breakdown of the traditional social classes and the development of the new tertiary sector) ought naturally to favour the non-ideological message of the 'centre' and to promote the values espoused by 'liberalism' (neither of which have the same connotations as in English, see below, pp. 122-3). That Giscard has been a prominent politician throughout the Fifth Republic stems partly from his skilful exploitation of favourable historical circumstances, partly from the originality of the political position he has generally succeeded in occupying (as head of an alternative, non-Gaullist centre of gravity for the right-wing coalition), and partly from his personal qualities, especially in relation to his toughness and durability, qualities demanded of any successful *présidentiable* in the Fifth Republic. It also reflects the fact that Giscard represents a deeply-rooted political and philosophical current within French history, that of the Orleanist right.

* *Raymond Barre*

The most serious obstacle to Giscard's renewed ambitions after 1981 was Raymond Barre, who had been Giscard's second Prime Minister from 1976-81. In a manner typical of the technocratic Fifth Republic, Giscard announced Barre to be the 'best economist in France', and named him Prime Minister despite the fact that he was a university professor with little prior formal political experience.[25] As Giscard's Prime Minister, Barre created the public image of being a loyal servant of the President, and consecrated his efforts to introducing a series of deflationary economic packages designed to combat spiralling inflation. The unpopularity of this economic medicine made Barre into the most unpopular Prime Minister of the Fifth Republic: a surprising base from which subsequently to become without question the UDF's most popular presidential candidate for 1988, and to be for a long time considered as Mitterrand's most formidable opponent. His emergence as a serious *présidentiable* probably owed more to the fact that his management of the economy while Prime Minister was vindicated post facto by the Socialists' economic U-turn of 1982-83 than it did to anything else: this transformed Barre's vigorous economic management into a political project in itself, legitimised by the behaviour of the Socialist adversary in government. Moreover, Giscard's discredit after his 1981 defeat proved stubborn and durable, whereas Chirac's intransigent style of opposition facilitated Barre's task in appealing to the *déçus du socialisme* more effectively than the RPR leader.

This is not the place for a detailed analysis of Raymond Barre's career: the interested reader will find this documented elsewhere.[26] To summarise, three closely related aspects characterised Barre's political activity from 1981-88: his Gaullien conception of politics and political parties, which led him to distance himself considerably - and ultimately fruitlessly - from the UDF; his cultivation of a precise image which placed his claimed economic credibility at the centre of his discourse and presidential message; and (linked to the first) his defence of the institutions of the Fifth Republic, associated prior to 1986 with dire predictions of institutional disorder in the event of *cohabitation*. In all three spheres, Barre attempted to position himself as a providential recourse to rescue the nation from predicted (economic or institutional) crisis. His ultimate failure rested at least in part on his misrepresentation of both the economy and the institutions, and the failure of the announced crises to materialise.

* *Jean Lecanuet*

Jean Lecanuet has acquired the cachet of being the Grandfather of centrism. At various stages throughout his career, he has occupied a number of prestigious political positions: President of the MRP from 1962-66, President of the Democratic Centre from 1966-76, and of its successor the CDS from 1976-82, President of the UDF from 1978-88. Despite this, he has failed to occupy any of the real summits of political power. The most important historical role performed by Lecanuet was as the centre's first presidential candidate in 1965: by failing to win through to the second ballot against de Gaulle in 1965 - to the benefit of François Mitterrand, the united left's candidate - Lecanuet illustrated the obstacles facing the independent centre in a bipolarising Fifth Republic.

As the most prominent centrist after 1965, Lecanuet was behind all of the various attempts to construct the independent centre as a viable alternative to both left and right, until finally inciting the centrists to support Giscard in 1974 and then to join the UDF in 1978. Lecanuet was President of the UDF from 1978 until Giscard took over in 1988. Once President of the UDF, Lecanuet withdrew somewhat from his identification with the CDS he had helped to found, resigned the presidency of the party in 1982 and made clear his belief that the CDS would have no future outside of the UDF. As argued below, his functions as President were largely symbolic, overshadowed by those of Jean-Claude Gaudin, President of the UDF group within the National Assembly. Despite this, he performed an important background role in permanently attempting to reconcile the frequently opposing fractions of the UDF.

* *Simone Veil*

Simone Veil is another personality strongly associated in the public mind with the UDF. She was for long one of the most popular French politicians, rising to the public's attention as Giscard's Health minister in 1974, when she had the difficult task of forcing the legalisation of abortion through the National Assembly, against the opposition of Gaullists and many Giscardians. Her strong public profile incited Giscard to entrust Simone Veil with leading the UDF list for the 1979 European election, at which the confederation registered its best ever score (27.39 per cent, compared with 16.09 per cent for the RPR). She was again head of a European list in 1984, this time a joint UDF-RPR list. That she was able to impose a joint list upon her reluctant colleagues (including Giscard and Léotard) testified to her political muscle: it also earned her the enmity of many within the UDF.

During the Mitterrand *septennat*, Veil remained symbolic of a spirit of tolerance which appeared often sadly lacking within the right-wing opposition. This was typified notably by her strong reaction against local UDF-RPR parties which sought to strike electoral bargains with the National Front, and by a firm anti-racist discourse which others - for tactical reasons - found inconvenient. After Mitterrand's re-election, Veil appeared as one of the centre-right politicians most likely to respond to Mitterrand's call for an opening up of the presidential majority to incorporate centrists, as well as being one of the most favourable to the creation of an autonomous, pro-Barre centre party. In June 1989, she led the unsuccessful autonomous centre list at the European election. Her future, in national politics at least, appears uncertain.

* *François Léotard and Pierre Méhaignerie*

Usually considered as second-rank leaders, these *frères-ennemis* have presided over the Republican Party and the CDS respectively since 1982.

François Léotard made a brilliant entry into political life in 1977, when he was elected as mayor of Fréjus (Var), followed in 1978 by his election to the National Assembly as a deputy for the Var department. He took over as leader of the Republicans in September 1982, with the clear consent of Giscard (who was anxious to renew his image by surrounding himself with young turks). Once in control, however, Léotard made it clear that the Republican Party was to be *his* political vehicle and undertook vigorous efforts to install his own followers at all levels of the party.

Despite this, his control over the Republican Party since 1982 has often appeared shaky. His personal initiatives have frequently been erratic, inconsequential or contradictory, such as his bluffed threat to run his own list against an official RPR-UDF one in 1984, or his controversial behaviour as Minister of Culture in Chirac's government. Despite forwarding himself as a *présidentiable* with great fanfare, no-one outside his tightly-knit band of followers took this claim seriously. Notwithstanding these shortcomings, Léotard did contribute towards presenting a youthful, dynamic image for the Republican Party after the early discredit of Giscard's defeat in 1981. His presence at the head of the PR symbolised the advent of a new political generation to posts of responsibility. His position has appeared gravely weakened since September 1989, when his arch-rival Charles Millon (the architect of Barre's campaign, and the man Léotard defeated for the party leadership in 1982) gained control of the UDF parliamentary group against Léotard's challenge. Léotard's decision to stake his political reputation on becoming President of the UDF-group was tactically inept for a politician aspiring for the status of a *présidentiable*.[27]

Pierre Méhaignerie succeeded Lecanuet to the presidency of the CDS in May 1982. He was firmly committed to retaining the CDS within the UDF. Méhaignerie's style of leadership has been very much in the aggregate, somewhat self-effacing Christian-democratic tradition, reflecting deeply rooted suspicions of strong personal leadership. This sets the modest, provincial Pierre Méhaignerie apart from the ebullient, *énarque* François Léotard. It was perhaps surprising, then, that under Méhaignerie's leadership, the CDS gradually became seduced by Raymond Barre and began to conceive of itself as a presidential party. Hardly a *présidentiable* himself, Méhaignerie proved a competent minister in Chirac's government, and an acceptable, if unexceptional leader to the various currents irrigating the CDS. His national profile was raised considerably when, after Mitterrand's re-election, he was instrumental in encouraging the creation of an autonomous centre group (UDC) and urging the party to adopt the 'autonomous' strategy which performed with such mediocre results in the European election of June 1989.

Ideas, Ideologies and Policies

It is customary to locate the UDF as occupying the centre right of the political spectrum in France. Following René Rémond's now classic formulation of the right in France, observers have tended to situate the UDF as forming part of the 'Orleanist', or liberal right, as opposed to the Bonapartist tradition sometimes ascribed to Chirac's RPR.[28] Rémond's Orleanist right (which first prevailed during the constitutional monarchy of

Louis Philippe, 1830-48) is characterised by a commitment to moderate constitutionalism, to the rights of the individual, and of the *corps intermédiaires* as opposed to those of the state, or the 'people'. This extends especially to a belief in the merits of free enterprise and an acceptance of Guizot's maxim *enrichissez-vous*.[29] This is combined with a cautious acceptance of necessary social change, allied with a respect for hierarchies based on wealth and talent, making this variety of French conservatism naturally defensive of liberal capitalism, and the role of the bourgeoisie within it. The UDF, the Republicans in particular, can best be portrayed as the latest historical manifestation of the *modérés* - in some senses the republican variant of older Orleanist traditions. The heyday of the *modérés* was in the Third Republic. They were cautious, conservative republicans, in theory suspicious of excessive centralisation and defensive of local provincial autonomy against the centralising tendencies of Paris. Likewise, prominent Republicans today are frequently provincial notables presiding over often-impregnable local power bases. It should be pointed out, however, that the UDF has reconciled the older Orleanist and conservative republican traditions with newer features deeply rooted within the Fifth Republic: many of the leading personalities within the UDF - for example Giscard d'Estaing, or Léotard - are products of the technocratic, Parisian background typical of the political elite in the Fifth Republic. Finally, whereas the Orleanist tradition stresses a belief in the merits of non-authoritarian representative, parliamentary institutions, the term Giscardian, while accepting all of the above, has also implied an approval of the institutions of the Fifth Republic, especially the directly elected presidency, which was initially condemned by many conservatives (those who remained within CNIP) as Bonapartist and dictatorial. The Giscardian right can therefore best be understood as a modern expression of the Orleanist tradition, modified to suit the political regime of the Fifth Republic.

This description of the Orleanist right fits certain of the component elements of the UDF more obviously than others, the Republicans more than the CDS. In fact, the range of ideological opinions represented by the component parties of the UDF is considerable (with diverging opinions sometimes being expressed within as well as between parties). The ideological consistency of all of these organisations, and their precursors, has never been particularly great; they have prided themselves instead on their flexibility and their adaptability to new ideas. Moreover, ideology, in the broad definition of the term, has never traditionally been as important for these parties as it has for the parties of the left, or even, arguably, for the Gaullist Party. Despite this, each formation within the UDF can trace its genealogy back to a particular strand of thought, deeply rooted in past French history. These ideological currents have occasionally occupied opposing positions on the political spectrum, notably social catholicism, anti-clerical radicalism and 'laissez-faire' liberalism.

The parties which came to together to form the UDF in 1978 implicitly accepted the objectives of President's Giscard's political testament, *La démocratie française*, published in 1976 as a theoretical justification for his presidency.[30] Although Giscard claimed to be both a 'centrist', and a 'liberal', these notions should not be understood in the Anglo-Saxon sense, but in a continental European and more specifically French one. The idea of the centre has classically had conservative connotations in France, where, partly as a by-product of the legacy of the French revolution, the notion of the right has been removed from the acceptable ideological lexicon (except at the extreme), and even today no self-respecting moderate conservative will admit to being a Man of the Right, preferring to take refuge in the 'centre'. The notion of liberalism is even more vague: it has usually been associated with the economic, free-market variety, rather than the political genre.

As President, Giscard attempted, to some extent, to combine both political and economic liberalism. The early emphasis during his presidency on social justice, and on political liberalism and the promotion of civil liberties was given expression, for example, in the liberalisation of divorce, the legalisation of abortion, the lowering of the age of majority to 18, the reform of the Constitutional Council and a number of other liberal societal measures.[31] In his book *La démocratie française*, Giscard outlined four main objectives of the 'advanced liberal society': social justice, civil and political liberties, respect for representative institutions, and decentralisation. As President, Giscard was generally regarded as more liberal than most of his lieutenants, including most of his Republican supporters. Indeed, unlike UDF platforms in the 1980s, Giscard's proposed 'advanced liberal society' contained an element of progressive social reform. This was symbolised, for example, by the attempted introduction of a capital gains tax, despised by the 'true' economic liberals in the RI/RPR, as well as by a number of welfare measures, aimed in particular at improving the position of working women. Left-wing critics dismissed this as largely 'liberal window-dressing', which was counterbalanced by a distinctly illiberal stance on immigration, on state-security, on civil and judicial rights, but it should be pointed out that even Giscard's limited reformism was unwelcome to many right-wing deputies. Despite considerable hype, it was difficult to reconcile the professed objectives of his 'advanced liberal society' with the achievements of his term in office. To take one example, for all his talk of political liberalism and restored constitutionalism, under Giscard presidential interventionism reached unprecedented, occasionally ridiculous new heights; this was far more important than his symbolic tinkering with parliamentary reform. The few liberal societal or political reforms that did materialise generally aroused greater enthusiasm amongst the left-wing parties than they did amongst the President's own supporters, and occasionally (as with abortion) depended upon the former for their enactment. However genuine the reforming aspirations of President Giscard had been in 1974, by 1976 - and especially after the 1978 parliamentary elections, once that the left's challenge had been fought off - his administration succumbed to a more conservative preservation of the status quo in all areas of society, and a vigorous economic management under Raymond Barre. Arguably, Giscard had no alternative: the fate of the early reformist measures illustrated unambiguously that his parliamentary majority (composed of Republicans, centrists and Gaullists) was a conservative one, hostile to any attempts by the state to interfere in property rights (witness the fate of Giscard's proposed capital gains tax of 1976, introduced by Chirac, which was rendered innocuous after stiff opposition from members of the presidential majority). The final period of the Giscard presidency witnessed a brutal and unexpected fall from grace, in which the President became implicated in a series of scandals and suspected abuses of power.

Just as the Orleanist right has classically been divided between more liberal and more conservative-inclined elements, so the UDF has contained within its ranks a broad variety of opinions, bordering the PS on its left and, arguably, the National Front on its right. Let us consider briefly the ideological identities of the UDF's two main families:

* *The Republican Party*

According to Frears, 'the Independent Republicans have been far more the instrument of Giscard d'Estaing than ever Gaullist parties were of de Gaulle'.[32] At its formative Congress in 1977, the PR announced its commitment to the principles of Giscard's 'advanced liberal society'.[33] It singled out a number of liberties as particularly worth defending, including: the freedom of private enterprise, freedom from excessive state intervention in the economic sphere, and the freedom of educational choice. These freedoms gave a clear indication of the ideological colouring of the Republicans' commitment to liberalism. This was coupled with a strong attack against trade unions and strikes. At an early stage, any assessment of the Republicans' beliefs was, perhaps, as Frears suggests, partly synonymous with charting the course of Giscard's philosophy, but this should not obscure the fact that divergences of opinion had always existed within the ranks of the Republicans: for example, in 1969, when four-fifths of Independent Republican deputies refused to follow Giscard in his rejection of de Gaulle's referendum. Moreover, the conservative provincial notables within the Republicans barely concealed their unease with Giscard's reforming measures, although usually publicly loyally supporting the President.

If it were at least partially true that the PR derived its *raison d'être* from supporting President Giscard until 1981, such a conclusion could no longer be maintained once that he had lost the presidency. Once in opposition the various components of the UDF, along with the RPR, underwent what must be described as a rightwards shift, in opposition to the radical policies of Pierre Mauroy's governments after May 1981. The Republicans were in the forefront of this 'liberal' re-evaluation, although even when the party appeared committed to the most uncompromising form of free-market liberalism, there remained dissenting voices against the leadership. A degree of ideological ecumenicism subsisted within the PR, but the dominant impression was that of the development in the mid-1980s of hardline 'liberalism', inspired by Anglo-Saxon conservatism. This culminated in the joint RPR-UDF common platform for the 1986 legislative election, the ideas of which were given full expression during Jacques Chirac's 1986-88 administration.

* *The CDS*

The CDS claims to be the inheritor of the social catholicism of the great party of the Fourth Republic, the Popular Republican Movement (MRP). In practice, this has meant that it has been somewhat less-inclined to accept the unregulated free market than other formations, and more anxious in relation to social protection, and the search for societal consensus. The 'social' aspect of the CDS and the past alliances of the old MRP with the Socialists probably helped the 'centrists' in their majority conviction that they represented the centre left of the political spectrum. In common with the old MRP, the CDS was ferociously favourable to European unity and the construction of a federal Europe. In fact, the CDS shared many of the problems which had beset its illustrious predecessor. The MRP had never really been able to choose between the natural reformist aspirations of many of its leaders and activists, and the conservative profile of its electorate. It had gradually sacrificed the former to the latter, but in so doing had lost the dynamic party activists it had initially attracted. Likewise, the natural sympathies of most CDS activists and politicians lay with a vaguely reforming social catholicism, but its electorate was largely composed of rural, conservative (disproportionately practising) Catholics.[34]

Once out of office after 1981 many of the specific characteristics of the CDS gave way to the general imperatives of the opposition: perhaps conscious of its weakness (it was reduced to 21 deputies in the 1981 elections), the CDS, under the influence of Méhaignerie's leadership, gradually silenced most of its policy differences with other components of the opposition. According to Dreyfus, the CDS abandoned - albeit temporarily - certain salient aspects of the Christian-democratic tradition, in particular its emphasis on the priority need for social justice, its hostility to the unregulated free market and its cult of solidarity.[35] In its 1983 manifesto, the CDS declared 'France will become prosperous once again only if its enterprises lead the way', and accepted a battery of proposals, such as the privatisation programme, with which it would previously have felt ill at ease. This evolution reflected firstly the growing sympathy felt for Raymond Barre, whose commitment to classical economic liberalism was unquestionable; secondly, the influence of the West German CDU, whose success served as a model, and finally the rejection of the sectarianism of the 1981-82 period.

From the Advanced Liberal Society to the Liberal Project

There was much talk within the UDF, especially amongst the leaders of the Republican Party, but also from Barre, or Giscard, of the 'liberal project' (*projet libéral*), forwarded by its most fervent supporters as a panacea for the ills of socialism. This involved a commitment to liberalism as a precise economic project/dogma. It involved a belief in the virtues of the free market and in 'rolling back the frontiers of the state' in all areas of social and economic activity, a belief predicated upon 'liberal' experience in Thatcher's Britain, Reagan's United States and Kohl's West Germany. A series of precise measures were drawn up, which formed the core of the RPR-UDF common platform of February 1986, and subsequently provided a manifesto upon which Jacques Chirac's government acted.

The central tenets of this programme were based around the idea that the state should be reduced to its essential functions of defence and law and order; that privatisation of nationalised industries and deregulation of bureaucratic controls would stimulate market-based economic revival, as well as combatting unemployment and promoting the development of a popular capitalism (of the sort designed to favour conservative-style parties); that supply side fiscal reforms would stimulate investment; that public expenditure had to be strictly controlled in order to combat inflation and that all artificial constraints to the free operation of the market should ultimately be removed. In fact, as Andrew Knapp illustrates in the next chapter, in practice Chirac's government applied these measures in an uneven manner: despite a huge programme of denationalisation, for example, the state retained a large measure of influence over the new private sector industries.[36]

Was there, in fact, any difference between the much-vaunted 'liberal project' which underpinned the RPR-UDF common platform, and the activities of Chirac's government, and Giscard's 'advanced liberal society'? Despite the rhetoric informing the latter, there was little evidence to suggest that President Giscard had introduced any substantial degree of liberalism (lessening of state intervention) in the economic sphere. Rather, he continued with classic practices of industrial interventionism. In contrast, a modest degree of political liberalism and social reform took place under Giscard of a type which would have been quite alien to the 1986-88 government. The political project espoused in the RPR-UDF platform of February 1986 (fully supported by Giscard) involved a more forthright, if imperfect, commitment to economic liberalism, notably in the form of wide-scale privatisation and deregulation, counterbalanced by a strong measure of political conservatism (especially over immigration). The contrast between Giscard's 'advanced liberal society' and the activities of Chirac's government indicated that the French right had evolved, *to some extent* calling into question the traditional *dirigiste*-style policies of the Fifth Republic, under the joint impact of foreign experiences (in the UK, in West Germany, in the US) and the extreme unpopularity of the left's interventionism. The experience of the Chirac government also suggested, however, that the French right lagged far behind its counterparts in comparable nations in its commitment to economic liberalism.

The UDF: A Confederation of Political Parties, 1978-88

Since its inception, the UDF's main difficulty has been that of existing. In fact, it has never really existed as a cohesive political organisation, except arguably from 1978-81 when it was dedicated to supporting President Giscard. The UDF is in reality a confederation of independent parties, each with long histories and traditions. It has never succeeded in superimposing a federal identity upon the individual parties, mainly because these parties stoutly have refused any such outcome. Besides, even in its statutes, adopted in September 1983, the UDF defined itself as a confederation, an 'association of independent political parties'.[37] As with any confederation, the UDF's structures were extremely weak, aimed at ensuring a minimal acceptable degree of coordination between its constituent parties, especially on an electoral level. They were far weaker than in any other of the main political formations. The composite nature of the UDF almost inevitably provoked an ongoing debate as to whether it should attempt to become a genuine federation (with a large measure of binding central authority over constituent members) or even a single political party; or whether the confederal solution was the only which allowed the UDF to survive at all. Each party considered the UDF in terms of its own interests, and pledged its loyalty accordingly. From its inception, and especially after 1981, the two principal parties - the PR and the CDS - made it clear that any evolution towards a genuine federation would be unacceptable. The PR envisaged its role within the UDF as that of the leading party, and periodically demanded that the principle of 'one man, one vote' be respected, which would give it greater influence on the UDF's governing organs. But even the PR rejected a genuine federal solution, which would weaken its identity - despite Giscard's early pressure in this direction.[38] The CDS, for its part, feared losing its reformist identity in a fused conservative party or a genuine federation. The smaller parties, over-represented in the UDF's governing organs due to the confederal principle (respect for party autonomy, equality between individual parties), fiercely opposed pressures towards federation or fusion. In fact, only the direct members were consistently in favour of such an outcome.

A number of consequences flowed from the organisational structure of the UDF, testament to the weakness of the confederation. There existed - in reality if not in theory - two mutually reinforcing rules: those of unanimity and non-decision making. In theory, decisions adopted by a three-quarters majority were binding upon member parties, but in practice the only decisions which were effective were those upon which all member parties could agree. Where disputes arose between the UDF's constituent parties, decisions were either postponed or abandoned. This situation was aggravated by the over-representation of the smaller formations within the UDF, and by the often endemic opposition (especially over personality and political strategy) between the PR and the CDS. Moreover, party spokesmen would frequently give contradictory statements when responding to issues of immediate political concern. The result of these pressures was too often impasse, overcome only with the approach of elections.

The 'decision-making' organs of the UDF were reduced to a strict minimum. At the grass-roots level, the UDF was in practice synonymous with the local organisation of the respective member parties, with one party often being clearly predominant (for example the CDS in the east, the PR in the southeast). During the entire period from 1981-88, only one National Congress was held, despite this body being given responsibility in UDF statutes for defining general policy. Because the Pontoise Congress in October 1982 had been transformed into a pro-Giscard rally, the anti-Giscard forces within the UDF were determined to avoid any repetition in the future. The preponderance of *élus*, holders of public office, was obvious at each level of the confederation, from the base to the summit. This reflected the legitimacy conferred by public office within what was in reality a collection of cadre parties, such as described by Maurice Duverger.[39] This was obvious in relation to the UDF's two real 'decision-making' organs, the National Council (*Conseil national*) and the Political Bureau (*Bureau politique*). Within the National Council, given responsibility for defining general orientations, each member party had in theory the same number of representatives (four), in accordance with the confederal principle of equality between independent sovereign parties. The tiny PSD, with three deputies in 1988, thus obtained a parity of representation with the PR or CDS. The formal equality of the confederal principle was offset somewhat by the practice of inviting a number of ex officio participants to attend the National Council: these included representatives of UDF senators, deputies and European deputies, as well as members of the smaller Political Bureau. This in practice moderated the principle of parity, since the larger formations were better represented in these institutions.

At the apex of the UDF structure was the Political Bureau. This was in principle charged with executing the decisions reached by Congress and the National Council, but in practice it was the only really important (non-parliamentary) decision-making organ. The Political Bureau derived its status from the fact that the leaders of all of the constituent parties participated in its meetings. The same observations made in relation to the National Council apply to the Political Bureau:

* There is formal parity between component member-parties, with each naming two representatives, always including the party leader, who sit along with the President of the UDF.

* This is tempered by the ex-officio participation of the Presidents of the UDF group in the National Assembly, the UDF intergroup in the Senate, as well as that of Giscard (ex-President of the Republic) and Veil (ex-President of the European parliament). The rule of unanimity has usually limited the effectiveness even of the Political Bureau, unless there has been broad agreement amongst the party leaders, or else unless certain leaders have been prepared to compromise, as for example Léotard did in 1984 over the issue of a joint RPR-UDF list for the European election.

As an association of cadre parties, it is perhaps hardly surprising that the real focus of UDF organisation between 1978 and 1988 should lie with the parliamentary group in the National Assembly. All UDF deputies sat within one group from 1978 to 1988.[40] The parliamentary group was the only element of the UDF in which a 'federal' mentality genuinely prevailed. UDF deputies recognised the political value of adopting a common outlook, to preserve a degree of unity and tactical manoeuvre vis-à-vis the RPR. It was relatively easy for all UDF deputies to oppose the Socialist-led governments of 1981-86 with equal vigour, because there was little real policy disagreement between the constituent parties. It was rather more difficult to occult the profound divisions caused by *cohabitation* and the approach of the 1988 presidential elections. But the UDF group in the National Assembly remained remarkably cohesive, especially by comparison with the extra-parliamentary organs of the UDF and the component parties.

The creation of the centrist UDC parliamentary group in June 1988 (see below) seriously damaged the UDF's cohesion precisely because its deputies had performed such a central role within the confederation. The President of the UDF group in the Assembly from

1981-89, Jean-Claude Gaudin, performed a crucial coordinating role. His detached position allowed Gaudin to ease the tensions between supporters of rival *présidentiables* Barre, Giscard and Léotard, especially during the period of *cohabitation* and in the run-up to the 1988 presidential election. Indeed, he performed this role of UDF-arbiter more effectively than did Lecanuet, the official UDF President. The importance of the presidency of the parliamentary group was illustrated by the fact that prior to the legislative elections of 1986 and 1988, it was Gaudin who led the UDF team in electoral negotiations with the RPR.

Finally, the UDF was a highly efficient electoral cartel in legislative and municipal elections, if not in relation to the presidential contest. The institutional and political pressures constraining the constituent parties of UDF to join forces in 1978 were still intact ten years laters and would conceivably remain so in the foreseeable future. Even in 1986, fought under a system of proportional representation, the perspective of governing with the RPR after the election acted as a powerful inducement for the UDF to agree upon a comprehensive electoral pact with their future coalition partners. Electoral agreements with the RPR were reached in 1978, 1981, 1986 and 1988. The UDF structure facilitated electoral cooperation between the various formations of the moderate right (enabling them to secure a relatively harmonious division of constituencies amongst themselves), as well as providing a formal structure in their dealings with the RPR. But the UDF was far less effective in relation to the presidential contest: indeed, the cohesion of the confederation was rudely called into question by the problem of presidentialism.

The creation of the Union for France (UPF) as a confederation between the UDF and the RPR in June 1990 added a new dimension to the debate over the nature of the confederation as a political organisation. The two formations agreed to go beyond informal collaboration, and to coordinate their activity by means of a Political Bureau, composed of an equal number of representatives of each formation (15).[41] It remained to be seen whether this new 'confederation' would prove any more robust an organisation than that constituted by the UDF itself; a priori, the mere fact of adding together a still broader range of often-conflicting forces made such a prospect appear unlikely.

The Problem of Presidentialism

The UDF was formed in 1978 as a presidential-inspired confederation. Giscard's ultimate aim in creating the UDF went beyond the immediate one of saving the 1978 legislative elections. His aspiration was that the constituent elements of his presidential majority would fuse into one coherent centre-right formation able to provide support and inspiration for the President. The UDF, initially a substitute for the lack of a presidential party, would in time be transformed into such a party. After Giscard had been re-elected to the presidency in 1981, such a formation would become established as the main political force of the centre and right, forcing the RPR into a subordinate role. This strategic calculation was laid asunder by Giscard's defeat in the 1981 presidential election. Before 1981, loyalty to the President had acted as the main source of internal cohesion for the UDF, whereas after 1981 presidentialism had a corrosive, rather than a cohesive effect. During the first term of the left in power (1981-86), the UDF was seriously divided between the claims of its rival *présidentiables*, Giscard and Barre.[42] This situation became even more complicated after 1986, as Léotard, head of the Republican Party, declared that he might stand in the 1988 presidential election. Support for Chirac's presidential bid also developed within the UDF, especially within the Radical Party.

The UDF provides a model study for the potentially negative impact of presidentialism upon the cohesion of political parties in the Fifth Republic. The presidentialised character of the French regime has imposed its own laws upon the political parties. To be politically successful a party needs to stand a reasonable chance of electing its candidate to the presidency. Each serious party must have a credible presidential candidate, recognised as such in terms of opinion poll popularity and ability to cope with the media (see Chapter Two). But should any formation have more than one credible *présidentiable,* it is likely to be subject to intense internal pressures, as supporters of rival candidates organise to secure the maximum possible backing for their presidential favourite. Within the UDF, this problem was exacerbated by the almost total lack of any internal disciplinary procedures, which might have been used by one presidential contender to discredit or attempt to silence his main rival. Certain similarities existed between the rivalry which pitted Giscard and Barre against each other from 1983-87 to that which separated Mitterrand and Rocard for the PS nomination in 1981 (see Chapter Four).[43] There was, however, one critical difference: within the pre-1981 PS, there existed a statutory selection procedure for choosing the party's candidate, which meant that potential candidates had to address themselves not only to public opinion, but also to party activists. The party controlled its own selection procedure, at least in theory. This meant that both Mitterrand and Rocard had officially to respect an organised timetable and a minimum number of ground rules and had to take account of party opinion in refining their strategies. The difference between the pre-1981 PS and the UDF was that the former was a genuine party, the latter was not. Neither Giscard, nor Barre paid even lip-service to the UDF in justifying their presidential credentials. Because the central federal organisation was virtually non-existent, no one candidate could use disciplinary procedures and public warnings to attempt to discredit his rival. The party (UDF) had no influence over whether a particular candidate would decide to stand or not. And of course there was no formal selection procedure. The more the party (UDF) was under-valued, the less likely it would act as a constraint on the competing *présidentiables,* and in turn the more encouragement was given to politicians of a lesser calibre such as Léotard to chance their hand.

The UDF was an efficient electoral cartel in legislative elections, but could not pretend as much in relation to the presidential contest (the decisive election in the Fifth Republic). Unlike in legislative elections, where each party respected the UDF's federal authority, there were no formal means for arbitrating between the rival claims of different presidential contenders. The weak federal character of the UDF and the restrictive notion of the place of political parties shared by both Giscard and Barre meant that the 'party' was the last conceivable institution likely to be able to arbitrate between rival candidates. Both pretenders reiterated their belief that the idea of national unification embodied in the presidential office precluded any serious candidate from explicitly seeking the nomination of a political party.

Presidentialism had a divisive effect not only on the UDF as a confederation, but also split each constituent party into different factions supporting particular *présidentiables.* Competition between Giscard, Barre and Chirac for presidential supremacy on the right also had a divisive impact upon the relationship between the UDF and RPR (see Chapter One). It is not proposed to analyse the fine detail of the presidential strategies of Giscard or Barre towards the 1988 election: these lie beyond the sphere of competence, stricto sensu, of an analysis of the UDF. Rather, we shall illustrate how a disdain for the UDF weakened Barre's campaign. After a five-year period spent attempting to recover his lost popularity, Giscard finally announced in January 1987 that he would not be standing again at the next presidential election. For all of his efforts, the ex-President had never been able to overcome widespread public apathy, even antipathy towards his personality since

1981. Once Giscard had announced his decision not to stand again for the presidency in 1988, nothing (including the presumptuous Léotard) could prevent the UDF from declaring its support for Barre, whose 1988 campaign disappointed even his most fervent supporters.

It was remarked above that Barre's over-concentration on institutional questions and his refusal of *cohabitation* had proved a negative factor during the 1986 campaign. His catastrophic predictions of institutional paralysis and instability proved groundless. One consequence of the rigid institutional position adopted by Barre prior to 1986 was his refusal to create any movement which could be labelled as a party: that would transgress what he interpreted as the fundamental principles of the Gaullien notion of presidential legitimacy. No President, aspiring to represent the entire nation, should be beholden to the interests of a particular fraction of it. In fact, Barre misinterpreted the role and underestimated the usefulness of the presidential party. All Presidents of the Fifth Republic, excepting Giscard, had been able to call upon the electoral infrastructure provided by a political party to help organise their presidential campaigns: de Gaulle's UNR, Pompidou's UDR, and Mitterrand's PS. The only exception was Giscard in 1974. It should be noted, however, that Giscard's election had been greatly facilitated by the paralysis of the Gaullist UDR, and its division into reformist and conservative camps. And once elected President, Giscard attempted to construct the PR, and later the UDF into a genuine presidential party, able to articulate the President's will and intermediate between the head of state and the electorate.

Instead of relying on party, Barre had early on allowed his followers to create a national chain of support committees, the REEL network. The initiative to create the REEL committees was taken as early as 1984 by the pro-Barre minority within the PR, anxious to organise in support of its presidential favourite and to counter Léotard's influence. These committees were rather more like decentralised political clubs than anything else. They were suspected from all sides within the UDF, so much so that Barre announced their dissolution in February 1988 along with his decision to stand for President. They were replaced by official presidential support committees within which all elements of the UDF were represented. But Barre steadfastly refused to allow any of the party leaders to take independent initiatives in his favour, and excluded the UDF as an official organisation.

The potential advantage with such a flexible structure was that it confirmed his position 'above parties', which might have been an advantage for the second ballot of a presidential election, when the successful candidate has to appeal to as broad a spectrum of opinion as possible. But before reaching the decisive second round a candidate has to mobilise his natural supporters on the first ballot. The 1988 presidential election suggested that the support of a party remained a useful, arguably essential precondition for a successful presidential bid. By condemning political parties outright, Barre weakened the logistical bases of support for his candidacy. Although the UDF officially declared its support for Barre certain elements within the federation virtually refused to campaign for 'their' candidate, and did little to hide their preference for Chirac in the right-wing primary. This was notably the case for Léotard, and the Radical leader André Rossinot. The central paradox was that having derided parties for so long, Barre was eventually forced to call upon the UDF to mobilise support in favour of his flagging campaign. Thus, he participated in a series of rallies with prominent UDF politicians, and eventually accepted the creation of a Political Council, within which most UDF leaders participated. Despite this eleventh hour reversal, he ended up appearing as an isolated loner, lacking the support of any established political party.

Barre's mediocre performance (16.54 per cent) after years of promising opinion polls could not be traced primarily to his poor campaign, or even to the lack of committed party support. Rather, it stemmed from an unfortunate political conjuncture, and the strategic limitations of centrism. Mitterrand's successful positioning as President of all the French during the period of *cohabitation*, his appeal to *la France unie* during the campaign and his call for an 'opening up' of the presidential majority all enabled the outgoing President to attract centre-right support which might otherwise have rallied to Barre. Moreover, unlike Giscard in 1974 or 1981, Barre suffered from being reduced to appearing as a 'centre' candidate, rather than a conservative candidate seeking to attract centrist political support (which better corresponded to his actual position). This was unfortunate, since it weakened his appeal amongst conservative voters, who generally preferred Chirac. By criticising Chirac, Barre distanced himself from the 1986-88 government, which had proved extremely popular amongst the core conservative electorate. Reduced to representing the 'centre', Barre's electorate was squeezed between more powerful centre-left and neo-Gaullist alternatives. The centre did not constitute a sufficient core of electoral support to enable Barre to win through to the second ballot, where the opinion polls suggested he would have been a formidable challenger to Mitterrand.

The 1988 presidential elections (as well as those of 1974 and 1981) provided more than sufficient evidence to testify to the damaging effects of rival first-round candidates upon the right's cohesion as a whole. In June 1990, after much internal manoeuvring for position, Giscard and Chirac and their respective formations agreed to the creation of the Union for France as a new confederation between RPR and UDF, and to the organisation of US-style primaries prior to the next presidential election.[44] Whether the organisation of primaries would be sufficient to resolve the right's problems was uncertain: underlying divergences are rarely smoothed away by purely institutional remedies. It is plausible to contend that the divisions brought out into the open by a bitterly fought primary campaign might actually exacerbate pre-existing rivalries between candidates and make eventual cooperation more difficult. But the lamentable effect of presidential rivalries on the right's divisions meant that desperate remedies had at least to be attempted.

Future Perspectives

The problems which faced the UDF after the 1988 elections were of an unprecedented gravity. Barre's defeat deprived the UDF of the possibility of performing once again the role of 'presidential party' it had enjoyed from 1978 to 1981. Each component of the UDF suffered from the confusion created by Mitterrand's victory. By the beginning of the 1990s, a clarification of what had become an extremely confused situation appeared vital if the right was to recover its cohesion.

The immediate source of the UDF's malaise lay in the 1988 elections themselves. The CDS initially responded to Mitterrand's victory (and Barre's defeat) by declaring its interest in the former's proposed 'opening up' of the presidential majority. Centrist leaders had engaged in covert discussions with both Mitterrand and Rocard before and immediately after the presidential election.[45] Any chance of a formal coalition between a moderate Socialist government led by Rocard and the CDS evaporated when Mitterrand dissolved the National Assembly some five days after his re-election. The CDS reacted to this 'provocative' act by reaffirming its traditional alliance within the opposition, thus in practice signifying the end of hopes (entertained by some) for a change of coalition partner. The CDS's longings for autonomy and independence continued in practice to be moderated by the conservative nature of its electorate, and electoral realities which constrained it to alliance within the UDF, at least during an election fought under the second-ballot system.

Mitterrand's dissolution reinforced the need for electoral cooperation between the UDF and the RPR. In an attempt to minimise the expected PS landslide, the RPR and UDF agreed to present single candidates from the first ballot in the bulk of constituencies.[46] The UDF again showed its efficiency as an electoral cartel, both in terms of arbitrating between rival claims within the UDF, and in negotiating with the RPR. Under Giscard's initiative, the UDF and RPR formed the *Union du rassemblement et du centre* (URC), a comprehensive electoral agreement based on single UDF or RPR candidates from the first ballot. The URC alliance (with 40.52 per cent on the first ballot compared with 37.88 per cent for the PS) performed far better than expected: the PS landslide did not materialise.

But however well the UDF formed as an electoral cartel (and for the first time it returned more deputies than the RPR), it remained politically weak because seriously divided. The idea of centrist 'autonomy' (conveniently suspended during the election campaign to allow the CDS to reelect its deputies) reemerged after the June 1988 election. The CDS leader Méhaignerie officially announced the creation of a separate parliamentary group, the Union of the Centre (UDC), on 15 June 1988, only days after the second ballot. This initiative was fiercely resisted by both Giscard and Léotard, who demanded the exclusion of the CDS from the UDF. The formation of the UDC represented the most serious step so far in the dislocation of the UDF.

One of the great paradoxes of Mitterrand's re-election was that it facilitated Giscard's renewed authority within the UDF, as well as within the wider UDF-RPR opposition. Giscard's political credibility had been greatly increased by not standing in the 1988 presidential election. In a reverse movement to that which occurred in 1981, the defeat of Chirac and Barre left Giscard as the only national opposition leader untainted with failure. The good performance of the UDF in the June parliamentary election increased Giscard's prestige, and removed any obstacles which had previously stood in the way of his taking over as President of the UDF. Giscard was duly elected as President of the UDF on June 30 1988. Any analysis of the 'UDF' since the 1988 elections must consider the centrist UDC group as a separate entity from the maintained UDF. We shall thus consider in turn the UDC, Giscard's UDF, and the future prospects of the non-Gaullist right and centre.

By creating the UDC parliamentary group, the centre recovered a degree of autonomy, but its identity remained ambiguous. In the first year of the UDC's existence, as a general rule the centre continued to align itself more frequently with the right-wing opposition than with the government, but declared its opposition to be 'constructive', and did not hesitate in supporting Rocard's government when it considered it suitable to do so. It was unclear, however, whether this new autonomy was fully understood by public opinion. Moreover, autonomy brought in its wake serious divisions within the CDS. By mid-1989, the party was divided between those who urged the creation of one unified confederation of the opposition (ranging from CDS to RPR); those who proclaimed the need for continuing centrist autonomy, with an ultimate view to creating a new expanded centre formation (to include Barrists and dissidents from parties other than the CDS), and those who advocated a return of all CDS deputies to the UDF parliamentary group.[47]

The autonomous position adopted by CDS leader Méhaignerie and Veil eventually won through in the run-up to the European election of June 1989, but only after considerable support for the idea of a united opposition list led by one of *rénovateurs* (see below). Had the CDS not presented its own list, there would have been little rationale for the continuation of the UDC as a separate parliamentary group apart from the UDF. The decision to present an autonomous centre list appeared to represent a further step in the disintegration of the UDF, although the poor performance (8.42 per cent) of the centrist list at the European election presaged a difficult future for an independent centre. The European election result demonstrated the relative electoral weakness of the centre, even in an apparently favourable election fought under a system of proportional representation. It repeated the centrists' classic dilemma: the centre lacked sufficient electoral strength to be able to survive in the longer term as an independent political formation in a bipolarising political system, except in alliance with other parties. It was in recognition of this constraint that the UDC group began to adopt a more resolute opposition to Rocard's government after the European election and agreed to the creation of the UDC-UDF-RPR intergroup in the National Assembly in September 1989. The tougher stance adopted by the UDC after the 1989 European election suggested that the parenthesis opened by Mitterrand's re-election had given way to a more classical model of confrontation between the presidential majority and the various opposition forces.

It has been claimed that the introduction of a system of pure proportional representation would enable the centre to exist in an autonomous manner, but the CDS (as well as its predecessors) has too often used the electoral system as a scapegoat for its woes for this argument to be fully convincing. Moreover, the centrists' demand for autonomy could not conceal the fact that CDS deputies had been elected by conservative electorates in the June 1988 legislative election, as had centrist mayors in the municipal election of March 1989.[48] Finally CDS leaders could not ignore that there had traditionally been a divergence between the conservative-inclined CDS electorate and the reformist aspirations of its leaders. The 'centre' is not an isolated political space. Both the PS and UDF (and to some extent the RPR) claim to represent centre opinion and there is no logical reason why any 'centrist' ideological evolution of the electorate should benefit the centre party, rather than its larger neighbours. This was a lesson eventually learnt to its cost, for example, by the Liberal/Social Democrat alliance in the UK, as well as by the centrists in France. The old adage that in the Fifth Republic elections have traditionally been won in the centre but not by the centre remains as true as ever. All these constraints pointed in the direction of severe limitations on the autonomy of the centre in the longer run. In fact, the participation of the CDS in the RPR/UDF confederation, the Union for France, created in June 1990, implied a clear acceptance by the centrists that the classical electoral agreement would be renewed for the next legislative elections, scheduled in 1993.

The formation of the UDC parliamentary group had greatly weakened that of the 'maintained' UDF. Under Giscard's leadership, the UDF remained afflicted by problems similar to those it had known throughout its existence, but in an exacerbated form: the weakness of the confederation vis-à-vis the constituent parties, disagreements over policy, the divisive impact of personal rivalries, and divergences in strategic outlook. To these classic sources of division were added new cleavages, especially relating to the rise of a new generation of dynamic young politicians, the *rénovateurs*. In the year following Mitterrand's re-election, inter-generational conflicts overshadowed all other sources of division within the right-wing opposition. These are fully dealt with in Chapter Seven. In the context of the UDF they comprised: firstly, the perennial struggle for influence separating Giscard and Léotard; secondly, more cogently, the challenge posed by the *rénovateurs* to the established UDF (and RPR) leaderships after the municipal election of March 1989. The challenge represented by the *rénovateurs* could be interpreted both as an inter-generational and a political one. The *rénovateurs* considered that for as long as the right remained enclosed within its existing structures, fundamental questions relating to its identity, policy, intellectual priorities, and partisan structures would remain stifled. This was a direct challenge to the established leadership of the right, embodied by the personalities of Giscard and Chirac. Of course, neither Giscard, nor Chirac really had any interest in encouraging the sort of debate the *rénovateurs* were demanding, since reform would occur at their expense.

The impetus which lay behind the breakthrough of the *rénovateurs* was the success in the March 1989 municipal election of a number of dynamic young opposition politicians, symbolised by the victory of the RPR's Michel Noir in Lyons. In the aftermath of Noir's municipal triumph, a group of twelve *rénovateurs*, drawn from the CDS, PR and RPR, publicly demanded an early fusion between the UDF (including the CDS) and the RPR, and for a joint RPR-UDF list, led by younger members of the opposition, for the 1989 European election. They threatened, if necessary, to run their own alternative list against an official list sponsored by the RPR-UDF.[49] It should be stressed that, contrary to the centrist autonomists, the *rénovateurs* were primarily interested in reinvigorating the entire opposition, rather than any particular fraction of it.

The *rénovateurs* eventually backed away from presenting their own list in June 1989. This illustrated both the internal contradictions within their ranks, and a certain political naivety. In their own way, they were all loyal to the notion that the unity of the opposition was imperative, albeit within renewed structures. But having declared themselves favourable to union, it was difficult in practice for the *rénovateurs* to run a separate list aimed against the established UDF and RPR leaderships. There could have been no more certain way of dividing an already-divided opposition still further. Like everybody else on the right, the *rénovateurs* were themselves hopelessly divided, as Andrew Knapp illustrates in chapter seven. Once they had withdrawn their threat of a separate list, they allowed the political initiative to be recovered by the traditional 'historical chiefs' of the right and centre.

With the support of Chirac, a large majority of the UDF executive eventually endorsed Giscard as the leader of a joint UDF-RPR list for the European election. Immediately afterwards the CDS announced its decision to run its separate list. By approving the ex-President of the Republic as head of the European list, Giscard's rivals undoubtedly hoped and expected to exile him to Strasbourg, and remove him from the forefront of the domestic political scene. Such hopes were disappointed; indeed, contrary to many expectations, Giscard's list performed well in June 1989, comfortably outdistancing the PS list led by Laurent Fabius (28.88 to 23.61 per cent). By choosing to head a joint UDF-RPR list excluding the CDS, Giscard testified that his long-standing commitment in favour of the union of the opposition outweighed that he felt towards the UDF of which he was the spiritual father. The logical culmination of Giscard's relentless discourse in favour of the union of the opposition would be the creation of a single opposition party, federation, or, at the very least, confederation. By calling loudly for the formation of a unified party after the European election, Giscard staked a claim for his future influence (and possibly leadership) within such a party. A new unified party would be a more apt vehicle for his ambitions than the impossible UDF. In fact, Giscard's discourse advocating *l'union* was more than ever a tactical necessity in view of his eventual candidacy at the next presidential election, and the weakness of the UDF as an organisational base. The ex-President continued to make the running after the European election by calling for the holding of the States-General of the Opposition: these were to be initially a series of conventions bringing together representatives of all the opposition parties to promote areas of convergence on policy. In Giscard's scheme of events, these meetings would ideally precede a unification congress to be held in 1991 or 1992 - in time for the 1993 legislative elections.[50]

The European election was followed by ever more favourable opinion poll ratings for Giscard, so much so that by May 1990, some polls placed Giscard ahead of Chirac both at the first and second rounds of a presidential election.[51] In turn, this led to an offensive, anti-Giscard reaction from Jacques Chirac of a type the RPR leader had not felt necessary to engage in since 1981. Despite such animosities, the leaders of the mainstream right-wing formations, the RPR and UDF, were determined to prevent any repeat of their disastrous divisions preceding the 1981 and 1988 presidential elections. This lay behind the agreement reached in June 1990 to institute a system of primaries, in order to designate a unique candidate of the RPR/UDF before the first ballot of the next presidential election. The creation of the UPF confederation in June 1990, along with the decision to organise primaries, was conceived of - in part, at least - as a necessary rearguard action to defend the incumbent UDF and RPR leaderships (crystallised around Giscard and Chirac) from the continuing challenge of the *quadragénaires*, the younger generation of aspiring leaders within both the UDF and RPR. In particular, the formation of the UPF was a rejoinder to François Léotard and Michel Noir (RPR), whose joint initiative *La force unie*, which urged the fusion of all existing formations and the creation of a new unified right-wing party under a fresh leadership, was clearly aimed against both Giscard and Chirac. The formation of the UPF could be interpreted in various manners: as an attempt to regulate and rationalise traditional presidential rivalries on the mainstream right; as an effort to fight off the challenge of the *quadragénaires*; as a means of providing a broader base from which to make a right-wing bid for the Elysée in the next presidential election; and to prepare for the legislative elections scheduled for 1993 in as unified a manner as possible, with both formations conscious of the need to fight on two fronts (against the PS and the FN).

*

The underlying problems which had beset the right throughout the 1980s remained unaltered, and continued into the 1990s. Indeed, new tensions had been added to old ones. Despite Giscard's victory in the 1989 European election, and despite the creation of the UPF confederation in June 1990, the opposition's strategic impasse remained cruelly obvious. It lacked one uncontested leader, and remained divided in relation to future strategy and orientation. The problem of leadership had become even more acute since the emergence of the *rénovateurs*, and the challenge to the existing leaderships of a new rising generation of aspiring leaders.

In the midst of this relentless manoeuvring, many concluded that the UDF had become an anachronism, after barely more than ten years of existence. But whether or not the UDF survives as an organisation, it seems likely that a force embodying the French tradition of the Orleanist right will continue to exist in some shape or form. The survival in French politics of a formation committed to moderate conservatism is highly probable, whether this exists as an independent party, as part of a confederation, or as a component element of a broader unified 'right-wing' party comprising representatives of other historical traditions as well.

Notes

1. See Cole, A., and Campbell, P., *French Electoral Systems and Elections since 1789*, Gower, Aldershot, 1989, Chapters Six and Seven.

2. See Ysmal, C., 'Le difficile chemin du Parti républicain', *Projet*, no. 118, 1977; Colliard, J-C., 'Le parti giscardien', *Pouvoirs*, no. 9, 1979.

3. The strongly pro-Giscard *Clubs perspectives et réalités* remained outside of the Republican Party.

4. Schonfeld, W., 'Le RPR et l'UDF à l'épreuve de l'opposition', *Revue Française de Science Politique*, vol. 26, no. 1, 1986, p. 16.

5. *Le Monde*, 29 September 1981. See also Thiebault, J-L., 'Les caractéristiques organisationnelles d'une confédération de partis: l'exemple de l'UDF', unpublished paper presented to the Third National Congress of the French Political Science Association, Bordeaux, 5-8 October 1988.

6. *Le Monde*, 14 January 1982.

7. On divergences over *cohabitation*, see *Libération*, 20 December 1985. On the UDF-RPR programme, see *Le Quotidien de Paris*, 2 October 1985. On the right's ideological evolution during the 1980s, see Ysmal, C., 'L'UDF et le RPR à la fin des années 1980', unpublished paper presented to the Third National Congress of the French Political Science Association, Bordeaux, 5-8 October 1988.

8. There were joint RPR-UDF lists in 60 departments in mainland France, separate lists in 36. The latter were generally in the largest departments. The existence of united opposition lists sparked off the creation of many dissident right-wing lists.

9. *Le Nouvel Observateur*, 17 April 1986. Pierre Méhaignerie, the CDS leader, was the most prominent as Minister of Housing.

10. In June 1987, Léotard was publicly invited by Chirac to choose between his position as a member of the government, which involved the duty to exercise collective responsibility, and his belief that his status as leader of the Republican Party gave him the right to express opinions divergent from those of the government. Léotard refused to give way in front of Chirac, who relented, but who became the latest in a long line to have become alienated by Léotard. The honeymoon was over. See Carton, D., 'La bande à Léo sur plusieurs coups', *Bilan du septennat*, Le Monde: dossiers et documents, May 1988.

11. It is not proposed to include any analysis of the CNIP in the present chapter, that formation never having officially formed a part of the UDF.

12. See, inter alia, 'Les R.I.' in *Les Cahiers de l'Education Civique*, no. 37-38, November-December 1976.

13. Roland-Lévy, F., estimates in *Libération*, 1 July 1988, claimed party membership for the component parties of the UDF as follows: PR - 150,000; CDS - 49,980; Radicals - 15,000; PSD - 4,000; *adhérents directs* - 28,000. Given the nature of these parties - as *partis de notables* -these figures are probably a gross over-estimation.

14. Local 'mutual withdrawal' alliances in Bouches-du-Rhône between the UDF-RPR coalition (dominated by Gaudin's PR) and the FN in the June 1988 legislative election attracted considerable media attention, and illustrated that strategic decisions were often in practice taken by powerful notables whom the Parisian leadership found it difficult to discipline.

15. *Le Monde*, 15 October 1983; *Libération*, 1 July 1988.

16. Dreyfus, F-G., *Histoire de la démocratie chrétienne en France*, Albin Michel, Paris, 1988, p. 379.

17. *Libération*, 1 July 1988.

18. Charlot, J., *Les partis politiques en France*, FNSP, Paris, 1986, p. 44.

19. The illusion that the Radical Party could survive as an autonomous political force was shown to be totally unrealistic in the 1979 European election, when Radical leader Servan-Schreiber ran as head of an autonomous list which polled 1.8 per cent, as against 27.4 per cent for the official UDF list led by Simone Veil.

20. *Libération*, 1 July 1988.

21. *Libération*, 1 July 1988. On the 1989 municipal elections, see Habert, P., and Ysmal, C., *Elections municipales 1989*, Le Figaro/Etudes Politiques, Paris, 1989. The PSD lost two of the handful of sizeable towns it had previously controlled: Perpignan and Abbeville.

22. *Libération*, 1 July 1988.

23. The following account draws mainly on Frears, J., *France in the Giscard Presidency*, Allen and Unwin, London, 1981, pp. 6-10; Colliard, J-C., *Les républicains indépendents: Valéry Giscard d'Estaing*, PUF, Paris, 1971.

24. During the so-called Bokassa affair of 1980, President Giscard was accused of having accepted a gift of diamonds from the ruthless dictator of the Central African Republic, Colonel Bokassa. Amongst the other points of interest aroused by this affair was the fact that the close relations maintained between France, the ex-colonial power, and Francophone Africa frequently brought French Presidents into contact with insalubrious dictators.

25. On Raymond Barre, see, inter alia, Remilleux, J., *Les barristes*, Albin Michel, Paris, 1987; Gaffney, J., 'Raymond Barre: The Providential Loser' in Gaffney, J. (ed.), *The French Presidential Elections of 1988: Ideology and Leadership in Contemporary France*, Gower, Aldershot, 1989, pp. 121-139; Birnbaum, G., 'La faillite du barrisme structurel ou l'échec de l'homogénéisation de l'entreprise Barre', unpublished paper presented to the Third National Congress of the French Political Science Association, Bordeaux, 5-8 October 1988.

26. Gaffney, ibid., pp. 124-133.

27. The PR leader must have been opposed by a strong minority (at least 20) of deputies from his own party. Léotard owed his defeat to a tactical alliance struck between Giscard and the *rénovateurs* within the UDF group.

28. Rémond, R., *Les droites en France*, Aubier Montaigne, Paris, 1982. For a succinct summary of the arguments, see Ysmal, C., 'Nature et réalité de l'affrontement Giscard-Chirac', *Politique Aujourd 'hui*, no. 3-4, 1977, pp. 11-23.

27. Guizot, Prime Minister during the reign of Louis Philippe. His invitation to the French people - in fact the bourgeoisie - to enrichen themselves was symbolic of the Orleanist right's promotion of the rights of the capitalist bourgeoisie. In fact, despite the regime's spurious commitment to free trade, it protected indigenous capitalists from the 'vissicitudes of unlimited foreign competition'. See Magraw, R., *France 1815 - 1914: the Bourgeois Century*, Fontana, Oxford, 1983, pp. 51-78.

30. Giscard d'Estaing, V., *La démocratie française*, Fayard, Paris, 1976.

31. See Frears, *France in the Giscard Presidency*, for a fairly thorough treatment of the policy angle of Giscard's presidency.

32. Frears, *Political Parties in the French Fifth Republic*, p. 63.

33. Ysmal, C., 'Le difficile chemin du Parti républicain'.

34. Dreyfus, F-G., 'Place et poids de la démocratie chrétienne en France', unpublished paper presented to the Third National Congress of the French Political Science Association at Bordeaux, 5-8 October 1988, pp. 3-4.

35. Dreyfus, F-G., *Histoire de la démocratie chrétienne en France*, pp. 394-396.

36. See Bauer, M., 'The politics of state-directed privatisation: the case of France', *West European Politics*, vol. 11, no. 4, 1988, pp. 49-60.

37. *Le Figaro*, 18 October 1983. The past tense will be used in the remainder of this section in order to signify that it relates primarily to the UDF from 1978-88, prior to the creation of the autonomous centre UDC parliamentary group.

38. Thiebault, op. cit., pp. 9-21. The following section owes a good deal to the cited article.

39. Duverger, M., *Political Parties*, Methuen, London, 1964.

40. But not in the Senate, where UDF members were split between three different groups.

41. *Le Monde*, 28, 29 June 1990. According to the constitutive charter of the UPF, decisions were to be binding on both formations when approved by 75 per cent of more of the Political Bureau. Such provisions were similar to those governing official UDF statutes, but we saw above how in fact a non-written rule of unanimity prevailed. Would a similar outcome prevail in relation to the UPF? From its creation, the UPF was contested from sections of the UDF and RPR, notably by François Léotard, for whom it represented a tactical compromise between Giscard and Chirac to forestall calls for a more thorough fusion of the two formations. Along with Michel Noir of the RPR, Léotard had since April 1990 been urging the opposition to dissolve its existing structures, and fuse into a unified right-wing party, under the leadership of the *quadragénaires*, the rising generation in its forties. Problems of discipline were likely to persist. Despite Giscard and Chirac firmly and solemnly asserting that the UPF would refuse to engage in any electoral alliance with the National Front - at any level - Jean-Claude Gaudin announced that the creation of UPF would not prevent the UDF in the Bouches-du-Rhône from coming to an electoral agreement with the National Front in view of the 1993 legislative elections.

42. On the attributes of a *présidentiable*, see Duhamel, O., and Jaffré, J., *Le nouveau président*, Seuil, Paris, 1987, Chapter Three.

43. On the Mitterrand-Rocard conflict, see Cole, A., 'Factionalism, the French Socialist Party and the Fifth Republic: an explanation of intra-party divisions', *European Journal of Political Research*, vol. 17, no. 1, January 1989, pp. 86-91.

44. Giscard feared that any system of primaries based on direct popular suffrage, *à l'américaine*, might favour the RPR - the most strongly organised formation - to the detriment of the UDF. A system of indirect election, based on the *élus*, and likely to be more favourable to his challenge, was Giscard's preferred option. The method finally adopted was in fact a compromise between Chirac and Giscard. The system was a weighted one, involving both *élus* and electors declaring themselves supporters of the RPR/UDF: each candidate would receive one mandate for every 40 electors supporting his or her nomination. All *élus* (holders of public office) would dispose of one mandate each. The *élus* and representatives of the electors would come together to form a National Convention to nominate the right's candidate. Each pretender would have to make a commitment to respect the verdict of the primary procedure.

45. See Domenach, N., and Labro, M., 'L'histoire cachée d'une ouverture ratée', *L'Evénement du Jeudi*, 19-25 May 1988.

46. Cole and Campbell, op. cit., p. 161. In 1978 there was a generalised pattern of 'primaries'; in 1986 an electoral system based on proportional representation was used.

47. See *Le Quotidien de Paris*, 12 April 1989. The first stance was generally favoured by *rénovateurs*; the second by 'autonomists' led by party leader Méhaignerie, the third by 'traditionalists' who resented having deserted the UDF in the first place.

48. On the 1989 municipal elections, see Habert and Ysmal, op cit.

49. *Libération*, 24 April 1989. See the special issue of *Le Point*, 17 April 1989, on the *rénovateurs*.

50. At the time of writing, three such meetings had taken place, in January, April and May 1990, consecrated respectively to education, immigration and decentralisation. In these meetings, the differences of sensibility between the CDS on the one hand, and RPR/UDF on the other were obvious. Immigration in particular remained an area where conflict was ever present: CDS leaders opposed the tenor of the States-General on immigration held in April 1990, at which Giscard was suspected of courting Jean-Marie Le Pen, in view of the second-ballot of a presidential election. The philosophical reflection undertaken at these conventions was supposedly to provide a theoretical basis for the new confederation, the UPF.

51. See the SOFRES poll in *Le Nouvel Observateur*, 10-16 May 1990.

Bibliography

Baker, D., 'Giscard versus the Gaullists', *Contemporary Review*, vol. 231, no. 1340, September 1977.

Bell, D.S. (ed.), *Contemporary French Political Parties*, Croom Helm, London, 1983.

Bergeroux, N-J., 'De la coalition de 1978 au parti du président de 1981', *Le Monde*, 17 February 1979.

Bergeroux, N-J., 'L'UDF face à une crise majeure', *Le Monde*, 14 May 1981.

Birnbaum, G., 'La faillite du barrisme structurel ou l'échec de l'homogénéisation de l'entreprise Barre', unpublished paper presented to the Third National Congress of the French Political Science Association, Bordeaux, 5-8 October 1988.

Bresson, G., 'Les libéraux mettent le turbo', *Libération*, 29 January 1987.

Brossollette, S., 'UDF: les godillots du président', *L'Express*, 22 March 1980.

Carmouze, P., 'Mais que veulent les centristes? ', *Le Quotidien de Paris*, 12 April 1989.

Carton, D., 'La bande à Léo sur plusieurs coups', *Bilan du septennat*, Le Monde: dossiers et documents, May 1988.

Carton, D., 'Le CDS veut pratiquer une opposition intelligente', *Le Monde*, 17 June 1988.

Carton, D., 'La grande scène giscardienne', *Le Monde*, 15 April 1989.

Carton, D., 'M. Valéry Giscard d'Estaing reprend sa croisade pour l'union de l'opposition', *Le Monde*, 23 February 1990.

Cayrol, R., 'Les citoyens centrés', *Politique Aujourd'hui*, no. 10, January 1989.

Cayrol, R., and Ysmal, C., 'L'UDF: une et diverse', *Le Monde*, 22 March 1980.

Charlot, J., *Les partis politiques en France*, FNSP, Paris, 1986.

Chirac, J., and Lecanuet, J., 'UDF-RPR: accord pour gouverner', *Démocratie Moderne*, 11 April 1985.

Cole, A., and Campbell, P., *French Electoral Systems and Elections since 1789*, Gower, Aldershot, 1989.

Colliard, J-C., *Les républicains indépendents: Valéry Giscard d'Estaing*, PUF, Paris, 1971.

Colliard, J-C., 'Le parti giscardien', *Pouvoirs*, no. 9, 1979.

De Montvalon, D., 'Les états d'âme de M.Léotard', *L'Express*, 30 March 1984.

De Montvalon, D., 'Léotard: pourquoi il monte', *L'Express*, 13 July 1985.

Domenach, N., 'Accord RPR-UDF', *Le Matin*, 26 March 1984.

Domenach, N., and Labro, M., 'L'histoire cachée d'une ouverture ratée', *L'Evénement du Jeudi*, 19-25 May 1988.

Dreyfus, F-G., *Histoire de la démocratie chrétienne en France*, Albin Michel, Paris, 1988.

Dreyfus, F-G., 'Place et poids de la démocratie chrétienne en France', unpublished paper presented to the Third National Congress of the French Political Science Association at Bordeaux, 5-8 October 1988.

Duhamel, A., 'Les centristes ont le coeur à gauche mais ils votent à droite', *Le Monde*, 27 March 1971.

Duhamel, A., 'La dernière chance de l'UDF', *Le Point*, 20-26 October 1986.

Duhamel, A., 'Le choix de Giscard d'Estaing', *Le Quotidien de Paris*, 13 February 1987.

Duhamel, A., 'Le mystère centriste', *Le Quotidien de Paris*, 23 December 1988.

Duhamel, O., and Jaffré, J., *Le nouveau président*, Seuil, Paris, 1987.

Dupin, E., 'La quadrature du centre', *Libération*, 8-9 November 1986.

Duverger, M., *Political Parties*, Methuen, London, 1964.

Fauvet-Mycia, C., 'Les adhérents directs s'intérrogent sur leur représentation', *Le Monde*, 17 October 1983.

Frears, J., *Political Parties and Elections in the French Fifth Republic*, Hurst, London, 1977.

Frears, J., *France in the Giscard Presidency*, Allen and Unwin, London, 1981.

Gaffney, J., 'The Providential Loser: Raymond Barre', in Gaffney, J. (ed.), *The French Presidential Elections of 1988: Ideology and Leadership in Contemporary France*, Gower, Aldershot, 1989.

Giscard d'Estaing, V., *La démocratie française*, Fayard, Paris, 1976.

Giscard d'Estaing, V., 'Ma stratégie pour l'union', *L'Express*, 6-12 October 1989.

Habert, P., and Ysmal, C., *Elections municipales 1989*, Le Figaro/Etudes Politiques, 1989.

Hainsworth, P., 'From opposition to office: the French right after the March 1986 legislative elections', *Contemporary French Civilisation*, vol. 11, no. 1, 1987.

Huet, S., 'L'organigramme de l'UDF: un savant dosage', *Le Figaro*, 18 October 1983.

Jeambar, D., 'Le plan secret des rénovateurs', *Le Point*, 17 April 1989.

Pégard, C., 'La danse du centre', *Le Point*, 20 February 1989.

Pégard, C., 'Le centre en bataille', *Le Point*, 24 April 1989.

Pégard, C., 'Droite: succès, complots, gamberges', *Le Point*, 19 June 1989.

Portelli, H., 'Quel avenir pour l'UDF', *La Croix*, 26 July 1983.

Portelli, H., 'Les contradictions de l'UDF', *La Croix*, 14 November 1985.

Portelli, H., 'L'UDF entre la soumission et la surenchère', *La Vie Française*, 26 May - 1 June 1985.

Portelli, H., 'L'heure du centre', *La Croix*, 13 November 1986.

Portelli, H., 'Les contraintes de la Ve', *Politique Aujourd' hui*, no. 10, January 1986.

Rémond, R., *Les droites en France*, Aubier Montaigne, Paris, 1982.

Rémond, R., 'L'opposition de droite à l'épreuve des européennes', in Habert, P., and Ysmal, C. (eds.), *Elections européennes 1989*, Le Figaro/Etudes Politiques, 1989.

Roland-Lévy, F., 'Le PR: un parti en tenue Léotard', *Libération*, 27 September 1982.

Roland-Lévy, F., 'L'UDF malade de la cohabitation', *Libération*, 20 December 1985.

Roland- Lévy, F., 'L'UDF règle sa minuterie présidentielle', *Libération*, 10 September 1987.

Roland-Lévy, F., 'UDF: les turpitudes cachées de l'ouverture', *Libération*, 2 June 1987.

Roland-Lévy, F., 'L'UDF, combien de divisions?', *Libération*, 1 July 1988.

Roland-Lévy, F., 'Sept ans de faux départs pour le président du PR', *Libération*, 26 September 1989.

Schonfeld, W., 'Le RPR et l'UDF à l'épreuve de l'opposition', *Revue Française de Science Politique*, vol. 26, no. 1, 1986.

Searls, E., 'The French right in opposition, 1981-1986', *Parliamentary Affairs*, vol. 39, no. 4, October 1986.

Servent, P., 'La création du groupe de l'Union du centre', *Le Monde*, 17 June 1988.

Sichler, L., 'Léotard saisi par 'ivresse', *L'Evénement du Jeudi*, 4-10 September 1986.

Sur, S., 'L'assimilation progressive par les centristes', *Revue Française de Science Politique*, vol. 34, no. 4-5, August-October 1984.

Thénard, J-M., 'Les centristes lèvent l'ancre en solitaires', *Libération*, 24 April 1989.

Thiebault, J-L., 'Les caractéristiques organisationnelles d'une confédération de partis: l'exemple de l'UDF', unpublished paper presented to the Third National Congress of the French Political Science Association, Bordeaux, 5-8 October 1988.

Wilson, F.L., *French Political Parties under the Fifth Republic*, Praeger, New York, 1982.

Ysmal, C., 'Le difficile chemin du Parti républicain', *Projet*, no. 118, 1977.

Ysmal, C., 'L'UDF et le RPR à la fin des années 1980', unpublished paper presented to the Third National Congress of the French Political Science Association, Bordeaux, 5-8 October 1988.

Ysmal, C., 'L'impossible centrisme', *Politique Aujourd'hui*, no. 10, January 1989.

Ysmal, C., *Les partis politiques sous la Vème République*, Montchrestien, Paris, 1989.

Zemmour, E., 'UDF: Giscard tisse sa toile', *Libération*, 13 October 1988.

7 *Un parti comme les autres*: Jacques Chirac and the *Rally for the Republic*

Andrew Knapp[1]

French parties under the Fifth Republic have had to perform an impossible feat on a daily basis: to differentiate themselves clearly from their immediate rivals while also cultivating the broad, consensual appeal necessary to field a successful candidate at the second ballot of a presidential election. For de Gaulle's party, de Gaulle himself supplied both the unique qualities and the broad appeal. Since his departure in 1969, the Gaullist Party has had to adjust to playing the game by the same rules as its competitors - as *un parti comme les autres*, a major but no longer a dominant player.[2]

As well as the General's personal appeal, the Gaullist Party disposed of a trump card in the amalgam of policy, ideology and folk-memory it brought to government in 1958. The core of classical Gaullism had been forged in the collision between de Gaulle's own mystical, romantic conception of France and the reality of the defeat of 1940. De Gaulle's overriding concern was France's strength and independence on the world stage - hence his withdrawal from NATO and precocious pursuit of détente. The necessary condition for this was domestic cohesion. This required strong institutions, and particularly a powerful executive presidency linked directly to voters through universal suffrage; a vigorous economy fielding world-class industrial groups, whether public or private; and the encouragement of workers' 'participation' in their firms, as well as extensive social protection, in order to defuse class conflict and the appeal of communism.[3] In many ways these were not conventional policies for a European right-wing party; less European, less Atlanticist, more ready to accept state economic intervention, less trusting of private enterprise.[4] But they were highly successful. To French voters, the Gaullist Party offered a charismatic leader; the heroic aura of the Resistance; loyalty to institutions that offered stable government for the first time in the twentieth century; *gloire*; a sure barrier against communism, and economic prosperity. This allowed it to appear as the 'natural' party of government throughout the 1960s and above all to attract an appreciable proportion of the working-class electorate.

As the dominant force in French politics, Gaullism survived its founder by the five short years of the Pompidou presidency. Georges Pompidou won nearly 44 per cent of the vote at the first ballot of the 1969 presidential election. Since his death in 1974, no Gaullist has occupied the Elysée, and no Gaullist candidate in 1974, 1981 or 1988 managed a first-ballot score above 20 per cent (Table 7.1). In 1968, the Gaullist Union of Democrats for the Republic (UDR) won France's first ever single-party National Assembly majority:

twenty years later its successor, the Rally for the Republic (RPR) held fewer than half of the moderate right's minority of seats in the Assembly. A decade of Gaullist power - control of the presidency, premiership, and the lion's share of the ministries, an unprecedented dominance in parliament, and an impressive network of patronage positions reaching out from the top civil service into nationalised and private industry - gave rise to the phrase *L'Etat-UDR*. The left used *L'Etat-RPR* as a slogan in 1988, but the posts Jacques Chirac had filled, under President Mitterrand's watchful eye, during his two-year premiership since 1986 were scarcely comparable in depth and permanence. Only in two respects did the party look stronger in 1989. Membership, though notoriously hard to estimate, was almost certainly up. And the RPR's local implantation, the Gaullists' weak point in the 1960s, was much improved, starting with Chirac's own conquest of the Paris Town Hall in 1977. But this was no substitute for the commanding heights of State power.

Table 7.1:
Gaullist and right-wing percentages of votes cast, 1958-88[a]

		Gaullists %	Total right %	Gaullists/total right %
1958	(parliamentary)	21.1	53.4	39.5
1962	(parliamentary)	32.4	56.2	50.5
1965	(presidential) *(second ballot)*	43.7 *57.6*	64.9*b*	67.3
1967	(parliamentary)	32.1	56.4	56.9
1968	(parliamentary)	38.0	58.9	64.5
1969	(presidential) *(second ballot)*	44.0 *57.6*	67.4*b*	65.3
1973	(parliamentary)	37.0	54.2	68.3
1974	(presidential)	14.6	52.2	28.0
1978	(parliamentary)	22.8	47.5	48.0
1979	(European)	16.1	48.1	33.5
1981	(presidential)	21.0*c*	48.9	36.8
1981	(parliamentary)	21.2	43.2	49.1
1988	(presidential) *(second ballot)*	19.9 *46.0*	50.9	39.1
1988	(parliamentary)	19.2	50.3	38.2

Source: Ysmal, 1989, pp. 257, 263.
a Refers to first ballot except where indicated: only one ballot was held for the 1979 European poll.
b Note that centre votes (Lecanuet in 1965, Poher in 1969) are counted in the right-wing total for these years. Without them, the Gaullists' position would look even stronger.
c Chirac + Debré + Garaud. Chirac's own percentage was 18.0.

As well as its commanding political position, the Gaullist Party has lost its unique political appeal. By 1989 much that had been distinctive had either disappeared or been diffused throughout the French political system. The charismatic leader rested at Colombey: Pompidou and Chirac could not match his attraction. The Resistance legacy faded with time: and it was not Chirac, but his adversary François Mitterrand, who had actually participated in it. The Fifth Republic's basic institutions commanded something close to an all-party consensus, so that the Gaullists' traditional link with them was no longer all-party consensus, so that the Gaullists' traditional link with them was no longer remarkable. The Gaullist emphasis on national independence and *grandeur* won similarly wide acceptance: no basic differences on foreign or defence policy troubled the two-year *cohabitation* between a Socialist President and an RPR Premier in 1986-88. The claim to represent the only sure barrier against communism became irrelevant as electoral support for the French Communist Party (PCF) sank below 10 per cent of the vote. The claim to be the 'natural' party of government rang increasingly hollow as first Giscardians and then Socialists proved they could run the country without its descending into the chaos long associated by Gaullists with 'the régime of parties'. The appeal to 'participation' and to measures within firms limiting managers' absolute right to manage had a limited legislative impact: from the Pompidou presidency on, the appeal of the Gaullists was more straightforwardly conservative. The Gaullists' willingness to accept extensive state intervention in the economy was apparently undermined by the RPR's conversion to the free-market virtues of economic 'liberalism' in the early 1980s. And finally, the 'catch-all' qualities of high Gaullism had largely disappeared, with the RPR's strength increasingly confined to the most traditionally conservative sectors of the population.

The Gaullists had not only lost their charismatic leader: they had lost what had allowed him to square the circle of Fifth Republic party politics. Since Pompidou's death they have sought to shore up their diminishing electoral appeal by putting down local roots, reinforcing their organisation and changing their policies. This has allowed them to survive, but not - except under the constraining circumstances of 1974-76 and 1986-88 - to govern. In the rest of this chapter we shall consider the Gaullists' voters, their local implantation, their organisation and their political strategy. All four, however, need a brief chronological framework.

Gaullism Since De Gaulle: A Chronological Overview

1969-74: The Pompidou Presidency

Winning the presidency in the aftermath of de Gaulle's defeat in his last referendum, Pompidou moved the Gaullist Party several steps towards orthodox European conservatism. The new President, a former banker, improved relations with both the USA and with Europe, waiving de Gaulle's veto on Britain's EEC entry. As de Gaulle's Prime Minister from 1962-68, he had devoted much attention to the need to modernise and concentrate France's basic industries: this continued. Pompidou also had little time for 'participation'. For ideological or tactical reasons, some Gaullists opposed this move to right-wing orthodoxy. Pompidou's first Prime Minister, Jacques Chaban-Delmas, a 'baron' of the earliest days of Gaullism, positioned himself well on the left of the party, won considerable popularity - and was replaced by the less independent Pierre Messmer in 1972. Messmer's premiership marked the decadence of governmental Gaullism, with recurrent financial and property scandals and the beginnings of a succession struggle, as it became clear that the President was ill and would not last his term. At his death in April 1974 there was no clearly designated successor: the Gaullists were thus particularly ill-equipped to hold on to power.

Others were poised to take it from them. The Communist and Socialists' common programme of 1972 gave the left governmental credibility for the first time in the Fifth Republic. The following year the Gaullists lost the absolute parliamentary majority they had won in 1968, as well as much of their working-class vote. Messmer's parliamentary support now depended on centrist deputies and on Valéry Giscard d'Estaing's strengthened Independent Republicans. The Gaullists' competitors and adversaries alike saw enhanced party strength as a window of presidential opportunity.

1974-76: The First Chirac Premiership

The man with most reason to mourn the President was Jacques Chirac. A graduate of France's elite civil service college, the *Ecole nationale d'administration* (ENA), Chirac had joined Pompidou's private office (*cabinet*) in 1962. His energy and effectiveness were appreciated, and he rapidly established an almost filial relationship with de Gaulle's second Premier. Elected to a constituency in his family's native department of Corrèze in 1967 after a characteristically vigorous campaign, Chirac immediately entered the government as Secretary of State for Social Affairs. Barely a year later he was part of the May 1968 crisis team in the Prime Minister's office and played a key role in the negotiations with union leaders, effectively by-passing his minister and reporting direct to Pompidou. After the June 1968 elections he became Secretary of State for the Budget, working under Finance Minister Valéry Giscard d'Estaing till January 1971, when he became Minister for Relations with Parliament. His poor performance at this job was followed by a happier period as Agriculture Minister after the departure of Chaban-Delmas in July 1972: the Gaullists had specifically targeted farmers during the approach to the 1973 elections, and Chirac's generous subsidies and aggressive European negotiations were rewarded with praise and loyalty from their main unions. In March 1974 he moved to the Interior. Whether or not Pompidou had chosen him as his successor, the President's two powerful advisers, Pierre Juillet and Marie-France Garaud, almost certainly had. The Interior offered an excellent base for Chirac to move to the premiership a year later and the Elysée at the end of Pompidou's term in 1976.

But Chirac had no substantial following among Gaullists. His patron's death was thus a huge political blow as well as a personal loss. In the disarray that followed, Chirac used his ministerial position to play kingmaker. Chaban-Delmas declared his candidacy early: Chirac knew he had nothing to gain if Chaban-Delmas won, and in any case believed he would lose to Mitterrand. Giscard's candidacy immediately followed. After a botched attempt to put Messmer forward, Chirac then won over 42 Gaullist deputies to a veiled declaration of support for Giscard. The reaction of leading Gaullists was vituperative, but opinion polls (some of them supplied by Chirac's services at the Interior Ministry) soon showed Giscard pulling ahead. At the first ballot of the presidential election, Chaban-Delmas won 15.1 per cent to Giscard's 32.6 and Mitterrand's 43.2. Giscard won the run-off by just 200,000 votes. He appointed Chirac Prime Minister on 21 May 1974, seven weeks after Pompidou's death.[5]

The appointment was based on a mutual political misunderstanding - 'La double méprise', as Catherine Nay has called it. Giscard appointed Chirac in the hope that Chirac could deliver him the Gaullist movement, which would then be merged in a 'presidential majority'. Chirac accepted in order to ensure the survival of Gaullism under his own leadership. The two objectives were not compatible and the first Chirac premiership was marked by an increasingly bitter power struggle between the two men.

Policy differences played some part in the conflict. Many Gaullist deputies had little sympathy with the wave of liberal societal measures that inaugurated Giscard's presidency, and they hated his plans for a capital gains tax. But Chirac as Premier was generally a loyal public apologist of presidential policy. More important in the break was Giscard's willingness to extend presidential government at Chirac's expense. The Prime Minister exercised little authority over 'his' government, which the President constituted and twice reshuffled with no pretence of proper constitutional consultation of the Premier. No key minister was beholden to Chirac: Michel Poniatowski was Giscard's principal hatchet-man, and Jean Lecanuet, the centrist candidate from 1965, had finally joined the presidential majority in 1974. Giscard regularly sent ministers their working agenda. And his personal intervention in matters such as the Left Bank expressway in Paris made it clear that henceforth no area of policy lay outside the presidential 'reserved domain'.

Linked to this constitutional question was that of the future of the Gaullists and the 'presidential majority'. As soon as he won the premiership, Chirac started to win back leading Gaullists, helped by the party's tradition of support for its most eminent member. But the barons - Chaban-Delmas, Olivier Guichard, Roger Frey, Michel Debré, Maurice Couve de Murville, and Alain Peyrefitte, most of whom had been Gaullists when Chirac was still in short trousers - were not converted. They planned to take over the party by getting Guichard elected Secretary-General in place of the incumbent, Alexandre Sanguinetti, at the National Council meeting in November 1974. Chirac moved first, persuaded Sanguinetti to stand down, and won the support of Charles Pasqua, the Secretary for Organisation, who duly delivered enough votes to elect him Secretary-General with a two-thirds majority (Chirac took out a party card - for the first time - the following day).

At first Giscard approved, and Chirac was suspected of trying to 'giscardise' the UDR. Instead, he put his own men in key positions and began a membership drive. Poniatowski, and then Giscard, rightly saw in a revived, Chiraquian Gaullist movement a threat to their own plans to 'rebalance' the majority. Under presidential pressure, Chirac therefore stood down from the Gaullist leadership in June 1975, leaving a trusted lieutenant, André Bord, in his place. In March 1976, after big left-wing gains in cantonal elections, he sought and obtained the task of 'co-ordinating the majority' from Giscard. But within weeks, the two centre groups of the majority merged into the Centre of Social Democrats (CDS), led by Jean Lecanuet. This move, encouraged by Poniatowski to strengthen the non-Gaullist groups in the majority, was undertaken without consulting Chirac. His task of 'co-ordinator' withdrawn, Chirac now led neither government nor majority. His premiership had won him one prize - control of the UDR - but no more. His resignation in August 1976 was a recognition of this de facto situation. Raymond Barre immediately succeeded him.

1976-81: the Rassemblement pour la République

Chirac spent the autumn planning with Juillet, Garaud and Pasqua, pausing only to get re-elected to the Corrèze seat he had had to vacate on accepting the premiership. The RPR was launched in December 1976 before a crowd of 70,000. Its name was a deliberate reference to the Rally of the French People (RPF), the mass movement created by de Gaulle in 1947, after his resignation from the premiership. Chirac became the RPR's first President.

The RPR soon had an immediate, if only local, goal. A 1975 law had given Paris, from the March 1977 municipal elections, a mayor elected by the municipal council as in other French cities. In November 1976 Giscard broke an earlier agreement with the Gaullists (who dominated the right in Paris) for a compromise candidate for the post, and had his lieutenant Michel d'Ornano announce his candidacy from the Elysée. The Paris Gaullists put up their own favourite son, Christian de La Malène, but when Garaud and Juillet persuaded Chirac to stand, de La Malène duly made way for him on 19 January. The municipal elections of 13 and 20 March 1977 were a nationwide victory for the left, which won two-thirds of the country's city halls. But in Paris, they were a triumph for Chirac.

who overcame an early poor position in the polls to trounce d'Ornano at the first ballot and to beat the left convincingly at the second.

Chirac had proved his campaigning abilities in Corrèze in 1967: similar qualities of omnipresence, organisation, affability and ability to target clienteles and to press the flesh were shown to great effect in Paris. Over the next twelve years, he fought nine more major election campaigns - for parliamentary elections in 1978, 1981, 1986 and 1988; for presidential elections in 1981 and 1988; for European elections in 1979 (the RPR list amalgamated with the UDF in 1984 and 1989); and for municipal elections in 1983 and 1989. It was partly the respite after a decade and more of near-continuous campaigns that made the RPR seem so uncertain of purpose following the 1989 European elections.

The campaigns of 1978, 1979 and 1981 were marked by a growing willingness to risk the defeat of the right as a whole in order to preserve the RPR's position within it. Chirac's 517 election meetings in 80 departments dominated the majority's 1978 parliamentary election campaign despite the federation of the pro-Giscard parties into the Union for French Democracy (UDF) a fortnight before the poll. The reward - much helped by the left's own divisions - was a right-wing majority with the RPR still just the leading party, with 154 seats (out of 491) to the UDF's 135. Giscard made no concessions in government to reflect this continued ascendancy, however, and went on moving Gaullists out of strategic positions in the state apparatus to put his own men in.

Chirac reacted with increasingly shrill populist and nationalist attacks on the government, a line that reached its apogee in the 1979 European election campaign: its very poor result at the polls led to the departure of its authors, Juillet and Garaud. The prospect opened by 1979 was that of the RPR as junior partner in the presidential majority, with Giscard picking off leading Gaullists at will, cutting off the RPR's sources of patronage, and inflicting countless petty humiliations on Chirac himself. Chirac could do little about this in the immediate term: when the RPR deputies voted against the budget in 1979, Barre invoked article 49-3 of the Constitution and dared them to vote a motion of censure - knowing that Chirac could not afford to take the blame for overthrowing the government. But the danger Chirac faced coloured his presidential campaign in 1981. As a party leader he was almost bound to stand and measure his own strength: the alternative would be the fragmentation of the RPR vote between Giscard and the two Gaullists who announced early candidacies - Debré and Garaud. In addition, though, Chirac's behaviour was at least as germane to Giscard's defeat as it had been to his victory seven years earlier. His first-ballot campaign was notable for its anti-presidential diatribes. And after a creditable performance (18 per cent to Debré's 1.7 and Garaud's 1.3) he announced that while 'personally' he would vote for the incumbent at the run-off, his voters should follow their own consciences. Many leading Gaullists went further when talking to their activists in private. A quarter of Chirac's electorate either abstained or supported Mitterrand. The new President immediately dissolved Parliament, leaving Chirac - despite Giscard's denunciation of his 'premeditated betrayal' - as the opposition's de facto leader for the ensuing election campaign. The RPR saved 88 seats to the UDF's 63 in the Socialist landslide of June 1981: with Giscard and Barre discredited, Chirac's leadership on the right was confirmed. So was his position as France's 'recourse' for the time when the electorate saw the errors of Socialist policies, as they surely would.

1981-86: Opposition

Discontent was not slow to appear as the Socialists followed an ill-judged reflation with devaluations and austerity packages. The RPR reinforced its organisation, overtaking the

PCF's official membership figures by 1983, and electing a younger leadership team under Secretary-General Jacques Toubon the following year. The programme was also renewed, with a free-market, privatising thrust that took its inspiration both from Britain and the USA and from the widespread exasperation with the Socialist 'experiment'. At the 1983 municipal elections the RPR gained control of 26 towns of over 30,000 inhabitants, thus doing much to remedy its traditionally weak local implantation. Chirac's result in Paris was perhaps the most spectacular: in the face of government legislation aimed at weakening his authority by giving the mayors of the capital's twenty *arrondissements* increased powers, he managed to win a 'grand slam' - majorities, and thus pliant mayors, in all twenty. He thus retained a commanding position in an increasingly credible opposition.

He faced three problems, however. The first was that his own public image did not reflect his political strength. The public still saw him as unstable and aggressive: they increasingly preferred Raymond Barre, who positioned himself as the tough-minded economist whose necessary policies the Socialists were now having to adopt. His second, and wholly unexpected problem was the rise of Jean-Marie Le Pen and his National Front (FN). Chirac's attempt to assume a more responsible, presidential image unfitted him to play the role of visceral populist opposition leader that he had half adopted in the 1970s; Le Pen, financed by a large inheritance, was only too ready to step into the new space on the RPR's right and use the emerging issues of law and order and immigrants to expand it. At the 1984 European elections the RPR left him plenty of room by joining a joint list with the UDF under the centre-right leadership of Simone Veil: the Veil list won 42.8 per cent, but the FN obtained 11.1.

This compounded Chirac's third problem, the electoral timetable. A right-wing majority at the 1986 parliamentary elections would face the choice between provoking a constitutional crisis or forming a government of *cohabitation* - unprecedented under the Fifth Republic - with a left-wing President until the presidential elections of 1988. Mitterrand further weakened the right's position by getting the electoral law changed to a form of proportional representation, thus ensuring parliamentary seats for the FN. Chirac was converted to *cohabitation* by Edouard Balladur, Pompidou's former Elysée Secretary-General who became Chirac's close adviser after the departure of Juillet and Garaud. And while Raymond Barre remained resolutely opposed to the idea, Chirac won round the bulk of the UDF - especially François Léotard and the Republican Party - and signed a highly free market-oriented common platform of government in January 1986. But he was pursuing a high-risk strategy. He was uncertain, under the new electoral system, of winning an absolute RPR-UDF majority, and had had to make big concessions to the UDF in the choice of parliamentary candidates. And the waters of *cohabitation* were uncharted. The first part of the gamble paid off, narrowly. Together with a handful of 'various right' allies, the RPR-UDF lists won a seven-seat parliamentary majority on 16 March 1986. Four days later, Chirac became the first Prime Minister of the Fifth Republic to be appointed because the President had no other choice.

1986-88: Cohabitation

The second part of the gamble lay in performing well enough as Premier to win a commanding position against any possible left-wing candidate in 1988. This required, firstly, a successful record in government; secondly, solid support from beyond the ranks of the RPR; and thirdly, a constant mixture of restraint and vigilance in his relations with the President. Chirac's success in all three was partial.

Like the Socialists in 1981, the right overestimated public support for its programme. Certain elements of it were indeed popular. Privatisations attracted 6.5 million new shareholders. Tax cuts benefited the rich disproportionately, but everyone to some degree. The authoritarian law and order measures of Interior Minister Charles Pasqua were decried by liberals, but in time Pasqua produced significant results, particularly against the terrorist group *Action directe*. These successes, though, were balanced by three negative factors. First, the government's economic measures, and especially the abolition of the Socialists' wealth tax, looked like a restoration of government by the wealthy for the wealthy. Second, the other elements of the programme ran into trouble early on. The university reform, presented by the hapless minister Alain Devaquet but scripted by right-wingers in Chirac's own *cabinet*, was withdrawn in December 1986 after huge student demonstrations that left one student dead after a beating by police. Other right-wing projects such as the reform of the nationality laws soon suffered a similar fate. Third, free-market policies failed to deliver the vigorous, inflation-free growth that the government had hoped for. Chirac also faced great difficulty in winning the stature of a *rassembleur* of the whole right. Policies on law and order and immigration that would win voters back from the FN would alienate UDF centrists. Personally, while most people saw Chirac as 'energetic', he aroused more antipathy than either Giscard or Barre, and was seen as less of a 'good republican' than either.[6] The parliamentary right remained solid: Chirac had after all promised that Pasqua's electoral reform would give safe constituencies to sitting RPR-UDF deputies. But fault-lines widened within the government. The university reform fiasco brought out the impatience of younger ministers such as François Léotard (Culture), Alain Juppé (Budget), Philippe Seguin (Social Affairs), or Alain Madelin (Industry) with those of their elders who, like Pasqua, saw the demonstrations as a re-run of May 1968 and thus a 'threat to the republic'. And there was increasing alarm on the part of leading UDF figures that the RPR was resuming its old hegemonic habits and packing its own men in key jobs in newly privatised industries and the civil service, much as the Gaullists had done in their heyday. His two-year premiership did not enable Chirac to shake off an image that was first and foremost that of a party leader.

Mitterrand used this weakness to great effect. Helped by common ground in the key areas of foreign policy and defence, *cohabitation* worked better than almost anyone had expected, with neither protagonist wishing to take responsibility for a constitutional crisis. Both men's standing in the polls rose accordingly. But the President's rose rather faster, as he polished his newly paternal, reassuring image and played on his Prime Minister's every discomfiture - expressing sympathy for the students in December 1986, meeting rail strikers shortly afterwards, and refusing to sign decrees which he claimed endangered the unity of the nation. When Mitterrand declared he would run for re-election, in March 1988, he surprised his opponents by coming out fighting on precisely the issue - the danger inherent in the RPR's hegemonic designs - that would strike chords elsewhere on the right - for example, among 44 per cent of the Barre electorate in March 1988.[7] Chirac's task, caught between Barre and Le Pen, was inevitably delicate. He avoided humiliation, but sustained a resounding defeat - under 20 per cent at the first ballot and barely 46 per cent at the second. A quarter of Le Pen's first-ballot voters and 14 per cent of Barre's chose to support the President at the run-off. As in 1981, Mitterrand dissolved the National Assembly. At the ensuing parliamentary elections, the RPR won 128 seats to the UDF's 130.

1988-: fissures

The defeat placed the RPR in its most difficult position for nearly a decade. Chirac in 1988 was not a recourse, as in 1981, but a solution that had been tried - even if this diminished presidential credibility did not prevent him from winning a second Grand Slam in Paris the following March. The RPR's National Assembly representation had fallen below that of the UDF for the first time. The Rocard government offered moderation, consensus and thus no easy targets for the right.

Hard times encouraged unprecedented intra-party dissent. A stormy Central Committee meeting in June 1988 opened a phase of criticism of the RPR's leadership, policies and lack of internal debate from young *rénovateurs* like Philippe Seguin: this led to a partial democratisation of the RPR's structures at the Extraordinary Congress of January 1989. Emboldened by successes at the March 1989 municipal elections (notably a major victory in Lyon by former Trade Minister Michel Noir), the *rénovateurs* then threatened to run their own list at the 1989 European elections with similar figures from the UDF, and only withdrew under threat of expulsion from the RPR from the new Secretary-General, Alain Juppé. The following months saw a reintegration of most *rénovateurs* within the official RPR ranks, but at a price: Chirac conceded the right to form *tendances* - factional groupings - within the RPR in June 1989. A dissenting motion at the February 1990 National Conference, presented by the unlikely combination of Séguin and Pasqua, was the most direct challenge to Chirac's leadership since 1976: it won nearly a third of the delegates' votes.

The RPR at the opening of the 1990s was not, like the UDF, under threat of implosion from its own in-fighting. But it was no longer the united, dynamic, campaigning movement established by Jacques Chirac. Eighteen months of debate had brought about remarkable structural changes - including the creation of an RPR-UDF parliamentary intergroup and closer policy coordination at a series of meetings planned for 1990, grandiosely entitled the States-General of the Opposition. But the party remained prey to its own strategic drift and to divisions of an unprecedented openness. Both diminished the RPR's chances of attracting new voters to complement what was becoming a limited, declining, conservative electorate.

The RPR Electorate

French elections of the 1960s were dominated by the emergence of Gaullism as a dominant political force: those of the 1970s were marked almost as heavily by its decline following the General's departure. In the 1980s, as Appendix 1 shows, the RPR appeared as the one stable feature in an otherwise rapidly changing landscape. Between 1981 and 1988, the PCF lost over half its voters, the PS consolidated its leadership of the left, the UDF vote fell by over 10 per cent, and the FN emerged from nothing to the status of a major political force. The RPR - measured in 1981 by adding the votes of Debré and Garaud to Chirac's own 18 per cent - moved by barely one percentage point. This stability is remarkable: one would expect the FN's rise to hit the RPR's share of the vote directly. This section will assess whether the stable RPR score in fact conceals substantial voter movement. We will examine the size of the RPR electorate, its geography, its sociological composition, and finally its attitudes.[8]

Size

Writing at the end of the 1960s, Jean Charlot saw in the rise of the RPR's predecessor, the UDR, 'the creation of a large party of the right, with no great weakness in any particular region or any one social category, capable of assuming power alone'.[9] As Table 7.1 shows, the Gaullists had become the dominant party of the right and the results of the 1968 and 1969 elections, in which they first secured an absolute majority in the Assembly and then won the succession to de Gaulle, gave reason to believe they would continue to be so.

Two major factors had contributed to this hegemony - the cross-class electoral attraction of de Gaulle, visible from the Liberation onwards, and the disarray of the left. Neither lasted much beyond 1969. To win the presidency, Pompidou was obliged to incorporate a larger slice of the centre into his majority, thereby moderating the Gaullists' dominance of it. The left's common programme of 1972 put further pressure on centre voters. The advantages of incumbency largely concealed the Gaullists' diminishing hold on the right in the 1973 parliamentary elections, but in the following year's presidential poll, the UDR's share of the right-wing vote fell to barely a quarter. Recovery under Chirac was partial: if the RPR was the largest right-wing party in 1978, it still failed to win half the right-wing vote, and slumped dramatically in the European elections of 1979. The Gaullist record from 1973 to 1981 shows increasing dependency on local incumbents, with mediocre to disastrous scores at presidential or European elections, but over 20 per cent in parliamentary elections where local positions could be made to count. Writing in 1980, Johnson argued that there were 'considerable grounds for scepticism about Chirac's ability to halt the Gaullist decline', and that 'no other European state, indeed no other developed state, can exhibit such a personalist movement maintaining itself long after its author's demise'.[10] From this perspective, the RPR's record in the 1980s is impressive: against renewed competition on the right, Chirac did stop the numerical decline. But the sociological base was dramatically narrowed.

Geography

Just as remarkable as the RPR's stable overall share of the vote in the 1980s has been the extent to which this has been reproduced locally. In not one of the 96 departments of metropolitan France did Chirac's 1988 vote differ by more than 5 per cent from the Chirac-Debré-Garaud total of 1981. Once again, this stability should be seen against a background of substantial change in the 1960s and 1970s, as Gaullism first converged towards and then diverged from the traditional right-wing French electorate.

The major areas of strength of the traditional right showed little variation between the 'No' vote at the 1946 referendum on the Fourth Republic constitution and Giscard's support at the second ballot of the 1974 presidential election. Indeed, the main bastions were discernible at least as early as 1902: the west, the east, and the southern heart of the Massif Central. To these were added, in 1946, a number of departments linking west to east.[11] The variation between strong and weak areas has diminished in intensity over time as local tradition has weakened and French politics has become 'nationalised'. But the overall pattern remained very similar.

The map of the classic Gaullist vote resembled that of the old right only partially. To begin with, Gaullism was more successful in the north than in the south. De Gaulle's vote at the first ballot in 1965 exceeded 42 per cent of registered electors in 13 departments, all of which lie north of a line between La Rochelle and Geneva. The traditionally right-wing southern Massif Central barely figured on the Gaullist map. Some northern areas of Gaullist strength like Nord and Pas-de-Calais, as well as parts of the Paris region, were traditionally left-voting. The eastern and western strongholds were thus linked, not by a narrow corridor, but by a broad swathe of Gaullist territory.

The distinctive geography of Gaullism began to change with the 1969 presidential election. While Pompidou won approximately the same first-ballot vote as the General, the north-south divide largely disappeared from the map of his support. He lost ground in northern departments, but gained in the Massif Central. This was helped by a 'favourite son' effect - Pompidou was from Cantal - but the overall result was at least as close to the geography of the traditional right as to that of classical Gaullism. This was accentuated in 1973, when the parliamentary elections saw further big losses in those northern departments that had contributed to the specificity of Gaullism - and a parallel reinforcement in the Massif Central.[12] In 1974 the Gaullists lost the presidency on their weakest poll of the Fifth Republic. Chaban-Delmas's first-ballot support was heavily concentrated around his city of Bordeaux. After the dust had settled and Chirac had shaken the party back into life, it was left with a geographical distribution of support that bore the - somewhat faded - traces of the Gaullien and Pompidolian electorates, as well as the strong imprint of Chirac's own personal areas of strength.

The geographical spread by department of the RPR's electoral strength is fairly even. The share of votes cast won by its presidential candidates deviated from the average by over 5 per cent in just seven departments in 1981 and eleven in 1988. Candidates of other parties showed comparable geographical evenness: the nationalisation of politics has softened the sharper relief of earlier contests. Within these limits, Chirac has done well in three main areas. The first is the 'inner west', a chain of traditionally right-wing departments stretching from Cherbourg to La Rochelle, where Barre as well as Chirac polled strongly in 1988. Secondly, Chirac's rural heartland is Corrèze and surrounding departments of the Limousin. Those to the south-east of Corrèze are part of the traditional right-wing Massif Central. But those to the north, south and west are traditionally left-wing, returning both higher-than-average Chirac votes and consistent overall left-wing majorities. Thirdly, Chirac's urban heartland, representing 10 per cent of his electorate, is Paris and the two suburban departments to the west. Long-standing Gaullist positions in the capital, more recent ones in the suburbs, and Chirac's own role as mayor of Paris, all contributed to his 27.5 per cent score in 1988 here. Finally, a number of RPR notables like Robert Poujade in Côte d'Or or Jacques Médecin in Alpes-Maritimes have contributed to good RPR scores in a number of isolated departments. The map of the RPR's support in the presidential elections of 1981 and 1988, then, is a very specific one, marked by the fading Gaullist and Pompidolian heritages and Chirac's own personal influence. A comparison between 1981 and 1988 gives the impression that Chirac has halted the Gaullist decline by 'freezing' his electorate in regions of strength. The sociological and opinion-poll data tell a somewhat different story.

Sociology

The sociology of Chirac's support changed more in the 1980s than the size of his electorate. These changes were, however, less marked than those of the 1960s and 1970s.

De Gaulle's dominant position in French politics depended to a great extent on his working-class support (Table 7.2). This appeal, discernible from the Liberation and the RPF years, distinguished classical Gaullism both from its right-wing predecessors and from its Pompidolian and Chiraquien heirs. The claim of the early 1960s that a cross-section of

Table 7.2: *Social penetration of Gaullism and right, 1965-1988 (presidential elections, first ballot, percentage of votes cast)* [a]

	de Gaulle 1965	Pompidou 1969	Chaban 1974	Chirac 1981	*Giscard 1981*	Chirac 1988	*Barre 1988*	**Le Pen 1988**
Total	44	44	15	18	*28*	20	*17*	**15**
Men	40	35	13	19	*23*	19	*15*	**17**
Women	46	46	16	18	*32*	21	*18*	**10**
Age								
18-24 *b*	-	-	-	11	*23*	17	*19*	**15**
25-34 *b*	-	-	-	18	*16*	13	*16*	**11**
21-34 *b*	36	38	16	-	-	-	-	-
35-49	36	38	15	18	*27*	17	*15*	**17**
50-64	48	41	14	24	*28*	29	*17*	**14**
65+	61	54	13	11	*48*	31	*17*	**12**
Profession of head of family								
Peasants	37	47	17	36	*33*	36	*16*	**18**
Shopkeepers, artisans	n.a.	n.a.	17	29	*35*	23	*23*	**31**
Liberal professions, Upper managers Industrialists *c*	{34*d* 45*f*	{44*d* 43*f*	{25	{36	*{24*	35*e* {27*g*	*16e* *{22g*	**21*e*** **{14*g***
White-collar, Junior managers *h*	{39	{35	{13	{18	*{17*	n.a. 18*h*	n.a. *17h*	**n.a.** **16*h***
Teachers, social workers *i*	n.a.	n.a.	n.a.	n.a.	*n.a.*	12	*16*	**6**
Office employees *i*	n.a.	n.a.	n.a.	n.a.	*n.a.*	15	*15*	**11**
Shop employees *i*	n.a.	n.a.	n.a.	n.a.	*n.a*	13	*21*	**21**
Blue-collar *j*	42	32	13	10	*18*	7	*7*	**16**
Low-paid, *j* unskilled	n.a.	n.a.	n.a.	n.a.	*n.a.*	9	*10*	**15**
Unemployed	n.a.	n.a.	n.a.	n.a.	*n.a*	10	*10*	**19**
Housewives, retired	57	51	13	16	*35*	23	*18*	**12**

Sources: Charlot, 1971, p. 74: Goldey & Knapp, 1981, p. 28 (IFOP poll): Le Monde, *Election présidentielle 1988* (Bull/BVA poll).

a INSEE, the French statistical office, changed several social classifications for the 1982 census: hence the many figures that are either not available or not strictly comparable.
b Voting age lowered to 18 in 1974 led to new age classification.
c First two categories amalgamated 1965-69: all amalgamated 1974-81: last two amalgamated 1988.
d Liberal professions and upper managers.
e Liberal professions only.
f Industrialists only.
g Upper managers and industrialists.
h White-collar divided after 1982 into four separate categories: 1988 figures junior managers only.
i First two categories amalgamated 1965-69: all amalgamated 1974-81: last two amalgamated 1988.
j Blue-collar divided after 1982 into skilled and semi-skilled vs. low-paid, unskilled.

Gaullists resembled 'the rush-hour crowd on the Metro' had considerable justification. They were, it is true, older than the adult population, and included more women. But overall de Gaulle's supporters, like the Socialists in the 1980s, managed a very even social penetration - a strong showing in every social group.

Pompidou only inherited part of this broad support. His electorate was as weighted towards women as de Gaulle's, and slightly younger. Above all, though, Pompidou won more support from peasants, the liberal professions and upper managers, somewhat less among white-collar workers, and much less among the blue-collar working class. What followed almost immediately was precipitate decline. The Chaban-Delmas electorate reveals a flat, low landscape, with a single modest peak among the urban bourgeoisie. Chirac in 1981 shows greater relief, and apart from the closing of the gender gap, the tendencies observed in 1969 are broadly reinforced. Overall, Chirac won just two-fifths of de Gaulle's popular vote. However, his levels of support are twice the average - and thus almost are strong as the General's - among peasants and the upper middle classes. Conversely, Chirac in 1981 won barely half his average vote, and less than a quarter of de Gaulle's, among blue-collar workers.

Changes in employment categories make changes in electoral sociology in the 1980s hard to measure, but some tendencies are still noticeable. The Chirac electorate has weakened in the 25-34 age category, but gained in all the others, most notably the over-65s (corresponding to gains among 'housewives and the retired') but also, to a lesser extent, the under-24s. Chirac's strength among peasants and the upper middle classes remains - he was ahead of all other candidates in these groups. It also seems clear that he has lost ground to Le Pen among his more modest urban voters. Le Pen attracted twice as many workers as either Chirac or Barre, and nearly twice as many of the unemployed: he also came ahead of all the candidates among shopkeepers and artisans, among whom Chirac lost six percentage points. Chirac in 1988 thus appears very much as the candidate of pensioners and peasants, the upper middle classes, shopkeepers and artisans. This is a long way from the classical Gaullist cross-class appeal. He should be concerned that his support was nearly twice as high among over-35s as among under-35s; that Barre's electorate in 1988 was younger and more sociologically balanced, and that he was very weak among all wage- and salary-earners below junior manager level. And there is reason to believe that Le Pen has accelerated Gaullism's decline among working-class and lower middle-class city-dwellers. For the FN has proved particularly attractive to RPR sympathisers.

Beliefs

Does the RPR electorate share a distinctive set of partisan attitudes? The specificity of classical Gaullism arose from the implications of de Gaulle's nationalism. National unity, even if it meant extensive social and economic intervention by the state, was more important than free-market capitalism. National independence set a limit to the depth of France's alliances and meant prickliness and suspicion towards NATO and Europe. Both were unusual for a European right-wing party.

Opinion-poll data shows little trace of such typically Gaullist attachments among the RPR electorate of the 1980s. By 1984, the vast majority of RPR sympathisers were strongly in favour of the EEC and NATO, including an integrated European defence, more pro-American than supporters of any other party.[13] They were barely more responsive to traditional Gaullist evocations of the General or the institutions of the Fifth Republic, and by 1988 a plurality even had a positive opinion of May 1968.[14] If not very distinctively Gaullist in their attitudes, RPR sympathisers do appear as more right-wing and more partisan on many issues. They have been more ready to identify themselves as right-wing, to give 'socialism' a negative connotation, and to support free-market policies than those of the UDF - though both groups appeared less attached to radical right-wing economics as the 1986 elections approached.[15] Stronger partisanship shows in the attitudes of RPR sympathisers to alternation in power. Between 1981 and 1986, RPR sympathisers were consistently more favourable than those of the UDF to an early end to the Socialist 'experiment', including early parliamentary elections, Mitterrand's resignation if the right won, and, for 12 per cent in 1983, any other legal or illegal means that might do the job.[16]

What really distinguishes the RPR electorate from that of the UDF, at least in 1983-85, is its greater receptiveness to the message of the FN. In 1984, a clear majority of RPR sympathisers approved of Le Pen's positions on immigration, Europe, anticommunism and law and order: UDF supporters only agreed with the FN on law and order, by a narrow majority. RPR supporters have also shown greater 'sympathy' for Le Pen (37 per cent to 24 for the UDF in 1985).[17] And immediately after the FN's first major breakthrough at the Dreux municipal by-election in September 1983, a clear majority of RPR sympathisers wished to see a local, national and governmental alliance with the FN, while a similar UDF majority rejected such ideas.[18] Not surprisingly, many RPR supporters have voted for the FN. A quarter of FN voters in 1984 said they had voted for Chirac in 1981. And 20 per cent of RPR sympathisers said they had voted for Le Pen at the first ballot in 1988 - twice the proportion of UDF sympathisers.[19] The real defection rate was probably higher than these figures indicate: some defectors, after all, must have stopped calling themselves RPR sympathisers and transferred their full allegiance to the FN.

The RPR's right-wing populists concluded that they should be won back by policies that emulated those of the FN: between ballots in the 1988 presidential campaign Pasqua claimed that the two parties shared 'the same values'.[20] Such statements risked alienating UDF support at the second ballot. The problem of wooing back FN defectors while retaining the UDF's second-ballot support explains many of the policy zig-zags between 1986 and 1988. In the end, the first objective was hardly achieved at all. RPR supporters surged to Le Pen just before the first ballot in April 1988, and only three-quarters of Le Pen voters who voted at the run-off cast their vote for Chirac. Chirac did a somewhat better job on the UDF: 23 per cent of its sympathisers voted for him at the first ballot, and 86 per cent of Barre's voters supported him on the run-off.[21] But it was far from sufficient, and certainly light years away from that Gaullist dominance of the right that had seemed so assured twenty years earlier.

Conclusion

De Gaulle's broad appeal, already skewed towards traditionally right-wing groups under Pompidou, has all but disappeared under Chirac. He is now supported by a classic conservative electorate - the elderly and old, the bourgeois, the peasants. And they have shown themselves more markedly right-wing in their attitudes than their UDF allies. This has resulted in greater vulnerability to the attractions of the FN, and an almost insoluble problem for Chirac as a presidential candidate.

The RPR electorate nationally appears as significantly more stable than any other in the 1980s. But this apparent stability is belied both by continuing change in its sociology, and by the evidence of departures to the FN as well as more or less compensating arrivals from elsewhere. The explanation lies at the local level, in two senses. Firstly, statistics on a smaller scale than the department may reveal bigger geographical variations than those noted above: there is not the space to consider this in detail here. Secondly, the local influence of the RPR may have helped to hold up the level of its support, even where the composition of that support was changing. Such local influence would depend both on the strength of the RPR organisation and - what in some cases amounts to almost the same thing - on the power of the RPR's notables.

The RPR's Implantation

For years after the Gaullists lost the presidency and their domination of the right-wing electorate, they retained a large number of their deputies. Both 1962 and 1968 saw the Gaullists win a comfortable majority - with Giscardian allies in 1962, and alone in 1968. In effect, they were winning parliamentary power from the top down on de Gaulle's coat-tails. Incumbency then placed Gaullists well for less favourable elections, whether they negotiated with their allies in order to run a single candidate from the first ballot, as in 1967 and 1973, or whether they fought a first-ballot contest against the Giscardians, as in 1978. Thus with the exception of the Socialist landslide of 1981, the Gaullists have always been more or less over-represented in the National Assembly relative to their first-ballot share of the vote.

Neither de Gaulle's prestige nor incumbency could guarantee parliamentary seats indefinitely, however. Most of this section will deal with the Gaullists' attempts to build a representative structure more conventionally, from the bottom up, particularly after they lost the commanding heights of national power.

The RPR and Local Government

Local government is particularly important in French politics for three reasons. First, there is a great deal of it: over 36,000 communes, 96 metropolitan departments and 22 regions, all with directly elected councillors. The French generally know who their mayors are, trust them, and vote at local elections (the 1989 municipal turnout of 73 per cent was considered low). Second, French local authorities enjoy considerable power. Major local elected officials played a crucial role in shaping France's rapid post-war urbanisation. The 1982 decentralisation acts reinforced their powers. Third, most national politicians are also local politicians. A traditional political career would start with a modest municipal post and move up through the offices of mayor and departmental councillor (*conseiller général*) to a national seat in the Assembly or the Senate - without relinquishing any of the local posts. Mitterrand's first four Prime Ministers have all held local offices as well as the premiership. This *cumul des mandats*, though limited after 1988 to one major local and one national position per office-holder, is still very much alive, and helps explain both the successful resistance of French local authorities to restructuring and the very great informal influence wielded by many mayors.

The earliest Gaullist electoral success was at the 1947 municipal poll. Ten years later, there was little trace of the strong local positions they won then: Chaban-Delmas was still mayor of Bordeaux, the Gaullists were strong on the Paris council, but at the March 1958 cantonal elections they elected just 60 departmental councillors out of some 1,500. The situation after 1958 was thus unprecedented: a national majority party with very few local roots - and few were put down in the Fifth Republic's first municipal elections in March 1959. The remedy lay in inverting the traditional cursus honorum. Chirac's own political debut is an excellent illustration of this. It was by using the resources his positions in Pompidou's *cabinet* commanded that he was able to target the backward and traditionally

Table 7.3: *Gaullists in the National Assembly, 1958-88*

Date	Total seats in National Assembly	Gaullist deputies (no.)	Gaullist deputies (% of total)
1958	552	212	38.4
1962	482	233	48.3
1967	487	200	41.1
1968	487	297	61.0
1973	487	184	37.8
1978	491	150	30.5
1981	491	85	17.3
1986	577	148	25.6
1988	577	130	22.5

Source: Lancelot, 1988; *Le Monde*.

Table 7.4: *Mayors of French towns of over 30,000 inhabitants, 1965-89*

Party	1965	1971	1977	1983	1989
Gaullists	25	30	19	47	40
Giscardians/ Centre *a*	n.a.	38	24	41	44
Socialists and allies	33	40	83	68	79
Communists	34	45	72	56	43
Other *b*	65	39	23	5	9
TOTAL	**158**	**192**	**221**	**217**	**217**

Source: Le Monde

a UDF in 1983 and 1989, its future components before then.
b Chiefly centre left and centre right: many become Giscardian/Centre from 1971.

left-wing department of Corrèze, and within it the difficult constituency of Ussel, to get himself appointed to the regional development council in 1964, and to win successively a municipal seat in Sainte-Féréole, a parliamentary seat in 1967, and finally a seat on the departmental council (*conseil général*). The Gaullists also attempted to improve their chances in France's towns and cities by changing the electoral law for municipalities of over 30,000 inhabitants. This abandoned proportional representation for a winner-takes-all system intended to reproduce the growing bipolarity of the national political system, squeezing the mass of Socialist and centrist incumbents between Gaullists and Communists.

Table 7.5: *Gaullists and moderate right in cantonal elections, 1961-88*

Year	Gaullists				Centre plus Giscardians (= UDF from 1976)				Total seats available for re-election
	First-ballot votes (% of votes cast)	Seats (no.)	Seats (%)	Presidencies	First-ballot votes (% of votes cast)	Seats (no.)	Seats (%)	Presidencies	
1961	12.8	166	11.0	7	9.4	142	9.4	5	1504
1964	12.2	123	7.9	7	13.4	229	14.7	5	1562
1967	14.5	220	12.9	8	12.1	249	14.6	19	1710
1970	15.7	206	12.8	13	14.3	293	18.2	22	1609
1973	12.7	244	12.7	9	14.8	336	17.4	28	1926
1976	10.8	171	9.5	11	20.3	425	23.4	25	1801
1979	12.3	172	9.7	11	21.1	347	19.5	31	1776
1982	17.9	323	16.6	13	18.8	460	23.6	34	1945
1985	16.6	399	10.4	21	18.1	519	26.5	40	1954
1988	15.9	352	18.2	22	17.2	436	22.5	45	1936
Total seats held, 1988		**754**	**19.8**			**933**	**24.5**		**3808**

Source: Lancelot, 1988, pp.110-112; *Le Monde*, September-October 1988. Figures for 1961-64 include overseas territories: the rest are for metropolitan France only.

But their success in remedying their poor local implantation was slow, as Tables 7.4 and 7.5 show. In the Gaullists' years of greatest national strength, they controlled only 15 per cent or so of France's towns and cities of over 30,000 inhabitants - and a much smaller proportion of the total number of communes. And their attempts to squeeze the centre merely resulted, after much hesitation on the part of the Socialists, in the Union of the Left being extended to the local level. This led to a famous municipal victory for the left in 1977, when the RPR lost a dozen cities - in effect compounding the decline of Gaullism with the right's overall weakness in that year. The single - enormous - exception to this record was Chirac's victory in newly reformed Paris, a precursor of later local conquests. These were achieved chiefly in 1983 and in a handful of by-elections (usually following ballot-stuffing by Communist incumbents) thereafter. They concerned both Paris suburbs and provincial cities, of which the largest in 1983 was Grenoble, won from the Socialists by the young and energetic Alain Carignon. RPR mayors held on to most, though not all of these gains in 1989: Nantes and Brest were the major losses. By the end of the 1980s RPR mayors ran 18.5 per cent of towns of over 30,000 inhabitants: in effect, the party's weakened national position and strengthened local one had converged to a roughly equivalent numerical level. The 18.5 per cent included Grenoble, Lyon - won by Michel Noir from an ageing UDF incumbent in 1989 - Paris and an impressive clutch of its suburbs.

The RPR's positions in the departmental councils reveal a similar record of sluggish growth in the 1960s and early 1970s, losses after Pompidou's death, and breakthroughs after the Socialist victory in 1981. Cantons have traditionally been the stronghold of centrist notables, increasingly willing from the mid-1960s to regroup under the Giscardian banner. Voters were unwilling to support Gaullists, who in the cantonal elections of 1967 and 1973 won barely a third of the vote they attracted at parliamentary elections in the same year.[22] And it took the arrival of the Socialist government, and the use of local elections to express national discontents, to bring the RPR's representation on the departmental councils to the level of its national support. Even in 1989, the RPR had only 22 presidencies to the UDF's 45.

Does local notability make a difference to national political performance? Two sets of figures suggest that it does. In the first place, as Table 7.7 shows, the RPR is now entirely wedded to the *cumul des mandats* and the traditional cursus honorum of building national elective office on the basis of local posts. In every parliamentary election since 1978, over 70 per cent of successful RPR candidates in metropolitan France have held local office as mayors, departmental councillors, or both. If we add parliamentary incumbency into the equation, the results are even more striking: anything between 78 and 97 per cent of successful candidates had already been elected as mayors, departmental councillors or deputies in their constituencies. The best-implanted, predictably, survive hard times best: in 1981, practically all the successful candidates were incumbents and half were *députés-maires*. But the 1986 result is also remarkable. Both the prospect of big gains and the closer central office control over candidate selection usually entailed by proportional representation apparently offered a fine opportunity to inject new blood. In fact, fears that notables who felt cheated of their rightful places on RPR lists might join competing lists led to considerable restraint from the candidacies committee: the proportion of notables among successful candidates was not much lower than at other elections in the 1980s.[23]

A second indicator of the importance of local positions for the RPR is the strength of Chirac's presidential vote in towns held by the RPR. The sample in Table 7.7 consists of the 67 towns and cities, including Paris, of over 20,000 inhabitants where an RPR incumbent was re-elected mayor in 1989 - in other words, towns that elected an RPR mayor twice in the 1980s. The presence of an RPR mayor offered Chirac a clear premium in votes, though no miracles. Chirac came first at the 1988 first ballot in 12 of the 67 towns, but he also came fourth in four; and in the majority (40), he came second, just as he did nationally. Even at the second ballot, Chirac only had a majority against Mitterrand in 30 of the 67. Taken as a whole, however, local notability showed clear advantages.

Table 7.6: *RPR notables in the National Assembly, 1978-1988*

	1978 no.	1978 %	1981 no.	1981 %	1986 no.	1986 %	1988 no.	1988 %
Mayors	59	*41*	39	*49*	67	*49*	59	*48*
City mayors (over 30,000 popln.)	12	*8*	8	*10*	22	*16*	10	*16*
Conseillers généraux a	73	*51*	39	*49*	72	*52*	77*e*	*63*
Both cons. gen. *and* mayors	31	*22*	18	*23*	39	*28*	42*f*	34
Total mayors *or* cons. gen. *or* both	101	*70*	60	*76*	100	*72*	93	*76*
Incumbent deputies *b*	99	*69*	75	*95*	81*b*	*59*	100	*82*
Députés-maires c	42	*29*	39	*49*	51*c*	*37*	50	*41*
Both cons. gen. *and* députés-maires *d*	22	*15*	18	*23*	30*d*	*22*	34*g*	*29*
Total in any of above categories	123	*85*	77	*97*	107	*78*	119	*98*
Total deputies in metropolitan France	**144**	***100***	**79**	***100***	**138**	***100***	**122**	***100***

a Includes Paris councillors, and 10 regional councillors in 1988.
b Includes 17 former deputies in 1986.
c Includes 12 former *députés-maires*, 1986.
d Includes 7 former deputies, 1986.
e Includes 10 regional councillors, 1988.
f Includes 5 regional councillors, 1988.
g Includes 4 regional councillors, 1988.

Table 7.7: *The Chirac vote in major RPR municipalities, 1981 and 1988*

Category of municipalities (all over 20,000 inhabitants, with an RPR mayor re-elected in 1989).	Number	Chirac vote April 1981 (%)	Deviation from 1981 national average (=18.02)	Chirac vote April 1988 (%)	Deviation from 1988 national average (=19.94)
RPR mayor since 1983 or later	39	18.3	+ 0.31	21.0	+ 1.02
RPR mayor since 1977 or earlier, excluding Paris	27	22.0	+ 4.02	26.8	+ 6.90
RPR mayor since 1977 or earlier, including Paris	28	25.0	+ 6.93	29.6	+ 9.66
Total excluding Paris region	35	19.0	+ 1.02	22.7	+ 2.71
Total excluding Paris	66	20.0	+ 1.94	23.5	+ 3.61
Paris region excluding Paris	31	21.5	+ 3.46	25.0	+ 5.07
Paris region including Paris	32	24.9	+ 6.90	29.1	+ 9.12
Hauts-de-Seine, Yvelines	16	25.7	+ 7.65	31.2	+ 11.24
Paris, Hauts-de-Seine, Yvelines	17	26.6	+ 8.61	31.5	+ 11.53
Paris	1	27.0	+ 8.95	31.6	+ 11.63
Total	67	22.7	+ 4.66	26.6	+ 6.66

Sources: both tables calculated from *Le Monde*. Table 7.7 - % of votes cast.

The group of 67 towns gave Chirac 22 per cent of the vote in 1981 - 4 per cent up on his national average - and 26.6 per cent in 1988. The second figure compares with a national average of 19.94 per cent, and averages of 19.5 per cent in towns of 20,000 to 100,000 inhabitants and 17.5 per cent in towns of over 100,000 inhabitants.[24]

The benefits of local office thus appear to increase with time. The gap between the national average and the result in the sample was greater in 1988 than in 1981. Both the addition of new towns won in 1983 and the maturing of municipalities won before then made a difference. And municipalities won in 1977 or earlier showed a bigger difference than those won more recently.

The benefits to Chirac were greatest in and around his Parisian bastion. Thus towns outside the Paris region show the smallest difference from the average in both 1981 and 1988. In the Paris suburbs, the difference is somewhat greater, and greater still in the two key departments to the west of the capital, Yvelines and Hauts-de-Seine. Paris itself, finally, shows the largest Chirac bonus of all.

Is the difference made by notability a critical one? The sample represents just over 8 per cent of all votes cast in 1988, and just under 11 per cent of Chirac's total vote - scarcely an overwhelming proportion. But the marginal difference could be vital: it was precisely in the Paris region, where the bonus of notability has been greatest, that the RPR pulled decisively ahead of the UDF in 1986, ensuring its dominance of the right-wing parliamentary coalition and thus of the *cohabitation* government.

The case of Paris deserves closer attention. In the first place, it is very big: each of its twenty *arrondissements* could pass for a 'large' provincial town. The Paris budget is equivalent to that of a large government ministry: the city employed over 40,000 people in 1983, and directly or indirectly controls tenancies to tens of thousands of housing units. The opportunities for patronage are vast. At the same time, the status of Paris as the capital city renders it particularly attractive as a political bastion. Its wealth ensures that Parisian ratepayers are lightly taxed, but often enjoy a generous level of provision, thanks in part to centrally financed amenities, for example in the area of culture. The mayor reaps a considerable public relations benefit, particularly as Paris was run before 1977 by a prefect and city council, neither of which were particularly image-conscious. Foreign heads of state pay courtesy calls on the mayor of Paris almost automatically. Finally, Paris does not simply have a large number of civil servants: the prefectoral past means it can recruit them from ENA. The mayor can offer close collaborators an unrivalled range of secure, interesting, well-paid jobs close to the summits of national power.

Chirac is an active, popular mayor with a high profile. The Paris Town Hall is where he lives full-time (even when he disposed of the Prime Minister's residence at Matignon), where he has retreated after electoral defeats, where he has a reservoir of loyal and competent supporters. He won all 20 *arrondissements* not only in the right-wing landslide of 1983, but also in 1989. Chirac has avoided the excesses of the Pompidolian era in architecture and planning, and also the politically unpopular decisions that the city arguably needs: private cars still roam and pollute freely.[25] The municipality has cultivated key groups like the liberal professions and shopkeepers assiduously, and has topped up family allowances and old-age pensions, except for immigrants. The opposition has been divided, inept and often ignored: municipal debates now take less than half the time that they did under the prefect. Chirac's municipal information service has both made the city's administration more user-friendly and burnished his own image. France's glossiest municipal bulletin reaches over half a million households every month. The municipal radio station occupies space in the Eiffel Tower. The press service draws the line between favourable and unfavourable journalists, and restricts the flow of municipal information (for example, the mayor's regular press conferences) to the former. Most remarkable, perhaps, is the synthesis Chirac has established between his positions in Paris, the RPR and - from 1986-88 - the government. This is symbolised by figures like Alain Juppé who have moved between high positions in the Paris council, the Paris bureaucracy, the 1986-88 government, and the RPR; or Jérôme Monod, the former RPR Secretary-General whose Compagnie Lyonnaise des Eaux won a favourable contract for the Left Bank's water distribution when the service was privatised in 1985. And in 1989, when Chirac created a 'communications cell' responsible to himself within the RPR, it grouped not only RPR services but also the information and press services of the Paris Town Hall.[26] Without operating a crude spoils system, Chirac has used Paris both to enhance both his hold on the RPR and his political position in the country.

Conclusion

Has the RPR become 'a conglomeration of local politicians', as Bell[27] suggests? To some degree, it clearly has. The Gaullists always knew that they could not indefinitely remain as they were in the 1960s, powerful nationally but weak locally. But they had little success in remedying their local weakness until several years after they had lost national power. The paradigm for the party's development in each case is offered by Chirac himself: moving downwards from Pompidou's *cabinet* to elected office in Corrèze, then, after the loss of national power, using a new local conquest - Paris - to initiate the process of reconstruction. What has resulted has been a more conventional party - one where most candidates for parliament hold local office and where holding local office clearly brings dividends in national elections. In this respect, the RPR has simply started having to play by the same rules as its competitors.

At the same time, the phenomenon of notability takes different forms and features in different parties. In the PCF, mayors are often treated with suspicion, excluded from the party's top decision-making bodies, and then used for their drawing-power to shore up the shaky Communist vote. Factional struggles within the Socialist Party have repeatedly formed around the big federations of Bouches-du-Rhône, Nord and Pas-de-Calais, each with a major Socialist town hall at its centre. The UDF has had significant success in regrouping moderate rural notables, but has been unable to unify them into a powerful electoral force. The most specific point about the RPR is Paris. It is an incomparable source of patronage, of daily electoral visibility, of expertise - in short, of almost all the scarce resources politicians need. Moreover, the conquest of the neighbouring department of Hauts-de-Seine under the leadership of the (erstwhile) loyal Charles Pasqua has strengthened the RPR's position from the city to the Paris region, making both into key sources of support both for the RPR and for its leader.

Although Gaullists have always been keen to win local positions, the logic of traditional Gaullism was never a municipal one. It rested on the unique relationship between the whole population and a head of state - not on parties, still less on the local resources party leaders could command. Reinforcing local positions after losing national power has perforce changed the nature of the RPR, adding to the grand, presidential, classical Gaullist concept of legitimacy, embodied in the presidency of the RPR, a series of competing local legitimacies. Conflict is to some extent limited by the fact that the biggest local conquest has been made by the RPR's President. But the appearance of provincial notables like Alain Carignon in Grenoble, Michel Noir in Lyon, or Michel Barnier in Savoie, who owe relatively little to Chirac and will not behave merely as cogs in a larger party machine, has placed unprecedented strains on the party organisation. These *rénovateurs* are based in the provinces, not Paris. In the year following June 1988, they brought about the greatest organisational changes the RPR had seen since its creation in 1976.

The 'RPR Machine'

As the policies of the RPR and the UDF converged in the 1980s, the main distinction between the two parties came to be seen as that of organisational style. The UDF was a federation of notables' clubs, the RPR a mass movement imbued with the leader principle: prominent members of each party often expressed the differences less kindly.[28] But despite its mobilising power the RPR has never functioned as a 'monolith', nor has the Gaullist Party organisation escaped major changes during its history. This section will assess both the organisational transformation of the Gaullist Party since it became the RPR, and the relative strengths of its leader and the centrifugal tendencies that have emerged since 1988.

History

The Gaullist movement has changed its names 10 times and its fundamental structures on four occasions. De Gaulle designed its first incarnation, the Rally of the French People (RPF) in 1947 as a mass movement that aimed to overthrow the Fourth Republic, effectively a mirror image of the Communists.[29] At its foundation, people queued up to join. The RPF's organisation attempted to be a near-military chain of command: its rallies typically featured martial music, stadiums, military uniforms, and gigantic Cross of Lorraine banners. It collapsed because the men it elected as deputies in 1951 were mostly conservative notables who used the RPF simply as a bandwagon to ride into the National Assembly. The lure of office and the reassuring conservatism of Antoine Pinay, who became Prime Minister in 1952, ensured their early desertion. A year later de Gaulle shut down the RPF: its remaining deputies became a small notable party called the Social Republicans, whose leader, Chaban-Delmas, joined several Fourth Republic governments, notably that of Pierre Mendès-France. Without the General, they were decimated at the 1956 elections. The party of de Gaulle's return to power was the Union for the New Republic (UNR). As Charlot has shown, it was 'first of all a ministerial team, then a central committee for the selection of candidates for the general election, then the largest parliamentary party in the National Assembly and finally - at last - a party'.[30] It also had an ambiguous relationship with de Gaulle. 'The situation is such that we must constantly serve him without ever being openly being commanded by him', said Albin Chalandon, the UNR's second Secretary-General.[31] The President of the Fifth Republic was supposed to be an *arbitre*, not another party chief. De Gaulle did not consult the party on the key political decisions of 1958: indeed, he did not give it his blessing until 1962, and then only indirectly. Unlike the RPF, the UNR filtered its membership with great care, partly to avoid *Algérie-française* entryism: it was never intended as a mass movement. But the UNR retained the RPF's tight central control. Each new deputy signed a 'declaration of fidelity' under the rules of the parliamentary group.[32] Co-opted majorities ran the top decision-making bodies. And in practice, the General's small entourage of 'barons' decided everything of substance.[33]

This changed somewhat with the Lille Congress of 1967, at which the party's name was changed to the Union of Democrats for the Fifth Republic (UDV^{e}) before becoming simply the Union of Democrats for the Republic (UDR) the following year. Lille was inspired by Pompidou: his main purpose was to ensure the movement a Pompidolian preparation for *l'après-de Gaulle*, the moment when it could no longer live on the prestige of its founder. Recruitment was widened and may have come close to the 150,000 mark. There were fewer co-opted or ex officio posts at the top, and the creation of a small Executive Bureau (*Bureau exécutif*) attempted to bring the real and the official decision-making bodies into line. Lille stressed the necessity for renewal rather than the heritage of the Resistance: the new Secretary-General was the 40-year-old Robert Poujade, future mayor of Dijon. But government members retained a real, if less tight, stranglehold on the movement.[34]

The UDR survived the shock of *l'après-de Gaulle* rather poorly. Its internal rivalries intensified with Pompidou's illness, and its collapse on his death was nearly total. Chirac himself spent that summer of 1974 winning back the support of the parliamentarians, many of whom found it hard to forgive his sabotage of Chaban-Delmas. Chirac's own election to the post of Secretary-General in December was followed by a flurry of all kinds of party activism designed to attract members back and to create a demand for 'a leader who took decisions'.[35] The ground was thus well prepared by 1976 for the party's re-launch.

Pasqua's model for the name and style of the renewed party was the RPF. For the first time, the movement had a President, a clear recognition that while not precisely in opposition (RPR ministers remained in government till 1981), it could not look for its 'natural', if unofficial leadership in the Elysée or Matignon. Like the RPF, the RPR has attempted to recruit massively: it claimed half a million members in 1977 and over 900,000 by 1986.[36] If it has never sought to overthrow the régime, it has shared the RPF's other main aim - its leader's return to power. At least until 1988, the membership saw this as a sufficient *raison d'être*.

Members

Accurate figures on party membership are as hard to find for the Gaullists as they are for any political party. Estimates for the total in the mid-1980s varied from the official claim of 900,000, to Bréchon, Derville and Lecomte's estimate of 310,000, to the actual number of cards found by the Harris polling institute when they examined the membership files, a mere 98,000.[37] Until such time as more research is done, it seems safe simply to state that the RPR is a mass-recruitment party and has many more members than any of its rivals on the right.

Who are the RPR's members? Their distribution does not correspond to the map of the RPR's electoral strength. Municipal implantation may help national electoral performance: but as Bréchon, Derville and Lecomte point out, high membership density has been neither a necessary nor a sufficient condition of electoral success.[38] Two exceptions stand out, however: RPR members are particularly thick on the ground in Paris and Corrèze, Chirac's own urban and rural heartlands.

Socially, as Table 7.8 shows, the RPR's membership is even less a cross-section of French society than its electorate. Caution is necessary with these figures. Most of them are official, and thus may simply correspond to the image the RPR wishes to give of itself (figures for 1970, 1975, 1977, and 1984 are the RPR's: those for 1984 delegates were researched by Bréchon, Derville and Lecomte, and the 1986 figures by Louis Harris polling). Moreover, both the RPR and INSEE, the national statistical office, have changed their sociological categories. With these reservations, four characteristics stand out. Firstly, men predominate - though less than in other French parties. Second, the self-employed (artisans, shopkeepers, and liberal professions) are heavily and consistently over-represented. Third, so are the upper and upper-middle classes - heads of firms and upper management.

Table 7.8:
Sociology of Gaullist Party members, 1970-86 (in %)

	UDR 1970	UDR 1975	RPR 1977	RPR 1984	**RPR 1984*a***	RPR 1986	*France 1982*
Sex							
Men		59	51	72	**80.0**	63	*48*
Women		41	49	28	**20.0**	37	*52*
Age							
Under 25				6	**4**	3	*14*
25-34				20	**14**	11	*21*
35-44				24	**34**	{	*16*
45-54				21	**21**	{70*b*	*16*
55-64				16	**20**	{	*14*
65 and over				13	**4**	16	*19*
Occupation							
Farmers	7	9	6	4	**3.5**	5	*4.0*
Heads of firms	3	3	{	4.5	**3.0**	{	*0.3*
Shopkeepers, artisans	16	17	{17*c*	13	**8.0**	{19*d*	*4.0*
Liberal professions	5	5	8	6	**9.5**	{	*0.6*
Upper management	3	4	10	12	**22.0**	{20	*3.0*
Civil servants	15	-	11	7	**-**	-	
Middle management/ 'Intermediate'*e*	6	11	-	-	**15.0**	11	*8.0*
Teachers	-	-	-	1	**6.0**	-	*8.0*
White-collar	9	20	-	13	**8.0**	11	*15.0*
Workers	15	22	20	3	**2.0**	5	*19.0*
Students	2	{	11	8	**2.0**	{	*5.0*
Retired, housewives, other (incl. no answer)	19	{ 9*f*	17	28	**21.0**	29*f*	*38.0*

Source: Ysmal, 1989, pp. 207, 209.

a Delegates to the 1984 *Assises nationales*, Grenoble (cf. Bréchon, Derville, and Lecomte, 1987).
b Includes ages 35-64.
c Includes heads of firms, shopkeepers, artisans.
d Includes heads of firms, shopkeepers, artisans, liberal professions.
e 'Intermediate', category introduced for the 1982 census, includes technicians, middle managers, social workers, etc. - but not teachers in this table.
f Includes students, retired, housewives, and no answer.

This is especially true of the 1984 delegates, and among them, of those exercising national responsibilities, where they accounted for 57 per cent.[39] Finally, the representation of white-collar and blue-collar workers, always lower than in the population as a whole, has decreased since 1976: again, this under-representation is particularly noticeable among 1984 delegates. If the over-representation of the upper categories is also typical of French parties other than the PCF, they tend to be managers or top civil servants in the RPR, as opposed to the university professors who people the upper reaches of the PS.[40]

The membership's sociological composition changed in part because of very rapid membership turnover in the 1980s. Bréchon, Derville and Lecomte have established that 34 per cent of the 1984 Grenoble Congress delegates, and fully 71 per cent of the 1986 Harris membership sample had joined the RPR since 1981: only 10 per cent of the Harris sample had joined before 1976. Only the small - but highly significant - group of elected officials retained some stability: in 1984, over half of this group had been members since before 1976.[41] With the turnover of members went a rightward shift in attitudes comparable to that observed for the electorate. The most direct comparison here is between Ysmal's sample of delegates at the 1978 Congress and their successors at Grenoble in 1984. The 1984 group are far more ready to place themselves, and the RPR, on the right of the political spectrum, further right than the UDF.[42] Support for state intervention in the economy and for reducing inequalities are common in 1978: by 1984, they have been replaced by a privatising zeal that applies to all nationalised industries and some public services.[43] Right-wing positions tend to be more pronounced among delegates who joined more recently: they are weaker among elected officials. Among the 1986 Harris sample, Bréchon has noted that 15 per cent felt 'close to' the FN after the RPR - a proportion second only to the Republican Party, with 40 per cent.[44]

The rank and file is not expected to participate in policy-making. Virtually every account agrees that the level of active participation within the RPR is very low, that meetings are dominated by office-holders, and that even many office-holders place a high priority on electoral mobilisation and winning support for the RPR, but a very low one on policy debates.[45] If a recurrent theme of successive party reforms has been winning more intensive participation from the rank and file, in practice the structure of the RPR as well as its culture have ensured that policy flows from the top.

Structure

Both external observers and internal actors have used the Leninist term 'democratic centralism' to describe the RPR's structure.[46] Like any mass party, the RPR reflects the country's administrative and political structures: it is present at local, constituency, departmental and (since January 1989) regional as well as at national levels. Party democracy resides in the election of a majority of the committees at each level by the level below. These committees are: the Constituency Committee (*Comité de circonscription*), the Departmental Committee (*Comité départemental*), the Central Committee (known since January 1989 by the rather less Bolshevik title of *Conseil national*) and the Political Bureau (*Bureau politique*). In addition, delegates at the National Conference (*Assises nationales*) elect the RPR's President. This systematic inclusion of elected members at each level was an innovation of the RPR in 1976, when the number of ex officio party office-holders was once again reduced. The RPR's centralism resides both in the party's official structures and in its unofficial functioning. Some dispositions are explicitly intended to reinforce central control. The Political Bureau is elected, but the Executive Commission (*Commission exécutive*), is appointed by the President and by the Secretary-General, himself the President's appointee. The Secretary-General appoints the Secretaries of the Departmental Committees. He can also sack party Secretaries and dissolve the Committees at both constituency and department level. A Central Control Commission (*Commission de contrôle des mandats*), elected by the Central Committee, monitors the federations' choice of delegates to the National Conference. Both the federations and the Secretary-General have the right to exclude party members under certain conditions. Though a right of appeal exists, through the National Commission of Conflicts (*Commission nationale des conflits*), elected by the Central Committee, it is not universal. Before 1990, only one annual report was presented to the National Conference, after a process of consultation similar to that obtaining in the PCF but without the - theoretical - opportunity for discussion in the party press.[47] In short, even a literal reading of the statutes makes it clear that intra-party democracy is more than tempered by central control.

And the reality is somewhat less democratic. Lawson's description of elections to offices at the lower level of the RPR is again reminiscent of Communist practice - one official candidate for each post being the rule. Schonfeld's account of how the 1977 Extraordinary Congress elected the Central Committee is also revealing: Chirac and his immediate *entourage* not only helped to draw up the list of 142 candidates from which the congress delegates elected 100 Central Committee members, they also proffered suggestions to influential delegates on how to vote.[48] No-one has ever opposed Chirac for the presidency: he has always been re-elected to the post by near-unanimous majorities. The National Conference does not begin to fulfil its function of 'fixing the general orientation of the movement': its job is to ratify, in appropriate pomp, decisions taken elsewhere. The Central Committee, at least before 1988, was also a rubber stamp: its key function of choosing parliamentary candidates was delegated to the RPR's election specialists, and its plenary sessions were so tedious that one Lawson interviewee declared that he had stopped going because he 'preferred to sleep at home'.[49]

Moreover, Chirac's personal advisers have often played a far greater role than that indicated by their official party title. The influence of Juillet and Garaud was critical throughout the 1970s. When Chirac finally let them go in 1979, he quickly turned to others. Pasqua, who has consistently held high office in the RPR, most notably as President of the Senate group, was the architect of the law and order policies designed to recapture the Le Pen electorate. Balladur held no such office but held regular individual meetings to advise Chirac on economic questions. With Juppé, he made a major contribution both to the RPR's conversion to the free market and to Chirac's conversion to *cohabitation*.[50] Superficially, then, the RPR is a good illustration of Michels's 'iron law of oligarchy'. The rank and file do not, and in many cases do not aspire to, play a policy-making role. And the President can exercise power to a formidable extent.[51] Yet between the base and the summit we find not only the leader and the led, but also a complex series of relationships between party officials, elected officials, and most frequently people who are both. Personal rivalries as well as party structures shape these relationships.

In each department, the key tandem is that of the President and the Secretary of the Departmental Committee. The President, elected by the committee, is usually a deputy, a departmental councillor, a mayor, or some combination of the three: he chairs the meetings of the committee. The Secretary, appointed by the RPR Secretary-General, sets the agenda for meetings and appoints the Treasurer.[52]

The potential for conflict is obviously great: the unfortunate Secretary may be caught between the notables on the committee and the demands of RPR Paris headquarters. Jacques Toubon, Secretary-General from 1984 to 1988, was particularly criticised for appointing Secretaries to the departments without local party approval. His successor Alain

Table 7.9: *The internal structure of the RPR*

Body/Post	Designation/Composition	Functions	Changes, 1989
President	Elected by *Assises nationales* (Chirac always above 97%).	National leadership of RPR: chairs national decision-making bodies.	
Secretary-General	Appointed by President	Assists President: may chair national bodies: RPR's legal signatory. May replace office-holders in departments.	Appointment ratified by *Conseil national*: (= old *Comité central*); makes annual report to *Conseil* which must be approved by it.
Bureau politique	President, Sec.-Gen., Treasurer, 20 members from Central C/ttee, former PMs, parliamentary leaders.	Assists President and Sec.-Gen. in leading RPR.	Treasurer no longer an ex officio member: now 30 members from new *Conseil national.*
Commission éxécutive	Membership and numbers chosen by President on proposition of Sec.-Gen.	Assists President and Sec.-Gen. in leading RPR.	All members referred to as *Secrétaires nationaux.*
Comité central	All national and European parliamentarians: all members of *Bureau politique*: former Secretaries-General and presidents of parliamentary groups: all *Délegués régionaux* and *Secrétaires départementaux*: 100 members elected on national list by *Assises*: members elected on regional basis by *Assises**.	Takes 'all decisions that may be required by the circumstances': decides on candidacies and second-ballot withdrawals at elections: decides on disciplinary measures with advice from *Commission nationale des conflits.* Fixes number of delegates to *Assises* from each department. Elects *Commission de contrôle des mandats.*	Renamed *Conseil national*: now 82 members from professional, youth and women's associations: between 1 and 3 members elected by each *Comité départemental*: former Prime Ministers: all members of *Commission éxécutive*: plus members of old *Comité central* less *Bureau politique* members and members elected on regional basis by *Assises.*
Conseil national	All members appointed by President and revocable by him.	Gives opinions on social, cultural and economic questions at meetings called by President.	Abolished.
Congrès extraordinaire	All RPR office-holders at department level or above.	Meetings called by Central Committee on proposition of President: Central Committee fixes agenda.	No longer *extraordinaire*: meets every year when no *Assises* held. Membership includes all *Conseil national* members plus Presidents of *Comités départementaux*, *Secrétaires de circonscription*, and youth/women/professional representatives.

Table 7.9: The internal structure of the RPR - *continued*

Body/Post	Designation/Composition	Functions	Changes, 1989
Assises nationales	All RPR members may attend. Voting members chosen by departments: number of votes decided by Central Committee for each department.	Meets every 2 years at 2 months' notice from Central Committee, which sends an agenda for comment from departments 2 months in advance. Composite report composed two weeks before *Assises*.	Meets every 3 years at least with 3 months' notice from new *Conseil national*: agenda sent to departments with 3 months' notice.
Comités regionaux	(not in 1976 statutes)	(not in 1976 statutes)	Structures analogous to those of Federations: the *Délegué régional* chosen by Secretary-General and charged with co-ordinating Federations.
Federations	One for each department under normal circumstances. *Comité départemental* consists of all elected officials above *conseiller général* level, and all Central Committee members from department, plus at least as many members elected by constituencies. President elected by *Comité*, Secretary appointed - and revocable - by RPR Secretary-General, Treasurer appointed by Secretary. Secretary-General may dissolve *Comité* in event of severe internal crisis. *Comité départemental* renewed before each *Assises nationales*.	May fix own internal operations. Chooses voting delegates to *Assises nationales* and elects some members of Central Committee. *Assises départementales* meet one month before *Assises nationales* to debate Central Committee's draft report. *Comité départemental* makes final decision on all membership applications.	*Comités départementaux* renewed in 3 months preceding each *Assises nationales*. *Conseil national* may dissolve Federations on proposal from RPR Secretary-General.
Constituencies	A *union de circonscription* for each constituency, composed of sections based territorially or on professional lines. *Comité de circonscription* consists of the constituency's elected officials (above mayor) and *Conseil national* members plus twice as many delegates elected by sections. *Comité* elects its own Secretary, and may be dissolved or its Secretary dismissed by RPR Secretary-General.	All membership applications made to constituency party. *Comités de circonscription* elect members to *Comité départemental*.	

Source: RPR, *Statuts nationaux*, December 1976 and January 1989.

* Members of Constitutional Council, ministers and current presidents of parliamentary groups excluded from party office unless exempted by Central Committee.

Juppé has been more conciliatory. Many Secretaries are themselves elected officials from the department, often relatively junior ones who are prepared to tolerate a fairly thankless job in the hope of being rewarded with a safe parliamentary seat.

The Departmental Committees also play a role in the choice of parliamentary candidates, and elected parliamentarians dispose of some margins of manoeuvre vis-à-vis the leadership. According to the statutes, candidates are chosen by the Central Committee, renamed the National Council (*Conseil national*) in 1989. The Central Committee delegates the final choice to a sub-committee, dominated throughout the 1980s by Pasqua. But circumstances have often obliged the subcommittee to take note of the notables' preferences. In both 1981 and 1988 the RPR was struggling to limit the damage of a Socialist victory. In 1978 it was struggling to stay ahead of the UDF. In 1986 it was doing this and fighting to head off defections of voters or even candidates either to the FN or to dissident Barrist lists. In all cases the Rue de Lille had to rely heavily on the candidates themselves to finance their own election - and local office is a powerful source of funds for the campaigns of any party.[53] Even in 1986 the rate of renewal was in fact rather low (see above). One of Chirac's first gestures towards his slim majority was to guarantee them all a clear run in safe constituencies for the next parliamentary elections. Voting discipline is generally respected, but frequently by a handful of deputies turning the Chamber's electronic voting keys for their absent colleagues. And exceptions are readily admitted where constituency interests impinge.

The two bodies at the top of the RPR, the Political Bureau and the Executive Commission, have identical statutory tasks of 'assisting the President and the Secretary-General in the direction of the movement'. In practice, their functions and activities differ greatly. The Political Bureau is convoked by Chirac roughly every two months: it includes the Secretary-General, the Presidents of parliamentary groups, the Treasurer (Robert Galley, former minister and *député-maire* of Troyes), all former RPR Prime Ministers and any other personalities whose support Chirac feels he needs. Its main purpose is to agree on major policy initiatives. Though these were generally formulated elsewhere, the Political Bureau is more than a rubber stamp: it is there to allow Chirac to note and if necessary head off or conciliate opposition to his activities from the most influential members of the RPR. The Executive Commission is the RPR's working management committee. Composed of the National Secretaries (*Secrétaires nationaux*) and chaired by the Secretary-General, it meets every Wednesday morning to review the week's events, to decide on the RPR's response to them, and to hear reports from individual members where appropriate. Thus while it does not exist formally to elaborate policy, its responses may in practice help to define the RPR's margins of manoeuvre. Parliamentarians dominate the top levels of the party. If the RPR limits the proportion of elected officials who are ex officio members of its governing institutions, there is no limit, as there is in the PS, for example, on the proportion of elected officials who may be appointed or elected on their own merits. In September 1988 nine of the eleven National Secretaries appointed by Juppé to sit on the Executive Commission were deputies. There is thus no hard and fast division between a party apparatus loyal to Chirac and a parliamentary group responsive to more local interests.

Nor, though, is there the extraordinary cohesion of the *compagnons* of the 1960s. Social origins encourage a sense of collegiality: the proportion of members of the *grande bourgeoisie* rises fast the higher the echelon in the party structure.[54] Long-standing networks of acquaintance also count: much of Pasqua's power resides in such networks, and in the number of people who owe him favours. So can personal animosity, as between Bernard Pons, the Secretary-General of the early 1980s, and his main competitor for air time,

Claude Labbé, President of the National Assembly group. An element of division, finally, can grow between the Parisians and the rest. For much of Toubon's time, not only the President and Secretary-General and the Presidents of both the parliamentary groups, but also most of the Executive Commission came from Paris or the Paris region. Part of the problem is one of logistics: the Parisian commitments of high party office risk losing a provincial deputy his seat. But the danger that provincial deputies may feel excluded from decision-making centres is real. It took striking shape with the appearance of the *rénovateurs* in 1988.

Tendances

The right's best-organised party was never a monolith. Its parliamentary notables broke the RPF in 1952. A minority of 'Left Gaullists' organised during the early Fifth Republic into a partly autonomous movement, the Democratic Union of Labour (UDT), alongside the UDR. The 'leftism' of the Chaban-Delmas premiership engendered a conservative UDR parliamentary group, *Présence et action du gaullisme*. Pompidou's death almost provoked the break-up of the UDR. More recently, several RPR elected officials, including François Bachelot and Bruno Mégret, left to join the rising FN at a high level. The novelty of the period after 1988 was that it saw the way opened for the appearance of identifiable factions (*tendances*) within the RPR on a pattern that owed more to Socialist practice than to the traditions of the leader-obsessed Gaullists.

The *rénovateurs*, who set much of the agenda for change between mid-1988 and mid-1989, tended to be young (of the immediate post-war generation), provincial, on the left of the RPR, and with friends in the UDF. They include Philippe Séguin, *député-maire* of Epinal and Social Affairs Minister from 1986-88, and Michel Noir, Foreign Trade Minister in the same period, deputy and (since March 1989) mayor of Lyon. Their UDF associates have included François d'Aubert, deputy for Mayenne, and Charles Millon, *député-maire* of Belley and (since September 1989), President of the UDF group in the National Assembly. The association began with the Socialist nationalisation bills, which the four deputies opposed with a round-the-clock spate of speeches and amendments that earned them the sobriquet of the 'four musketeers'. It was perpetuated by an informal group known as the 'Cercle', dedicated to breaking down the right's party divisions.[55] The RPR's *rénovateurs* emerged as a force for party reform at the first Central Committee meeting following the 1988 parliamentary elections, when their proposals for the avoidance of further electoral defeats took two main lines. Greater party democracy would bring the RPR closer to its electorate and avoid policy errors which had offered easy ammunition to the Socialists; and an early merger with the UDF would avoid the *querelles des chefs* - squabbling among over-ambitious leaders - which had cost the right so dear in 1988.

In 1988-89 the *rénovateurs* made no direct challenge to Chirac's leadership. But their calls for reform echoed through the federations as Juppé undertook his inaugural tour as Secretary-General in autumn 1988. And in January 1989 an Extraordinary Congress made three major changes to the statutes (see Table 7.9). The old National Council (*Conseil national*), which had been very much the President's creature, was simply abolished - the least important measure, as it had had little power. The name was now given to the former Central Committee. Secondly, the Extraordinary Congress was regularised: Congresses are now held annually when there is no National Conference (*Assises nationales*). Fixing the timing of Congresses removes the President's prerogative of effectively calling a Congress when he liked - a right Chirac had used against Chaban-Delmas in 1978. Finally, the Secretary-General, though still the President's appointee, must now also present an annual report to the Central Committee (renamed *Conseil national*), who debate and vote on it. While a defeat for the Secretary-General in this vote of confidence is unlikely, the provision for such a debate is a major innovation. The Secretary-General's position now resembles that of a Fifth Republic Prime Minister, appointed by the President and responsible to parliament - and thus potentially very uncomfortable.

The *rénovateurs* were much less successful in establishing themselves as an independent political force or in seizing commanding heights in the RPR. True, Juppé appointed fewer Parisians and more provincials to his Executive Commission. But Séguin was narrowly defeated by the older and more conservative Bernard Pons for the presidency of the parliamentary group in the summer of 1988. The following spring, following their successes at the March 1989 municipal poll, a group of RPR and UDF *rénovateurs* signed a declaration in favour of a list of younger opposition politicians, removed from any *querelles des chefs,* to fight the European elections. The declaration was signed by the 'Four Musketeers' as well as by Etienne Pinte, RPR deputy from Yvelines, Michel Barnier, President of the departmental council of Haute-Savoie, François Fillon, deputy for Sarthe, and Alain Carignon, *député-maire* of Grenoble. Juppé's response was swift: the Central Committee declared that RPR members who joined any unofficial European list would have 'placed themselves outside the party', a line reminiscent of the PCF in the early 1980s, which served to by-pass the cumbersome official exclusion procedures.[56] It worked: the *rénovateurs* were absent from the European elections. This defeat showed their weaknesses rather openly: they had no common or coherent policy, no organisation, no common strategy, and no single leader. Deflecting the direct challenge with a mixture of concessions and threats has thus been relatively straightforward for Juppé.

He had neither coopted nor crushed the *rénovateurs*, however. They continued to attract support both within the RPR and among voters, and without acting as an organised group, they set much of the RPR's policy agenda for the rest of 1989. Their ideas on relations with the UDF moved two steps forward with the organisation of a parliamentary intergroup in October 1989, and preparations for the States-General of the Opposition, to be held in 1990. Their policy preferences were advanced as the RPR 'rediscovered' its social dimension and the Gaullist commitment to workers' 'participation'. And in June 1989 the leadership allowed for the organisation of *tendances* for the first time.

As a result, no fewer than eight 'contributions' were defended at the Central Committee meeting that prepared the February 1990 National Conference, including one from Carignon, one from Seguin, two from conservative groupings, and one 'official' one from Juppé.[57] Juppé managed to produce a synthesis that satisfied most of their authors. Séguin, however, remained the loose cannon on the deck, detached from the mainstream *rénovateurs* but in no way tied down by the leadership. His sudden alliance with Pasqua, the leader of the RPR's right-wing, was the main surprise in the run-up to the National Conference. The Pasqua-Séguin motion (submitted late in December) criticised the leadership for allowing the RPR to lose the initiative after 1988, called for the RPR's relaunch as a 'new *rassemblement*', and prayed Chirac to leave its presidency the better to prepare his next presidential campaign. Pasqua and Séguin claimed that their challenge was to Juppé, not to Chirac himself: Chirac refused to see it in this light, and threatened to resign if the official text won less than two-thirds of the delegates' votes. He got his two-thirds - just - at a National Conference punctuated by wholly unprecedented open factional campaigning. The delegates' vote resolved little. With over 30 per cent, Pasqua and Séguin remained strong. And a week later, the composition of the new Political Bureau accommodated both their supporters as well as those of Michel Noir. By March 1990, the *compagnonnage* of traditional Gaullism had been laid to rest, and faction had well and truly arrived in the RPR.

Conclusion

Unlike the pre-1969 Gaullist Party, dominated by a charismatic leader and his small, loyal entourage, the RPR has been both a machine aimed at regaining the presidency and a collection of politicians concerned to consolidate power bases that owe little either to the General and his legacy or to Chirac. The RPR's statutes reflected its first mission: the more flexible practice and the strong position given to elected officials in the leadership reflect the second. Despite 'democratic centralism', the RPR leadership has not stifled dissent in the manner of the PCF. The first mission failed in 1988, at least for the moment: it is not surprising, then, that the second has grown in importance, with one element of the RPR's 'notable' side being able to effect durable change to the statutes. The question is whether this will lead to a structural change in the balance of power in the RPR and will moderate in practice the centralisation and hierarchy that have distinguished it from other parties of the right and whether the arrival of faction will bring the RPR the benefits - and drawbacks - of an open debate on policy that it has so far tended to eschew.

Political Strategy

'Our method', Philippe Seguin told the Central Committee after the 1988 elections, 'was the following. We had a leader. This was our hope. It was also, very often, our only certainty. And from one election to another, according to what was fashionable at the time, or which adviser was influential, we chose the ideas that seemed to offer the best chance of electing our leader or his partisans'.[58]

The RPR's policy revisions in its first fifteen years were indeed dramatic, tempting some authors to assert an abandonment of its Gaullist heritage. This is overstating the case. There were plenty of precedents for policy change. As Charlot has noted, the free-market economics of de Gaulle's RPF years was a far cry from the interventionism of the Fifth Republic.[59] Leadership and a 'certain idea of France' had always been more important than specific policy questions to the Gaullists. Discussing policy change entirely in terms of fidelity to or betrayal of Gaullism is in any case of limited use. The context has changed, with some elements of high Gaullism either losing relevance or coming to command a very broad consensus. The onset of economic crisis in the 1970s led to major policy reappraisal throughout the developed capitalist countries. And France's loss of economic independence has given international developments a greater relevance to domestic policy. It remains true that the RPR did abandon many policies characteristic of the Gaullists' most successful years in government. This section aims to detail and explain this major revision. A postscript will assess a possible reversion to earlier doctrines after the 1988 defeat.

Programmes and Policies

Chirac's first premiership of 1974-76 could have done credit to a social-democratic government. A political context in which the left had come within an ace of winning the presidency and set much of the political agenda encouraged Giscard to call for a 'vast building-site of reforms'. Thus the first Chirac government saw the age of majority lowered to 18; more liberal laws on abortion, contraception and divorce; the break-up of the state television monopoly into three separate - though still very state-controlled - stations; a law giving Paris a mayor for the first time in a century, and another taxing high-density building in city centres, and the creation of a single middle-school system. Social Security was extended to virtually the whole population, the retirement age of manual workers lowered, and the old local purchase tax replaced by the *taxe professionnelle*, a business rate. Workers' pay rose faster than that of managers, and pensions reached half of the minimum wage in 1975. Redundancies required government authorisation, and unemployment benefit for the first year amounted to 90 per cent of previous income. Rivalry between President and Prime Minister helped ensure that austerity measures rendered inevitable by the 1973 oil crisis were applied hesitantly: consumption continued to grow, profits and investment fell.

Were these the President's policies, imposed on a reluctant Premier and majority? Chirac certainly opposed some reforms in private - for example, the change in the status of Paris, the source of so much of his own power after 1977. Gaullist deputies mauled Giscard's capital gains tax bill badly, rendering it almost unworkable as law. They also made sure to stifle the report commissioned by the President on 'participation' of the workforce. Abortion was legalised primarily with Socialist, not Gaullist votes. But Chirac still countenanced all the legislation for two years: power, rather than specific policy questions, was the main issue at his departure.

And when the Gaullists did seek to differentiate themselves from the government after 1976, they did not immediately do so from the right. Basic policy differences between the UDF and the RPR in the late 1970s were fairly clear. The UDF was more 'liberal' both in the American sense (in its positions on social issues) and in the French one (in its support for the free market), as well as being more supportive of NATO and the EEC. The RPR was more conservative on societal issues, but decidedly more interventionist on the economy as well as more defensive of French national sovereignty. Just before the 1978 elections, Chirac claimed that the RPR differed from the UDF in its commitment to national independence, its greater *volontarisme* in economic affairs, its concern for social welfare and - a more valid claim for the 1960s than for 1978 - its more 'popular' electorate.[60] The 1978 programme was classic left-wing Gaullism. It included reinforced planning to achieve growth of five or six per cent; increased workers' share-holdings and profit-sharing; tax concessions to small traders, and tax exemption for people on the minimum wage; a 'national environment bank', and a wealth tax. Almost the only element in common with later policies was the strong emphasis on law and order, on which Giscard was considered soft.[61] The traditional prickliness on sovereignty questions reached a paroxysm in the RPR's campaign for the 1979 European elections, which aped the Gaullist rhetoric of June 1940 in order to attack the government's European policy. Its failure was conspicuous: Chirac's European list came in ten points behind Simone Veil for the UDF.

The 1981 presidential campaign began the move to a more orthodox conservatism. For the first time, Chirac's attacks on the President's record ('France is on the road to bankruptcy and despair') came unambiguously from the right. He proposed spending cuts totalling some 2 per cent of GDP over two years, to be achieved chiefly by natural wastage of civil servants; major tax cuts - 5 per cent for all households, and total exemption for incomes below 3,300 francs; enhanced tax concessions for capital investments, and the abolition of the *taxe professionnelle* and the capital gains tax, both instituted under his own premiership. Chirac argued that his fiscal and other measures would stimulate growth, reduce unemployment and increase the state's income while diminishing the calls on its expenditure - a classical supply-side thesis. This was not yet the conservative orthodoxy of the mid-1980s. Cuts in personal taxation were weighted towards lower, not higher incomes. The wealth tax was now rejected as being 'inappropriate in current circumstances'. 'Participation' was still mentioned. So was planning, though Chirac stressed that he meant indicative planning. But this was a radically different programme from anything the RPR had suggested hitherto.

Five years later, the RPR's social conservatism and the UDF's economic 'liberalism' (expressed, but barely applied, in the 1970s) converged in the 'common platform' of February 1986. The platform's most striking feature was a very large programme of privatisations, starting with the major banks and industries nationalised by the Socialists in 1982 and including the whole of the 'competitive sector' of the economy plus most state television and radio channels. It also called for deregulation of prices, bank lending, foreign exchange and rented property, cuts in taxes and social security contributions (this time to benefit top income groups most), a reform of the *taxe professionnelle*, some limited incentives to investment, and a greater role for the private sector in building and running infrastructure. New employment legislation would end the government authorisation of redundancies, encourage temporary contracts, decentralise pay negotiations, and end indexation of the minimum wage. Nods to the FN agenda included the return of random police identity checks, the immediate custodial return to the frontiers of illegal immigrants and convicts at the end of their sentences, more spending on the police, and a new nationality law ending the automatic acquisition of French nationality by children born in France of immigrant parents.[62] Other key proposals included the immediate restoration of the two-ballot parliamentary electoral system, and greater autonomy for universities. In foreign and defence policy, the platform confirmed a departure from traditional Gaullism as remarkable as the conversion to economic 'liberalism'. It proposed to accelerate the realisation of a single European market and monetary system; to support further institutional reforms to improve the functioning of the EEC; to increase defence spending to a steady 4 per cent of GDP, and to integrate France's nuclear strategy with the rest of Europe and the USA.

This was arguably the most right-wing programme put forward by a major French political grouping since the Liberation, and one that had more in common with 'Anglo-Saxon' conservatism than with Gaullist policy of the recent past. Much of it was applied by the second Chirac government. The stock market successfully digested eight large groups and three medium-sized banks, worth roughly 100 billion francs: they included banks that had been in the public sector since 1945. The wealth tax and the governmental authorisation for redundancies were abolished, all personal and business taxes diminished, and the Stock Market further deregulated. An amnesty for customs and tax frauds encouraged the return of capital to France. The first television channel was privatised, and defense spending programmed to 1991. Interior Minister Pasqua restored random identity controls, won significant successes against the *Action directe* terrorist group, and expelled illegal - and some legal - immigrants with relish. At the same time there were limits to the programme's application. The university reform was withdrawn in the face of student protest. Shortly afterwards, both the nationality reform and Justice Minister Chalandon's project to build private prisons were shelved: both were highly controversial, and likely to damage the consensual credentials Chirac the presidential candidate was trying to build. Moreover, as Michel Bauer has noted, the privatisations were characterised more by the creation of 'a new economic technocracy close to the Gaullist Party' than by that of a genuinely free market.[63] In these two very different respects, Gaullism as a movement aimed at winning power prevailed over newly discovered ideological purity.

Accounting For Policy Change

Whether or not the RPR's policies of the 1980s, with their exaltation of private enterprise and their calls for greater European and Atlantic integration, were fundamentally at odds with the General's own Gaullism, they certainly had little in common with the record of the 1960s - of the years, in other words, when the Gaullists had enjoyed their greatest political success. Given the RPR's failure to regain power, or broad support across the country, or indeed very much support at all among wage- and salary-earners, with the new policies, it is worth asking why it adopted them at all.

The first reason was the change in the domestic and international context. The first half of the 1980s also saw the PS move from a strategy of 'rupture with capitalism' to deregulating the Stock Market and engaging in discreet denationalisations. Only the PCF failed to change its policies, losing half of its voters in the process. The left no longer dominated the political agenda. On social questions, and particularly anything concerned with immigration, the agenda was increasingly set by the FN. No party had formulated a strategy to deal with that. On economic problems it was set by Margaret Thatcher and Ronald Reagan, as the centre ground of politics moved sharply rightwards in Britain, the USA and Germany as well as France.

This ideological space on the right opened up at a critical moment for the RPR. Attacks on the UDF from exaggeratedly Gaullist positions had met with little success: they had brought an honourable result in 1978 but a very poor one in 1979, and the RPR was no closer to regaining power than at its launch. Nor was it succeeding very well in tapping the discontent on the right with Giscard's obsession with occupying the centre ground. Right-wing opposition to government policy took on a new breadth and intensity after the Socialist victory of 1981. By positioning itself on the orthodox right, the RPR was offering an alternative governing programme that was not a re-run of the Giscard presidency.

Policy change was not preceded by any major debate within the party. As we have seen, the structure of the RPR is designed for winning power rather than debating policy. Moreover the early 1980s also saw massive turnover in party membership, from the rank and file to leading positions: this diminished the risk of damaging traditionalist sympathies; indeed, new members were markedly more right-wing than the old. The danger, however, was that the party would then perform its function of linking a potential government to the electorate rather badly. Much of the free-market economic platform was defined by political clubs like the *Club de l'horloge* and the *Club 89* (as well as by Balladur as Chirac's adviser after the departure of Juillet and Garaud). The *Club 89*'s policy statement, *La double rupture*, written by Juppé in 1983, was quite explicit about the need to break both with Mitterrand's socialism and with the quasi-socialism it saw as preceding it - and about the need to seek economic inspiration in Britain and the USA. By adopting many of its recommendations in February, the RPR was saddling itself with a set of policies that even the right-wing electorate - however much it disliked the Socialists - viewed with reserve: and its success with peasants, small businesses and the independent professions was gained at the expense of the denser ranks of workers and the salaried middle classes.[64]

What is important is less that the RPR had not kept its policies of the 1960s as that it has found nothing to replace the unique appeal it enjoyed under the General's leadership. Nothing Chirac has done has filled this vacuum. Entertaining when Jean Baudouin calls 'an opportunistic relationship to ideology', the RPR in general, and Chirac in particular, have had a price to pay in terms of basic political credibility.[65]

Postscript: Faction and Strategy

Programmatic debate took second place after 1988 to questions of party strategy, and particularly to the problem of relations with the UDF and FN. In many ways, the RPR's position resembled that of the Socialists in the early 1960s. To regain power, they needed to win votes both from the party on their extreme flank (the PCF for the Socialists, the FN for the Gaullists) and from the centre. Attempting to so both at the same time had been tried during *cohabitation*, with less than conclusive results. Choosing a priority - to expand towards the extreme or towards the centre - was to run the risk of losing voters at whichever pole was neglected. The leading *rénovateur* Michel Noir clearly chose a centrist option in his *Force unie* initiative of March 1990, aiming for an early union with the UDF and having no strategy at all for winning back FN voters. Carignon went further in June 1990, inviting RPR voters to support the Socialist candidate against the FN at a run-off in a cantonal by-election from which the RPR candidate had been eliminated. He was immediately subjected to a statutory expulsion procedure. Pasqua and Séguin were closer to the rightist choice, stressing the importance of stopping departures to the FN - though Pasqua became increasingly hostile to any form of electoral or governmental pact with the FN. The leadership has, for the moment, concentrated more upon its relations with the UDF, holding several joint meetings under the name of the States-General of the Opposition and moving towards a form of confederation: this would stop short of Noir's plans for fusion but would include Pasqua's idea of a 'primary' that would give the right a single candidate from the first ballot of the next presidential election. It is no nearer than in 1988 to finding the right strategy for defeating the FN. To adopt the equivalent of François Mitterrand's strategy of the 1960s would, of course, mean a binding national alliance with Jean-Marie le Pen, with major concessions to his agenda and the promise of ministries. This option has not so far been openly discussed within the RPR

Ultimately, the strategic debate is linked to a policy debate. The Rocard government, by choosing the safe, consensual ground of the New Caledonia referendum and the minimum income for the poor, offered few policy openings for the right-wing opposition in the short term. The *rénovateurs*, the leadership, and Pasqua were all in varying degrees ready to renew calls for a more 'social' Gaullism, and implicitly or explicitly to accept that the 1986-88 government had done too little for ordinary wage and salary earners. The debate, then, was more likely to turn on the FN's agenda of law and order and immigrants than on questions of economic policy.

There remain grounds for scepticism on the RPR's capacity to learn from recent misfortunes. The party's 'culture of debate' is slight: this has been a source of weakness as well as strength, and it cannot acquire one overnight. Chirac's main policy initiatives of 1989-90 were to rally to calls for a more 'social' Gaullism, to launch a petition against highly putative Socialist plans to offer immigrants the vote at municipal elections, and to propose a 'shadow cabinet' of the whole right - a plan greeted with considerable scepticism even within the RPR. All smack more of the old Chirac, reacting fast to unfolding events, than of a man who has reflected deeply on the causes of his own defeat and charted a new course.

Conclusion

Mitterrand's victory in 1988 was to a considerable extent that of the patient strategist over the frenetic tactician. The RPR has not been alone in realigning itself as the political centre ground tilted sharply rightwards in the early 1980s. But there is little sense, in the record of Chirac and his party over the 15 years following Pompidou's death, of objectives and policies clearly defined and consistently pursued. As Liffran has pointed out, success as Mayor of Paris does not demonstrate presidential qualities.[66]

Chirac's energy, dynamism, and assiduous cultivation of clienteles and fashions failed to compensate for a failure to communicate a coherent sense of vision or purpose. Such a vision would have stood him in better stead both to react more effectively to the major new challenge of the 1980s, the rise of the FN, and to present a credible alternative to Mitterrand's patriarchal appeal of May 1988. For the moment, Séguin's assessment at the beginning of this section must stand.

General Conclusion

How successfully have the Gaullists adjusted to life without the General? Assessing whether the RPR's record is one of wasted opportunities or amazing survival is partly a matter of calling the glass half-empty or half-full. Chirac's performance in 1988 was both undistinguished as an absolute figure and worrying in its social composition. The fact that the RPR had fewer parliamentary seats than the UDF was without precedent in the Fifth Republic. The continued strength of the FN reflected the RPR's failure to define a coherent strategy to win back its lost right-wing voters, and represented as big a problem for the right as a whole as the PCF's strength had to the left before 1981. The post-election debates of 1988-89 and the demobilisation of the RPR's activists left the party weaker and more divided than at any point in the 1980s. No French party, though - and certainly not the UDF - escaped internal disputes and activist demobilisation in 1988-89. And the RPR still controlled the largest National Assembly group on the right, the largest group of any in the Senate (reinforced by 13 seats in September 1989), the Town Halls of Paris, Lyon, Bordeaux and Grenoble, and the presidencies of five regional councils and 22 departmental councils. This is an impressive power base for a movement whose very survival had been in doubt the previous decade. Whether as an independent grouping or as a key component in a larger right-wing federation, the RPR is likely to remain a major player for the rest of the century.

Less certain is the extent to which the 'Gaullist' Party has retained its identity. Policies, we have seen, have changed radically under Chirac - though not for the first time. So has the electorate. So have the movement's sources of strength. Under de Gaulle's presidency, they lay in the General's own incomparable standing, in the ideology and policies he represented, and in a near-monopoly of positions at the summit of the state. The RPR's force lies in its organisation and membership, in its local and regional positions, and in the Senate - the one summit body that eluded Gaullist dominance in the 1960s - more than the National Assembly. The RPR's descendence from classical Gaullism, though unquestionable appears remote.

One way to conceptualise the continuity that does exist is as a varying balance between heroic Gaullism, governmental Gaullism, and notable Gaullism. The first is the exalted campaigning Gaullism of the RPF years and of the May 1968 counter-demonstration - the Gaullism of a mass party, existing primarily to win and then to make or keep France great The second is what Mitterrand campaigned against in 1988 - *L'Etat-RPR*, the colonisation (attempted by every party in power, particularly successfully by the RPR) of a core of top positions in government, the civil service, public enterprise and private industry. The third represents the Gaullists' local and parliamentary roots. These three manifestations of Gaullism may frequently converge: the fulfilment of Chirac's presidential ambitions seemed desirable, in general terms, to both ministers and mayors of the RPR between 1986 and 1988. But at times they may pull the party in different ways, organisationally and politically. It is very clear that the purpose for which the RPF was founded was of secondary importance to some RPF deputies elected in 1951 beside the defence of the franc and of their own careers. Chirac's attempts to distinguish the RPR from the UDF in the late 1970s were not always well received either by those RPR members who remained in the Barre governments or by mayors who worked with municipal UDF colleagues. It is also clear that at the foundation of the RPR, the heroic, campaigning manifestation dominated: the Gaullists had lost the Elysée and Matignon, and were in the middle of a series of local set-backs (with the signal exception of Paris) that were to last until 1982. The RPR was modelled on the RPF, even if Chirac and his entourage were increasingly unable to supply more than an *ersatz* heroic leadership to replace the real band of resistance fighters who had run the movement for thirty years.

In the second half of the 1980s the heroic mode became less dominant. Part of the 'heroic' audience was attracted to a new competitor, Le Pen, who attempted to cultivate a very similar appeal and who won over some of the warmest frequenters of Chirac rallies. And while much of government policy during the second Chirac premiership was dictated by the need to produce tangible results in time for 1988, the purposeful expansion of governmental Gaullism was ultimately a liability at the presidential election. Finally, the defeat of 1988 left the heroic mode appearing, at least temporarily, incapable of producing a result, while the 1989 municipal and senatorial elections significantly reinforced the notables. The potential result is the disappearance, or more probably moderation, of that 'monolithic' style that distinguished the RPR from the UDF, as the RPR leadership is bound to be more responsive to the rest of the party apparatus and the admission of *tendances* opens the possibility for notables based on local bastions competing for high office as leaders of such *tendances*. In such a contest, it is true, Chirac would hold many trumps: as well as being the party President, he is the biggest notable of them all. It would nonetheless be a radical departure from the RPR's earlier organisational style.

The brief verdict on the RPR in its first thirteen years must be that it has been remarkably successful in surviving (especially since many predicted the demise of the Gaullist movement with its founder) and in reinforcing its positions in the country's local institutions, but remarkably unsuccessful in developing either coherent policies or a coherent political strategy that would return it durably to national power. If this record owes something to the abilities of Chirac's political opponents, especially Mitterrand, it also reflects Chirac's own personal abilities: an able tactician, an energetic administrator, a competent shaper of policies to suit specific clienteles, but not, so far, the bearer of a 'certain idea of France'. He still has time. There is at least a fair chance that in 1995, Chirac will be the second 62-year-old in recent French history to embark on his third presidential campaign.

Notes

1. The author wishes to thank both RPR head office and M. Antoine Rufenacht for their help with the research for this chapter.

2. I have used the term 'Gaullist Party' for all the various incarnations of the movement up to and including Chirac's RPR.

3. See Wilson, F., *French Political Parties under the Fifth Republic*, Praeger, New York, 1982, pp. 127-133 for a fuller discussion of the nature of classical Gaullism.

4. See Bauer, M.,'The politics of state-directed privatisation: the case of France', *West European Politics*, vol. 11, no. 4, October 1988, p. 50 for de Gaulle's position on nationalisations and welfare measures and on his relations with big business in 1942-46.

5. The best available biography of Chirac is Giesbert, F-O., *Jacques Chirac*, Seuil, Paris, 1987. For Pompidou's death and the election that followed, cf. ibid., pp. 196-216. See Bell, D.S., 'A Hunger for Power: Jacques Chirac', pp. 101-120, in Gaffney, J. (ed.), *The French Presidential Election of 1988: Ideology and Leadership in Contemporary France*, Gower, Aldershot, 1989, for a short account in English of Chirac's career to 1988.

6. See SOFRES, *Opinion publique - 1984*, Gallimard, Paris, 1984, pp. 95, 100; SOFRES, *Opinion publique - 1986*, Gallimard, Paris, 1986, p. 94.

7. See SOFRES, *L'état de l'opinion - 1989*, Gallimard, Paris, 1989, p. 108.

8. In doing so we will refer chiefly to data on presidential, rather than parliamentary elections. This has clear disadvantages. The Communist vote, for example, has varied very widely in the consecutive presidential and parliamentary elections of 1981 and 1988, particularly at the local level. However, in both 1981 and 1988 the UDF and RPR ran common parliamentary candidates in the vast majority of constituencies, and in the proportional system of 1986 they ran combined lists of candidates in two-thirds of departments. While the choice of candidates may indicate the two parties' respective strengths in different constituencies, the candidates won votes as candidates of the whole right, not just the RPR. To find another election where the RPR was able to measure its own forces, one must go back to 1979 (the first direct European poll) or the 1978 parliamentary elections, when separate RPR and UDF candidates contested some 330 seats.

9. Charlot, J., *The Gaullist Phenomenon*, Allen and Unwin, London, 1971, p. 83.

10. Johnson, R.W., *The Long March of the French Left*, Macmillan, London, 1981, pp. 98 and 100.

11. Goguel, F., *Chroniques électorales*, FNSP, Paris, 1983.

12. Ibid., p. 31.

13. SOFRES, *Opinion publique - 1985*, Gallimard, Paris, 1985, pp. 232, 235, 254-255.

14. SOFRES, *Opinion publique - 1984*, p. 104; *Opinion publique - 1986*, p. 91; *L'état de l'opinion - 1989*, p. 108.

15. SOFRES, *Opinion publique - 1984*, pp. 84, 86; *Opinion publique - 1985*, pp. 97, 257; *Opinion publique - 1986*, p. 62.

16. SOFRES, *Opinion publique - 1984*, pp. 77, 112; *Opinion publique - 1985*, p. 48.

17. SOFRES, *Opinion Publique - 1985*, pp. 178, 180, 183.

18. SOFRES, *Opinion publique - 1984*, pp. 81-82.

19. 1984 figure from Plenel, E., and Rollat, A., *L'effet Le Pen*, La Découverte/Le Monde, Paris, 1984, p. 125; 1988 figure from SOFRES, *L'état de l'opinion -1989*, p. 77.

20. *Le Monde*, 3 May 1988.

21. Goldey, D., and Johnson, R.W., 'The French presidential election of 24 April - 8 May and the general election of 5-12 June 1988', *Electoral Studies*, vol. 7, no. 3, December 1988, p. 209: Habert, P., and Ysmal. C, *Election présidentielle 1988*, Le Figaro/Etudes Politiques, Paris, 1988, p. 16.

22. This pattern contrasts with that of the Communists, who attract far less suspicion locally than nationally, and have thus consistently over-polled by 2-3 per cent in cantonal elections.

23. See Goldey, D., and Johnson, R.W., 'The French general election of 16 March 1986', *Electoral Studies*, vol. 5, no. 3, December 1987, pp. 234-235, and Knapp, A., 'Proportional but bipolar: France's electoral system in 1986', *West European Politics*, vol. 10, no. 1, January 1987, p. 99 for the construction of right-wing lists in 1986.

24. Habert and Ysmal, op. cit., p. 37.

25. The revision of the land use plan (*Plan d'occupation des sols*) may, however, lead to a renewed orgy of speculative office-building in the 19th and 20th *arrondissements*, which have so far retained some of their working-class character.

26. *Le Monde*, 16 September 1989.

27. Op. cit., p. 116.

28. Frémontier, J., *Les cadets de la droite*, Seuil, Paris, 1984, pp. 181ff.

29. On the RPF, see Charlot, J., *Le gaullisme d'opposition*, Fayard, Paris, 1983; and Purtschet, C., *Le RPF*, Seuil, Paris, 1965.

30. Charlot, J., *L'UNR: étude du pouvoir au sein d'un parti politique*, Armand Colin, Paris, 1967, p. 23.

31. Ibid., p. 258.

32. Ibid., p. 143.

33. Ibid., pp. 302-305.

34. Charlot, *The Gaullist Phenomenon*, pp. 129-133, 156.

35. Offerlé, M., 'Transformation d'une entreprise politique: de l'UDR au RPR, 1973-77', *Pouvoirs*, no. 28, 1984, pp. 12-13.

36. Ysmal, C., *Les partis politiques sous la cinquième République*, Montchrestien, Paris, 1989, p. 162.

37. Ibid., p. 167.

38. *Les cadres du RPR*, Economica, Paris, 1987.

39. Ibid., p. 36

40. Ibid., p. 33.

41. Bréchon, P., 'Adhérents et militants gaullistes', unpublished paper presented at the Third National Congress of the French Political Science Association, Bordeaux, October 1988, pp. 11-12.

42. Bréchon, Derville and Lecomte, op. cit., pp. 134, 138-139.

43. Ibid., pp. 159, 163-165.

44. Bréchon, op. cit., p. 18.

45. Bréchon, Derville and Lecomte, op. cit., pp. 71, 126-127; Ysmal, C., *Demain la droite*, Grasset, Paris, 1984, p. 36; Guiol, P., and Neveu, E., 'Sociologie des adhérents gaullistes', *Pouvoirs*, no. 28, 1984, pp. 91-106; Portier, P., 'Les militants du RPR: étude d'une fédération', *Pouvoirs*, no. 28, 1984, pp. 107-122; Lawson, K., 'The impact of party reform on party systems: the case of the RPR in France', *Comparative Politics*, July 1981, pp. 401-419.

46. See Guiol and Neveu, op. cit., p. 105.

47. The February 1990 National Conference broke with the past, however, by allowing a variety of contributions.

48. Schonfeld, W.R., *Ethnographie du PS et du RPR: les éléphants et l'aveugle*, Economica, Paris, 1985, p. 6; Lawson, op. cit., p. 406.

49. Lawson, op. cit., p. 411.

50. Giesbert, op. cit., pp. 328, 359.

51. It was under Chirac's impulsion that a wholesale renewal of cadres took place between 1975 and 1977. See Schonfeld, W.R., 'La stabilité des dirigeants des partis politiques: le personnel des directions nationales du Parti socialiste et du mouvement gaulliste', *Revue Française de Science Politique*, vol. 30, no. 3, June 1980, p. 503. Or again in 1978, it was Chirac who called an Extraordinary Congress to exclude persons holding high public office from high positions in the RPR, following the election of Chaban Delmas to the presidency of the National Assembly against RPR opposition in 1978. Lawson, op. cit., p. 410.

52. The job of Departmental Secretary is considerably more important than the largely honorific post of Regional Delegate (*Délégué régional*), reflecting the respective importance for the RPR of these two territorial levels.

53. The sources of RPR finance are as murky as for any French party. Until 1988, business contributions to campaigns were illegal, but universal. Government office offered numerous channels for funds. The favourite technique used at local level has been for a municipality to commission non-existent 'studies' for sums that then find their way into election coffers. Even with these means at their disposal, many deputies claim that they have to spend their own money to win and retain their seats. Sums paid directly to candidates by RPR headquarters (*Rue de Lille)* often amount to no more than FF10,000-20,000.

54. See Bréchon, Derville and Lecomte op. cit., p. 36.

55. Frémentier, op. cit., pp. 192-195.

56. See René Rémond in Habert, P., and Ysmal, C., *Européennes européennes 1989: résultats, analyses et commentaires*, Le Figaro/Etudes Politiques, Paris, 1989, p. 19.

57. *Le Monde*, 21 November 1989.

58. *Le Monde*, 5 July 1988.

59. See, for example, Baudouin, J., '"Gaullismes" et "chiraquismes": réflexions autour d'un adultère', *Pouvoirs*, no. 28, 1984, pp. 53-66, for the abandonment thesis. See also Charlot's contribution in Bréchon, Derville and Lecomte, op. cit., p. 1.

60. *Le Monde*, 4 March 1978.

61. *Les élections législatives de mars 1978*, Le Monde: dossiers et documents, 1978, pp. 27, 45; Ysmal, C., *Les partis politiques sous la cinquième République*, p. 106.

62. See *Les élections législatives du 16 mars*, Le Monde: dossiers et documents, 1986, pp. 44-46 for analysis of the RPR-UDF common platform. The Paris town hall had already excluded immigrants from its family allowance programmes in March 1985. See Liffran, H., *Les Paris de Chirac*, Ramsay, Paris, 1989, p. 137.

63. Bauer, op. cit., p. 66.

64. SOFRES, *Opinion publique - 1986*, p. 62.

65. Baudouin, J., 'Le moment néo-libéral du RPR: essai d'interprétation', unpublished paper presented at the Third National Congress of the French Political Science Association, Bordeaux, October 1988, p. 9. I am indebted to this article for many of the ideas expressed in this section. On this point also see Bell, op. cit., p. 116.

66. Liffran, op. cit., p. 238.

Bibliography

Anderson, M., *Conservative Politics in France*, Allen and Unwin, London, 1974.

Ambroise-Rendu, M., *Paris-Chirac*, Plon, Paris, 1987.

De Baeque, F., 'L'interpénétration des personnels administratifs et politiques' in de Baeque, F., and Quermonne, J-L. (eds.), *Administration et politique sous la cinquième République*, FNSP, Paris, 1981.

Baudouin, J., '"Gaullismes" et "chiraquismes": réflexions autour d'un adultère', *Pouvoirs*, no. 28, 1984.

Baudouin, J., 'Le moment néo-libéral du RPR: essai d'interprétation', unpublished paper presented at the Third National Congress of the French Political Science Association, Bordeaux, 5-8 October 1988.

Bauer, M., 'The politics of state-directed privatisation: the case of France', *West European Politics*, vol. 11, no. 4, October 1988.

Bell, D.S., 'A Hunger for Power: Jacques Chirac', in Gaffney, J. (ed.), *The French Presidential Elections of 1988: Ideology and Leadership in Contemporary France*, Gower, Aldershot, 1989.

Bréchon, P., 'Adhérents et militants gaullistes', unpublished paper presented at the Third National Congress of the French Political Science Association, Bordeaux, 5-8 October 1988.

Bréchon, P., Dervale, J., and Lecomte, P., *Les cadres du RPR*, Economica, Paris, 1987.

Capdevielle, F. et al., *France de gauche vote à droite*, FNSP, Paris, 1981.

Charlot, J., *L'UNR: étude du pouvoir au sein d'un parti politique*, Armand Colin, Paris, 1967.

Charlot, J., *The Gaullist Phenomenon*, Allen and Unwin, London, 1971.

Charlot, J., *Le gaullisme d'opposition*, Fayard, Paris, 1983.

Charlot, J., 'Tactique et stratégie du RPR dans l'opposition', *Pouvoirs*, no. 28, 1984.

Colombani, J-M., 'Qui est à la droite de qui?', *Pouvoirs*, no. 28, 1984.

Crisol, P., and Lhomeau, J-Y., *La machine RPR*, Fayolle, Paris, 1977.

Derville, J., and Lecomte, P., 'RPR - génération 86. Processus de mobilisation et système de représentations des adhérents récents du RPR', unpublished paper presented at the Third National Congress of the French Political Science Association, Bordeaux, 5-8 October 1988.

Desjardins, T., *Un inconnu nommé Chirac*, La Table Ronde, Paris, 1983.

Desjardins, T., *Les chiraquiens*, La Table Ronde, Paris, 1986.

Duhamel, A., *La république giscardienne*, Grasset, Paris, 1980.

Frémontier, J., *Les cadets de la droite*, Seuil, Paris, 1984.

Frémontier, J., 'Les jeunes élus du RPR: des héritiers ou des parricides?', *Pouvoirs*, no. 28, 1984.

Giesbert, F-O., *Jacques Chirac*, Seuil, Paris, 1987.

Goldey, D., and Knapp, A., 'Time for a change: the French elections of 1981', *Electoral Studies*, vol. 1, nos. 1, April 1982, and 2, August 1982.

Goldey, D., and Johnson, R.W., 'The French general election of 16 March 1986', *Electoral Studies*, vol. 5, no. 3, December 1987.

Goldey, D., and Johnson, R.W., 'The French presidential election of 24 April - 8 May and the general election of 5-12 June 1988', *Electoral Studies*, vol. 7, no. 3, December 1988.

Goguel, F., *Chroniques électorales* (3 vols.), FNSP, Paris, 1981 and 1983.

Guiol, P., 'Le RPF ou la difficulté de rassembler' in Lavau, G. et al. (eds.), *L'univers politique des classes moyennes*, FNSP, Paris, 1983.

Guiol, P., and Neveu, E., 'Sociologie des adhérents gaullistes', *Pouvoirs*, no. 28, 1984.

Habert, P., and Ysmal, C. (eds.),

* *L'élection présidentielle 1988: résultats, analyses et commentaires*, Le Figaro/Etudes Politiques, Paris, 1988.
* *Elections législatives 1988: résultats, analyses et commentaires*, Le Figaro/ Etudes Politiques, Paris, 1988.
* *Elections municipales 1989: résultats, analyses et commentaires*, Le Figaro/Etudes Politiques, Paris, 1989.
* *Elections européennes 1989: résultats, analyses et commentaires*, Le Figaro/Etudes Politiques, Paris, 1989.

Haegel, F., 'Les modes de gestion de la référence gaulliste au RPR: mémoire, héritage, filiation', unpublished paper presented to the Third National Congress of the French Political Science Association, Bordeaux, 5-8 October 1988.

Hartley, A., *Gaullism: the Rise and Fall of a Political Movement*, Outerbridge and Dienstfrey, New York, 1971.

Juppé, A., *La double rupture*, Economica, Paris, 1983.

Johnson, R.W., *The Long March of the French Left*, Macmillan, London, 1981.

Knapp, A., 'Proportional but bipolar: France's electoral system in 1986', *West European Politics*, vol. 10, no. 1, January 1987.

Knapp, A., 'Paris: le système politico-administratif local, 1977-1987', *Annuaire des Collectivités Locales, pp. 65-90.*

Lancelot, A., *Les élections sous la cinquième République*, 1st and 2nd editions, PUF, Paris, 1983 and 1988.

Lancelot, A., *1981: les élections de l'alternance*, FNSP, Paris, 1986.

Lancelot, A., and M-T., *Annuaire de la France politique*, May 1981-May 1983, and 1984, FNSP, Paris, 1984.

Lawson, K., 'The impact of party reform on party systems: the case of the RPR in France', *Comparative Politics*, July 1981.

Le Monde: dossiers et documents:

* *Les élections législatives de mars 1978*, Paris, 1978.
* *Les élections législatives de juin 1981*, Paris, 1981.
* *Les élections législatives du 16 mars 1986*, Paris, 1986.
* *Les élections municipales de Mars 1983*, Paris, 1983.
* *Election présidentielle, 24 Avril-8 Mai 1988*, Paris, 1988.
* *Spécial élections municipales*, Paris, 1989.

Lecomte, P., 'The Political Forces of French Conservatism: Chirac's *Rassemblement* and the President's Party' in Layton-Henry, Z., *Conservative Politics in Western Europe*, Macmillan, London, 1982.

Liffran, H., *Les Paris de Chirac*, Ramsay, Paris, 1982.

Mayer, N., and Perrineau, P., *Le Front national à découvert*, FNSP, Paris, 1989.

Nay, C., *La double méprise*, Grasset, Paris, 1980.

Offerlé, M.,'Transformation d'une entreprise politique: de l'UDR au RPR, 1973-1977', *Pouvoirs*, no. 28, 1984.

Passeron, A.,'Le parti d'un homme', *Pouvoirs*, no. 28, 1984.

Ponceyri, R., 'Le RPR et l'achèvement de la banalisation électorale du gaullisme', *Pouvoirs*, no. 28, 1984.

Portelli, H., 'L'activité internationale du RPR', *Pouvoirs*, no. 28, 1984.

Portier, P., 'Les militants du RPR: étude d'une fédération', *Pouvoirs*, no. 28, 1984.

Purtschet, C., *Le RPF*, Seuil, Paris, 1965.

Rassemblement pour la République, *Libres et responsables: programme de gouvernement*, Paris, 1984.

Rassemblement pour la République, *Statuts nationaux adoptés par les Assises extraordinaires du 5 décembre 1976, mis à jour après le Congrès national de Paris du 7 Décembre 1986.*

Rassemblement pour la République, *Statuts nationaux adoptés par le Congrès extraordinaire du 29 janvier 1989.*

Rémond, R., *Les droites en France*, Aubier Montaigne, Paris, 1982.

Schonfeld, W.R., 'La stabilité des dirigeants des partis politiques: le personnel des directions nationales du Parti socialiste et du mouvement gaulliste', *Revue Française de Science Politique*, vol. 30, no. 3, June 1980.

Schonfeld, W.R., *Ethnographie du PS et du RPR: les éléphants et l'aveugle*, Economica, Paris, 1985.

Schonfeld, W.R., 'Le RPR et l'UDF à l'épreuve de l'opposition', *Revue Française de Science Politique*, vol. 36, no. 1, February 1986.

Searls, E., 'The French right in opposition, 1981-1986', *Parliamentary Affairs*, vol. 39, no. 4, October 1986.

Sigoda, P., 'Les cercles extérieurs du RPR', *Pouvoirs*, no. 28, 1984.

SOFRES, *Opinion publique*, 1984, 1985, 1986, Gallimard, Paris, 1984-86.

SOFRES, *L'état de l'opinion - 1989*, Seuil, Paris, 1989.

Szafran, M., *Chirac ou les passions du pouvoir*, Grasset, Paris, 1986.

Williams, P.M., *French Politicians and Elections, 1951-1969*, Cambridge University Press, Cambridge, 1970.

Williams, P.M., and Harrison, M., *Politics and Society in De Gaulle's Republic*, Longman, London, 1971.

Wilson, F., *French Political Parties under the Fifth Republic*, Praeger, New York, 1982.

Wright, V., *The Government and Politics of France*, 3rd Edition, Unwin Hyman, London, 1989.

Ysmal, C., 'La résistible ascension du RPR', *Projet*, no. 178, September-October 1983.

Ysmal, C., *Demain la droite*, Grasset, Paris, 1984.

Ysmal, C., 'L'univers politique des militants RPR', *Pouvoirs*, no. 28, 1984.

Ysmal, C., 'L'UDF et le RPR à la fin des années 1980', unpublished paper presented at the Third National Congress of the French Political Science Association, Bordeaux, 5-8 October 1988.

Ysmal, C., *Les partis politiques sous la cinquième République*, Montchrestien, Paris, 1989.

8 A New Chapter in the History of the French Extreme Right: The National Front

James G. Shields

In a study of contemporary French political parties, none presses its claim to consideration more forcefully than the National Front (FN). When, in April 1988, Jean-Marie Le Pen won 14.4 per cent of the vote in the first round of the presidential elections, he took the extreme right to an unprecedented height of electoral achievement in post-war France.[1] This personal performance marked the culmination of a series of electoral successes which had brought Le Pen and his party to the forefront of European political attention. Such an upturn in the fortunes of the French far right, with its newly attested capacity to compete in the full range of national and local elections, has raised compelling questions for politicians and psephologists alike. Yet the same difficulty in coming to terms with the presence of Le Pen's party is as evident now as it was in the mid-1980s, when the National Front first emerged as an important force in French politics.

The purpose of this study is not to attempt any detailed analysis of the multiple and complex causes underlying the success of Le Pen and his movement.[2] It is rather to review some of the changes that have been wrought both within and beyond the National Front by the new electoral opportunities opened up to this party in recent years. It is [illegible] much affirmed by political commentators that the extreme right in France ha[illegible] to the brink of extinction when the left acceded to power in 1981. A politic[illegible] was thought not to exist could afford to be ignored; and ignored it was, [illegible] commentators alike. When, writing in the mid-1970s, Malcolm Anderson [illegible] the electoral holocaust of the extreme Right in 1962', he articulated a complacency about the Fifth Republic's resistance to the incursions of right-extremism which characterises political analysis from the early 1960s through to the mid-1980s.[3] With the loss of the Algerian cause, reflected Anderson, the extreme right saw its political *raison d'être* severely diminished and its heartlands of support disintegrate. The standard image of the far right in the years following the establishment of the Fifth Republic and the Evian Accords (1962) granting independence to Algeria was as an array of factions, associations and leagues occupying an irrelevant place in the democratic process and serving at best as a means of political initiation for a militant youth which became, with predictable regularity, absorbed into the mainstream parties the moment real political opportunity beckoned.[4] If the far right represented, as Anderson puts it, 'a "purer", less corrupt form of politics', it was a form of politics whose integrity remained the very measure of its failure.[5]

While the analysis provided by Anderson in the 1970s is accurate within a historical perspective, it takes no account of the extreme right's capacity to update its programme and appeal. On the contrary, the tendency among commentators at large was to consign the far right in France to an opprobrious past from which escape was deemed impossible. In its perpetual appeals to a by-gone age, its obdurate refusal to 'embrace its century', it was argued, lay both the driving force and the crucial weakness of the French extreme right.[6] As William R. Tucker argued in 1968, the 'frustrating impediment' of right-extremist movements in France was precisely that they remained 'the victims of their own past'.[7] So far indeed was right-extremism consigned to the annals of political history that John Frears was able to assert, in a study published in 1977, that the Fifth Republic had 'virtually no native extreme Right at all.'[8] The conclusion drawn by Frears was that movements whose aim was to set the clock back could have no place in a thriving democracy with stable institutions and a successful economy.[9] Issues which had provided the *casus belli* for an earlier generation of right-extremists (decolonisation, economic modernisation, fiscal reform, the accelerated transition from agricultural to advanced urban society, the shoring up of France's military strength and international influence, the 'containment' of the Marxist threat) had, by the 1970s, been resolved, by-passed or appropriated by the incumbent right. If attention was focused upon extremism, it was, Frears rightly points out, upon the extremism associated with 'the fear of a Left-wing victory at the polls which would bring the Communists into government.'[10]

It is in the extent to which it deviates from this whole analysis, the extent to which it marks a new departure in the history of the French far right, that the Le Pen phenomenon assumes its full significance. Until the emergence of the National Front in the European elections of 1984, the conviction remained unshaken that right-extremism was a spent force in terms of its access to popular support in France. That it took some time to appreciate the full complexity of the Le Pen vote is attested by the earliest interpretations of it. The first reflex reaction of political commentators was to look to Vichy, Poujade and *Algérie-française* as ready points of reference.[11] While such points of reference undoubtedly do have a place in any overall analysis, they betrayed an initial failure to address the Le Pen question on its own terms, to recognise in it an array of issues particular to the 1980s and calling for a much more sophisticated interpretation than narrow historical comparisons would allow. As Le Pen has progressed with varied success through the whole range of European, cantonal, municipal, regional, parliamentary and presidential elections, consolidating his party structure and national base of support, the tendency to see in him a latter-day Poujadism of ephemeral appeal has given way to the recognition that here is a movement which admits of no easy classification within the traditional parameters of French right-extremism. It is for this reason that Jean Jacob, in an article published in 1987, takes issue with Alain Rollat's assertion that the political and social policies of Jean-Marie Le Pen fit perfectly within the tradition of French right-wing extremism. To claim as much, Jacob points out, is to lose sight of the fact that 'this extreme right makes no appeal to violence and has no recourse to street politics. It is not, like fascist organisations of the past, fiercely anti-capitalist. It does not call into question the established institutions, does not set its face against the parliamentary process and does not reject democracy.'[12] If the National Front is to be defined as an extreme-right movement, it is, Jacob contends, a movement which displays few of the classic hallmarks of French right-extremism as it is documented by political historians.

Breaking the Historical Mould

This very difficulty of defining the National Front's place within a historical perspective is testament to the success of Le Pen's long-term strategy. The creation of the party in October 1972 was to have been more than the 'latest attempt at regrouping the forces of the extreme right' described by *Le Monde* of 28 February 1973.[13] Though convened with the express purpose of contesting the legislative elections of March 1973, this fledgling movement was to mark a new departure in political strategy for the far right, the renunciation of street politics and the pursuit of electoral legitimacy. While attracting to its ranks many representatives of the right-extremism which had ploughed a different course in the 1960s, the National Front set itself an agenda which marked it apart from its sister-movements on the far-right fringe. Such indeed was the change in attitude and policy which crystallised in the formation of this party that commentators could now write of the extreme right's 'absorption into the system', a notion quite inconceivable only a few years before.[14] As René Chiroux observed in 1974, 'the extreme right no longer articulates a coherent programme, distinct from that of the conservative right. This was particularly true of the National Front during the legislative election campaign of March 1973.'[15]

To argue as much is to underplay the differences of tone, style and substance which were evident then, and remain evident still, between these two political camps. Yet the parliamentary elections of 1973 did mark an important rapprochement in the relative profiles of the orthodox right and the extremist right as represented by the National Front. The borders between these tracts of the French political landscape had never, of course, been hermetically sealed. The so-called 'new right' which bourgeoned in the 1970s, with its clubs, think-tanks and assault on the ideological hegemony of the left, did much to highlight the common ground that already existed between the moderate and extremist forces of the right.[16] What was novel in the run-up to the parliamentary elections of 1973, however, was the quite conscious effort now being made by the extreme right to excise, or at the very least disguise, the more repellent elements in its political repertory in order to court broader support among the electorate. Set up in 1969 to succeed the newly disbanded *Occident*, the far-right organisation *Ordre nouveau* made its first impact as the legatee of a tradition of violent agitation.[17] By the time its second Congress came round in June 1972, however, a new set of imperatives had superseded the old. The talk now was of renouncing 'all recourse to clandestine action', of respecting 'the judicial order and the letter of the law', of playing 'the law and order card [...] within the framework of the established institutions'.[18] Tame pronouncements indeed from a movement which had laid claim at its inception to the mantle of the violent *Occident*, only to join the National Front on a new path towards electoral acceptability some three years later.[19] The purpose was to effect a break with a past that had become a crippling liability and to redefine its image. The matter was put in no uncertain terms at the said congress of June 1972:

> What attitude should be adopted for the next parliamentary elections due in March 1973? We have for over a year now declared our intention to put up candidates in the full awareness of the importance of this contest. The problem is one of maximising our chances of success by presenting the best possible image and trying to appeal to as broad a constituency as possible. One central question is at issue: how can we emerge from the political ghetto in which we find ourselves still, how can we break down the barriers which the mass media have erected between us and our potential supporters, how can we overcome the isolation to which the propaganda of our adversaries and the popular press conspire to condemn us?[20]

The reason for this change of policy was to be sought not just in a *prise de conscience* resulting from the extreme right's continued failure, in its isolation, to bring any meaningful influence to bear upon the course of French politics. It lay also, and more significantly, in events which had recently taken place in neighbouring Italy. There, in the parliamentary elections of May 1972, the far-right *Movimento Sociale Italiano* (MSI) had registered a notable success, with almost three million votes and an 8.7 per cent share of the poll, which brought home to its French counterparts the sterility of their own approach and the gains to be had from an electoralist strategy.[21] The example of the MSI delivered the impetus required to set part at least of the French far right on a new course. The secessions and internecine hostilities which marked the history of this 'family' were perceived now as political short-sightedness of the highest order.[22] Success by any standard, it was argued, was to be achieved by forging a broad base of membership and support, by sinking doctrinal differences in favour of political efficacity. The MSI of Giorgio Almirante, a party which sought to encompass all shades of rightist persuasion in a single 'destra nazionale', with an electoral success which had almost doubled its parliamentary representation from 30 to 56, provided the paradigm:[23]

> It is clear that the MSI, while broadening its base of support, has conserved the full force of its militancy, that its lack of 'outward' sectarianism is perfectly in keeping with its search for greater 'internal' cohesion... It is in such a spirit that our own fusion with other components of a vast popular movement engaged in 'active' struggle is to be achieved. We must banish sectarianism as we must banish all woolliness in our thought and our ideology.[24]

Thus the new discourse embraced by *Ordre nouveau* and, at its creation, the National Front. With the MSI as its model and Le Pen at its helm, the latter posed from the outset as a federator of the many and diverse ideological currents which traversed a perennially disunited extreme right.[25] At its third Congress in June 1973, those factions of *Ordre nouveau* who held fast to the strategy of cooperation outlined above, and who advocated to that end a close association with the recently created National Front, summed up clearly the new state of affairs on the far right:

> The primary function of the National Front is to serve as a rallying-point, to bring together all currents of national and nationalist opinion... The National Front must therefore provide and continue to provide a forum for the whole of the national opposition in its broadest sense, in order that we may mount major political campaigns with the maximum chance of success... To transform the National Front into a monolithic party-machine would be to run the risk of serious error and would be tantamount to denying the conditions which have given rise to its formation.[26]

Nothing could be clearer than this statement of the place early occupied by Le Pen's party in the far-right scheme of things. The National Front, it was urged, with its unifying role and its image of democratic respectability, was well placed to carry the extreme right forward into a new era of electoralism.[27] In his appeals for tolerance and cooperation on the far right, Le Pen himself set a new tone, placing political expediency above ideological entrenchment. The unitary strategy to which he lent his endorsement was never more vividly illustrated than by his call in May 1973 for a 'sacred union' of the far right. 'Let us solemnly undertake to tolerate one another,' he exhorted. 'The time has come to bind together in unity all the forces of nationalism so that France may be heard to speak with a free and strong voice.'[28]

The Fruits of Electoralism

All of the foregoing is crucial to an understanding of the National Front in the 1980s. For in its earliest endeavour to escape the confines of any narrowly defined political heritage, and to open its ranks to the broadest possible membership and support, we find the source of our difficulty in defining the precise nature of Le Pen's movement today. Though its early attempt to serve as a rallying-point for *Ordre nouveau* and other similar movements was short-lived and far from trouble-free, the National Front has remained true to its initial ambition of grouping around itself the varied components of the French far right.[29] The net effect of such an ambition has been to blur the contours of the party's ideological profile, making it a ready haven, as Christian de Brie argues, for right-extremists of every hue:

> Nationalists, legatees of Pétainism, of Poujadism and of French Algeria - causes to which the National Front and its leader remain firmly attached; traditionalist and 'integralist' Catholics from the movements *Occident* and Counter-Reform; monarchistic survivors of *Action Française*; long-standing fascists from the collaboration era, neo-nazis and Europeanists. Such is the reservoir from which have been drawn many of the party's leading figures, many of those who play a prominent role in the political network which surrounds the National Front, and many of the publications through which its ideas are disseminated.[30]

It is this 'open door' policy which has ensured the National Front a margin of political manoeuvre free of narrow doctrinal constraints and, ipso facto, rare among French right-extremist movements. Seeking to escape the incriminating connotations of Vichy or the OAS and the sectional interests of Poujadism, Le Pen's party has pressed its case on lines calculated to exert maximum appeal for the far right, without compromising the potential for an opening towards more mainstream right-wing sympathisers. Nationalism, the moral order, socio-economic decline, and the conjoined threats of communism and Islamic Arab immigration have from the outset constituted the rudiments of the party's message. In its initial programme, 'Défendre les Français', notes René Chiroux, the National Front 'laid stress above all upon the moral and political crisis besetting France, and proposed to put a stop to this "process of decadence" by revitalising the fundamental values of the family, school, work, the nation, and by redefining the proper functions of the national state.'[31] That there is nothing to separate such objectives from the aims set out in the 'Passeport pour la victoire' which served as a manifesto in Le Pen's 1988 presidential campaign, or in the various policy statements which have been issued by the party in the 1980s, is a point which bears emphasis.[32] For the general, quite 'timeless' nature of many of the policies articulated by Le Pen and his party have given them a durability which transcends the specific, and often short-lived, causes with which the extreme right has historically been associated. Le Pen has been cautious to tie his fortunes irrevocably to no single 'cause' of this type. From Poujadism through the Algerian question to the *Comités TV* and the bitter anti-Gaullism of the sixties, Le Pen has left himself free to move on when the 'cause' in question lost its purpose or momentum. That such an ability was denied Poujade or Tixier-Vignancour is attested by their failure to recover from the respective parliamentary and presidential setbacks of 1958 and 1965.[33] Le Pen has proved, in this important sense, a rare survivor among his political *confrères*.

It is this ability to adapt his militancy to the changing issues of the day, whilst remaining true to the directing principles of his political philosophy, that is perhaps the single most important feature of Le Pen's career. The will with which the leader of the National Front has embraced the full range of current social and political issues - from Middle Eastern terrorism to the unification of Europe, from domestic crime and unemployment rates to drug addiction and the AIDS virus - demonstrates his readiness to move with the times, to shift his focus from issues which no longer exercise a popular mobilising appeal and exploit those by which they have been supplanted. Such opportunism, while it may be condemned by the *purs et durs* on the far right, goes a long way towards accounting for Le Pen's recent electoral successes. His eye for the main political chance, moreover, has dictated that the posture of democratic respectability adopted by the National Front in the early 1970s be sustained. Le Pen has been scrupulous throughout in his observance of the democratic process. For all his periodic bouts of verbal intemperance and numerous court appearances as prosecutor and defendant alike, he has striven to project an image of unassailable legitimacy.[34] As Monica Charlot observes, Le Pen has taken care from the earliest 'not to compromise himself through involvement in violent activism. He has never belonged to any movement whose goal was to overthrow the republic (such as the OAS); he has never overstepped the bounds of legality.'[35]

This question of legitimacy lies at the heart of the evolution which the National Front has undergone over the course of almost two decades. From an irrelevant fringe movement, able to muster barely 1 per cent in the parliamentary elections of 1973, Le Pen's party has assumed the status of a major force in French national politics.[36] The transition testifies at once to the tenacious strategy of the National Front and to the far-reaching changes which have taken place in French politics over the period in question.[37] For the first ten years of its existence, Le Pen's party failed to make the slightest impact upon the course of political affairs. In the parliamentary elections of 1978, it fared dismally, attracting only a fraction of the nugatory support to which it had laid claim in the 'electoral disaster' of 1973.[38] Some three years later, in the elections which followed Mitterrand's presidential victory in 1981, the combined forces of the extreme right were to experience worse still, polling less than a hundred thousand votes in all and witnessing the accession to power of an absolute Socialist majority and a government comprising a number of Communist ministers.

Such was the state of extreme debilitation in which the extreme right found itself at the beginning of the 1980s. Yet, within the space of few years, the National Front was to put itself firmly on the electoral map. A series of isolated successes in the municipal elections of 1983 presaged the breakthrough of Le Pen's party at national level in the European elections of the following year. The 2.2 million votes (11 per cent of the national ballot) cast in favour of the National Front on 17 June 1984 established a support-base upon which the party was to build in the subsequent parliamentary elections of 1986 (2.7 million) and 1988 (2.3 million), elections in which its proportion of the vote remained stable at just under 10 per cent. Arresting though such statistics are, they pale alongside the 4.4 million votes garnered by Le Pen in the first round of the presidential elections on 24 April 1988. With 14.4 per cent of the ballot, the leader of the National Front mounted a serious challenge to Raymond Barre (16.5 per cent) and Jacques Chirac (19.9 per cent), and contributed substantially to the eventual defeat of the latter in the run-off against Mitterrand.[39] That the National Front proved able to sustain a serious presidential campaign at all is remarkable; that it fared so well in the event alongside the 'presidentialist' parties of the RPR and UDF provides a solemn commentary on the current state of the French right. Had Chirac won some 3 per cent less and Le Pen some 3 per cent more, it is - the thought is a sobering one - the leader of the National Front who would have gone through to challenge for the presidency on 8 May.

Such are the bare statistical facts of the National Front's rise to political prominence in the 1980s. Whether or not Le Pen is able to replicate these successes in future elections, an indisputable fact emerges: he has closed, or at the very least substantially reduced, the 'credibility gap' - to borrow the expression of Cerny and Hainsworth - which has dogged the best endeavours of the extreme right to enlist popular support for its policies among the French electorate.[40] The motley ranks of far-rightists who make up the *noyau dur* of the National Front have been swollen beyond all proportion by a popular constituency which the party found itself denied in the first decade of its existence. That pre-election polls throughout the 1980s should so signally have underestimated the strength of this constituency testifies to the residual stigma attaching to a vote for a party of the far right. Yet this unwillingness of would-be voters to declare open support for the National Front must be set against the fact that so many have chosen, for whatever reason, to endorse it through the ballot-box. In the process of electoral legitimation from which the National Front has benefited, there is no more significant event than the entry of its 35 deputies into the National Assembly in 1986. Present thus for the first time in its history at the highest political level, Le Pen's party was to see its representation (which it owed, technically speaking, to the system of proportional representation instituted by Mitterrand in the run-up to these elections) decimated in the wake of the legislative elections of June 1988, when it was reduced, through the return of the two-round majority voting system, to a single seat in the Assembly. What is important, however, is not the length of time during which the National Front exercised its long-coveted parliamentary role: it is the fact that its electoral endeavours in 1986 should have been so handsomely rewarded, and the influence which it was able subsequently to exert upon the political direction of Jacques Chirac's slender right-wing majority.

There can be no doubt that the years 1986-88 consecrated the political legitimacy of Le Pen's party. Far from unleashing some hydra-headed demon into the National Assembly, the National Front's newly formed parliamentary group presented itself as a very model of democratic respectability. In one or two instances only (most notably the 'hysterical night' of October 1987) did the authoritarian edge break through in the parliamentary demeanour of the National Front deputies.[41] At all other times, Le Pen's group (an assortment of far-right activists, lawyers, doctors, academics, journalists and others) conducted itself according to constitutional convention, sat on parliamentary commissions, traded its support for the governing right-wing majority, and brought a significant influence to bear upon government policy. Having avoided by the narrowest of margins the prospect of being forced into some parliamentary deal with the National Front, Chirac found himself hard pressed by Le Pen's group in the National Assembly. In matters of law and order, rights of entry and residence for foreigners, and prevention of crime and terrorism, the pressure from the far right upon Chirac's legislative programme was clear.[42] The choice of Charles Pasqua as Minister of the Interior, while it occasioned some misgiving among more centrist elements of the majority, was widely seen as a tactic to offset the influence of the National Front. It was Le Pen's claim, indeed, that the presence of Pasqua alone represented 'a bulwark preventing part of the RPR electorate from defecting to the National Front'.[43]

The loss in 1988 of his parliamentary group, with all its attendant political and financial benefits, came as a blow to Le Pen. The return of his party to its former position 'outside' the system was compounded by the relatively, if understandably, poor performance of the National Front in the cantonal elections of September-October 1988 and the municipal elections of March 1989. These elections, if they are to be interpreted as setbacks, should nonetheless be seen in context. Both are highly localised ballots in which success depends upon solid local implantation. As though in answer to those who were proclaiming its demise, Le Pen's party used the much more expedient occasion of the European elections of June 1989 to put itself firmly back on the electoral map. With little short of 12 per cent (a result second only to Le Pen's 14.4 per cent on 24 April 1988), it bettered its overall performance of 1984 and retained all of its ten seats in the European Assembly, finishing third behind the RPR-UDF and PS lists, in advance of the Greens, the centrists and the PCF. This shows beyond question the continued strength of Le Pen's party in a national ballot where proportional representation renders the *vote utile* redundant. Most notable among its results were those in the south-eastern departments of Alpes-Maritimes, Bouches-du-Rhône and Var, where the National Front once again scored between 20 and 25 per cent, and came close to outdistancing the combined forces of the RPR and UDF. That the party could pull off such a result after five years of intense electoral activity, and after the relative setbacks of autumn 1988 and spring 1989, confirms its staying power and the fact that it can no longer be compared with 'surge' movements such as the Poujadism of the 1950s. Viewed as the receptacle of a passing protest vote in 1984, the National Front has established its claim to be taken seriously as a potentially permanent feature of the French political landscape.

Both the presidential and the parliamentary elections of 1988 provided evidence of the solid electoral implantation which the National Front had secured throughout the whole of France. The outstanding feature of the Le Pen vote in the first round of the presidential elections on 24 April 1988, in relation to the European elections of June 1984 and the parliamentary elections of March 1986, was a swelling of support - sometimes dramatic - in every one of France's 96 departments.[44] As in those previous elections, support for Le Pen was strongest along the Mediterranean coastal belt (Alpes-Maritimes, Var, Vaucluse, Bouches-du-Rhône, Gard, Hérault, Pyrénées-Orientales), in heavily industrialised areas of the north and north-east (Bas-Rhin, Haut-Rhin, Moselle), and around the major conurbations of Paris and Lyon (Seine-Saint-Denis, Seine-et-Marne, Val d'Oise, Rhône).[45] Predominantly urban in character, the Le Pen vote is high in industrial areas with large immigrant communities and in those regions of the south where many French *pieds-noirs* were resettled in the aftermath of the Algerian War. Such areas have been hard hit by economic recession and by the attendant problems of unemployment, housing shortages, and increased rates of crime and petty delinquency. Where competition for scarce social and economic resources is compounded by the tensions of coexisting cultures, Le Pen is assured a ready audience. His claim to represent the immediate concerns of the common Frenchman in the face of an indifferent establishment has struck a chord in constituencies which feel ill-served by the mainstream parties of right and left alike.

Though the National Front lost its parliamentary group in the legislative elections of June 1988 (stark evidence of the effects of the double-ballot majority voting system upon a party such as Le Pen's), the value of the two years spent in the National Assembly, in symbolic and real political terms both, should not be underestimated. More than a decade and a half after its formation, the National Front achieved its earliest goal by becoming established as a full-fledged participant in, and beneficiary of, the democratic process. The legislative programme to which it contributed, moreover, has served (despite the Rocard government's endeavours to temper the perceived excesses of its predecessor) to shift the political balance, on the issues of immigration and law and order notably, further to the right. In addition to the leverage which Le Pen was able to apply to the RPR-UDF-*divers droite* majority in the National Assembly, his relations with the mainstream right in the 1980s greatly contributed to the transition of the National Front from a protest party to a political broker of sorts. At every major election, and in a number of notable by-elections, since 1984, the question of a potential agreement between the mainstream right and Le Pen's movement has occupied the political headlines. Though the national leadership of the right has repeatedly declared its opposition to any such dealings with the National Front, the door has been left open to local agreements which have, in a number of cases, brought the RPR and UDF into alliance with Le Pen's party in order to secure victory for the right. The 1986 regional elections saw several right-wing notables retain control of Regional Assemblies only at the cost of complicity with the National Front. In the parliamentary elections of June 1988, attention came to rest upon a number of south-eastern constituencies around Marseille, where the strength of the National Front made alliance the only alternative to defeat for the joint RPR-UDF forces, or URC, under Jean-Claude Gaudin.[46] If the deal proved in practice to be beneficial only to the URC, it nonetheless afforded Le Pen the satisfaction of seeing his party treated as a component of the right and an acceptable political ally.[47]

The National Front within the Contemporary French Right

The 1980s have been a period of great political change and development in France. In the case of the National Front, these years attest to the manner in which a fringe party may, in favourable circumstances, capitalise upon apparently short-term gains in order to e[illegible]lish a firm footing in the political arena. The danger for a movement such as the [illegible] Front was that it should be condemned to the status of a political pressure gr[illegible] national campaigns on national questions but out of touch with the local issues u[illegible] so much of French political power is founded. The unbroken series of elections w[illegible] has contested since 1983 shows the degree to which Le Pen's party has sough[illegible] overcome this problem at its source. A striking measure of the success with which th[illegible] party has been able to expand its base lies in the number of candidates which it fielded in local elections between the early and mid-1980s. In the cantonal elections of 1982, with some 2,000 seats at stake throughout France, the extreme right put up a token 65 candidates who attracted 0.2 per cent of the total vote, the endorsement of 25,273 electors.[48] A mere three years later, in the corresponding elections of March 1985, Le Pen's party was able to field some 1,500 (not, as Schain puts it, 500) candidates who, though standing for only three-quarters of the cantonal seats at stake, accounted for 8.8 per cent of the total national vote.[49] With an average score of 10.4 per cent in those cantons where it was represented, the National Front secured over a million votes on that occasion, polling between 20 and 30 per cent in a considerable number of constituencies throughout France, and upwards of 30 per cent in isolated cantons of Marseille, Toulon and Nice.[50] Despite its failure to turn such support into seats - a clear measure once more of the crushing effect of the two-ballot majority voting system - these elections demonstrated the National Front's ability to respond to the exigencies of local as well as national electioneering. Adversely affected by a record 51 per cent abstention rate in the first round of the more recent cantonal elections of September-October 1988, the National Front nonetheless kept its share of the vote above 5 per cent, displaying once again its resilience and its capacity to compete in an electoral contest whose strictly local character does little to favour the success of a party such as Le Pen's.[51] Since then, the party has been present in a succession of cantonal and municipal by-elections which have permitted it to remain at the forefront of public attention, to test its local base of support and to keep up pressure on the RPR and UDF in constituencies where a challenge from the extreme right poses acute questions of conscience and political strategy.[52]

Other measures, too, confirm the broadening of the party's local base. Having seen a dramatic increase in its membership over the course of the 1980s, the National Front now boasts an impressive campaigning and communications network, disseminating its message through a number of far-right publications (*National Hebdo, Présent, Minute*), a newsletter (*La Lettre de Jean-Marie Le Pen*), a radio broadcasting service, a 'minitel' information line, and a host of clubs and political coteries.[53] With its well-organised party structure and its network of regional bases and local offices, Le Pen's movement has sought with some success to develop the implantation which it lacked in the early 1980s.[54] Having forced its way in 1986 into positions of influence in a number of regions, holding the balance of power in five of France's 22 regional Assemblies, the National Front also enjoys representation now on many of France's municipal councils. Over one third of the 392 towns in France with upwards of 20,000 inhabitants now have National Front representatives on their council.[55] In the presidential elections of 1988, it was notable that Le Pen gained ground throughout the length and breadth of France, appealing beyond what might have been considered the established boundaries of National Front support.[56] That his support in virtually every socio-professional category exceeded 10 per cent is a fact not to be overlooked in assessing the broad and very varied profile of his electorate.[57] The setting-up of a 'Euro-right' in Strasbourg, moreover, has brought the possibility of closer international links with far-right movements such as the Italian MSI and, latterly, the German Republican Party. While Le Pen's real power continues to lie less in what he can achieve himself than in what he can exact from others, notably the Gaullist RPR and centre-right UDF, he has established the French far right on a firmer political and electoral footing than could have been imagined at any time since the Liberation.

The style in which the National Front hosted its eighth National Congress in Nice over the weekend of 30 March - 1 April 1990 was not that, certainly, of a party in decline. Its stated objective, as always, was to present itself as a credible political force capable of commanding widespread support among the French voting public. Under the slogan "The conquest of power", some 1600 delegates devoted themselves to debating the central themes not of immigration or law and order - on which their stance is already well-defined - but of ecology and social policy. Here was a party intent upon extending the frontiers of its popular appeal. With a rousing endorsement, they voted the re-election to the leadership of the sole candidate, Jean-Marie Le Pen, and returned to their constituencies to work for the 30 per cent of votes on which the party has set its sights for the parliamentary elections of 1993.

All of this leaves the French political establishment confronting still questions which have exercised it since the mid-1980s. What is the political future of the National Front, and what long-term changes does the breakthrough of this party herald in the French political landscape? Though such questions are ridden with imponderables, it is clear that the emergence of the National Front has seriously destabilised the overall *rapports de forces* between left and right. While the traditional bipolar interpretation of the French political map was already complicated in 1981 by the overwhelming predominance of the Socialists on the left and the damaging divisions between the Giscardian and Gaullist currents on the right, Le Pen's party has brought about a need to reassess the whole party political system. The already acute political and personal rivalries between the major formations of the right have been compounded by the strategic dilemma of how best to respond to the challenge of the National Front. The ambiguities of the right's stance on this question have seriously undermined its credibility and cohesion. For Le Pen has split the right not along traditional party political lines, but according to a much more complex - and a potentially more damaging - pattern. The gaping disparities between the electoral opportunism of Jean-Claude Gaudin (UDF), the Le Pen-style populism of ex-Interior Minister Charles Pasqua (RPR), and the stern refusal by figures such as Simone Veil (UDF) and Michel Noir (RPR) to countenance any rapprochement in word or deed with the National Front, highlight the difficulty of evolving an easy common strategy. As Jean-Louis Bourlanges stresses, in his unsparing analysis of the contemporary French right, Le Pen represents a pole in what appears more than ever to be an over-extended and critically fragmented political family:

> No longer can any means be found to counteract the centrifugal forces which divide the conservative camp into extremists and moderates, the moderates into RPR and UDF, the RPR into ancients and moderns, and the UDF into conservatives, liberals and centrists.[58]

Le Pen is more, however, than some remote pole of attraction, the neatly symmetrical counterpoint to an ill-defined and somewhat abstract 'centre'. While the mainstream right in its broadest sense remains divided into what are popularly dubbed 'résistants' and 'collabos', the inescapable fact is that Le Pen's party now accounts, in hard electoral statistics, for a very substantial proportion of the right's combined strength.[59] The 1988 presidential and parliamentary elections testify clearly to the dimensions of the problem. In both cases, the combined right won over 50 per cent of the votes in the first ballot, only to see this statistical advantage evaporate in the second round. In the presidential run-off against Mitterrand, Chirac found himself beaten by one of the widest margins (54 to 46 per cent) in the history of presidential elections under the Fifth Republic. The problem of the contemporary right could not have been more starkly dramatised. The bitter rivalry between Giscard and Chirac contributed substantially to the Socialist victory in 1981. Almost a decade later, the traditional divisions between centrist and Gaullist camps are not only sharper than ever, but are aggravated by a new tripartite geography of the right-wing landscape (UDF/RPR/FN) which threatens any prospect that the right can concert its forces for a return to power when Mitterrand's mandate comes up for renewal in 1995 at the latest.

The electoral breakthrough of the National Front, taking place as it did in a period of perceived social and economic crisis, admits of no easy explanation. To ascribe the success of the National Front to economic recession, immigration or the problems of law and order is to provide a quite inadequate account of the factors underlying the rise of this party. For it is to take cognisance neither of the situation prevailing in the period prior to Le Pen's success, nor of the very specific political context within which this success was achieved. The ravages of economic recession were by no means peculiar to the 1980s: if Valéry Giscard d'Estaing inherited an unemployment rate of some 2.3 per cent in 1974, he presided over a period during which the figure soared to all of 7.4 per cent.[60] As with unemployment, so with inflation, which proved resistant to the stiffest austerity measures of Prime Minister Raymond Barre. The opinion poll ratings of Giscard d'Estaing on the questions of unemployment, inflation and living standards bear eloquent witness to the economic problems encountered between 1974 and 1981.[61] Nor is the problem of law and order new, as the public order measures of Giscard d'Estaing's administration equally testify.[62] The terms 'austerity' and 'security,' as Machin and Wright point out, came to occupy an increasingly salient place in the discourse of the Giscard régime.[63] What, then, of the single most frequently cited cause of Le Pen's success, the immigration question?

This, it must be recognised, is itself something of a misnomer, since there has been no immigration in France on any major scale since the mid-1970s. Perceived as an aggravating factor in economic recession and as a stimulus to racial tensions, immigration was brought sharply under control by Giscard d'Estaing as early as 1974. Throughout the latter's presidency, indeed, restrictive immigration policy remained the order of the day, as government measures sought to clamp down on illegal immigration and to offer repatriation incentives to bona fide foreign residents in France.[64] As G.P. Freeman documents, evidence of animosity towards immigrants has been lacking neither in French society nor in French political discourse since the earliest mass intake of North African labour in the 1960s.[65] To claim therefore that these issues, whether considered separately or collectively, are responsible for the National Front's success is to lose sight of the fact that this party languished in electoral obscurity for more than a decade after its foundation in 1972. It was to take a political upheaval of major proportions to permit Le Pen to capitalise at last on social and economic issues which had failed to win his party electoral recognition throughout the 1970s. The *alternance* of 1981 disrupted what had appeared to be the neat equilibrium of the French party system, abruptly reversing the established roles of the right- and left-wing coalition blocs. Nor did it take the newly elected administration long to fall from grace in the eyes of an electorate all too accustomed, after five years of Barrist government, to the language of economic austerity. Disenchantment at the Socialists' failure to curb unemployment and their recourse, in a quite dramatic economic U-turn, to the politics of 'rigour' did much to erode public support. Wage claims and industrial action, rising inflation, a perceived drop in living standards, and the inflammatory issues of state jurisdiction over private (Catholic) schools and the freedom of the press, all contributed to a climate of public protest.[66] An amnesty to a large number of illegal immigrants and the promise of a vote for foreign residents in municipal elections presented the government's opponents with an opportunity to politicise as never before the immigration debate.

The failure of the established parties of the right to mount a convincing challenge and to present themselves as an attractive alternative to the Socialists in office provoked a crisis of political confidence which, between 1982 and 1984, opened the way for the National Front. Opinion poll after opinion poll in the mid-1980s attest a deepening disillusionment with political élites, while election results and exit polls chart an increase in the electoral volatility from which Le Pen's party has clearly benefited.[67] The rank opportunism which has been exposed at times among the established parties of the right with regard to Le Pen has served only to undermine the credibility of the mainstream right and further enhance the new-found legitimacy of the National Front. The issues upon which Le Pen has secured his electoral platform, and which have been co-opted in varying degrees by the established parties, betoken a marked evolution in electoral attitudes towards established political parties and the problems confronting French society. The oxygen of publicity has served Le Pen well. Immigration and law and order, while they are not new, now occupy a salient place on the domestic political agenda; other themes popularised by the National Front, from the fight against terrorism to the nationality question, find a resonance in the agendas of the major parties of right and left alike.

Much has changed in the French political theatre since the Mauroy government's traumas of 1982-84; yet Le Pen's party holds doggedly still to the high level of support which it first attracted during that period. Through the very fact that it is deprived once more of its potential for bringing any direct influence to bear upon the processes of government, the National Front, it may be argued, is well placed to build on its successes to date, exploiting disillusionment with the institutional parties and presenting itself as a ready channel for discontent among voters across the political spectrum. As Jean-Louis

Bourlanges argued in 1988, towards the end of the party's brief spell in the National Assembly, 'the National Front exercises a genuine power of attraction as a "tribune" party only insofar as it remains outside the mainstream right, appearing first and foremost as an anti-system force.'[68]

This does not mean, however, that the National Front has settled for isolation as a political strategy. Le Pen's party will continue to exploit the divisions and tensions of the right and to force itself, wherever possible, upon the RPR and UDF as the alternative to defeat at the hands of the left. The many instances of electoral cooperation that have been witnessed in the 1980s have already done much to break down the taboo implicit in such a prospect. All of this depends, of course, upon the capacity of the National Front to retain the ground which it has won over the past few years. Since its resounding successes of April 1988 and June 1989, the party has entered a new phase in which its staying power is likely to be more severely tested than ever. The relative media silence which resulted from the loss of its parliamentary mandate proved damaging, but not critically so. The remarkable performance of the National Front in the parliamentary by-elections of Marseille and Dreux in November-December 1989 showed once more the capacity of this party to confound political commentators and pre-election pollsters. With 33 per cent of the vote in the 2nd constituency of the Bouches-du-Rhône department on 26 November, Marie-Claude Roussel brought the National Front to second place behind the UDF (39.2 per cent), well in advance of the Socialist (13.1 per cent) and Communist (7.4 per cent) candidates. In the first round of the Dreux by-election, which took place on the same day in the 2nd constituency of the Eure-et-Loir department, the statistics were more arresting still: National Front - 42.5 per cent, RPR - 24.5 per cent, PS - 18.1 per cent, PC - 3.9 per cent. These results warrant consideration, for they demonstrate clearly the National Front's continued ability to mount electoral challenges to the major parties in selected constituencies where it has built up a strong - and, it seems increasingly, a durable - base of support. They also, and more significantly, assured the election to the National Assembly as deputy for Dreux of the National Front candidate, Marie-France Stirbois, widow of the late Secretary-General of the party, Jean-Pierre Stirbois, and continuator of the latter's hardline policies in a town with a large proportion of immigrants and rising anxieties over crime and unemployment levels.

The signs are, then, that the National Front, far from being exhausted as a political force, will continue to vie with its Communist counterpart as the voice of 'redemptive' politics, the purveyor of certitudes and panaceas in a climate of political uncertainty and electoral volatility. The lessons of the 1980s counsel against rash prediction. What seems certain, however, is that the National Front has opened up a political space which requires now to be filled. Whether this is done by Le Pen's party alone, by a radicalised segment of the mainstream right, or by a combination of the two, it is clear that France is obliged to address a social agenda for the 1990s over which the shadow of the National Front hangs as never before. Howard Machin is correct in his assertion that, like the Communist Party at the opposite end of the ideological spectrum, the National Front occupies a marginal place in French politics, able to 'compete only for the possibility of parliamentary leverage, influence on public opinion, a voice in the European Assembly, organisational self-preservation, and some local council seats.'[69] Such marginal status, however, does not preclude the capacity of Le Pen's party to bring to bear a political weight that is not always commensurate with its power in real terms. The electoral alliance between the mainstream right and the National Front in the municipal by-election of Le Luc on 11 February 1990, though of limited significance in itself, was symptomatic of the problem which has bedevilled the RPR and UDF since the first such deal was struck for the municipal by-election of Dreux in September 1983. While the National Front retains the potential to compel such local alliances, or to exact a heavy price by refusing to give the mainstream right a clear run in cases where cooperation is refused, it will remain a force which cannot be discounted. With his performance in the presidential elections of 1988 standing as testament to what may be achieved, Le Pen is of no mind to relinquish his claim to a meaningful place in the annals of Fifth Republican politics. His ambition is to make the National Front the major force of the right in France, attracting between 15 and 30 per cent of the total national vote. While such an objective seems highly unrealistic, a glance at the electoral maps of 24 April and 5 June 1988 demonstrates the number of departments in which Le Pen and his party are capable of commanding such a telling proportion of the vote.[70]

The breakthrough of the National Front can be ascribed, in part at least, to a collapse of confidence in government and institutional opposition alike. While the Socialists have staged a remarkable recovery since the nadir of their popularity between 1982 and 1984, the right has done little to put its house in order and to see off the challenge of Le Pen. Having failed to harness the protest which gave impetus to the success of the National Front, the RPR and UDF no longer enjoy a monopoly over right-of-centre support. Yet such a monopoly appears ever more a statistical imperative if they are to wrest power from the Mitterrand-Rocard diarchy. Few entertain the prospect that, without some fusion of the right-of-centre forces to replace the shaky coalition that prevails, the mainstream opposition can mount an effective challenge either to the governing Socialists or to the National Front. While the Gaullist RPR and Giscardian UDF remain, for all their increasingly urgent talk of 'union', as fundamentally divided as ever, Le Pen has no reason yet to fear that his political fortunes are on the wane.

Notes

1. See Shields, J.G., 'Campaigning from the Fringe: Jean-Marie Le Pen', in Gaffney, J. (ed.), *The French Presidential Elections of 1988: Ideology and Leadership in Contemporary France*, Gower, Aldershot, 1989, pp. 140-157.

2. See on this question Schain, M.A., 'The National Front in France and the construction of political legitimacy', *West European Politics*, vol. 10, no. 2, April 1987, pp. 229-252; Mitra, S., 'The National Front in France: A Single-issue Movement?', *West European Politics*, vol. 11, no. 2, April 1988, pp. 47-64; Shields, J.G., 'The Politics of Disaffection: France in the 1980s', in Gaffney, J., and Kolinsky, E. (eds.), *Political Culture in France and West Germany*, Routledge, London, forthcoming. Among studies which seek to analyse the composition and voting motivations of the National Front electorate, see Perrineau, P., 'Le Front national: un électorat autoritaire', *Revue Politique et Parlementaire*, no. 918, 1985, pp. 24-31; Jaffré, J., 'Front national: la relève protestataire', in Dupoirier, E., and Grunberg, G., *Mars 1986: la drôle de défaite de la gauche*, PUF, Paris, pp. 211-229; Platone, F., 'Histoire de l'électorat Le Pen', *Le Journal des Elections*, no. 1, 1988, pp. 23-24; Grunberg, G. et al., 'Trois candidats, trois droites, trois électorats', in *L'élection présidentielle*, Le Monde: dossiers et documents, May 1988, pp. 41-43; Mayer, N., 'L'"effet Le Pen" s'est nourri de l'"effet premier tour"', ibid., p. 44. The joint publication under the direction of N.Mayer and P.Perrineau, *Le Front national à découvert*, FNSP, Paris, 1989, provides full and detailed analyses of many aspects of the Le Pen phenomenon. See in particular Orfali, B., 'Le droit chemin ou les mécanismes de l'adhésion politique', pp. 119-134; Ranger, J., 'Le cercle des sympathisants', pp. 135-149; Blondel, J., and Lacroix, B., 'Pourquoi votent-ils Front national?', pp. 150-170.

3. Anderson, M., *Conservative Politics in France*, Allen & Unwin, London, 1974, p. 279.

4. For more than one notable politician, the road from the OAS and *Occident*, as Paul Hainsworth puts it, 'apparently led to the benches of the *majorité*'. See 'Anti-Semitism and Neo-Fascism on the Contemporary Right', in Cerny, P. (ed.), *Social Movements and Protest in France*, Frances Pinter, London, 1982, p. 159. See also on this point Chombart de Lauwe, M-J., *Vigilance: vieilles traditions extrémistes et droites nouvelles*, EDI, Paris, 1987, pp. 72-74.

5. Op. cit., p. 297.

6. Chiroux, R., *L'extrême-droite sous la Ve République*, Librairie Générale de Droit et de Jurisprudence, Paris, 1974, p. 236.

7. Tucker, W.R., 'The new look of the extreme right in France', *Western Quarterly Review*, vol. 21, 1968, p. 95.

8. Frears, J., *Political Parties and Elections in the French Fifth Republic*, Hurst, London, 1977, p. 162.

9. See ibid., pp. 162-165.

10. Ibid., p. 165.

11. See, for example, Rollat, A., *Les hommes de l'extrême-droite: Le Pen, Marie, Ortiz et les autres*, Calmann-Lévy, Paris, 1985, pp. 134-141; Plenel, E., and Rollat, A., *L'effet Le Pen*, La Découverte/Le Monde, Paris, 1984, pp. 166-177.

12. Jacob, J., 'L'extrême-droite revue et corrigée par Jean-Marie Le Pen', *Revue Politique et Parlementaire*, vol. 89, no. 927, January-February 1987, pp. 36-37. Cf. on this point Rollat, op. cit., p. 134.

13. Cited by Chiroux, op. cit., p. 210.

14. See ibid., p. 212.

15. Ibid., p. 215.

16. See Rollat, op. cit., pp. 145-162; Hainsworth, op. cit., pp. 155-158; Chombart de Lauwe, op. cit., pp. 69-74, 103-123.

17. The importance of this movement is stressed by Dumont, Lorien and Criton, who write: Au début des années soixante-dix, Ordre Nouveau *est* l'extrême-droite'. See *Le système Le Pen*, EPO, Antwerp, 1985, p. 89.

18. See Chiroux, op. cit., p. 212 n. 732.

19. See Chebel d'Appollonia, A., *L'extrême-droite en France: de Maurras à Le Pen*, Editions Complexe, Brussels, 1988, pp. 311-312, 316-318; Camus, J-Y., 'Origine et formation du Front national (1972-1981)', in Mayer and Perrineau, *Le Front national à découvert*, pp. 17-22.

20. Cited by Dumont, Lorien and Criton, op. cit., pp. 92-93.

21. On the history of the MSI and the 1972 election as its high-water mark, see Caciagli, M., 'The Movimento Sociale Italiano-Destra Nazionale and Neo-Fascism in Italy', in *Right-Wing Extremism in Western Europe*, edited by K. von Beyme, special issue of *West European Politics*, vol. 11, no. 2, April 1988, pp. 19-33.

22. The new note of pragmatism in the discourse of *Ordre nouveau*, its capitulation to the exigencies of realpolitik, is striking: 'Un vieux mythe doit être condamné une fois pour toutes: "Etre soi-même", qui a autorisé toutes les excommunications et tous les sectarismes. La seule loi d'un révolutionnaire est la loi de l'efficacité; pour lui, la fin justifie réellement les moyens et tout doit être subordonné à la victoire de la cause. "Etre soi-même" a toujours été le mot d'ordre de ceux qui baptisaient "Esprit révolutionnaire" la crainte panique d'être supplantés par des gens plus capables et plus intelligents. Or, l'exemple du Movimento sociale italiano montre, une fois encore, combien une telle attitude correspond à une myopie politique complètement stérile [...]' Cited by Rollat, op. cit., p. 53.

23. See ibid., p. 53; Dumont, Lorien and Criton, op. cit., p. 93.

24. Cited by Rollat, op. cit., p. 53.

25. 'Ce n'est d'ailleurs pas un hasard,' notes B. Brigouleix, 'si l'emblème du Front national - des flammes tricolores - est exactement, en remplaçant le bleu-blanc-rouge français par le vert-blanc-rouge italien, celui du MSI'. See *L'extrême droite en France: les 'fachos'*, Fayolle, Paris, 1977, p. 172.

26. Cited by Rollat, op. cit., pp. 58-59.

27. '[...] le Front national, de par sa vocation unitaire et son image favorable, représente l'outil le mieux adapté pour mener le combat politique sur le terrain classique, type de combat qu'il est indispensable de poursuivre, même s'il apparaît qu'il ne faut pas s'y cantonner'. Cited in ibid., p. 59.

28. Ibid., p. 58.

29. See Charlot, M., 'L'émergence du Front national', *Revue Française de Science Politique*, vol. 36, no. 1, 1986, pp. 30-33; Camus, op. cit., pp. 17-22; Brigouleix, op. cit., pp. 174-176.

30. De Brie, C., 'Le terreau de l'extrême droite', *Le Monde diplomatique*, May 1988, p. 13. On the composition of the National Front, see Birenbaum, G., and François, B., 'Unité et diversité des dirigeants frontistes', in Mayer and Perrineau, *Le Front national à découvert*, pp. 83-106; Ysmal, C., 'Sociologie des élites du FN (1979-1986)', ibid., pp. 107-118.

31. Op. cit., pp. 213-214.

32. See, for example, Le Pen, J-M., *Pour la France: programme du Front national*, Albatros, Paris, 1985.

33. See Chebel d'Appollonia, op. cit., pp. 288-289, 291-295, 319; Brigouleix, op. cit., pp. 61-63, 72-74.

34. Witness his description of the holocaust as a 'point of detail' in the Second World War, or his grotesque reference to the Minister of Public Functions, Michel Durafour, as 'Durafour-crématoire' - 'four crématoire' being the French for 'crematorium furnace'. See *Le Monde*, 4-5 and 6 September 1988.

35. Op. cit., p. 30.

36. For a full breakdown of the National Front's performance in 1973, see Chiroux, op. cit., pp. 218-231.

37. On the 1981-86 period notably, see Schain, op. cit.; Shields, 'The Politics of Disaffection: France in the 1980s'.

38. See Chiroux, op. cit., p. 217; Dumont, Lorien and Criton, op. cit., pp. 103, 146.

39. See Shields, 'Campaigning from the Fringe: Jean-Marie Le Pen'.

40. See Cerny, P., 'Non-Terrorism and the Politics of Repressive Tolerance', in Cerny, op. cit., p. 99; Hainsworth, ibid., p. 167.

41. See Schneider, R., 'La nuit hystérique de Jean-Marie Le Pen', *Le Nouvel Observateur*, 16-22 October 1987, pp. 32-33. On the occasion in question, a number of National Front deputies disrupted the proceedings of the Chamber in protest against parliamentary absenteeism during a debate on new legislation to combat drug trafficking.

42. See Fysh, P., 'Government policy and the challenge of the National Front - the first twelve months', *Modern and Contemporary France*, no. 31, 1987, pp. 9-20.

43. *Le Monde*, 29-30 March 1987. Cited by Fysh, op. cit., p. 20 n. 48.

44. See *L'élection présidentielle*, Le Monde: dossiers et documents, May 1988, p. 34.

45. On the electoral geography of the National Front, see Mayer, N., 'Le vote FN de Passy à Barbès (1984-1988)', in Mayer and Perrineau, *Le Front national à découvert*, pp. 249-267; Platone, F., and Rey, H., 'Le FN en terre communiste', ibid., pp. 268-283; Etchebarne, S., 'Le FN dans le Nord ou les logiques d'une implantation électorale', ibid., pp. 284-306; Viard, J., 'Le dérangement marseillais', ibid., pp. 307-321; Ysmal, C., and Habert, P., 'Les terres de mission', ibid., pp. 322-342.

46. See Shields, 'Campaigning from the Fringe: Jean-Marie Le Pen', p. 149; Perrineau, P., 'Front national: la drôle de défaite', in Habert, P., and Ysmal, C. (eds.), *Elections législatives 1988: résultats, analyses et commentaires*, Le Figaro/Etudes Politiques, Paris, 1988, pp. 30-31.

47. See Guyomarch, A., and Machin, H., 'François Mitterrand and the French presidential and parliamentary elections of 1988: Mr Norris changes trains?', *West European Politics*, vol. 12, no. 1, 1989, p. 207.

48. See *Le Monde*, 16 March 1982.

49. Op. cit., pp. 245, 249. See Perrineau, P., 'Les étapes d'une implantation électorale (1972-1988)', in Mayer and Perrineau, *Le Front national à découvert*, pp. 45-47.

50. See Rollat, A., 'Le Front national confirme son implantation', *Le Monde*, 12 March 1985.

51. See *Le Monde*, 27 September 1988.

52. See Malaurie, G. et al., 'Enquête sur le Front national', *L'Express*, 23 February 1990, pp. 24-34. See also the article 'Recul de la gauche et progrès du Front national', *Le Monde*, 20 March 1990, p. 12.

53. See Malaurie et al., op. cit., pp. 24-34.

54. On the quasi-military character of the National Front, see Plenel, E., 'Les militants-soldats du Front national', *Le Monde*, 30 March 1990.

55. See Biffaud, O., 'Le Front national maintient ses positions du premier tour', *Spécial élections municipales*, Le Monde: dossiers et documents, April 1989, p. 6. For an analysis of the National Front's performance in the March 1989 municipal elections, see also Perrineau, P., 'Le Front national: une minorité de blocage', in Habert, P., and Ysmal, C., *Elections municipales 1989: résultats, analyses et commentaires*, Le Figaro/Etudes Politiques, Paris, 1989, pp. 27-28.

56. See Shields, 'Campaigning from the Fringe: Jean-Marie Le Pen', p. 142.

57. See ibid., p. 144; Grunberg, G. et al., 'Trois candidats, trois droites, trois électorats', op. cit., pp. 41-43; Mayer, N. 'L'"effet Le Pen" s'est nourri de l'"effet premier tour", ibid, p. 44.

58. Bourlanges, J-L., *Droite, année zero*, Flammarion, Paris, 1988, p. 25.

59. See Algalarrondo, H., 'Le Pen casse la droite', *Le Nouvel Observateur*, 22-28 May 1987, pp. 26-27.

60. See McCormick, J., 'Thorns among the roses: a year of the Socialist experiment, *West European Politics*, vol. 6, no. 1, 1983, p. 47.

61. See Machin, H., and Wright, V., 'Why Mitterrand won: the French presidential elections of April-May 1981', *West European Politics*, vol. 5, no. 1, 1982, pp. 22-23.

62. See Frears, J.R., *France in the Giscard Presidency*, Allen & Unwin, London, 1981, pp. 185-187; Cerny, op. cit., pp. 116-120; Hainsworth, op. cit., pp. 162-163.

63. Op. cit., pp. 14-15.

64. See Frears, *France in the Giscard Presidency*, pp. 157-158.

65. Freeman, G.P., *Immigrant Labor and Racial Conflict in Industrial Societies: The French and British Experience, 1945-1975*, Princeton University Press, Princeton, 1979.

66. See Shields, 'The Politics of Disaffection: France in the 1980s'; Rémond, R., 'The Right as Opposition and Future Majority', in Ross, G. et al. (eds.), *The Mitterrand Experiment: Continuity and Change in Modern France*, Polity Press, Oxford, 1987, pp. 133-134.

67. See Schain, op. cit., pp. 232-234.

68. Op. cit., p. 72.

69. 'Stages and dynamics in the evolution of the French party system', *West European Politics*, vol. 12, no. 4, 1989, p. 59.

70. See *L'élection présidentielle*, Le Monde: dossiers et documents, May 1988, p. 34, and *Les élections législatives*, Le Monde: dossiers et documents, June 1988, p. 38.

Bibliography

Books

Algazy, J., *L'extrême-droite en France de 1965 à 1984*, Editions L'Harmattan, Paris, 1989.

Anderson, M., *Conservative Politics in France*, Allen & Unwin, London, 1974.

Bourlanges, J-L., *Droite, année zéro*, Flammarion, Paris, 1988.

Brigouleix, B., *L'extrême-droite en France: les 'fachos'*, Fayolle, Paris, 1977.

Cerny, P. (ed.), *Social Movements and Protest in France*, Frances Pinter, London, 1982.

Chebel d'Appollonia, A., *L'extrême-droite en France: de Maurras à Le Pen*, Editions Complexe, Brussels, 1988.

Chiroux, R., *L'extrême-droite sous la Vᵉ République*, Librairie Générale de Droit et de Jurisprudence, Paris, 1974.

Chombart de Lauwe, M-J., *Vigilance: vieilles traditions extrémistes et droites nouvelles*, EDI, Paris, 1987.

Dumont, S., Lorien, J., and Criton, K., *Le système Le Pen*, EPO, Antwerp, 1985.

Dupoirier, E., and Grunberg, G. (eds.), *Mars 1986: la drôle de défaite de la gauche*, PUF, Paris, 1986.

Frears, J.R., *Political Parties and Elections in the French Fifth Republic*, Hurst, London, 1977.

Frears, J.R., *France in the Giscard Presidency*, Allen & Unwin, London, 1981.

Freeman, G.P., *Immigrant Labor and Racial Conflict in Industrial Societies: The French and British Experience, 1945-1975*, Princeton University Press, Princeton, 1979.

Gaffney, J. (ed.), *The French Presidential Elections of 1988: Ideology and Leadership in Contemporary France*, Gower, Aldershot, 1989.

Le Pen, J-M., *Pour la France: programme du Front national*, Albatross, Paris, 1985.

Mayer, N., and Perrineau, P., *Le Front national à découvert*, FNSP, Paris, 1989.

Plenel, E., and Rollat, A., *L'effet Le Pen*, La Découverte/Le Monde, Paris, 1984.

Rémond, R., *Les droites en France*, Aubier Montaigne, Paris, 1982.

Rollat, A., *Les hommes de l'extrême-droite: Le Pen, Marie, Ortiz et les autres*, Calmann-Lévy, Paris, 1985.

Articles and Book Chapters

Caciagli, M., 'The Movimento Sociale Italiano-Destra Nazionale and Neo-Fascism in Italy', in von Beyme, K. (ed.) *Right-Wing Extremism in Western Europe*, special issue of *West European Politics*, vol. 11, no. 2, 1988.

Cerny, P., 'Non-Terrorism and the Politics of Repressive Tolerance', in Cerny, P. (ed.), *Social Movements and Protest in France*, Frances Pinter, London, 1982.

Charlot, M., 'L'émergence du Front national', *Revue Française de Science Politique*, vol. 36, no. 1, 1986.

De Brie, C., 'Le terreau de l'extrême droite', *Le Monde diplomatique*, May 1988.

Eatwell, R., 'Poujadism and Neo-Poujadism: From Revolt to Reconciliation', in Cerny, op. cit.

Frears, J., 'The 1988 French presidential election', *Government and Opposition*, vol. 23, no. 3, 1988.

Fysh, P., 'Government policy and the challenge of the National Front - the first twelve months', *Modern and Contemporary France*, no. 31, 1987.

Grunberg, G., et al., 'Trois candidats, trois droites, trois électorats', *L'élection présidentielle*, Le Monde: dossiers et documents, May 1988.

Guyomarch, A., and Machin, H., 'François Mitterrand and the French presidential and parliamentary elections of 1988: Mr Norris changes trains?', *West European Politics*, vol. 12, no. 1, January 1989.

Hainsworth, P., 'Anti-Semitism and Neo-Fascism on the Contemporary Right', in Cerny, op. cit.

Jacob, J., 'L'extrême-droite revue et corrigée par Jean-Marie Le Pen', *Revue Politique et Parlementaire*, vol. 89, no. 927, January-February 1987.

Jaffré, J., 'Front national: la relève protestataire', in Dupoirier, E., and Grunberg, G. (eds.), *Mars 1986: la drôle de défaite de la gauche*, PUF, Paris, 1986.

Levy, D.A.L., and Machin, H., 'How Fabius lost: the French elections of 1986', *Government and Opposition*, vol. 21, no. 3, 1986.

Machin, H., and Wright, V., 'Why Mitterrand won: the French presidential elections of April-May 1981', *West European Politics*, vol. 5, no. 1, 1982.

Machin, H., 'Stages and dynamics in the evolution of the French party system', *West European Politics*, vol. 12, no. 4, 1989.

Mayer, N., 'L'"effet Le Pen" s'est nourri de l'"effet premier tour"', *L'élection présidentielle*, Le Monde: dossiers et documents, May 1988.

McCormick, J., 'Thorns among the roses: a year of the Socialist experiment', *West European Politics*, vol. 6, no. 1, 1983.

Mitra, S., 'The National Front in France - A Single-issue Movement?', in von Beyme, K., *Right-Wing Extremism in Western Europe*, special issue of *West European Politics*, vol. 11, no. 2, 1988.

Perrineau, P., 'Le Front national: un électorat autoritaire', *Revue Politique et Parlementaire*, no. 918, 1985.

Perrineau, P., 'Front national: la drôle de défaite', in Habert, P., and Ysmal, C. (eds.), *Elections législatives 1988: résultats, analyses et commentaires*, Le Figaro/Etudes politiques, Paris, 1988.

Perrineau, P., 'Le Front national: une minorité de blocage', in Habert, P., and Ysmal, C. (eds.), *Elections municipales 1989: résultats, analyses et commentaires*, Le Figaro/Etudes politiques, Paris, 1989.

Platone, F., 'Histoire de l'électorat Le Pen', *Le Journal des Elections*, no. 1, 1988.

Rémond, R., 'The Right as Opposition and Future Majority', in Ross, G. et al. (eds.), *The Mitterrand Experiment: Continuity and Change in Modern France*, Polity Press, Oxford, 1987.

Schain, M.A., 'The National Front in France and the construction of political legitimacy', *West European Politics*, vol. 10, no. 2, 1987.

Shields, J.G., 'Politics and populism: the French far right in the ascendant', *Contemporary French Civilization*, vol. 11, no. 1, 1987.

Shields, J.G., 'Campaigning from the Fringe: Jean-Marie Le Pen', in Gaffney, J. (ed.), *The French Presidential Elections of 1988: Ideology and Leadership in Contemporary France*, Gower, Aldershot, 1989.

Shields, J.G., 'The Politics of Disaffection: France in the 1980s', in Gaffney, J., and Kolinsky, E. (eds.), *Political Culture in France and West Germany*, Routledge, London, forthcoming.

Tucker, W.R., 'The new look of the extreme right in France', *Western Quarterly Review*, vol. 21, 1968.

Appendix 1

Parliamentary and Presidential Election Results in the Fifth Republic[1]

Table 1
The 1958 legislative election
(mainland France only)

Registered Voters	27,244,992		
Abstentions	6,218,450	22.82	
Valid Votes	20,492,367	75.18	
Party	**Votes**		**%**
PCF	3,870,184		18.9
SFIO	3,171,459		15.4
Radicals/Centre	2,347,989		11.5
MRP/Christian Dem.	2,378,788		11.6
UNR (Gaullist)	3,603,958		17.6
Conservatives	4,092,600		20.0

Source: Interior ministry figures as given by Goguel, F., *Chroniques électorales: la cinquième République du Général de Gaulle*, FNSP, Paris, 1983, p. 20.

Table 2
The 1962 legislative election
(mainland France only)

Registered Voters	27,526,358		
Abstentions	8,608,199	31.28	
Valid Votes	18,333,791	66.60	
Party	**Votes**		**%**
PCF	4,003,553		21.84
Extreme left/PSU	427,467		2.33
SFIO	2,298,729		12.54
Radicals	1,429,649		7.79
UNR/UDT (Gaullist)	5,855,744		31.94
MRP	1,665,695		9.08
Conservatives *a*	2,493,525		13.60

Source: Goguel, op. cit., p. 244.

a CNIP and *modérés*. Includes Giscard's pro-Gaullist Independent Republicans.

APPENDIX

Table 3
The 1965 presidential election
(mainland France only)

First ballot

Registered voters	28,233,167	
Abstentions	4,231,206	14.98
Valid Votes	23,757,669	84.16

Candidate	**Votes**	**%**
De Gaulle	10,386,734	43.71
Mitterrand	7,658,792	32.23
Lecanuet (centre)	3,767,404	15.85
Minor candidates *a*	1,944,739	8.16

Second ballot

De Gaulle	12,643,527	54.50
Mitterrand	10,553,985	45.50

Source: Goguel, op. cit., pp. 384, 402.

a Tixier-Vignancour (extreme right - 5.27%), Marcilhacy (independent - 1.73%), Barbu (independent - 1.16%).

Table 4
The 1967 legislative election
(mainland France only)

Registered voters	28,291,838	
Abstentions	5,404,687	19.10
Valid Votes	22,392,317	79.15

Party	**Votes**	**%**
PCF	5,029,208	22.46
Extreme left	506,592	2.26
FGDS (Socialist)	4,207,166	18.79
UNR/RI *a*	8,453,512	37.75
Democratic Centre	2,864,272	12.79
Others	1,330,967	5.95

Source: Goguel, op. cit., p.467.

APPENDIX

Table 5
The 1968 legislative election (mainland France only)

Registered voters	28,171,635		
Abstentions	5,631,892	19.99	
Valid votes	22,138,657	78.38	
Party	**Votes**		**%**
PCF	4,435,357		20.03
FGDS (Socialist)	3,654,000		16.50
PDM (centre)	2,290,165		10.34
UDR/RI/*majorité*	10,201,024		46.05
Others	551,398		2.48

Source: Goguel, op. cit., pp. 501, 505.

Table 6
The 1969 presidential election (mainland France only)

First ballot

Registered voters	29,513,361		
Abstentions	6,614,327	22.41	
Valid Votes	22,603,998	76.59	
Candidate	**Votes**		**%**
Pompidou (Gaullist)	10,051,816		44.47
Poher (centre)	5,268,651		23.31
Duclos (PCF)	4,808,285		21.27
Defferre (SFIO)	1,133,222		5.01
Rocard (PSU)	816,471		3.61
Others	530,924		1.80

Second ballot

Pompidou	11,064,371		58.21
Poher	7,943,118		41.79

Source: Goguel, F., *Chroniques électorales: la cinquième République après de Gaulle*, FNSP, Paris, 1983, pp. 13-14.

APPENDIX

Table 7
The 1973 legislative election (mainland France only)

Registered voters	29,883,748		
Abstentions	5,595,163	18.72	
Valid votes	23,751,424	79.47	
Party	**Votes**		**%**
PCF	5,084,824		21.40
PS/MRG	4,919,426		20.71
Reformist Movement	3,048,824		12.83
URP	8,224,447		34.62
Other *majorité*	784,985		3.30

Source: Goguel, op. cit., p. 22; Goldey, D., and Johnson, R.W., 'The French general election of March 1973', *Political Studies*, vol. 21, no. 3, September, p. 336. Goldey and Johnson estimate that the URP vote divided as follows: UDR (Gaullist) 5,700,000 (23.9%); RI, 1,650,000 (6.9%); CDP 900,000 (3.7%).

Table 8
The 1974 presidential election (mainland France only)

First ballot

Registered voters	29,778,550		
Abstentions	4,492,715	15.1	
Valid votes	25,285,835	84.1	
Candidate	**Votes**		**%**
Mitterrand	10,863,402		43.3
Giscard d'Estaing	8,253,856		32.9
Chaban-Delmas	3,646,209		14.6
Others *a*	2,294,104		11.0

Second ballot

Candidate	**Votes**	**%**
Giscard d'Estaing	13,082,006	50.7
Mitterrand	12,737,607	49.3

Source: Goguel, F., and Grosser, A., *La politique en France*, FNSP, Paris, 1980.

a A total of nine candidates: only Royer (3.2%), Laguiller (2.3%), and Dumont (1.3%) crossed the 1% barrier. Le Pen polled 0.7%.

APPENDIX

Table 9
The 1978 legislative election (mainland France only)

Registered Voters	34,402,883		
Abstentions	5,729,750	16.65	
Valid votes	28,105,239	81.70	
Party	**Votes**		**%**
PCF	5,793,139		20.61
PS	6,412,819		22.82
MRG	603,932		2.15
Greens	612,100		2.18
UDF	6,007,383		21.37
Other pro-Giscard	657,962		2.34
RPR	6,329,918		22.52

Source: Goguel, op. cit., p. 63. Cf. also Goldey, D., and Johnson, R.W., 'The French general election of March 1978: the redistribution of support between left and right', *Parliamentary Affairs*, vol.31, no. 2, Summer 1978, p. 302.

Table 10
The 1981 presidential election (mainland France only)

		First ballot	
Registered voters	35,517,816		
Abstentions	6,519,319	18.35	
Valid votes	28,517,660	80.30	
Candidate	**Vote**		**%**
Giscard d'Estaing	7,933,963		27.82
Mitterrand	7,439,577		26.08
Chirac	5,141,063		18.02
Marchais	4,415,028		15.48
Lalonde	1,118,885		3.92
Laguiller (LO)	661,532		2.31
Crepeau (MRG)	639,238		2.24
Debré (diss. Gaullist)	469,249		1.64
Garaud (diss. Gaullist)	380,815		1.33
Bouchardeau (PSU)	318,319		1.11
		Second ballot	
Mitterrand	15,541,965		52.22
Giscard d'Estaing	14,219,051		47.78

Source: Goguel, op. cit., pp. 145, 166.

APPENDIX

Table 11
The 1981 legislative election (mainland France only)

Registered voters	35,536,041		
Abstentions	10,353,065	29.13	
Valid Votes	25,182,262	70.86	
Party	**Votes**		**%**
PCF	4,003,025		16.12
PS/MRG	9,376,853		37.77
Greens	270,792		1.09
RPR	5,192,894		20.91
UDF	4,756,503		19.16
Other right	660,990		2.66
Extreme left/PSU	330,344		1.33
Extreme right	90,026		0.36

Source: Goguel, op. cit., p. 180.

Table 12
The 1986 legislative election (mainland France only)

Registered voters	36,605,381		
Abstentions	7,883,577	21.53	
Valid votes	27,485,667	75.10	
Lists	**Votes**		**%**
PCF	2,663,734		9.69
PS/MRG/Soc *a*	8,663,734		31.61
MRG [sep.lists]	70,526		0.25
Other left	248,726		0.90
RPR/UDF *b*	11,553,945		42.03
Other right *c*	745,803		2.71
FN	2,694,233		9.80

Source: *Les élections législatives de mars 1986*, Le Monde: dossiers et documents, Paris, 1986.

a Includes candidates supported by the PS.
b RPR lists 3.14 million & 11.5%; UDF lists 2.33 million & 9.53%, RPR/UDF lists 6.02 million & 21%.
c Mainly dissident RPR or UDF who rejoined their parties' parliamentary groups once elected.

APPENDIX

Table 13
The 1988 presidential election (including DOM-TOM)

First ballot

Registered voters	38,128,507		
Abstentions	7,100,535	18.62	
Valid Votes	30,406,038	79.74	
Candidate	**Votes**		**%**
Mitterrand	10,367,220		34.09
Chirac	6,063,514		19.94
Barre	5,031,849		16.54
Le Pen	4,375,894		14.39
Lajoinie	2,055,995		6.76
Waechter	1,149,642		3.78
Juquin	639,084		2.10
Laguiller (LO)	606,017		1.99
Boussel (ext.left)	116,823		0.38

Second ballot

Mitterrand	16,704,279	54.02
Chirac	14,218,270	45.98

Source: *L'élection présidentielle*, Le Monde: dossiers et documents, May 1988.

Table 14
The 1988 legislative elections (including DOM-TOM)[2]

Registered Voters	37,945,582		
Abstentions	13,000,790	34.26	
Valid Votes	24,432,095	64.39	
Party	**Votes**		**%**
PCF	2,765,761		11.32
PS/allies	9,176,708		37.55
Green *a*	86,312		0.35
UDF	4,519,459		18.49
RPR	4,687,047		19.18
Other right	697,272		2.85
Total URC/allies			40.52
National Front	2,359,228		9.65

Source Ministry of the Interior figures for 575 constituencies (mainland France plus DOM-TOM), excluding French Polynesia (two seats).

a Only a handful of Greens stood.

APPENDIX

Notes

1. Except for the 1988 elections, these figures concern mainland France only. This is in order to avoid the distortion in *real* party strengths by accepting at face value the grossly distorted figures which occur in certain of the overseas territories and departments. For further information, cf., Cole, A., and Campbell, P., *French Electoral Systems and Elections since 1789*, Gower, Aldershot, 1989, pp. 180-1. DOM-TOM is included in the 1988 figures because of the difficulty experienced in tracing the official ministry figures for mainland France only.

2. Interior figures used for the 1988 elections do not distinguish between metropolitan France and DOM-TOM. These figures therefore slightly underestimate PS mainland strength, and overestimate that of the URC parties. PCF figure overestimates strength in mainland France; FN figure underestimates strength.